D0843086

Terrifying
Transferences

Terrifying Transferences

Aftershocks of Childhood Trauma

LAWRENCE E. HEDGES, PH.D.

CLINICAL MATERIAL CONTRIBUTED BY

Linda Barnhurst, John Carter, Shirley Cox, Jolyn Davidson,
Virginia Hunter, Miguel Reyes, Audrey Seaton-Bacon,
Sean Stewart, Gayle Trenberth, and Cynthia Wygal

JASON ARONSON INC.
Northvale, New Jersey
London

This book was set in 11 pt. Goudy by Alpha Graphics of Pittsfield, NH, and printed and bound by Book-mart Press, Inc. of North Bergen, NJ.

Library of Congress Cataloging-in-Publication Data

Hedges, Lawrence E.
    Terrifying transferences : aftershocks of childhood trauma /
Lawrence E. Hedges : with a foreword by Sanford Shapiro ; and
clinical material contributed by Linda Barnhurst . . . [et al.].
      p.   cm.
    Includes bibliographical references and index.
    ISBN 0-7657-0225-8
    1. Transference (Psychology)   2. Psychotherapist and patient.
3. Regression (Psychology)   4. Psychic trauma in children.
I. Title.
RC489.T73H43   1999
616.89'14—dc21   99-17470

Printed in the United States of America on acid-free paper. For information and catalog write to Jason Aronson Inc., 230 Livingston Street, Northvale, NJ 07647-1726, or visit our website: www.aronson.com

To my family

Breta, Dustin, Gerardo, Michelle, Ray

Contents

Part V
Working Through Terrifying Transferences

Foreword

Patients whose problems are rooted in early trauma are stuck in the early relational paradigms related to their trauma that are not accessible to verbal interpretations or insight. These patients require a special connection, a new relational experience, before they can learn new relational paradigms.

Before they can process their early childhood experiences of pain and trauma, these patients need relationships that feel safe. Unfortunately for these patients, as Dr. Hedges points out, to feel connected and safe is an oxymoron. While they desperately seek connection, their experience of connection is one of violation and humiliation.

The therapist is like the pet lover trying to console and reassure an abused puppy. The little dog huddles in a corner and snaps at the hand offering to pet and to comfort. The pet owner must be patient, must not interpret the snapping as anger, or punish the dog for growling and biting. Instead, he must slowly wait and earn the frightened animal's trust and confidence.

Once a patient feels safe, however, the therapist is suddenly confronted with experiences of abuse and humiliation from the patient. Because patients' traumas are encoded in nonverbal, procedural memory, they must find behavioral ways to communicate their histories. Identifying with early traumatizing figures, they model the behavior they were subjected to. However, their behavior is not the expression of innate, sadistic strivings; it is a desperate attempt at communication and connection.

In 1967, when I began my psychoanalytic training, I already had a busy psychotherapy practice. I was limited in my work then by a lack of understanding of transference, of the special connection that develops between analyst and patient. As my appreciation of the transference relationship developed, I began to listen differently and to understand my patients better. As a result they came to appointments more frequently, they stayed in therapy longer, and they got better in a more fundamental way. But when it came to patients who suffered from primitive or psychotic anxieties and who were compelled to engage with me in primitive, terrifying transferences, my analytic training was limited.

A revolution in my thinking and my practice started when a supervisor much like Dr. Hedges introduced me to the work of Harold Searles (1965). Reading Searles, I discovered that the process—the ways of connecting and the types of attachments that develop between analyst and patient—is more significant than the content of what the patient is saying. These ways of attaching are at the center of what terrifies the patient with early trauma and, in a successful therapy, structure the development of the transference. In doing so, they come to terrify the analyst as well.

Countertransference reactions—feelings stirred up in me during the work—were often, I learned, reactions to unconscious communications from my patient. For example, the feeling that I was going crazy, or that I hated my patient, did not necessarily mean I was failing but in fact was a sign that my patient was engaged with me in a process of self-integration by identifying with my capacity to withstand a barrage of fragmentation-fostering experiences (Searles 1965).

Now, thirty-one years later, Dr. Hedges, like Dr. Searles, has started another revolution in psychoanalytic education. A gifted supervisor who has the ability to teach, and to remain calm in the face of terror, Dr. Hedges here addresses four crucial issues:

1. Therapists who have the courage to stay connected with a traumatized patient's deepest fears will come to experience stark terror. In this book, Dr. Hedges shows us how to look into the face of such terror, to hold steady, and to work through these feelings safely.

2. Shame and embarrassment are typical reactions of therapists who believe that their experiences of feeling fear, hate, and vulnerability are viewed as evidence of their personal shortcomings. These feelings of inadequacy may be intensified by supervisors who know what the therapist should have done or should be doing to forestall these overwhelming experiences. Supervisors, unfortunately, are often unaware of how their own fears are stimulated when supervising such patients, and they react defensively with an authoritarian "I know better" attitude—an attitude that stifles both the therapist's and the patient's creative explorations.

All therapists are vulnerable to feeling overwhelmed by these patients, and it is too much to expect of therapists that they deal with primitive anxieties by themselves. They need the support of colleagues and supervisors to feel strong enough to maintain the self-esteem necessary to stay connected with their patients. In this book we see how a master supervisor works.

3. Therapists who work effectively with these patients know that, even though they are doing superior work, they would be criticized by many of their colleagues as doing inferior work should they reveal what they do and what they feel. So they keep their work secret to protect themselves, and they deprive their students and colleagues of the opportunity to learn about developments in technique and understanding. In this book Dr. Hedges and his colleagues share, often with great personal discomfort, their courageous work.

4. Most practicing therapists are handicapped by a lack of training in treating such patients. Little has been written to guide developing therapists in facing primitive anxieties and overwhelming terrors, or of the therapist's role in their resolution. Similarly, little has been written to guide supervisors in helping therapists treat such patients.

A supervisor who can see that the therapist's task is to survive the onslaught rather than worrying about making the right interpretation is to be highly valued. Such a supervisor is, unfortunately, hard to come by.

In Dr. Hedges we are fortunate to have such a teacher and supervisor. In this book he courageously demonstrates how to stay focused and connected during the inevitable storms that characterize successful therapy with such difficult patients. Dr. Hedges is a role model for all of us.

Sanford Shapiro, M.D.
September 1999

Acknowledgments

Nearly 300 Southern California therapists have participated in a research process that has spanned two decades focused on listening to depth issues in psychotherapy with narcissistic, borderline, and organizing (psychotic) level personality structures. *Terrifying Transferences* is in many ways a culmination of that joint work. Most of these therapists have been credited in previous volumes of theoretical and clinical work. Those who have been actively involved in helping me think through the issues of this book are:

Cristine Bates
Brandt Caudill
Charles Coverdale
Barbara Davis
Jeffrey Diefendorf
Cecile Dillon

Jeanne Lichman
Alexander Lowen
Edward Muller
Christine Panik
Roxie Persi
Dolly Platt

Arlene Dorius
Leslie Drozd
Gary Dylewski
Barbara English
Tim Gergen
Jacque Gillespie
Cheryl Graybill
James Grotstein
Jeanne Haislett
Robert Hilton
Virginia Wink Hilton
Linda Holley
Masaru Horikoshi
Joyce Hulgus
Jane Jackson
Robert Jacques
Cathearine Jerkins-Hall
Steve Johnson
Helen Kaufman
Michael Kogutek
Patsy Koos
Steve Lawrence

Jack Platt
Karen Redding
Helen Resnick-Sannes
Margo Robinson
Georgiana Rodiger
Howard Rogers
Fern Ross
Sandra Russell
Sabrina Salayz
Karyn Sandburg
Vincentia Schroeder
Steve Shehorn
Jackie Singer
Marion Solomon
Mary E. Walker
Marijane Ward
William White
Robert Woods
Cynthia Wygal
Colleen Yoder
Jean York

I am greatly indebted to the people who have generously contributed clinical and theoretical material to this book: Linda Barnhurst, John Carter, Shirley Cox, Jolyn Davidson, Virginia Hunter, Miguel Reyes, Audrey Seaton-Bacon, Sanford Shapiro, Sean Stewart, Gayle Trenberth, and Cynthia Wygal.

As always, my daughter Breta Lynne Bonham has assisted in assembling and preparing the manuscript. But the bulk of credit for this book goes to Gerardo H. Arechiga for mastering the computer, deciphering my handwriting, and managing all of us in putting together what has been an extraordinary project. Ray M. Calabrese makes the business and finances of the project work for us.

Judy Cohen, senior production editor for Aronson Publishers, has brilliantly made it all come together. Thanks also to Sigrid Asmus for fine-tuned copy editing and to Judie Tulli for art work.

Jason Aronson has been my ongoing inspiration and support for these two decades. It was Hedda Bolgar and he who first saw and understood the nature of this project and who have both provided ongoing consultation and advice on how it should be sculpted and presented.

To all of you and the many others previously named who have kept us all going so long by collaborating so well, I give heartfelt thanks.

Lawrence E. Hedges
Modjeska Canyon, California
September 1999

Contributors

Linda Barnhurst, Psy.D., is in private practice in Orange County, California, where her clinical work is informed by intersubjective and object relational perspectives. She is an instructor at Trinity College of Graduate Studies.

John Carter, Ph.D., is Dean of Doctoral Studies at Trinity College of Graduate Studies. He received his Ph.D. from the Graduate Faculty, The New School for Social Research, New York City. He has authored and co-authored two books and over a dozen articles on psychology and spirituality, and is in private practice in Santa Ana, California.

Shirley Anne Cox is a therapist in training at the Georgiana Rodiger Center, Inc., in Pasadena, California. She received her master's degree in marriage and family therapy from Phillips Graduate Institute, and is currently a doctoral candidate at the California Graduate Institute in Los Angeles. Her primary occupation is teaching. She has been employed by the Pasadena Unified School District for thirty years. Under the supervision of Georgina Rodiger, Ph.D., she has been counseling patients for several years. Her orientation is object relations.

Jolyn Davidson, B.S.N., L.C.S.W., B.C.D., is a child, adolescent, and adult psychotherapist in practice since 1977. She currently practices in Covina, California, providing both brief and long-term psychotherapy to individuals, families, and couples. She has extensive background providing mental health services and training internationally. She has served as a university faculty member, training both graduate and undergraduate students for professional work in the fields of psychiatric nursing, mental health, education, and human resource development.

Lawrence E. Hedges, Ph.D., ABPP, is a psychologist-psychoanalyst in private practice in Orange, California, specializing in the training of psychotherapists and psychoanalysts. He is director of the Listening Perspectives Study Center and the founding director of the Newport Psychoanalytic Institute. He holds faculty appointments at the California Graduate Institute and the University of California, Irvine, Department of Psychiatry. Dr. Hedges holds diplomates from the American Board of Professional Psychology and the American Board of Forensic Psychology. He is the author of numerous papers and books on the practice of psychoanalytic psychotherpy.

Virginia Hunter, Ph.D., L.C.S.W., author of *Psychoanalysts Talk*, is in private practice in child and adult psychotherapy and psychoanalysis in Long Beach, California. She is on the faculties of the Kansas City Institute for Contemporary Psychoanalysis and the Newport Psychoanalytic Institute, Tustin, California, where she is also a training and supervising analyst.

Miguel Reyes, Ph.D., currently practices in Upland, California as a marriage and family therapist intern. He has completed his doctoral work at the Graduate School of Psychology of Fuller Theological Seminary and serves as a consultant in the counseling center at The Crystal Cathedral.

Audrey Seaton-Bacon, Ph.D., is a psychotherapist in Hacienda Heights, California. She completed her academic training in clinical psychology at Rosemead School of Psychology, Biola University, and was recently licensed as a psychologist in the state of California. She works with an ethnically and racially diverse population, performing individual, couple, family, and group psychotherapy.

Sanford Shapiro, M.D., is a psychoanalyst in private practice in La Jolla, California. He is a training and supervising psychoanalyst at the San Diego Psychoanalytic Institute and at the Institute of Contemporary Psychoanalysis in Los Angeles. He is an Associate Clinical Professor of Psychiatry at the UC San Diego School of Medicine. Dr. Shapiro is the author of *Talking with Patients: A Self Psychological View.*

Sean Stewart, Psy.D., M.F.T., has fifteen years of experience in psychotherpy and is currently in private practice in Seal Beach, California, working with individuals, couples, and families. He earned his B.A. in psychology at Southern California College, and his M.A. in marital and family therapy at Azusa Pacific University. Dr. Stewart received his doctorate in psychology from the American Behavioral Studies Institute.

Gayle Trenberth, Ph.D., has been a psychologist in private practice in Seal Beach, California for the last twenty-one years. She graduated from the California School of Professional Psychology, Los Angeles, in 1976, and did post-doctoral training at the Newport Psychoanalytic Institute and the Southern California Institute for Bioenergetic Analysis. She has been a certified bioenergetic analyst for the last thirteen years, supervising both interns and trainees.

Cynthia Wygal, M.A., M.F.T., has been practicing psychotherapy in Orange County, California for ten years. An active advocate for the understanding of early childhood trauma and its effects, she presents seminars for the public and workshops for the California Association of Marriage and Family Therapists, colleges, and hospitals. Her private practice includes adult, child, and couple therapy.

PART I

PRIMITIVE ANXIETIES IN LIFE AND PSYCHOTHERAPY

1

Introduction:
Encountering
Primitive Anxieties

You are about to encounter a series of terrifying experiences reported by therapists and clients in psychotherapy. While the experiences recounted here include one sudden death, a suicide, and a homicide, the focus of this book is not on unusual or unsettling events, or on tragic consequences of therapeutic encounters. Rather, there is a level of stark terror known to one degree or another by all human beings. It silently haunts our lives and occasionally surfaces in therapy. It is this deep-seated fear—often manifest in dreams or fantasies of dismemberment, mutilation, torture, abuse, insanity, or death—that grips us with the terror of being lost forever in time and space or controlled by hostile forces stronger than ourselves. Sometimes these overpowering forces are perceived as coming at us from the outside world. At other times we may be frightened that the source of the overwhelming terror is inside ourselves. Or worse, we may be caught wavering somewhere in between, not really feeling sure whether the danger is out there or somewhere inside. Will we be tortured, attacked, mutilated, or killed?

Or will we fragment in wild and uncontrollable insanity? Whether the terror is felt by the client or by the therapist, it has a disorienting, fragmenting, crippling power. How we can look directly into the face of such terror, hold steady, and safely work it through is the subject of *Terrifying Transferences*.

The episodes and struggles written about in this book are ones that therapists often wish had not occurred. They are seldom written down, much less ever systematically reported to colleagues. But psychotherapy is a very human process, and consequently, terrifying, treacherous, and traumatic experiences indeed do occur. And we need to know about them in order to enrich and expand our work and in order to make it safer and saner.

Many therapists do everything in their power to keep the therapy process interpersonally clean, theoretically sound, and rationally comprehensible. In working hard to keep things totally neat and tidy such therapists never allow confusing, fragmenting, and frightening regressions to occur. More courageous therapists may tiptoe to the brink or even drop into the mire. But then they may become so confused, discouraged, disoriented, frightened, or even ashamed that they struggle through in silence as best they can. Then they try to put the whole painful and upsetting set of circumstances as far behind as possible.

Shame or embarrassment is a frequent response to regressions that are deeply trying because therapists too often believe that they should somehow be on top of all situations that arise in therapy. Or therapists believe that they should know how to conduct therapy in such a way that confusion, fragmentation, and terror do not result. But in the midst of the kinds of episodes that try one's soul, all therapists know that they have done things they probably should not have done, that they have made decisions they probably should not have made. And therapists would rather not have to deal with those unpleasant uncertainties.

Another group of therapists have been doing deeply disturbing work quietly, courageously, and efficiently for years. But they have felt a need to remain in the closet about it. That is, their human compassion and intuition has successfully pointed the way through some difficult and traumatizing pieces of therapy. But since they have never read about such cases in textbooks or never heard about such strange work in their therapy training, they are understandably shy about revealing their work and its many trials and uncertainties to anyone. Additionally, they may feel guilty or incompetent because they fear they don't know enough about what they are doing or that they should have called on colleagues for help. Perhaps they fear that if they had referred the client to "someone more knowledgeable" the work would not have been so difficult, or not have taken so long, or not have ended so badly.

For nearly thirty years I have consulted on difficult cases with therapists who have expressed all of the above feelings . . . and more. I have worked with therapists who feel they barely got through some difficult situations by the skin of their teeth. I have been called upon to witness for therapists who were doing their best when the situation collapsed with them inadvertently ending up in a legal or ethical investigation.

The most tragic cases involve therapists who have attempted to stay with a desperate client in order to do a difficult piece of work but in psychological areas where they had some limitation in their understanding, training, or therapeutic technique. The client needed to transfer some deep, horrible, abusive life situation into the therapeutic relationship. But these therapists simply did not have the training or understanding to enable them to protect either the client or themselves from the coming disaster. Most clinical training fails miserably at teaching therapists about how to recognize and to work with deep and treacherous transferences. As a result, therapists sometimes get caught in a frightening crossfire of psychotic anxieties and then end up in an investigation that may completely wreck their careers and personal lives.

This book takes us directly into the darkest recesses of the psychotherapy situation, where primitive psychotic anxieties silently await a rendezvous with therapist and client. I am convinced that such primitive anxieties are, at least to a limited extent, universal—except that ordinary life protects us from encountering them most of the time. But the psychotherapy engagement seeks relational representation of all the psychological forces that impinge on our lives, including the dark and dangerous ones.

Psychotherapy is an invitation for the forgotten, hidden, silent anxieties of childhood and for traumas suffered in infancy to be reawakened—transferred onto the therapist and into the therapeutic relationship. Therapists willingly make themselves inviting targets, sitting ducks for the transfer or for the projection of primitive anxieties—for the aftershocks of childhood trauma. Clients and therapists never know when they start therapy what kinds of terrifying and treacherous experiences they are setting out to liberate from the darkness of the past. Each alarming account in this book challenges us with disarming candor to rediscover for ourselves what depth psychotherapy is truly about.

OUR BEGINNING

I want to sketch some rough maps—mind–body maps of our deepest fears and how they operate. But I don't know you. I don't know why you picked up a book called *Terrifying Transferences*. I don't know what you fear or what you think about fears. So where shall we begin?

I usually start my thoughts at the point where two people are approaching each other without having the slightest idea of what they are going to do with each other or how they are going to get along. One reaches out in some way and the other reacts. We might say that one speaks and the other listens and responds. We each bring to this moment of speaking and listening all that we are or have become in a lifetime. And so our encounter or conversation begins.

Books used to be easy to write. We could have one person who knows something write to another person who wants to know more. But books like this don't serve us so well anymore. Now we need a writer or a speaker who can find a way into some part of our inner selves and stir us somehow, who can cause us to feel something we haven't quite felt before. We need a writer who can point us toward new ways of experiencing ourselves. We need a writer who doesn't pretend to know, but who can somehow lead us into experiencing something of the unknown. So what kind of a map can orient the adventurer without presuming to know what the adventure will be like? What kinds of maps suggest possibilities, places to begin, while expecting that the imagination and creativity of the journeyer will make the trip enriching, worthwhile, and fulfilling?

I will attempt some maps. But you must let your creative resources run free—thinking, exploring, imagining, and feeling. This book is about the fears that haunt our lives, many of them silent, irrational, and elusive, but nevertheless quite powerful in their effects on us.

I am a psychotherapist who has learned what I know primarily from many people engaged in psychotherapy, so it's probably best if I keep my ideas close to the psychotherapy encounter where I have achieved some degree of comfort and familiarity. In therapy we have a speaker, a listener, and a conversation about their encounter. Where better to begin to think about two people and how their encounter is bound to arouse fear?

We now know that traumatic experiences early in life leave emotional scars that affect our later relationships. When over- or understimulating traumas occur in infancy—or even before birth—a particular kind of scar is left. The situation is quite simple. A baby experiences some need and begins some sort of extension, movement, or signal to express that need. Since conception the baby's needs have been signaled and responded to. But at some point the need–fulfillment cycle becomes traumatically impinged upon or somehow interrupted. When the unmet need then gathers momentum, intensity, agitation, and distress result. After a period of distress marked by various attempts to signal its needs—restless stirring, screaming, thrashing, arching its back, holding its breath, or throwing up—the baby may finally give up, stop the signaling altogether, and weaken or wither in fatigue or defeat. Or, in the process of extending a distress signal, the baby may encounter some sharp pain—perhaps something from the environment such as a loud angry shout, a tight squeeze, or a slap. Or perhaps the baby encounters something from its body like a sharp hunger or gas pang, an uncontrollable itch, an unquenchable thirst, or an overwhelming rage response. A contraction or constriction process begins, tightening various parts of the baby's musculature. At first the tightening seems to control or quell the pain. But in time the self-protective contracting or constricting process itself becomes painful. With repeated experiences the constriction or contraction response comes to be chronically held for fear of encountering the initial (and in the child's mind) life-threatening need or signal pain again.

Whether the baby's early response to trauma is of the weakening, withering, giving-up kind or the tightening, contractive, constrictive kind, a strong message is permanently inscribed on the nascent neurological system—"Don't go there again, don't reach, don't express that need or that part of yourself again because if you do it will be unbearably painful." A block to further relating to others in specific ways is thus set up in the foundation of the child's mind. No one can know at the time what the future implications of that block will be or how in later life that basic neurological blockage may become mentally represented. But we do know that it will be marked by fear, signal pain and agitation, and will bring about a chronic avoidance of various kinds of interpersonal relating.

Whether the trauma is caused by a neglectful or abusive environment or by the unavoidable realities in the infant's early life—an incubator, a cleft palate, an allergy to milk, an alcoholic or depressed mother or father, family stress, or Holocaust conditions—the child creatively blocks the paths that have brought in the frightening, painful, or traumatic experiences. Later psychotherapy seeks to discover how that blockage lives on in the person's mind and body to systematically limit relationships and life experiences. When these primitive blockages are at last brought forth in the therapeutic relationship for analysis and transformation, the memories that must be relived in the here-and-now relationship are body–mind experiences of unbearable physical and psychical pain and unspeakable terrors of being retraumatized.

Depending on the person's overall ego development, on her or his current life situation, and on the nature and viability of the current trust relationship, the person may or may not be able to negotiate a full body–mind memory of the infantile pain and trauma so that it can be experienced and worked through in the present relationship. We now know from considerable clinical experience that at these moments of intense body–mind remembering, there is often excruciating pain and overwhelming terror. And that the fear of and resistance to further experiencing traumatic memory becomes directed at the only other human being present–the therapist or other person in the trust relationship who invited and called forth the pain *by being present and available for intimate relating and somatopsychic remembering.*

If the therapist does not fully understand the process of trauma recreation or is not prepared to move profitably and creatively forward with the client through the re-experiencing of the physical pain and psychological terror and the accusation that the therapist is responsible for it, then we are in for trouble. The client feels the pain, knows that the therapist is responsible for eliciting it, and, from the primitive place being experienced at that moment, *cannot fully distinguish* the emerging past body–mind memory from the present experience of pain and terror in relation to the therapist. The inevitable conclusion? It is the therapist who is hurting me.

So the secondary and background theme of this book is how terrifying transferences that have been successfully elicited by trust relationships of various kinds, but not fully worked through in the context of that relationship, can and do give rise to false accusations against the therapist or the other person in the trust relationship. These accusatory cries are a regular part of the working-through process and are at high risk for being acted out in the outside community as charges of misconduct against the therapist or other trusted and/or admired persons.

Another theme that runs throughout this book is how people in trust relationships go about conceptualizing what is happening as pain, terror, and distorted accusatory cries tumble about in seemingly pell-mell fashion. And how the person in a therapeutic role in the relationship can respond creatively and effectively to the emergence of these traumatic memories, keep his or her calm and sanity more or less intact, and promote a working through of the terror and constriction that has in devious ways limited all aspects of the client's life and relationships.

2

The Ethic of Relating

THE LESSON

I have something I want to teach. I have been working on it for years. In my previous books I have surveyed the work of many other therapists. I have asked colleagues to submit their work for roundtable discussion. I have presented samples of my own work. But at the center of it all I am always teaching an ethic. I hope in this book to clarify what that ethic is. It is an ethic of relating.

Most of us grow up assuming that other people are more or less like us, that each person is a freewheeling, freethinking, independent center of initiative not unlike ourselves. The grammar of our language and the ideas of our culture assume that each person is an independent actor or agent doing, speaking, thinking, interacting, or being.

It comes then as a bit of a shock in psychotherapy training when one discovers that this belief in our individual freedom and independence doesn't quite hold water and that people aren't quite so free and independent psychologically as it might seem. "Yes, we know we are tied by the demands of many relationships. But don't we choose which people we want to relate to and under what conditions we want to be bound to relating to them? Oh, that isn't quite so either? Why not?"

The simplest answer to the riddle of how we are affected by relationships is: "we are beings conceived and born into an interacting milieu from which we cannot escape. Nevertheless, our individual consciousness strives to gain a measure of freedom and independence within our significant relationships. And we are successful in this in many regards. But we delude ourselves if we believe that we can ever be completely free of our past conditioning and the influence it holds over us." Okay. But so far we haven't said very much.

A more sophisticated answer might be: "All of our experiences of relating to others teach us how to be and how not to be when considering how to make our own choices and how to achieve our own aims in life. We learn ways of interacting that serve us as young children. We later modify those ways to suit our needs as we grow up." Yes, but we still haven't said much.

How about: "We are creatures of habit. Based upon our earliest significant relationships, we develop emotional habit patterns of relating to others that persist throughout our lives. As the twig is bent so grows the tree." Better? Perhaps, at least for now.

And what about the automatic pilot side of all of this? We know from our dreams and slips of the tongue that we have an unconscious side. "The unconscious, too, belongs to a creature of habit. Except that unconscious habits are the worst ones to try to give up, because we never quite know how those knee-jerk responses got conditioned in the first place and so we can't know very much about how to uncondition them. We have only to think of very basic, everyday habits to see how resistant to change unconscious habit is. The ways we eat, drink, sleep, move through the day, greet family and friends, and think about ourselves are all so seemingly fixed that we consider these unconscious habits a part of our fundamental character makeup. We are only too painfully aware of how little power we have to change long-standing, automatic patterns."

Depth psychology has, over the last century, made the observation that large portions of our lives are silently and automatically governed by long-standing and entrenched habits of relating. Psychotherapy has evolved as a practice or as a discipline geared toward exposing those habits and seeing what kinds of creative transformations might be possible. Unfortunately, the legitimate consciousness-raising goals of psychotherapy have been corrupted by market pressures oriented toward promoting concepts of illness, disease, and cure. When we consider as some form of sickness the inevitable limitations of our unconscious habits of relating—formed in early childhood as they were—we easily fall into yet another bad habit! Then we get sidetracked wondering "What's wrong with me that I always . . . ?" It's hard to pay close attention to who we are and how we operate in relationships when the minute something odd about ourselves catches our attention we label it as an indication of weakness, craziness, or as a symptom of some kind of disease or illness.

Also thwarting the consciousness-raising goals of psychotherapy is the wish to be objective about a person's subjective self—certainly a contradictory endeavor. It's not that we can't find systematic and helpful ways for studying our subjectivity, but let's not call that science! Certainly the overall practice of psychotherapy lends itself to scientific scrutiny. But studying personal subjectivity and working on consciousness-raising about one's relational habits is not a science but a creative narrational activity. Psychotherapy, it turns out, is a form of storytelling—the oldest and most respected of all human communication and knowledge-enhancing activities. Whatever vital truths about our nature have been passed down through the generations have been embedded in narrations—stories, myths, archetypal experiences—that we come to appreciate in various ways.

Psychotherapists have realized from the beginning that if we want to know better who we are, we must tell and re-tell our personal stories. We can't simply tell our story once, or in one way. Nor can we expect it to be coherent or sensible when we do tell it, because we have numerous stories to tell, many of which don't make the slightest bit of sense! Other stories we tell about ourselves are embellished, outlandishly exaggerated, or blatantly untrue. But they exist for a reason and serve some of our purposes. Many of our stories contradict one another. Others have huge gaps in time, place, memory, continuity, and meaning that we can't quite account for. Nevertheless, we endlessly occupy ourselves trying to create seamless narratives that flow coherently, make perfect sense, and are eminently plausible. We crave a sense of coherence and certainty though we know our entire existence is marked by incoherence and uncertainty.

If we buy into the notion that we are essentially flawed beings, that there's something fundamentally wrong with us or sick deep down there somewhere, then we run into other problems. We soon come to believe that if we could just remember—if we could only find a way to get to the bottom of it all, then we would find out what really happened to us and then we could be okay. But once again we lose sight of the fact that our quest is to discover how our unconscious, automatic emotional patterns affect our *present* everyday relationships. In trying to remember in order to get better, we end up searching for the truth of a forever elusive historical past and how it somehow ruined us. And if we go very far in this search for the Grail, the Cure, the Way, we are very likely to come to believe that there is a royal road to self-discovery and perhaps that we now know what it is! Needless to say the "how to do it right" ground is a fertile place for religious zealots, peddlers of dogma, charlatans, and marketeers. "If you are weak, wounded, despairing, or worn out searching for the truth of what ails you, then come to me because I have the answers and the way." This may at times be appropriate in religion but it makes for poor psychology.

If what we are looking for are ways of noticing and dealing with our entrenched emotional habits of relating, then there must be many ways of attaining our own personal enlightenment. There must be many ways of discovering and defining our subjective truths, many ways of allowing our consciousness of ourselves to expand. Simply adopting another fixed set of metaphors—like medical or scientific ones—to replace the old personal ones we want to be free of may well put us ahead in the short run of the self-discovery game. But in the long run our flexibility will still be severely limited because we haven't been absolutely truthful in noticing all of the expectable uniqueness and strangeness that is ourselves.

If we are to grasp the essentials of consciousness-raising, perhaps it's time to stop and think a minute about the meaning of consciousness in the first place. "Consciousness" comes from the ancient Greek meaning "knowing together." Consciousness then, or knowing together, constitutes its own special and personal form of truth. We certainly do know that when two or more are gathered together under a single banner or a single thought, or when two or more move forward with a single purpose, a new consensus, a new consciousness, and new forms of shared truth do emerge. Each partnership and every grouping of people does indeed evolve its own point of view, its own perspective, its own ideas, its own character, and its own consciousness of what seems perfectly clear, obvious, and true to the participants.

Psychotherapy is then a narrational enterprise in which two or more are gathered together with designated speaker(s) and designated listeners(s) for the purpose of expanding consciousness. The storytelling begins. Each listener questions the story from the vantage point of his or her own life experiences, trying to extract the messages, themes, puzzles, and codes of the evolving and emerging narratives. Each listener is attentive to the emotional load of the stories—from the nonverbal content and body reactions that accompany the narrations through the sequencing, the pacing, the language employed, the tone of voice, and the various other physical movements, to emotional expressions, energetic vibrations, and muscular constrictions.

The psychotherapy dialogue expands as both speaker and listener attend to the evolving stories and to the ways they are coming to consider those stories and their reactions together. In time, a complex collaboration or joint cooperative endeavor evolves. This collaboration in developing meaning, in struggling to define themes and movements *is* expanded consciousness itself. Listener and speaker might agree to focus, to interact in many different ways depending on who they are and on what their past experiences have been. But the consciousness expansion or consciousness-raising that has come to characterize psychotherapy arises from a dialogue centering on personal relationships and personal modes of meaning and relatedness, using stories and the interpersonal relationship of therapy itself as a jumping-off point.

Is it so outlandish to think that in human life the very unconscious habit structures that determine the flow of our minds and of our consciousness itself have to do with relationships? Is it really so strange to imagine that the entrenched habits of our emotional life revolve around how we have come to experience ourselves in relation to various others who have been important to us? And is it such a far reach to say that how we experience and relate in the present must surely be strongly colored by how we have learned to relate in the past? *Psychotherapy is about noticing present patterns and the way they operate in the here-and-now to color all of our meaningful relationships, especially the psychotherapy relationship.*

We engage in storytelling rather than, say, playing tennis, taking a hike, or noticing how we sit in a chair for two reasons. First, because storytelling is the oldest and most richly evolved form of human communication and therefore has the highest possible yield in terms of information about a person's unconscious relatedness habits. And secondly, because good stories are full of imagination, nonverbal associations, subtle motivations, and varying contents that all point toward lively self-definitions that may be useful in the development and expansion of the joint consensus of the psychotherapy consciousness-raising endeavor.

"And just what are we trying to raise to consciousness by partaking in therapy?" Psychotherapy seeks to define the unconscious relational habits or patterns that govern the way we live all of our relationships every day. Without a working knowledge of these repetitive, characterological patterns or mechanisms, we haven't got a ghost of a chance of altering them, of exploring options, or of developing novel and creative approaches to how we live our relationships.

"But people have real symptoms—nervousness, tension, sexual dysfunctions, memory lapses, concentration difficulties, attention deficits, addictions, chronic fatigue, and eating problems—to mention only a few. What do all of these symptoms have to do with meaning and consciousness-raising, with emotional habits of relating?" That question has given rise to one of the most ingenious marketing strategies ever devised. By convincing people to consider psychological issues as symptoms of some hidden or mysterious illness or disease process, we psychotherapists can then sell our wares. We can then promise an understanding and a cure. Not that psychological issues don't interface with various constrictions and disease processes in our bodies, because they certainly do. But failing to appreciate how profoundly our physiological processes are reciprocally influenced by psychological processes blinds us to the ways that our emotional-relatedness habits influence, to a greater or lesser extent, all that we are and everything that we do—in every relationship every day of our lives! *Whatever is going on with us is not so very mysterious and it isn't a disease process. It is the diversity and uniqueness of who we are. And no-*

ticing how we are connected mentally and relationally to others and to our bodies is what counts.

"So if we can just straighten out our relationships we'll be okay?" I didn't say that. I said that it is folly to think of ourselves as other than mind and body inextricably linked together and interacting at all times, striving to relate to others. From before birth human beings know about relationship and how, in order to get our needs met on this planet we must relate, and we must do it well. In vitro fertilization studies have shown us that a dozen or more eggs often become fertilized. Many of them immediately attach themselves to the intrauterine wall and, if conditions are hospitable, begin developing. Those who survive must compete in effective relating to the maternal body. They must start an immediate and robust communicating and relating process or they will die. And so on from there—relate, relate, relate! All aspects of our minds and bodies are oriented toward relating to others. Our entire beings, all of our emotional (mind and body) patterns and habits, come to be structured according to the ways of relating that are required for the infant, the toddler, the child, the adolescent, and the adult in order to survive and thrive—given the specifics of each person's immediate emotional environment.

"So what is this ethic you were talking about earlier?" The ethic which is becoming clarified by modern psychotherapy is simply the imperative in human life to relate! "But what exactly does that mean? Relate?" To relate means to recognize that each person who approaches us or who speaks to us is living out, in the way he or she relates to us, the full history of his or her emotional patterns of relatedness. Every person's history is unique, diverse, and rich in its own way. Every person's story is unique. And every person's consciousness about his or her personal automatic patterns of relating is limited in a variety of ways. Psychotherapeutic listening means relating—working hard to see, to define, to understand, and to respond to all of the relationship habits brought to the encounter by both speaker and listener in as many ways as we can.

"But shouldn't relating be free and spontaneous? Why do you speak of hard work?" You're right. We most enjoy ourselves when we are in a relationship with a free, spontaneous, and enjoyable flow. But let's not be naive. Those are the delicious moments of our lives. All day we struggle with myriad kinds of relationship demands that aren't always so spontaneous and delicious. And in any meaningful, ongoing relationship we need to be fully prepared for periods of turmoil, strife, struggling together, and conflict resolution.

"Then this consciousness-raising you are talking about can occur in the hard work of relating in any relationship." Yes it can and it does. But the trials and tribulations of our days as well as our need for a certain amount of solace in our significant relationships at the end of the day make it difficult for us to keep up the hard work of relating that is required to keep both parties alive to each other every minute. We tend to become lazy and sloppy in our close relationships. And for this reason it is not uncommon for our relationships to fall into various kinds of trouble. But over time it has become increasingly clear that the value of studying our patterns of relating is so great and the personal gains so significant that we are willing to dedicate a great deal of time and energy to the cause of therapy and to designate a professional listener whom we are willing to pay. With that listener we hope to become more able to spell out in consciousness how we typically approach people, how we set up expectations for our relationships, and how we systematically engineer relationship disasters that profoundly affect our minds and our bodies. Systematic consciousness-raising can be a part of any relationship. And good relationships are always rewarding in this way. Therapy is simply a special form of two or more people coming together dedicated to the process.

"But back to this ethic of relating . . ." Yes. The psychotherapeutic situation has forced therapists to systematically examine the problem of relatedness for more than a century. Because mind is interesting and the role of healer often prestigious and lucrative, and because helping people has its own personal rewards, some extraordinary people have devoted themselves to the study of relatedness over the last hundred years and have left a formidable body of ideas that continues to evolve. The bottom line, as psychotherapists have learned, is that if you can't see or feel where people are coming from with their emotional-relatedness patterns, then you certainly can't relate very personally to them or help them see how they are relating to you, to themselves, or to others. So the study of relationship and relatedness has had to occupy center stage in order for psychotherapy to prosper.

"So that's what relatedness is all about, prospering?" Yes, I believe so. I believe that striving, thriving human beings prosper in all ways in their lives by paying close attention to how they relate to themselves and to other people in their lives. It is through studying all of their unconscious habits of relating that truly enlivened people learn how to cultivate new options for themselves. The psychotherapeutic dialogue teaches us how to create greater flexibility in relating to others for more joy, richness, and fulfillment in life.

3

Love—The Impossible Dream

Psychotherapy is about relationships and love. Love is about reaching out and receiving back. As children we learned many ways to reach out and to receive love back. In childhood we each struggled to develop regular, reliable, and workable ways of seeking and finding the love we needed—or at least the love we could get. From the people who raised us we also learned where and when love was and was not to be found. We learned about unreliable, painful, and unrealistic ways of reaching that did not work so that we had to constrict or to withdraw. We learned in early relationships how, when, and where it was safe to expand and under which conditions it was necessary to contract.

As young children we soon built fortresses to protect our vulnerable selves. We built living structures for our love based on knowing how we could safely reach out and find. But we also built our castles of love with the limited knowledge we had at the time about when to retreat behind our walls and when to pull up the drawbridge. Unfortunately, we continue to carry this castle of love with its drawbridges—

so painstakingly constructed by the tender heart of a young child—with us wherever we go for the rest of our lives. Until and unless we choose to do something about it.

The trouble with the love castles or the protective fortresses we carry with us is that these instinctive, automatically operating structures built in childhood continue to decide for us today who will be admitted and who will be refused. The love decisions we make as adults are based on silent, unconsciously operating expectations and rules learned from our experiences in early childhood. Is it any wonder that we find friends and lovers who resemble our mothers and fathers, brothers and sisters? Is it any wonder that we soon feel resentment and hatred toward the friends and lovers admitted into our lives on the basis of our childish hopes and our infantile tolerances of pain?

Love castles built in childhood are an inevitable part of the human condition. We all built love castles. We all learned when it was safe to let down the drawbridge of our fortress and to welcome someone into our lives. But we also learned how to maintain our protective walls in order to survive the depriving, rejecting, and abusive conditions we were raised in—no matter how good our family was. This means that the expectations we bring to love are a hangover from early childhood and truly make love "the impossible dream." We continue to stay holed up in our fortresses, never daring to reach out in ways once found frightening and painful. And we allow admittance only to dangers and pains that were once found tolerable. We choose for lovers people who, according to our predetermined castle and fortress rules, promise good things and who only offer disappointment and pain in ways we believe we can endure.

But what of all of the passersby on life's journey who may have much to offer us, who call to us, who knock on our castle doors, who beg to be let in but whom we refuse because they don't look or feel familiar? Because their ways of reaching don't conform to our preset rules for admission? Because their forms of villainy appear to us to be unduly treacherous? How great the potential loss!

What is bound to be wrong with those whom we do admit into our castles of love? First, the people we admit to our love will certainly disappoint us because we expect that they will respond to us, that they will take care of us in ways that will make us feel loved according to the hopes and expectations we learned in childhood. But it is only a matter of time before we learn that it is impossible for them to meet our deeply personal, preset expectations. Our illusion of hope slowly crumbles into resentment and despair. Secondly, the people whom we admit to our love castles will disappoint us because we thought we could endure the familiar forms of insensitivity, neglect, and hurt they seemed to offer us. But this illusion too crumbles as we are confronted with unfamiliar forms of neglect, insensitivity, and injury. We find the unexpectable intolerable because we fail to notice that we are no longer helpless children without options.

So it is only a matter of time with any intimate friend or lover until we discover that our hopes, expectations, and anticipated intolerances in love fail us. We discover we have made a mistake. We find that we have let someone in who does not conform to our unspoken rules. We have admitted someone into our intimate circle who does not receive our reaching out in the desired ways. Someone who does not reach back in the longed-for ways. Someone who feels hurt by us when no hurt was intended. And someone who hurts us in ways we find puzzling and unbearable. Moreover, what we experience as missing when we reach out creates a painful longing in us.

Frustrating or unsatisfying relationships heighten our desire for a love that meets us where we need to be met. We soon cry out in pain and agony, "Is this really too much to ask? I only want to love and to be loved. I only need small considerations. Do I really deserve to be so disregarded, so ignored, so degraded, so abused?" It's hard not to feel like a victim when the conditions we have set for our love are not being met and the pain—long conditioned by childhood neglect and abuse—is steadily rising.

And so we find another friend or lover—and another, and another—only dimly perceiving that it is we ourselves who, by constructing our love castles and fortifications in the first place, have frustrated the fulfillment of our own desires. We then realize, along with Don Quixote, that our love is indeed an "impossible dream" that we senselessly and relentlessly pursue. Love is "impossible" because the more we search for what we so desperately desire and believe we must have, the less we are truly able to love and to be loved by another real and available but unfamiliar person.

Philosophers and poets throughout the ages have considered the differences between the mundane forces of everyday reality and the human capacity for inspiration by and transcendence to the ideal. In no area of our lives does the power of the ideal affect us more than in love. Like a love-smitten adolescent we are all prey to fanciful reveries of experiences of self-affirmation and personal worth and power when it comes to love. We attain a special sense of who we are, of who we desire to be, and of how the infinite can play into our lives when we imbibe the ideals, hopes, promises, and passions of love! But when the transport is over, the infatuation is gone, and the moment of infinite self-realization has passed, we once again descend into the ordinary. We no longer soar on the wings of an infinite and ideal love. Because we harbor dreams of endless love, and because of the internal love castles and fortifications we maintain, we find ourselves prisoners within the same familiar relationship traps we have known for so long. Yet we know that somehow our sense of the infinite, the passionate, the powerful, and the ideal cannot be totally wrong—the dream is too compelling within us. We also know that our sense of emptiness, depletion, weakness, and discouragement with our mundane and unsatisfying everyday reality cannot be totally right. How can we account for, how can we deal with these discrepancies? How can the ideal and the real be reconciled in love?

The paradox of love is that we experience the fullness of passion, the inspiration of the infinite, and the supreme goodness of the ideal only through real relationships. In the act of loving and being loved we experience an infinity of being that transcends our sense of the temporal, the known, the causal, and the certain. But the joy of loving only comes to us as we risk pain and uncertainty—as we dare to be fully alive through risking passionate loving and terrifying pain. And we cannot allow ourselves the risk and the uncertainty of truly loving in the present until we have learned how to assess and resonate with the inner pathways that hold us in bondage to past loves.

THE SEVEN PATHWAYS OF LOVE

In considering love we can conceptualize, more or less in the order we first encountered them, seven pathways that have served to fix our relationship habits and thus to limit our possibilities.

1. Searching for someone who is there.
2. Reaching out and interconnecting with someone.
3. Finding and being found by someone special.
4. Pushing for independence my own way.
5. Pulling for self-affirmation and self-acceptance.
6. Negotiating triangular love relationships.
7. Impacting and being impacted by love in a group.

How can we consider these developmental pathways of human love in relation to sensuality, sexuality, desire, and fear?

SENSUALITY AND SEXUALITY

In 1905 Freud labeled the line of human development he wished to study "infantile sexuality"—on an *a posteriori* basis. That is, he took human sexuality to be biologically based and labeled the developing love and sensual functions of childhood on the basis of where they would eventually end up—adult sexuality. He may also have wished to scandalize and reprimand Victorian society a bit by opening people's eyes to the soon to be sexualized intentions and vulnerabilities of young children. But whatever his purposes, Freud certainly ended our collective fantasy that children's sensual strivings are innocent—in the sense of being free from sexual intentions of a sort.

As psychoanalytic research progressed, the familiar oral, anal, urethral, phallic, and oedipal phases of psychosexual development became delineated on the basis of an unfolding sequence of developing erogenous body zones. This particular way of defining phases of libidinal instinct has served particularly well in the classical and ego psychological conflict models for conceptualizing psychoanalytic work with oedipal level (4- to 6-year-old) relatedness patterns. The formulation "instincts versus defenses" allows an analyst to speak, for example, of oral or anal level conflicts in the context of an oedipal/neurotic relatedness pattern.

With the scope of psychoanalysis widening to include analytic understanding of a range of preoedipal relational patterns and concerns (age before birth to 3 years) the conflict model of instinct versus defense has become a less compelling way to think and to talk. The current prevailing thought paradigm in psychoanalysis revolves around relationship and relatedness (Hedges 1992). Dynamic formulations featuring the ways the subject experiences (or represents) self in relation to experiences or representations of others now capture the central core of our thinking. Jacobson (1954, 1964) and Mahler and her colleagues (1968, 1975) have provided developmental schemas that allow for conceptualizing an array of progressively complex self-and-other experiences in the earliest months and years of life. Again, the "self-and-other" line of development is labeled *a posteriori*, because distinctions, conceptions, and representations of "self" in contrast to "other" are at first not clear to the infant but only gradually come to be the optimal end result of human relational development.

Where have sensuality and sexuality gone in the history of our growing concerns with relationships and love? How does personal desire operate in the relatedness paradigm? It would seem that along with a waning emphasis on biological instinct there has been a corresponding lessening of emphasis on the concrete aspects of erogenous zones both as organs and as metaphors to describe the development of sensual and sexual interests. Instead there is an interest in describing phases or levels of relationship, with the implication that the diversity of human sensuality, sexuality, and love evolves in the context of available opportunities for and experiences of arousing others in relationships.

According to this contemporary relatedness approach we can conceptualize a developmental series of human desires along with their accompanying fears. The implication would be that the richness, diversity, and personal specificity of human sensuality, sexuality, and love arise from within an overall context of individual relatedness experience. Table 3–1 shows what the seven pathways of love might look like when considered from the vantage points of desire and fear.

In my work with Virginia Hilton in *The Seven Deadly Fears* (Hedges and Hilton, in press), we take the position that all people develop conditioned fears or "fear reflexes" in the relationships of early childhood. We sketch seven developmental stages or phases of relationship development, pointing out the kinds of fears that typify the relatedness issues of each normal childhood era. We show how the relatedness fears we establish at each level of development are both mental and physical, and how in time our fears become automatic conditioned reflexes that can easily become triggered later in life when similar emo-

Table 3–1. The seven pathways of love from the vantage points of desire and fear

Relationship Strivings: The Sensual/Sexual Desires	Relationship Inhibitions: The Seven Deadly Fears
1. To reach out and touch	Nobody will be there.
2. To connect	I will be hurt.
3. To bond with another	I will be abandoned.
4. To assert my autonomy	I will be crushed.
5. To be affirmed as a person	I will be unacceptable.
6. To succeed or fail in competition	I will be injured.
7. To thrive in a group	I will be rejected.

tional threats arise. Which of us can get through a day without experiencing relationship threats, any one of which can trigger a tightness in our jaw, a tensing of our stomach, a sick feeling in our gut, a pain in our neck or back, or cramps in our arms, hands, legs, and feet? In *The Seven Deadly Fears* we offer a series of simple body exercises designed to help the reader contact the ways different types of relationship fear affect his or her body. Patterns of automatic fear response are like a personal fingerprint: they are unique to each person. The book shows how to form an individualized body mapping of personal patterns of fear response, as well as how to track one's personal patterns in order to learn ways of releasing fear constrictions as they occur in various relationships during the course of the day. We call the seven universal types of constrictive fear response *deadly* because of the disastrous long-term consequences for health and mental well-being that our personal patterns of constrictive fear inevitably have for each of us.

These seven pathways of sensual and sexual desire with their corresponding seven deadly relatedness fears have, in various forms, become the central focus of transference, resistance, and countertransference studies in the contemporary relatedness approach to depth psychotherapy. *The dream of actually finding someone to love and to be loved by can only become realized when one has learned the residual childhood patterns of his or her relatedness strivings and relatedness fears enough to transcend the familiar pathways of love, sexuality, and fear into the breathtaking and risky uncertainty of loving and being loved now by someone who is unfamiliar.*

4

Listening Perspectives and Terror

Four distinctly different listening perspectives in psychotherapy have evolved for listening and responding to the relatedness qualities that each person lives out on a daily basis. These perspectives are essentially metaphors derived from observing relationship developments in early childhood. They have been found to be especially useful as differential frames for the listening activity of psychotherapy. But since these listening perspectives have evolved for grasping various qualities of interpersonal relatedness, they can also be used for thinking about relationships in arenas other than psychotherapy.

FOUR RELATEDNESS LISTENING PERSPECTIVES

1. The Organizing Experience.

Infants require certain forms of connection and interconnection in order to remain psychologically alert and enlivened to themselves and to others. In their early relatedness they are busy "organizing" physical and mental channels of connection—first to mother's body and later to her mind and to the minds of others—for nurturance, stimulation, evacuation, and soothing.

2. The Symbiotic Experience.

Toddlers are busy learning how to make emotional relationships (both good and bad) work for them. They experience a sense of merger and reciprocity with their primary caregivers, thus establishing many knee-jerk, automatic, characterological, and role-reversible patterns of relatedness.

3. The Self–Other Experience.

Three-year-olds are preoccupied with using the acceptance and approval of *others* for developing and enhancing *self* definitions, *self* skills, and *self*-esteem. In their relatedness strivings they make use of the admiring, confirming, and idealized responses of significant others to firm up their budding sense of self.

4. The Independent Experience.

Four- and 5-year-olds are dealing with triangular love and hate relationships and are moving toward more complex social relationships. In their relatedness they experience others as separate centers of initiative and themselves as independent agents in a socially competitive environment.

Since we have all passed through these four periods of relationship development, we have all established our personal forms of relatedness habits characteristic of each era. Our relationship habits silently and automatically persist into adult life in various ways to color all of our significant relationships.

Four levels or perspectives is an arbitrary number based on logical considerations of self-and-other relationship possibilities. But when, for example, we consider love and sexuality, the transference of desire and fear into later life, we find it helpful to divide three of the stages so that we expand the number of perspectives to the seven we have already considered. The number doesn't matter so much as the contrasts and comparisons that developmentally based categories allow us to create in order to enhance our listening to relationships.[1] See Table 4–1.

Table 4–1. Listening Perspectives and the Seven Deadly Fears

The organizing experience	1. The fear of being alone
	2. The fear of making connections
The symbiotic experience	3. The fear of abandonment
	4. The fear of self-assertion
The self–other experience	5. The fear of being unacceptable
The independent experience	6. The fear of failure and success
	7. The fear of being fully alive

TERRIFYING TRANSFERENCES

Relationship experiences from all four levels of self-and-other development—the organizing, the symbiotic, the selfother, and the independent—are emotionally transferred, and re-experienced in relation to the therapist in long-term, intensive psychotherapy. Whether they are explicitly talked about and interpreted in the here-and-now of the therapeutic relationship or whether they are ignored and acted out depends upon the cleverness and insightfulness as well as the purposes and goals of both speaker and listener.

Any child could have been exposed to intrusive, traumatic, or terrifying experiences at any age and might need to relive that fear later in psychotherapy with the therapist assuming a variety of roles in the re-creation of the emotionally traumatic experience. But by the time a child is 2½ or 3 years old, he or she has a wealth of resources avail-

---

1. I have considered these four levels of relationship experience and their implications for psychotherapeutic listening in detail (Hedges 1983), and have summarized the listening perspective approach to psychotherapy elsewhere (Hedges 1994a, 1996).

able for dealing with frightening, fragmenting experiences, so that fear becomes progressively less likely to totally overwhelm the existent ego or self-structure.

Truly terrifying and deeply traumatic experiences are therefore more characteristic of the earliest stages of development—the organizing and the symbiotic experiences. And it goes without saying that a child (or anyone) subjected to overwhelming terror during an earlier phase of life is vulnerable to having a similar overwhelming level of terror restimulated in later frightening or fragmenting circumstances. A corollary of these two propositions—(1) that a propensity to experience overwhelming terror is most likely to begin very early in life, and (2) that people terrified early in life are highly vulnerable to later retraumatization—would be that (3) people are more likely to be able to recall with some clarity later traumatic experiences that occur after perception and memory are well developed, whereas early overwhelming trauma usually cannot be directly recalled and recounted because when it took place ordinary forms of perception, judgment, and memory were not yet in full operation.

In the "recovered memory" controversy a few years back we had a whole group of therapists colluding with their clients trying to image through "truth serum," hypnosis, and guided imagery what was at the bottom of their lifelong dissatisfaction. The images that were conjured up to convey the sense of what horrors had happened to them in infancy repeatedly turned out to be a series of archetypal stories and pictures masquerading as recovered memories. Through body-shaking memories of past lives, alien abductions, and childhood molestations to the dissociations of multiple personality, out-of-body experiences, and satanic ritual abuse, speaker and listener were jointly conveyed to realms of horror and terror by the images and drama that emerged. What was missing, of course, was a careful study of how these same terrors were emerging concurrently in relation to the therapist and to the pressing psychotherapeutic demand to relate emotionally. Both speaker and listener could be transported to "way back then," struggling to remember exactly what atrocities occurred and identifying just who perpetrated them. Both participants could then react with disgust, horror, and outrage, thereby enabling themselves to collude in engaging in activities allied with resisting or avoiding the task at hand, that is, the revival in the here-and-now trust relationship of the transference terrors associated with interpersonal emotional intimacy and the transfer into the present of the accusatory cries of the past.

I want no one to misunderstand me. Plenty of childhood abuse has occurred—much more than any of us would like to think about. But as the various task forces of the mental health professions have reported: (1) most seriously abused people have memory for some or all of the childhood abuse, (2) not all memories of abuse are about things that actually happened, (3) the earlier and more vivid the recovered memory, the less likely that it actually happened in the exact way it is recalled, (4) infantile abuse is remembered in somatic and relational modes, not narrational and pictorial modes, and (5) construction of memories that reflect emotional truths is not uncommon.

Remembering, Repeating, and Working Through Childhood Trauma (Hedges 1994b) studies how focal as well as cumulative strain trauma in infancy leaves imprints on the personality that are likely to be recalled later through (1) archetypal narrations, (2) replicated interpersonal interactions, and (3) deep and terrifying somatic abreactions. A brief word is in order about each, as these forms of memory are related to terror being reexperienced in the transference of psychotherapy and other trust relationships.

1. *Archetypal narrations* are stories of trauma that serve like dreams to condense, symbolize, and represent the emotional sense of the remembered trauma. Archetypal narrations such as abduction, ritual abuse, and past lives serve as metaphors to express the emotional sense of "what I know I must have gone through at one time long, long ago."

2. *Replicated interpersonal interaction* is a well-known form of memory accomplished by re-creating, living out, and acting out in contemporary personal relationships—usually again and again—the traumatic situation that one was once caught up in, exposed to, or trapped by. This compulsion to repeat earlier trauma in present relationships is presumably based on an attempt to master the trauma through repetition with the hope of a better outcome, or, through a role reversal, to turn an enduring sense of passive defeat into active victory.

3. *Deep somatic abreaction* such as shaking, convulsing, vomiting, breath holding, ritualistic obsessions, panic attacks, hysterical paralysis or blindness, and other psycho-physical manifestations may *be* critical memories of infantile trauma, although there is often some event, story, or interpersonal context that is relevant to the triggering of the

somatic abreaction. These reactions can be sudden, dramatic, and at times even dangerous to both client and therapist, but they usually emerge in a context of threatened or successful interpersonal contact, connection, or intimacy. *That is, it is in the anticipation of or in the wake of some successful move by both participants in the relationship to achieve some form of viable and meaningful interpersonal connection that the somatic abreaction occurs.* As such, it expresses terror of contact and functions to rupture, to prevent, and/or to foreclose the interpersonal connection that is forbidden by primordial conditioning. *The physical abreaction itself is the memory, and whatever narration accompanies it usually serves as a decoy concern to derail the intimacy being approached or achieved by the two in the moment.* That is, intimate relating in the past was the instrument of the abuse or trauma, and therefore it is intimate connecting in a true interpersonal interaction in the present that is feared.

TERROR

Shifting slightly to consider childhood fears that might have been experienced in the extreme at any particular moment, let us move to begin thinking about terror.

Webster defines terror as stark fear and as a running from fear. We may say we are terrified of being somehow disabled, helpless, or trapped. We may feel a terror of not being able to move, to breathe, to think, or to speak. We may awake terrified from a nightmare in which we cannot pass an examination, cannot talk or scream, cannot escape an approaching disaster, or are paralyzed in the face of overwhelming and unavoidable danger. A "reign of terror" is a frightening, oppressive, and damaging political situation that cannot be escaped.

I have long suspected that those enamored with murder mysteries, suspense stories, and horror films are somehow rehearsing or attempting psychologically to master an escape from fear, much in the same way that we all do in our dreams. The fear is allowed to slowly intensify with the knowledge that there will be a denouement, a moment of relief in which we once again feel safe and unafraid. Pornography often features a buildup of fear as a part of sexual arousal—fear of being hurt, tortured, penetrated, bound up, helpless, chased, raped, dominated, mutilated, subjugated, murdered, followed by the orgiastic release.

Fear is known to all of us. Although it may be externally triggered, fear itself is a natural physiological response that arises from *within* our bodies to alert us to potential danger, thus making the fear response itself adaptively important and somehow inescapable. And yet our *experience* of fear is invariably linked to some external stimulus, an outside threat that elicits, triggers, or causes it. We may be suddenly startled and then relieved when we realize there is really nothing to be afraid of.

Certain situations may elicit fear for prolonged periods of time until we find some escape, some safety, some relief. But for many people chronic fear has been conditioned into their minds and bodies by the ongoing and frightening circumstances of their childhoods. Some people have experienced severe traumas and major disasters later in life that leave them perennially vulnerable to being once again seized by panic and terror. One observation just now being made is that survivors of the Holocaust and other traumatic stress survivors who may have been able to manage or control their conditioned fears for most of their lives once again become prey to terrifying experiences and memories in the weakness of old age. It is as though a propensity toward the experience of terror is difficult if not impossible to eradicate.

The dream I wakened to this morning, knowing that I was going to write about terror today, featured some unknown but powerful human force or group (like the Mafia) which was out to get me. As I moved in and out of sleep the scenario changed as I attempted to control the fear. Someone whispered in my ear not to start my car because sometime soon there was going to be a bomb going off. "Have the maid start it instead." I pictured the poor housekeeper sent to the garage to start the car only to be helplessly blown up. Carnage and tattered pieces of maid's uniform splattered everywhere. That didn't work. Perhaps I won't drive for a while, then the bomb threat won't work. But then there was the threat that my wife or my teenage daughter might forget the threat and accidentally start the car. Blood and guts all over the garage again. But if they couldn't get me that way what would they try next? I had apparently innocently done something to offend them. Just living my life the way I do had put me in jeopardy. Whoever I am is important enough to stalk and torture or kill. Next my little boy is swinging happily in the park. I am pushing him higher and higher when suddenly his head is blown off and shattered by a sniper shot. Vulnerability, helplessness, and terrifying threat were all coming from unknown powerful, vengeful, and out-of-control forces—from evil-intentioned people. There was nothing I could do, nowhere I could go that was safe. There was no way to protect my loved ones, no way to save myself. Sooner or later they would get me. This sort of vulnerability and terror are an ongoing part of our lives, whether we like it or not.

Needless to say, our media play endlessly on our many terrifying vulnerabilities—real and imagined. The fears we feel have a constricting effect on our minds and bodies. Chronic fear leaves us paralyzed and crippled and increases our vulnerability to stress, fatigue, and disease. We cringe with arthritic fear. We shake with heart-stopping terror. Our eyes open wide in sudden shock and horror. We clench our fists. We try to scream or run. We freeze with fright, get cold feet, shiver, curl up in a ball, double over with pain, curl our toes, hold in our breath, pull into our shell, strike out in panic, fight for our lives, run for safety, hang on for dear life. Body–mind terror is not so far away as we might like it to be!

ABOUT THIS BOOK

The case reports in *Terrifying Transferences* will be formulated primarily in terms of the organizing and/or the symbiotic listening perspectives, since it is at these levels of listening that experiences of overwhelming terror can be expected to emerge. Other formulations may strike the reader. Each contributor to this book is a professional colleague of mine. Each has described an evolving relationship with a psychotherapy client that led to the emergence of terrifying experiences—sometimes for the client, sometimes for the therapist, but usually for both. Some chapters have actually been written by the therapist. Others are edited verbatim recordings of consultation sessions with me or of case conference seminars held in my office with groups of therapists. Each case situation is unique and compelling in its own way and each seeks to focus on different elements of terror as they emerge into the transference–countertransference dimension of the therapy process. I will make comments as we go before and after each case presentation.

The symbiotic listening perspective has evolved in the psychoanalytic community for listening to so-called borderlines. Based on the work of Mahler and her colleagues (1968, 1975), Kernberg (1975), Searles (1979), Giovacchini (1979, 1997), Winnicott (1953), Stolorow and his colleagues (1992, 1994), and the work of many others, it has become possible to listen to people in terms of their self and object representations, their split affects, primitive mental states, diffuse identity formations, and false self formations. *Interpreting the Countertransference* (Hedges 1992) surveys the symbiotic listening perspective in the context of a paradigm shift to an emphasis on considering relating and relationship as the foundation of the human mind. The symbiotic listening perspective is often seen as the royal road to understanding and analyzing the merger experience through the interpretation of the countertransference because so much of the nonverbal material of the early symbiotic era is projected into the therapist and manifests as countertransference. Understanding internalized relationship scenarios and role reversals in the transference–countertransference exchange allows an understanding of what Bollas (1987) has called "the unthought known." *Strategic Emotional Involvement* (Hedges 1996) consists of a series of intensive case studies by twelve therapists that show how countertransference works differently at each developmental level but is crucial to the interpretation of the symbiotic internalized structure.

Therapists at Risk (Hedges 1997), co-authored by Robert Hilton, Virginia Wink Hilton, and attorney O. Brandt Caudill, outlines the ethical and legal risks entailed these days in doing intensive, in-depth psychotherapy. The critical risks are the personal ones, the moments when one's personality is on the line, when one is accused, when one is asked to believe recovered memories, when one must speak disturbing countertransference feelings, or when one is battling a transference psychosis and at risk of failing.

Working the Organizing Experience (Hedges 1994c) puts forth a working theory of the organizing experience and is illustrated by numerous clinical vignettes provided by many therapists. The organizing experience records our earliest relatedness strivings and describes the way imprints from our earliest interpersonal connections live on to affect our later relationships. The critical feature from the organizing experience that becomes central to *Terrifying Transferences* is the re-creation in contemporary relationships of deep-seated fears conditioned by relationship-related traumas experienced in infancy. As Winnicott (1949) has shown us, in utero and in the earliest months after birth the infant mind can be characterized as having a sense of "going on being" that allows it to evolve unperturbed. Intrusive impingements of intensity, frequency, or duration into that nascent sense of continuity and well-being leave a mark on the infant mind by forcing it to react to strong external stimulation before it is ready. Significant intrusive impingement constitutes trauma for the infant because the nascent and developing ego–self structures cannot adequately receive, process, and attribute meaning to overwhelmingly strong stimulation. We hear a loud, sudden noise and watch the infant awake—startled, tense, constricted, wide-eyed, terrified. And then comes the cry, the clamor to be picked up, the need to be soothed, the plea to be allowed to return to preconscious reverie, to a sense of personal well-being and to the safety of mental continuity. Paradise is made of such fruits and we all yearn for them. But whenever we were prematurely and/or abruptly cast from paradise a scar was formed—a scar of conditioned mind–body fear and, in its extreme form, primordial terror.

THE CLAMOR

In trying just now to visualize terrifying infantile trauma and the mind-body constrictions it gives rise to, I have alluded to the clamor that over- or understimulation inevitably gives rise to. We hear it incessantly in depth psychotherapy. I don't know what else to call it. I know the clamor comes from deep distress and pain. And I don't mean to sound pejorative—but it is a clamor, and our psychotherapy rooms are filled with it. Clamor to me implies two things. First, an incessant cry or demand for more, for special consideration, for "what I legitimately need and have a right to *now*—before I fragment or die." But secondly, clamor is a cry that is so intense and so intrusive as to be annoying, alienating, and contact-rupturing. Undoubtedly the original function of the cry was to signal distress and to demand that the mothering partner restore a mind–body state that could be enjoyed or tolerated. But when the cry becomes a conditioned part of an infant's life that cannot be adequately calmed it can become a conditioned response to any perturbation. Subsequently the clamor is systematically paired with or conditioned to a sense of the presence of the (m)other who is failing to relieve the perturbation or pain. So through simple conditioning the trust relationship itself becomes the object of terror, in proportion to whatever extent it was originally unsuccessful in quelling the rising tide of overwhelming distress and pain. Later trust relationships or trust situations are then imbued with this conditioned fear and its accompanying clamor. The clamor thus comes to serve as an alienating wedge between people to prevent the danger of intimate relating.

Clamor takes myriad forms. But in therapy it functions to produce a breach in interpersonal connection or to limit the possibility of sustained connection. Therapists with good training in empathy try to ride out the cry, to empathize with the need—the demand associated with the clamor—and with the frustration that it is not being adequately met. But paradoxically, empathy with the content of the clamor serves to escalate its intensity, delay its punch, and reinforce its alienating function. What is not being realized by such a limited form of empathy is that the *content* of the clamor cannot be satisfied because, as cry, it is a memory with a purpose but not necessarily a relevant content. *The clamor is an angry memory of what I needed and didn't get. But the conditioned clamor-memory now functions in the service of preventing intimate or reciprocal interconnections that in the past were known to be traumatic.* What is remembered is the pain of a previous relation or connection that was experienced as dangerous or terrifying. Muscular constriction to withdraw from, ward off, or quell the pain then provides its own form of permanently conditioned pain response—which, over a lifetime, the person comes to fear. The trust relation rouses this contiguous physical-psychological pain response. The cry or clamor serves to ward off present and future connections by alienating the other and creating a safety zone to prevent future relationship trauma. *Once an expression of pain in relationship, the clamorous cry now functions as a defense against relationship retraumatization through foreclosing meaningful emotional connections.* The person is terrified of connections, of relationship, because interconnectedness in the primordial past was known to be hurtful. To connect in the present is to run the risk of stimulating pain again. There are many ways to prevent relatedness—one is a clamorous cry for "more," for "what I deserve," for how "you're not treating me right," for

how "you're not giving me what I need," or for how "I can find somebody better who will." "Abandonment!" in one form or another is the
cry. But it is essentially bogus because it is used *not* to promote relating, *not* to search for ways of separation and re-establishing empathic
attunement, but for purposes of preventing connection or creating a
break in connections!

One man who was born with a birth defect that prevented sucking sought older women prostitutes and then complained that he
couldn't orgasm with them. Soothing sensual contact was what had
been missing, and when he now goes for it in ways that are self-limiting,
he then focuses on his sexual dysfunction rather than on his self-
frustrated yearning for closeness and his terror of relationship. A woman
client who had been mechanically managed by her mother out of a
sense of obligation and duty in infancy begged her therapist for physical touch because she was internally prevented from feeling his mental presence and touch. He knew that the soothing physical touch that
she longed for was available to her in many ways in her life. Her clamor
for physical touch from him not only kept him uneasy and distant in
the relationship, but prevented the very mental and emotional closeness and soothing that would allow her to participate in transformational relating. Another man maintains a schizoid or bored demeanor
in relationships until the other almost forcibly approaches him with
overriding, warm, affirming interest. He thinks he is afraid to approach
others because he might be rejected, but in fact his manner staves off
the possibility of connection that he is terrified of. When there are brief
moments of connection with his therapist he suffers terrifying nightmares and phobias. He remains stuck in the belief that others "don't
relate well, don't approach me right." Numerous therapy relations end
with the client bitterly complaining about the shortcomings of the
therapist. Yet when the interaction is closely scrutinized we can see that
the clamor and accusatory cries only serve to justify the client's retreat,
and that there was an unwillingness or inability to continue negotiating the relating. Appendix E contains an informed consent form that
seeks to alert clients in advance to this possibility and to specify a course
for productive resolution.

The desperate plea, "You've got to believe that really happened
to me" confused a number of therapists during the recovered memory
controversy a few years ago. Of course, the memory was of trauma that

resulted from close interpersonal contact in infancy or childhood. Insofar as the clamor for the recovered or constructed memory to be literally believed troubled or derailed the therapist, it thus functioned to ward off the terror about to be experienced in the trust relationship of the therapy. A terror of contact can be transferentially replicated and worked with if therapists are willing to maintain empathy with relationship fears and accusatory cries instead of getting lost in the content of the reported memory or other content or symptomatology that the client finds impelling.

The plea is always somehow "Don't abandon me, I need you." But the plea comes in the form of a clamor bound to alienate and replicate the original abandonment. *The clamor stems not from abandonment fear, as the client is inclined to claim, but from the terror of meaningful connections.* The memory expressed in this way is the danger of connecting, the terror of a deeply personal I–thou exchange that has the power to transform. The content of the clamor invariably revolves around some charge—aimed at the therapist or at others—of rejection, neglect, abandonment, misunderstanding, or abuse. The therapist is thrown some tantalizing bone to chew on which serves as resistance to the two experiencing the full impact of the terrifying transference—thus derailing the therapeutic process. The content is designed to fend off intimate and meaningful relating. A variation of this resistance to intimate connecting appears when the therapist is told how the previous therapists failed, blundered, or behaved inappropriately. How easy it is for the present therapist to ignore what the relational problem really is by tracking the content of the break—and narcissistically assuming that "I am a better therapist"!

In Search of the Lost Mother of Infancy (Hedges 1994a) is a series of in-depth case reports by eight therapists that demonstrate how the theory of the organizing experience and the conditioned scars of relationship terror can be applied in various kinds of interpersonal circumstances. The listening perspectives approach and the theory of the organizing experience is used to understand avoidance, withdrawal, and disconnecting rage and terror in the case material. The clinical study of Sandy especially illustrates the extent to which countertransference plays an unsettling part in this terrifying type of engagement.

But it is with Paul in Chapter 17 of this book that we can at last see with clarity and in detail the nuts and bolts of this way of considering and working the organizing experience. It is here that the relation between close interpersonal encounters and the emergence of psychotic anxieties is portrayed in its subtlety. I realize that many psychothera-pists and psychoanalysts would not choose to be so active, or intrusive, or directive as I have been with Paul. I also realize that many will greet this work either as folly, or with a "Ho-hum, what's new?" attitude. But I hope that the work with Paul and with other individuals throughout this book succeeds in *clarifying a frame developed for the purpose of securing for analysis the organizing transference* or what others have called the transference psychosis.

Let us now shift our focus in order to move to the heart of the problem of *Terrifying Transferences*, the way the organizing experience emerges in psychotherapy. I will first tell you a story that terrified me, and set out the letter I wrote to a state licensing board in an attempt to master my fear. The letter will be a strong and tightly condensed description of the organizing transference that threatens both partici-pants—speaker and listener—in the psychotherapy experience.

5

The Letter

Howard left word on my voice mail requesting the name of an attorney who defends psychotherapists. I left the name of the best attorney I know on his recorder, adding that I hoped this wasn't for him! A few weeks later on a Tuesday I received a call from an investigator employed by the State of California. She explained that she was investigating a complaint of sexual misconduct against Howard made by one of his former psychotherapy clients. Howard told her that he had consulted with me ten years previously regarding this case. Had I indeed supervised him at one time? Yes. Could she ask me a few quick questions over the phone about Howard and his work? I explained that I could not say anything to her until I had obtained a release from him. I also stated that I thought she and I needed to meet in person, considering the potential importance of our time together. We set up an appointment in two weeks to discuss her concerns.

I was immediately sick to my stomach. I knew too well how grave this situation was. I hardly slept for two nights—and I'm usually a good sleeper. I tossed and turned with tortured nightmares. I dreamed of being in Berlin in 1938, smelling burning flesh and with everyone around me saying there was nothing they could personally do, thus choosing to blind themselves to the atrocities that were occurring right under their noses. I saw the Nazi Gestapo in high black boots knocking on doors in the middle of the night. I saw the lines of those waiting to be burned.

I know too well our administrative justice system. I know that therapists are tried daily under conditions totally lacking in civil rights. Licensing boards for psychotherapists have sadly become courts of inquisition in which bizarre complaints of highly disturbed, disgruntled consumers are allowed to wreck the lives of hard-working, honest, well-intentioned therapists. Administrative justice as it is practiced today in California and most other places strips therapists of their professional dignity, their right to discovery processes, their right to a trial by jury, their right to practice their profession, their peace of mind, and the financial security they have worked a lifetime to establish for their families and for their retirement.

In agonizing over Howard's plight, I knew too well that people who sit in judgment on state licensing boards are political appointees to represent consumers, people who have absolutely no training or experience in long-term, intensive psychotherapy. There's no way they would ever be able to understand his case. The same is true for state investigators and attorneys general—no relevant training, no expertise, no professional supervision, no understanding whatsoever of processes they are being called upon to deal with and make judgements about. Even the handful of licensed therapists who are sprinkled in the boards and the "experts" hired by the boards to examine accused therapists lack the systematic supervised training that would make them qualified to render opinion on the deep transferences stirred up by depth psychotherapy. I have written textbooks, published numerous articles, and lectured endlessly on this topic to little avail. An administrative monster continues to grind out injustices that destroy the lives of my professional colleagues, creating hopelessly untenable situations against which therapists cannot even be insured.

Howard is now being called upon to account for himself in this Inquisition-like setting. He has been accused of sexual misconduct by a woman who undoubtedly would have been burned at the stake as a witch by the Grand Inquisitor! I'm a miserable wreck just thinking about it. I've seen too much of this to even hope it will turn out okay.

Howard's attorney accompanies him for a two-hour interview with the state investigator. Afterward he tells Howard the situation is grim. The accusations are serious. It's next to impossible to defend oneself against unsubstantiated claims before state licensing boards. How do you prove you didn't do something you are accused of when the licensing board has significant political motivations and financial incentives to find you guilty? Administrative justice is set up so that the licensing boards simultaneously serve as accuser, prosecutor, judge, jury, sentencer, and penalty collector. Howard's attorney sees no way out and advises him to prepare for the worst. Disciplinary actions for sexual misconduct usually result in loss of license or, at best, five years of probation with huge expenses for required therapy, supervision, and ongoing education as well as steep financial penalties—not to mention public humiliation.

In the past when I have witnessed such travesties of justice firsthand, it has been as a hired witness for total strangers. This was strikingly different. Howard I know—very well, in fact. I trust his personal and professional integrity almost more than my own. I know the case well. I had heard about Francine off and on for eight years. Howard had presented his work with her to more than twenty professional colleagues in case conference seminars that I either led or attended. I had heard him present his work to three visiting, internationally renowned, experts. His colleagues called her "Howard's case from hell."

Suffice it to say that Francine had been stalked and raped on a nearly daily basis throughout her childhood by every member of her family including her mother. Not surprisingly, she later became the victim of numerous other sexual assaults. Every time she saw Howard she announced in one way or another that she wanted to "jump his bones." The infernal saga tormented Howard endlessly for years as Francine slowly began to trust, gradually learned to connect with him, and finally began to develop a personal life with some rewards and some sanity. Then Prozac came along to give her just the added boost to motivate her to stop therapy, though the decisive working-through process was by no means complete.

Several years later when Francine ran into some difficulties at work her managed care provider would not support her going back to see

Howard, instead offering her time-limited in-house crisis counseling. When Francine began recounting her sexualized agony and torment in her previous therapy with Howard, her newly licensed counselor working for the managed care company advised her to report Howard to the licensing board for misconduct—no one should ever have to feel so sexually overstimulated or be so tortured in therapy. It apparently never occurred to the counselor that childhood trauma might be getting mixed up in Francine's accounts of her therapy.

Frantic after the disturbing call from the state investigator and two sleepless nights, I arrived Thursday morning at a case conference seminar that I lead. I knew I couldn't sit passively by and watch Howard burn, but I dreaded what might be entailed if I tried to stand up to the power of the state. I asked the group to give me their time today as I was in crisis. During the ninety minutes I allowed myself to free associate and ultimately to break down. Everyone there knew I had been suffering with these issues for some time. All were familiar with my writings and lectures on the subject. They could feel my distress and urged me to talk freely, to let it all hang out, and I did. I found my heart racing, my hands perspiring, and my voice tense and strained as I swore at the "fuckin' boards," at the farce of administrative justice, at the uselessness of all my books, at the needless damage that board stupidity continues to foist on patients, at the atrocities I have seen boards commit against therapists, at the misery of therapists and their families I have seen suffer, and at the utter audacity of the licensed professionals—the "expert witnesses"—who unethically allow themselves to be used as pawns in this whole devastating process. Did I scream and yell? Probably. I don't know. But I began tearing shortly after John quietly said, "There's more, Larry, this runs deeper. . . ." I was thrown back to second and third grade to Butch Prather, the school bully who often targeted me. I vividly recalled the day Butch caught up with me on my bicycle on the way home. "He took me down, but none of his cronies were with him that day and I beat the shit out of him. I was miserable then just like I am now." Jane said, "He forced you to hit him . . . he made an animal out of you!" "Yes, and I cried all the way home and sobbed with my head on my mother's lap. I had bloodied him and left him alone crying in a ditch. I never wanted to hit him. You're right. There was no choice, he made me fight him. And now damn it, I have to do it again." I was feeling deep fear and dread. I recalled similar emotions when I finally had to stand against the abusive force of my father and others. I definitely did not want this task. But I could find no escape. I protested, "Those state guys all have a police mentality—blind, ignorant, vindictive. They are dangerous. All I have to do is to make myself a target and I'll be crushed." "That's what the Germans said about the Nazis," someone who remembered my dream chimed in. "It's too late, Larry," John reminded me. "You are already a target because of your papers on dual relationships and false accusations."[1] "Thanks for reminding me. But the investigators and boards haven't understood it so far, why would I think more protest would do any good?"

The group's support was strong and I begin to calm down, to relax. I was fighting an imperative I couldn't avoid. I was dreading the prospects of moving forward. If the accusations against Howard were allowed to stand, who would be next? I thought of all the therapists who for nearly thirty years have brought to me their most difficult cases for consultation. Most of these cases were high risk.

I said, "Every one of us is vulnerable to this type of accusation, the kind that emerges from deep transference work. As you know, I have already been involved in civil courts representing accused therapists on a number of these cases. But at least in civil court there is a discovery process, and a judge and jury to appeal to. In administrative law—after the politically and economically motivated board has made an accusation—and if the therapist has thirty thousand dollars, cash in pocket—an appeal can be made to a state appointed commissioner who will hear the case. But the commissioner's decisions are not binding and are frequently overturned by the boards. More than half of the judges' decisions were reportedly overturned in 1990 and the figure has risen steadily since.

"In the past few years I have done considerable expert witness work attempting to help falsely accused therapists. In every case in which I have been given full access to the court's records and been given the time to study and to formulate, each accusation I have tagged as likely to be false on the basis of transference considerations has been dropped by the administrative law judge. I assume from those results that I have

---

1. See Appendices A, B, and C.

at least been successful in creating reasonable doubt. But in case after case the licensing boards of California and several other states have ignored the findings of the commissioner and have gone ahead to sustain the accusations and to mete out severe disciplinary actions against the therapists. That's the current state of things. Anyone who's not terrified by that isn't dealing with reality!"

As I talked freely in the consultation group I felt the relief of support from colleagues. I still felt dread, but I also felt the necessity of biting the bullet and forging out something that had the hope of being effective. Howard's case was in itself moving to everyone, but beyond that were the broader issues of patient care and therapist safety for us all.

> *John:* There's no one better prepared than you are to do this. You have the credentials. You've written the books and articles. You have the research data. You have the experience and the courage. . . .
>
> *Jane:* If you don't do this, then who will, who can? There isn't really a choice. You're prepared. You can do it. And so you must. We'll all help you in any way we can.
>
> *Larry:* It scares the shit out of me. I feel fear and dread.
>
> *John:* Of course you do. That's appropriate. But there's also plenty of support. People know you. Your work is credible. You are articulate and people respect what you have to say. Your fundamental good will in this is evident and known.
>
> *Larry:* But how do I dare start to tackle this monster if so far my words have fallen on deaf ears?
>
> *John:* Your protest is falling on sympathetic but deaf ears now. You are in it too deep. We all see you're not going to be able get out of this!

I had less than two weeks to get my act together before talking to the state investigator. Ventilating with the group underlined that I must act and act now—quickly, decisively, and effectively. Being able to air my feelings and to feel supported helped me clarify that *my enemies aren't the boards, the attorneys general, the investigators, the ethics committees, or anyone else. My enemy is simple ignorance—a certain lack of knowledge in critical places.* For more than twenty years I have been conducting clinical research into these deep transferences. It is clear that there is indeed a widespread knowledge gap and that ignorance of cutting edge thinking is hurting clients and therapists in many ways. In my role as a professional educator I deal every day with knowledge gaps and problems of ignorance. I began to see this as simply another educational challenge—and it was true that I was up for it. Something inside me began to calm and to take hold.

I could clearly see that I had two tasks before me that were separate but interrelated. The problem of getting myself ready to meet with Howard's investigator was one. And the broader problem of how to call for a widespread educational campaign was another. The tasks were related in that the accusation against Howard was inexorably propelling me to get the road paved in Sacramento well in advance of Howard's case coming to the attention of the board.

The format I selected to begin the educational campaign was a letter to Sherry Mehl, Executive Director of the California Board of Behavioral Sciences, with copies to be sent to a number of key administrative people in California and national organizations. What the fallout would be I did not know. But it wasn't my job to speculate about that. I needed to simply get down to the business of clarifying the problem and calling for accountability.

Morning, noon, and night over the next two weeks I pounded on my computer. I printed out numerous revised drafts to read to friends, colleagues, consultation groups, and classes for feedback. Drafts were faxed all over the country asking for ideas and suggestions. The response was swift and enthusiastic. Everyone saw the need to get this straightened out as soon as possible. It's great to be able to count on people when you really need them. I sought professional consultation from several experts in law and ethics. Especially helpful was Muriel Golub, Chair of the California Psychological Association's Ethics Committee. Dr. Golub knows these issues well and gave up considerable time on a holiday weekend to fax follow-up memos back and forth helping me to clean up and focus my arguments.

By the time of my appointment with Howard's investigator, I was imbued with a rare sense of high energy, inspiration, and purpose, a firm feeling of widespread support, and an absolute sense of the rightness of what I had to say to her. Fortunately, she was a wonderful woman with a lot of common sense who had done this kind of work for many years. She had somehow been spared the deadening effects of the "civil servant syndrome." She had just come from having her nails done at a beauty salon she was investigating. In the morning she had interviewed people in a chiropractor's office about a complaint there. Now it was sexual misconduct allegations against a therapist. The investigator was up front in saying that she knew next to nothing about therapy—so if I was going to get technical on her I had to go slow and explain as I went! She immediately grasped the sincerity of my intent, my level of sophistication in what I was talking about, and my passion for what I believed. To her credit she asked good questions and stopped me often to be sure she was getting what I was saying correctly. It was a good meeting and I was heartened. But I had seen too much to be optimistic. It was now her job to recommend that the board make charges against Howard or that the allegations be dropped.

You are about to read "the letter," as it came to be known locally. It was the powerful thinking of a hundred plus people in this letter that fueled my interview with Howard's investigator. But even with all the energy that went into this confrontation, I was still shocked and incredulous when, a few weeks later, I came home and heard Howard's voice on my answering machine. "I don't know what you said to that lady, Larry. But I received a letter today from her indicating that she was closing my case! The accusation will not go to the Board. God bless you and thank you so much. I'll be talking with you soon."

And God bless everyone who has helped me in this journey over the years. When something is wrong we have to stick together and stand up for what's right. Yes, I'm still scared. And the educational campaign has just begun. But I'm breathing much easier now that the problem is clearly articulated and out in the open. Having loving support makes all the difference.

As you will shortly see I don't believe this is simply a case of bad justice for therapists, but of grave misunderstanding even by most therapists about the nature of deep transferences and the terrors and dangers they stir up. The ultimate concern here is for the well-being of the client and for the usefulness of the therapeutic process in helping to resolve issues of childhood trauma. I hope you find the letter interesting and that you pass copies of it along to your friends and colleagues who might be interested. You will feel as you read the letter the power of many voices behind me enriching, clarifying, and sculpting the final text. I hope you enjoy it.

June 24, 1997
Sherry Mehl, Executive Director
Board of Behavioral Sciences
Department of Consumer Affairs
400 R. St. Suite 3150
Sacramento, CA 92814

Re: Increasing awareness of how the "Organizing" or Psychotic"
transference operates in the accusation and investigation
processes.

Dear Ms. Mehl,

As we discussed on the telephone, I am writing concerning a
matter that has weighed heavily on me for some time. It is my belief
that consumers as well as psychotherapists are currently being
misled and damaged by a critical gap in knowledge about the
nature and operation of transferences caused by infantile trauma.
My primary professional activity for twenty-five years has been
coaching therapists through their most difficult cases—in individual
tutorials as well as in case-conference groups. I have consulted on
more than fifty cases involved in some type of complaint process in
five states and have served as an expert witness on a series of
cases brought before licensing boards. I have tried (not always
successfully) to limit my work to cases in which I believed the
therapists were doing an average, expectable job with their clients.
And in which the therapy process had fallen prey to primitive
transferences giving rise to distorted, faulty, and/or false
accusations against the therapist.

In the course of my work I have witnessed many serious
breaches in law and ethics on the part of therapists who were
abusing and taking advantage of their clients. I wholeheartedly
support our investigation processes and believe that prompt and
effective disciplinary measures should be taken against all who
violate our legal and ethical standards.

It is clear to me that licensing boards and ethics committees
have a very difficult task. It is also clear that the current knowledge
base and operating policies allow most circumstances to be
handled effectively and appropriately. For this I congratulate those
who devote their time and energy to insuring that psychotherapy

remains a viable, effective, and safe professional enterprise in our society. However, a glaring gap in one particular area of knowledge and expertise needs to be addressed.

THE KNOWLEDGE GAP

There exists a widespread lack of awareness regarding a psychological structure referred to as "the organizing transference." This transference structure is formed in early childhood in response to infantile trauma during the organizing period of development. In our literature this phenomenon has been assigned the label "*transference* psychosis" because it emerges as a deep transference structure in long-term, intensive psychotherapy. And called "*psychotic* transference" because, when the client transfers this early emotional scar into the psychotherapy situation and onto the person of the therapist, the client's capacities for ordinary perception and reality testing are eclipsed. *Under these conditions the person experienced in the past as perpetrator of the infantile trauma is confused with the object of the transference in the present—the therapist who has worked hard to elicit the transference.* The current acute distress at having to reexperience in therapy the deep psycho-physical trauma is "blamed" on the therapist—for, after all, it is he or she who has been active in bringing the long forgotten past agony into the experiential present.

Since many otherwise sane people have a history of some kind of infantile trauma and are occasionally subject to such deep transference-memory regressions, I do not like the term "psychotic," which implies some sort of wild, crazy madness. The terms "organizing experience," "organizing memory structure," or "organizing transference" better describe the origin of the experience that is being revived for therapeutic work. That is, a fetus or an infant while *organizing* psychological channels to the environment for nurturing, soothing, and tension relief is met with some form of invasive trauma. A traumatized infant typically reacts with agitation and, in extreme cases, terror. Intense fear in infancy is painful and accompanied by physical constrictions, diffuse physiological stress, and severe emotional withdrawal. It is the revival and working through of these regressive psycho-physical experiences in the present psychotherapeutic transference that permits eventual recovery and growth.

Most licensed therapists may never encounter the organizing transference because they are doing short-term work, cognitive or behavioral interventions, family or couple counseling, industrial or forensic consulting, or support groups of various types. But any therapist who has been seeing individual clients for very long inevitably attracts some people who need extended care. Psychotherapeutic relationships which last for more than a few months raise the likelihood that in time a significant emotional relationship will develop. It is the deepening of the therapeutic relationship that makes possible the perception and analysis of the well-known narcissistic and borderline transferences as well as the little understood organizing transference.

Many competent therapists doing long-term work have, in the course of their professional development, made it a point to seek out additional supervision and continuing education as needed in order to successfully bring out the merger fantasies, split affects, dissociations, and projective identifications involved in deep work. And ethics committees and licensing boards are becoming accustomed to dealing effectively with complaints arising from narcissistic and borderline transference structures. However, in areas of deeper regression to the organizing transference understanding remains limited.

TRANSFERENCE MEMORIES
OF INFANTILE TRAUMA

There exists a significant and growing group of clients whose therapeutic needs press them to explore the deeper or "more primitive" transference structures that contain the memories of infantile trauma. Infantile trauma can result from the many kinds of overt or covert molest, abuse, or neglect that we already know about. But infantile trauma—either experienced in utero or in the earliest months of life—can also result from such things as toxemia in pregnancy, fetal exposure to alcohol and drugs, premature birth,

birth trauma, birth defects, separation from the biological mother, adoptions, incubators, foster placements, medical procedures, parental or familial distress, Holocaust conditions, maternal depression, and myriad other highly stressful conditions. Infantile trauma can be focal and acute, or it can be diffuse and cumulative in its effect on the developing child.

THE TERROR OF HUMAN CONNECTIONS

What is it that characterizes this group of clients who have experienced severe infantile trauma? Terror—a deep-seated, nonconscious terror that if they reach out for interpersonal emotional connection they will be retraumatized. *The transference expectation insures that they will experience terrifying, body-shaking, soul wrenching trauma in response to close emotional contact. The very nature of this transference alerts these people to the threat that, if anyone approaches them in emotionally significant ways they will once again feel injured. Every cell in their bodies yells out "Danger! Danger!" whenever they dare to experience the possibility of the human connections that have the power to heal them. Since intimacy was the original instrument of the abuse or trauma, it is deeply feared.*

I frequently travel and lecture, conduct classes and seminars, and I meet privately every day with groups of therapists, teaching them about the effects of infantile trauma. I attempt to show them the ways that *the organizing transference asserts itself as a terror of empathic connections.* The knowledge expansion in the field of psychotherapy over the past three decades has taught most therapists the empathic skills involved in "connecting," "holding," and "containing" techniques appropriate for narcissistic and borderline transferences.

But therapists generally do not know, nor is it intuitively obvious, that many clients who were traumatized before ordinary forms of communication and memory developed, have no choice but to experience the connecting overtures of the therapist as seductive, frightening, and painful. Nor is it intuitively obvious that ordinary empathic connections—which most therapists have been taught to value—paradoxically function in the organizing transference as intrusive retraumatizations that the client must avoid as much as possible, fend off, and eventually rage about and/or flee from in terror.

Is it any wonder that so many of these clients cry out in pain and seek public redress for their experienced injuries? Therapy promised them healing. The therapist promoted relationship. And relationship led to terrifying and painful regressive transference experiences that they could not bear. Reality testing weakened. Then, in the revival of the confused and traumatized state of infancy, the therapist was experienced as the perpetrator.

I coach therapists daily as they struggle with their clients through this most treacherous of passages—through deep body–mind terror—on the way toward learning how to make and to sustain human connections that have the power to cure. Much of our work is devoted to learning how the specific client characteristically desires and approaches the therapist for the human warmth and connection that they have been deprived of for so long. We study week after week, month after month, exactly how each client begins to experience the connection to the therapist. Then we wait and watch exactly how the client instinctively falls into deep fear, physical symptoms, disorientation, and contact avoidance. Studying in each client the operation of the pre-defense fear mechanisms common to all mammals—freeze, fight, or flee—aids us in the discovery and working-through process toward safe interpersonal connections and emotional interactions that allow growth and healing. Accusations of therapists are a regular part of reviving the accusatory cry of infant trauma for psychotherapeutic study.

At present we know of no way to determine in advance the exact nature of the trauma experienced at the base of a person's psycho-physiological being. Nor is there any way known to predict exactly how that trauma will reassert itself in the approach–avoidance matrix of the therapeutic situation as the transference–countertransference struggle unfolds.

It is clear that the terror of interpersonal connection these people experience is distinctly different from the fear of abandonment that people working on narcissistic and borderline transferences experience. Also clear is the agony of the accusatory cry revived from the traumatized infant self, "You hurt me when you came near me—when you touched me!" Or, in the reverse, there is the fighting clamor to the effect that the therapist did not "give" or "do" enough. A harshly accusatory or incessant cry and struggle for "more," of course, can serve to alienate the affections of the therapist so that deep emotional connections do fail—thus replicating the infantile trauma afresh. The struggle to get the therapist to be more attentive, or to do more, often purposefully functions to disturb or rupture the therapist–client empathy ties— which replicates the exact thing that produced the original trauma.

At the moment of reexperiencing the confused, regressive, psychotic transference, the perception and reality testing of the client are sufficiently eclipsed so that the traumatic psycho-physical memory resurfaces in the present in a form that contradicts reality. That is, it is caring, reaching out, and the desire for compassionate healing connections that the therapist is offering. This offering elicits the impulse to reach out to find human connection. But then, because of the nature of the organizing transference, the emotional connection will necessarily be experienced as terrifying and painful. *At such moments clients can actually perceive and believe that an abusive violation has occurred when in reality there was no such violation.* Rather, early trauma was reawakened and distortedly attached to what the therapist did or did not do.

The transferred infantile experience of sensual connection being traumatically intruded upon is thus, "You were loving me, encouraging me to open up to you, insisting that I trust you, and then you hurt me." The "then you hurt me" takes endless forms as the historical specifics of the client's infantile trauma emerge. *But the archaic, sensual body memory of trauma is now emerging in an adult with a fully sexually charged body.* And, given the sensuality of the original experience, the transferred experience is often felt to be a sexual or quasi-sexual intrusion.

Staying with such persistent and traumatic structures takes stamina on the part of both therapist and client. At any point in the process, therapist or client could, for any of a variety of reasons, falter in intent or determination. Or an outside unforeseen event could interrupt the working-through process with disastrous consequences. This is often the point at which complaints are filed. *There is a significant knowledge gap about the nature of this kind of transference remembering. And there is a knowledge gap regarding how therapeutic technique for this kind of work necessarily differs in major ways from work with narcissistic and borderline transferences.*

THE DAMAGE CREATED
BY THE KNOWLEDGE GAP

Consumers who approach psychotherapy with the hope of having their deep trauma wounds healed are being misled when many therapists haven't the slightest idea of how to even identify the organizing or psychotic elements in deep transference, much less how to work with them. For example, many "recovered memories" attributed to later events can undoubtedly be traced to the transference effects of infantile trauma that have been misunderstood by therapists. This is the subject of my text, *Remembering, Repeating, and Working Through Childhood Trauma* (Hedges 1994b). *Licensing boards have an obligation to consumers to address this knowledge gap in an aggressive and creative way before more damage is done.*

When training therapists I often say, "It's not just your own neck that's at stake if you naively conduct yourself in such a way that allows you to be the target of a transference accusation, but the progress and well-being of the client as well. No client was ever cured of infantile trauma in an investigation process or in a courtroom. If you don't know what you're doing you will bring disaster on yourself. And you will have failed in the trust relationship and the cure you had worked so hard to achieve."

A BRIEF HISTORY

The organizing (or psychotic) transference was first extensively studied by Sigmund Freud in his famed Schreber Case of 1911. Schreber, a well-known civil magistrate in Vienna, had

published his scandalous memoirs of several hospitalizations
for a severe and continuing paranoid psychosis. Among his
many confirmed false allegations were claims of repeated violent
and sexual assaults in the hospital by his treating physician
and caregivers which Freud successfully traced to transferred
infantile trauma.

Freud had earlier shown how the same kind of deficit
in reality appreciation in the 1882 treatment of Anna O. had
led her to blame her therapist for her false pregnancy. In
Freud's 1895 paper, Project for a Scientific Psychology, he
clarified the dynamics of how childhood molestation not only
leaves a person vulnerable to later molestations, but how later
intimate contacts can be psychologically confused with infantile
intrusive trauma.

I first summarized the basic literature on the organizing or
psychotic transference in my 1983 book, *Listening Perspectives
in Psychotherapy*. I have subsequently published (with Jason
Aronson Inc., of Northvale, New Jersey) seven additional textbooks
for psychotherapists, with clinical contributions from more than
200 therapists, addressing this subject. Most relevant to this topic
are: *Working the Organizing Experience* (1994c) and *In Search
of the Lost Mother of Infancy* (1994a). Dr. James Grotstein, a
Beverly Hills psychoanalyst and an internationally recognized
expert on psychotic transference, wrote a review of the literature
with an extensive bibliography as a forward to *Working the
Organizing Experience*. The recently published *Therapists at Risk*
(Hedges et al. 1997), co-authored with Robert Hilton, Virginia Wink
Hilton, and attorney O. Brandt Caudill, Jr., further elaborates the
dangers to consumers and therapists.

THE NEED FOR EXPERTISE
IN CLOSING THE KNOWLEDGE GAP

Enclosed please find a series of papers in which I have
specifically addressed the knowledge gap. "In Praise of the Dual
Relationship" looks at dual relationships somewhat differently than

you may be used to.[2] I take the position that the heart and soul of depth-transference interpretation rests on a principle of duality in which the real relationship is revealed to be distinctly different from the fantasied transference–countertransference relationship. On the opposite end of the duality spectrum lies the exploitation and damage created by engagements such as sexual acting out. There are many actions of therapists that clearly violate clients' boundaries in exploitative and damaging ways. Such violations should be disciplined firmly and appropriately.

But in the "gray area" of the duality spectrum between useful transference interpretation and destructive boundary violations lie many activities engaged in by therapists and clients aimed at (1) developing the real relationship and (2) elucidating the transference–countertransference relationship. *The intent and effects of activities and events in the gray area of the duality spectrum in long-term therapy can easily be misunderstood by outside observers. I take the position that ethically responsible professional opinion regarding the organizing or psychotic transference requires careful and studied thought. Responsible and ethical opinion can be rendered only by properly trained professionals who possess such expertise—which includes many years of personal experience in actually doing and supervising long-term, intensive therapy.*

In my paper studying dual relationships I specify the psychodynamic issues at stake and what such consultative expertise might look like, using the California Research Psychoanalyst Law as an already existing codified model of expertise. I asked the question if we could name even one licensed therapist who currently renders opinions on a licensing board or who is routinely hired as an expert witness by a licensing board who possessed such expertise. I expressed my belief that *a great many therapists are operating unethically in board-related activities*

---

2. "In Praise of the Dual Relationship" was published in *The California Therapist* July/August 1993 and reprinted in *Remembering, Repeating, and Working Through Childhood Trauma*. It appears as Appendix A of this book.

by rendering professional opinions in areas outside of their training and expertise.

Further, I called for the establishment of agreed-upon standards regarding what constitutes expertise in understanding the workings of organizing or psychotic transference. I suggested forming a preselected panel of such experts who could be called upon to provide education, advice, and experienced opinion to licensing boards and administrative law judges.

Following the newly instituted requirement that the decisions of the administrative law judge be held binding in cases in which the credibility of the accusing consumer is in question, I would now suggest that such expertise not only be available to support the work of the licensing boards, but also that it be a regular and mandated part of the administrative hearing in such cases.

Perhaps a task force comprised of members of the various boards and professions should be formed to study the situation, to seek out expertise, and to make recommendations. Infantile trauma is here to stay, and consumers who seek out therapy for such deep wounds have a right to know that this branch of psychotherapy is being appropriately monitored by the professions and by the state boards. Perhaps an in-service training or consciousness-raising day sponsored by each state board and ethics committee might be a first step in the recognition of the problem.

THE GOAL IS AN EDUCATIONAL ONE

I realize that my opinions and conclusions as well as my recommendations are offered at a time before state boards and ethics committees have had an opportunity to assess the nature and seriousness of the problem I am pointing toward. I further recognize that many professionals practicing psychotherapy may not even be aware of this knowledge gap. This is because only a relatively small sector of the therapist and client populations have as yet been impacted by the problem.

I wish to make clear that, as an educator, my primary concern is the dissemination of information and knowledge. As a trainer and as a consultant to psychotherapists I am concerned about a knowledge gap that is widely affecting therapists and consumers alike.

THE MAGNITUDE OF THE PROBLEM

Let me close by expressing my opinion as to the magnitude of this problem. I think of an avalanche slowly accumulating weight over a long period of time until one sparrow quietly settles on a small twig—adding just the right weight in the right place to precipitate an enormous disaster. I believe the avalanche is in place and that it is precariously balanced at present.

First, we have a large and frightened community of psychotherapists whose consciousness about these matters is slowly rising. Many are slowly aiming their sights toward licensing boards, which they believe to be the source of a serious danger that is not being addressed and which threaten them personally, and affect their professional practices and also what clients they feel safe working with.

Secondly, we have a large, politically powerful and incensed population of "seriously mentally ill" consumers who, first because of unenlightened treatment approaches, then because of the managed care industry, and now because of frightened therapists blaming licensing boards, feel that they are being denied treatment. These people have organized nationally and locally to lobby for protective legislation and are increasingly targeting the licensing boards as the current cause of their not being able to obtain treatment because therapists are afraid of the serious liability involved in taking them on.

Thirdly, we have a formidable group of pre-licensed trainees, graduate school educators, and training clinic personnel who are in acute distress because of the sudden drastic diminishment of apprenticeship opportunities. Many supervisors, even senior clinicians who have been involved in supervision and training for years, are now loath to involve themselves with pre-licensed training, or even to engage in case supervision of licensed therapists because of disturbing disciplinary actions of state boards that have held supervisors accountable for the inappropriate actions of people they are helping to train. Professionally responsible supervision and training is slowly grinding to a halt until more safety nets are in place for supervisors.

Finally, we live at present in a supercharged social atmosphere. Whether we choose to speak in terms of a "litigious society" or in terms of "an era of increased accountability," legislators, judges and jurors, governors, and the public at large are all concerned about liability and about damage to innocent victims. Therapists are running scared because they have no reassurance that their deep transference work will be understood and respected if an accusatory situation arises. Therapists are becoming innocent victims to unknowledgeable boards.

THE STATE BOARDS MUST BE ACCOUNTABLE

It is my purpose in this letter to begin a calling to account of the state boards and the ethics committees of the various professions by pointing out the serious liability that currently exists because of a critical knowledge gap regarding the dynamics of organizing or psychotic transference. Liability through ignorance is sometimes excusable, but continued thoughtless practices after one has been informed of their damaging consequences are not excusable. Boards and ethics committees now stand informed. How they will choose to curtail the ongoing damage being done by the knowledge gap remains to be seen.

In my lectures around the country on the subject of false accusations and the existing flaws in administrative law, I am regularly met with angry shouts of protest. Some say, "Let's sue the licensing boards!" And, as we know, suits against state boards regarding issues of discipline have begun and will likely increase. It seems only a matter of time before we have some class action suits involving millions of settlement dollars and widespread public embarrassment for licensing boards.

Others say, "We must take legislative action at once!" And as we know, this has already happened in Arizona where a grassroots movement of patients and therapists appealed to the legislature at "sunset time," successfully blocking a scheduled reauthorization of the state board. Sunset time in California is just around the corner and a massive letter writing campaign to the legislature or to the governor could have disastrous consequences.

MY APPEAL

I am appealing to you and to all people involved in the investigation and disciplinary processes for psychotherapists to help in closing the knowledge gap. It is my impression that the ethics committees of the professions have long practiced obtaining appropriate outside expert opinion on these matters so their position seems less critical. The professional organizations at present are so beleaguered with issues brought about by managed care that they may be slow getting around to this set of issues. *The welfare of many consumers is at stake as well as the board's liability for enforcing fair and appropriate disciplinary standards on therapists.*

The reality is that one disgruntled consumer or therapist could file an ethics complaint against all of the clinical members of all of the boards and all of the expert witnesses working for the boards who do not clearly possess the training and experience that would constitute expertise in this area. An ethics complaint against a number of licensed therapists would serve to create immediate pressure within the disciplines and within the boards to find ways of addressing the knowledge gap. But not without unfortunate consequences to the individuals involved.

In discussing my concerns with Muriel Golub, Ethics Chair for the California Psychological Association, it was her suggestion that this problem area be addressed in the most professional, ethical, and constructive manner possible. This would clearly involve educative efforts aimed both at individual licensees and at all participants who carry out the investigative and disciplinary processes. I completely agree.

It is my intent that this statement be the beginning of a dialogue to understand better the nature of infantile trauma and the way it affects the transference–countertransference relationship of long-term psychotherapy.

The goal is to initiate educational measures to help therapists deal more effectively with the organizing transference and to help investigative personnel at all levels discern its operation, seek appropriate consultation, and make the best decisions possible.

Thank you for your consideration of my concerns. I hope to be able to speak with you soon. In our brief telephone conversation several weeks ago you invited me to send you my papers on the subject. My offer to come to Sacramento for the purpose of discussing with you further the nature of the "organizing" or "psychotic" transference as it affects accusatory processes still stands.

Yours very truly,
Lawrence E. Hedges

Enc:

In Praise of the Dual Relationship (3 parts)
False Accusations Against Therapists
Prevention of False Accusations Against Therapists[3]
Curriculum Vitae

Several weeks later I received a letter from Ms. Mehl thanking me for my materials which would be placed in the library of the board. In a subsequent letter I requested some assurance that board members be notified of my concern and requested further opportunities to speak with her in person or by telephone. No response. So that's where we stand today. My interpretation is that a total lack of interest or concern for this serious matter exists at the board level. I sent copies of this letter to other California and state licencing boards and ethics committees and received no response except a letter from Dr. Muriel Golub, Chair of the California Psychological Association Ethics Committee, thanking me for at last bringing some clarity to this very difficult set of issues.

From this letter let us now move to a telling example of how the emergence of terrifying transferences inspires terrifying countertransferences—deep unsetting feelings and experiences in the therapist.

---

3. Because this matter of understanding how the organizing transference works to threaten therapists, I have reprinted these three previously published papers in the Appendices of this book.

PART II

THE STRUGGLE TO MAKE TERRIFYING CONNECTIONS

6

In Search of the Intolerable
Clinical Contribution by Gayle Trenberth

HEDGES' COMMENTS

Gayle's title conveys the essence of what *Terrifying Transferences* are about, a desperate search for what dare not be found, as well as some of the ways her client, Carla, had of making sure that the connections required to sustain life and growth could not be made.

"DON'T GO."

I was watching her eyes lose focus, shifting to the left and rolling up, her body tensing in an arch, one hand closing in a fist, the other pressing hard against her leg. My words startled her, her eyes darting to meet mine. I saw the longing in her eyes, and my body began to stiffen, my eyes began to close, my chest became tight, breathing shallowly. In a choked, panicked voice, she said, "Don't go!"

This exchange occurred seven years into the therapeutic relationship. We were exploring the powerful effect of *trying* to stay in contact with one another. I could feel her terror as she made contact with my eyes. Resonating to that terror, I began to shut down my connecting senses: my eyes, my skin, limiting the common air we shared by breathing shallowly. At this point in our relationship, she could express her longing for me to stay in the connection, but even as her words brought me back, she could not tolerate the contact, and broke it by shifting her eyes, and tensing her body. Carla's intense longing for contact, and her intense fear of it, became the core work of twelve years of psychotherapy.

I first heard about Carla when my office partner asked to have a short consultation with me. He revealed that he was treating a woman who had apparently developed a crush on me after seeing me in the waiting room. I was surprised to learn she was obsessed with me to the point of following me home. My colleague felt overwhelmed by Carla's stalking behavior, and brought up the possibility of referring her to me. His thought was that her obsession with me might ease if she had contact with me. He reassured me that while she had developed these obsessions with women before, she had no history of violence. At the time, I had been analyzing another case where a patient stalked me, and was curious about the possible similarities in the meaning of this behavior. As my understanding of Carla evolved, the stalking behavior proved to have a very different function than in the other case. For the other patient, the stalking was a way of tracking me as an infant will track mother with his or her eyes. For Carla, stalking me was her desperate search for the intolerable, *for contact with another.*

As Carla came to her first session with me, she was excited and frightened about seeing me. As she told me about her issues and her belief that I could help her, I was aware of the longing in eyes that would not look at me, and of an overall extreme tension in her body. I was also aware of a repellent smell she had. She was a heavy smoker, and the smell permeated her skin. While she was confessing to following me home, speaking her obsession that I had some magic that could save her, I simultaneously felt warded off, told by her body to stay away. She wanted to see me twice a week, as she felt she could not tolerate the time between sessions spaced a week apart. I felt a curious dread as I agreed to the schedule. Here was a woman who had stalked me, who seemingly had a crush on me. And in the first session, I felt repelled by her. I had fantasies of being engulfed by a sucking infant's mouth, whose smell made me nauseous. I questioned whether I could work with her while feeling so repelled, yet I was touched by what seemed like her need to find some meaning to her existence. Later, I was to discover that her need was to create enough of a "psychic skin" to be able to tolerate the contact with another she so longed for, yet intensely feared would destroy her.

Esther Bick, a British psychoanalyst, first coined the term *psychic skin* in her 1968 paper, "The Experience of the Skin in Early Object-Relations." After observing infant development, she theorized that on a sensory level it was the mother–baby interaction that begins to bind together the experiences of parts of the nascent self and develops the primitive ego. The application of experiences of a physically and emotionally "holding" and mentally "containing" other to the surface of the infant's body allows the baby to move toward integration into a cohesive sense of self. Bick describes this as developing a psychic skin, a containing function that is introjected from the external object. The external object *is* experiences of continuous interaction stimulating the sensory organs of the infant—particularly the skin—which, once introjected, create a sense of containment. This containment allows the concept of a space within the self, and the development of a boundary between self and other.

Bick, along with Frances Tustin (1990, 1991), and D. W. Winnicott (1960), assumes that psychic unintegration at the point of birth is a natural state of being, and that this state only becomes alarming to the infant if the holding and containing other is over- or understimulating. In the absence of a containing presence, there will be a breakdown of the continuity of sensory dominated experience, and the infant will experience unbearable terrors of falling or spilling away forever (Tustin), or fear of going to pieces, falling forever, having no relationship to the body, having no orientation in space (Winnicott). To defend against such unbearable terrors, the very young infant may develop a *second-skin* formation (Bick 1968), a pseudo-independence, through which the infant attempts to hold him or herself together. This archaic defense is often manifested somatically as disturbances related to the skin, or to the experience of the skin, such as skin rashes or numbing of areas of the skin. In the adult, second skin formation can manifest either somatically or in preoccupation with bodily sensations and symptoms. This can extend to compulsive behaviors such as eating and masturbation. These psychosomatic symptoms, preoccupations, and behaviors are attempts to create heightened experiences of a sensory surface in order to ward off feelings of loss of sensory cohesion, so that existence can be felt without the terror of falling or spilling into space, or going to pieces.

Hedges (1983, 1994a,c) has described the drive toward sensory and psychic cohesion as the *organizing level* of development. It is the infant's task to use all sensorimotor modalities to establish channels to the human nurturing environment, the interaction of which organizes the rudimentary sense of "I-ness." When there is an interruption of the organization of channelings through over- or understimulation, there is a momentary disruption of the infant's internal harmony and continuity. The infant has a sense of disorganization that to it seems like breakdown, emptiness, or death, and experiences terror. All adults have had in their infantile pasts these moments at the organizing level of development, and to a greater or lesser extent, have needed to find ways to defend against the catastrophic anxiety of loss of cohesion. In the consulting room, when working at the organizing level, the patient experiences a yearning for contact, but at the very moment of contact the transference memory of the over- or understimulating other appears, the fragile sense of self loses cohesion, and there is an experience of terror. The patient may break the potential for contact through splitting, obsessing, tangential affect or thought, somatic reactions or preoccupations, negativity, passivity, withdrawal, or more psychotic manifestations, such as delusions or hallucinations. Any defense can stop the threat that relationship presents to the fragile sense of "going-on-being" (Winnicott 1949).

In a recent session with Carla, she described this dilemma between the intense longing for contact, and the threat it represents to the vulnerable sense of self-cohesion. She was talking about her longing to be wanted by a group of friends, yet observed herself "flitting" from one person to another so they could "never pin her down." She then said, "I'm flitting with you right now." I acknowledged that, and told her my reaction was to wander in my thoughts, to then come back to working on connecting with her, then wander again, and it felt exhausting. She commented that she wanted me to work hard to "get" her, then she would feel wanted. My experience was that the harder I worked at the connection, the more I could not "pin her down." After some silence, she said she felt she was avoiding the connection, that she was avoiding the *intensity* of her wanting me. If she felt the intensity, she would shatter into a million pieces, or dive off a high rock into space. She looked at me intently, saying, "I don't want to get close, I want this [locking her hands together]. I want to be part of you." If she can psychically merge with me, she can avoid the space of relatedness, thus avoiding the unbearable anxiety of shattering or falling. If she cannot be part of me, then she must "flit" from me, avoid me so as to avoid the potential of relationship, and the transference memory of the over- or understimulating other that threatens the loss of self-cohesion. What was different in this session, after twelve years of working together, was that Carla could talk about her dilemma without splitting off or regressing into an autistic state. In the beginning this was not remotely possible.

THE CASE STUDY

Carla, a 43-year-old single woman, was in treatment for issues involving religious commitment, her attraction to a woman, and a sense of meaninglessness about her life. She lived alone, had never had a primary relationship, and had never had sex. She was confused about her sexual orientation, and her gender identity. She had a muscular, boyish body, a masculine face, and wore her hair very short. Except for her breasts, which she hid in large shirts, one might have thought she was a man. Later, she revealed that she felt she should have been a man, and in regressed states, would feel she had a penis, or had lost the penis she had when she was born.

Carla was one of six children. She had a brother a year and a half older, and a brother one year younger. Eight years after the birth of her younger brother, her parents had the first of the next three daughters. Carla wanted to be like her brothers, going on boyish adventures and playing sports, but felt shunned because she was a girl. She felt forgotten between the demands of her older brother, and the needs of her younger brother. She was sent to a Catholic boarding school in the seventh grade with the explanation that if she stayed home she would end up caring for her baby sisters. Her experience was that she had been replaced by cute baby girls and sent away. She felt ugly, short, and masculine. That first year in Catholic school, she developed a crush on one of the nuns, a pattern that was repeated over her years of schooling. She had no high school experiences with boys, and only superficial friendships. In college, she decided to be a nun and spent six years in a convent, but on the day of her final vows confessed to daily compulsive masturbation and was asked to wait on the vows until she could stop. Disheartened, she dropped out and came to California, becoming a teacher in Catholic school settings for the next seventeen years.

Carla's recollection of her childhood was scant, and communicated mainly through impressions. Her mother seemed too busy for Carla's needs, her father, distant and critical. The overall impression was of a child surrounded by potential connections that were never made. Carla began seeing me as I was completing my training as a bioenergetic analyst and beginning training in psychoanalysis, and I brought both modalities to her treatment. Bioenergetics is the study of human personality in terms of the energetic processes of the body. The body's available energy, and how that energy becomes constricted or expanded in the musculature is seen as mirroring the psychological defenses the individual created to handle the early childhood environment. In Carla's case, her body was short and compressed, with thick powerful muscles. She had a hunched back, a short, thick neck, flattened buttocks, and overdeveloped calves and quadriceps. Her skin was brownish in tone, yet her heritage was white. All these characteristics seemed an exact description of the masochistic character structure described by Lowen (1975). In his view, the masochist's body is fully charged, but the energetic charge is held back from expression through the overdeveloped, compressed musculature. This body structure mirrors the psychological inhibition against being independent and self-assertive. As Carla and I began working together, I discovered that while masochistic themes and defenses existed, her musculature was a mirror of even more primitive defenses, those of the second-skin formation described by Bick (1968).

I began bioenergetic therapy with Carla by working on the muscular holding in her neck, assuming she had a masochistic character structure that needed to be decompressed. I asked her to hit a couch with a tennis racket, and as she began, her back and legs cramped.

Again, thinking bioenergetically, I assumed this cramping was energy trying to move through chronically tense muscles. I asked her to breathe through the cramping. She collapsed to the floor, rolled onto her back and began hyperventilating, while her whole body spasmed. Suddenly, it seemed I was looking at a newborn infant in intense distress. I reached out to touch her to provide some containment, and she responded as if she were electrocuted by my touch. Pulling back, I directed her to breathe slowly, and paced her on her exhalation to counter the hyperventilation. She calmed down, opened her eyes, but had no words for this experience.

Wanting to explore the meaning of her experience, we began a series of sessions with her lying on her back. As she attempted to relax and deepen her breathing, her body would begin to cramp and spasm. The distressed newborn would reappear. Hyperventilating, her eyes closed, face scrunched-up, mouth and jaw alternating between locking and trembling, her arms and legs would flail, threatening to hit me if I did not keep my distance. It seemed she had no awareness of my presence, and often she did not respond to my voice. If I attempted a bioenergetic technique of contacting her head to provide a sense of containment, all the muscles under the surface of her skin would tighten, producing an impenetrable barrier. There were times when she would scream, as if into a void, "Just love me!" Then she would startle, jump up, rush into a corner of the office, hands in fists, glaring, "No! Leave me alone!" In all these maneuvers, I felt nonexistent as a person in the room. I was a painful stimulus or an absence of stimulation. I was often confused, trying to ride out the experience, looking for some moment when I could penetrate the autism.

In between sessions, Carla isolated in her apartment when she wasn't working. There she would sit in a favorite chair, sucking her thumb, compulsively masturbating, creating fantasies about being with me, being in me. At times she would sit in the office parking lot waiting for a glimpse of me between sessions, or walk around the neighborhood where I lived. This time between us was captured in Carla's journal when she wrote:

> You've helped unleash a monster with a thousand arms. All reaching at once a big hungry mouth—kicking legs, pounding, pounding, pounding—more, more, more—stay away from me—just let

me reach—don't let me get you. Don't let me touch you. DON'T
LET ME TOUCH YOU! I'LL GOBBLE YOU UP. GOBBLE
GOBBLE FIST FIGHT—ENERGY—finger tips, toes, feet, geni-
tals crotch/let me in/fuck you—penetrate—be part of you—inside
you—warm secure.

I felt tormented by the intense need expressed in her fantasies,
journal writing, and stalking behavior, yet the impenetrable autism in
the session. At times, I felt sadistic, wanting to use stressful bioenergetic
techniques to break that impenetrable barrier, and make me *exist* to her.
Exist, be a person in that consulting room, yet I had my own terror that
if I existed, I would be engulfed by the needy infant wanting to surround
me, be in me. After working in a session to make some sort of contact,
I would feel grateful that the session was over, and that little contact
had been made. Carla would leave, opening to contact now that the
possibility was over, and suffering that none was available. And so we
did our dance. Working toward connection, dreading it, being repelled
by it, finding ways to avoid it, yet somehow longing for it. Again, her
journal expresses the poignancy of the struggle:

I'm crazy in love with Gayle. I want to be with her all the time.
I want to call but have nothing to say. I came home twice today
and my machine light was on. I was hoping there was a call but
knew there wasn't because I hadn't asked for one. I was disappointed anyhow. I started to call again but said no. It's like—Let
her worry and wonder if I don't call. Let her wonder why. I can't
keep telling her I love her. I hate it that it's not reciprocal. I wish
she'd tell me she loves me and misses me but I know she never
will. So why am I in this position? I can't help it. I love her.
I went by the house and just walked back and forth. I wanted
to go in, but I know I won't. I want to watch her at home—see
what she's doing. She wouldn't even have to pay any attention
to me. I just want to watch her—just be there—actually it would
be great if I could be invisible, then I could be with her and not
bother her or annoy her. She wouldn't even have to pay any attention to me. On the other hand, I had this giant urge to roar
down the street blasting my horn—just to let her know I was
there. Of course, she wouldn't see me—I'd be gone! I was going

the wrong way on the street— I'd have to have been going the other way. I might not have been able to get out on the busy street fast enough.

Carla, as she approached the nearly impossible task of trying to find a way to connect with me, would experience intense hunger for me, followed immediately by an equally intense need to eliminate me. At the moment of potential connection, she would feel herself disintegrating or falling, and eliminating me would restore her fragile sense of being. She could destroy the connection, splitting off into a trance-like state, using intense and painful muscular tension to hold me out, as she held herself together. Her increasing self-stimulation at home was an attempt to create a heightened experience of a sensory surface in order to ward off feelings of loss of sensory cohesion.

At this point in my own training, I was being exposed to analytic formulations that led me to believe I needed to approach Carla's dilemma in a gentler way. I proposed that she come three times per week, but that we use the format of her lying on the couch, where she did not have to look at me, and where she could "flow" with whatever might come up for her.

She was immediately frightened of falling off the couch. As she would begin to lie down, she had sensations of falling into space that at times would lead to the reappearance of the distressed infant, and at other times would lead to body motions that seemed like a reenactment of birth trauma and falling out of the birth canal. If my chair was too close to the couch, she would panic. She needed to find just the right distance that gave her a sense of my presence without overwhelming her. As these fears subsided, she began to experiment with streams of consciousness, verbalizing anything that came to her mind. If the content of the verbalization exposed her needs or longings, she would become nauseous or need to go to the bathroom. She began wearing diapers, longing for and fearing the letting go. I again found myself feeling a curious dread. Would she vomit or urinate on my couch? What would I do with these "productions" if it happened? The repelled feeling reappeared. If I happened to touch her in session, I felt a compulsive need to wash my hands, as if some substance emanating from her was sticking to me. It was as though in trying to open a potential way of connecting, I was again being warded off by her body.

Eventually, she calmed, and we had periods of silence, breathing quietly together. She began to look at me from the sides of her eyes, creating a halo effect where she could see the shape of my head, but not the details of my face. She would occasionally ask that I sit closer, and could tolerate the closeness if she did not look at me. Once in a while, we would touch the tips of our fingers together and she felt comforted, not frightened. The dread and repelled feeling began to leave me, and moments emerged when we had the same thought at the same time, indicating a more symbiotic level of contact was beginning.

As these moments began to build, a surprising event emerged. I began falling asleep! I was not sleepy before or after her session, but struggled to keep myself awake during her session. Hedges (1994a,c) refers to this phenomena as the therapist having such empathy for the client's terror of contact that, as connection becomes possible, the therapist breaks the relatedness moment.

I shared my reactions with Carla, and suggested we begin to study the ways in which we were both disconnecting at the point of contact. She wanted to sit up and look at me. As we talked and looked at each other, one of us would note when the other was going away. I would watch Carla's eyes lose focus, shifting to the left and rolling up, as her body tensed, and one hand would close into a fist while the other would tap at her head. I would say, "Don't go." Other times, as I felt our connection, my body would begin to stiffen, my eyes would begin to close, my chest would tighten as I breathed shallowly, and Carla would find some way to say, "Don't go." We would examine together the fears around the moment of contact.

Carla began to bring in drawings that visualized her ambivalence about connection. She begin writing in her journal with her non-dominant hand, *backwards*, then would bring her journal entries in, hold them up to a mirror and read them to me. In this way, she could share her desires, fantasies, dreams, and feelings. It was a period of revelation of her secret self. She expressed her longing to have a penis, drawing a picture of the intense boy she felt she was. She shared her obsession with sex, with penises. She confessed to the frequency with which she walked by my house, and to her intense longing for me. She wanted to penetrate, to merge. In the act of her self revelation, I felt her attempts to build a bridge to me, and to take me in as a relational object in her world.

The backwards journal writing lasted nine months, a gestation period in which she seemed to be reordering channels of connection to me. The mechanism of optics is that our eyes receive visual information backwards and invertedly, and it is through interaction with the caretaking environment that we are taught to translate that visual information into what is considered normal perception. A young child will often turn a book upside down and correctly name an object on the page. The mother turns the book right-side up, and repeats the name of the object. The child learns perspective and "correct" up–down, right–left directionality through contact with mother's sense of orientation.

Winnicott (1971) refers to object presenting as one of the main ways the environment orders the world of sensation for the infant. The mother presents the object to the visual or tactile field of the infant, waits for a response, and mirrors the response, so that the child sees itself in the mother's face. The child knows the self's reaction to the object through the mirror of the mother's face.

Carla would stand at the mirror, reading her backwards writing, with me sitting behind her. She would read, look at my face in the mirror for a response, then continue to read. It seemed as if she were re-creating a holding environment that could respond to her productions and mirror back her reactions so that she could reorder her perceptual set. She could begin to know herself through the relational mirror of the other in a way that was not overwhelming for her.

Soon after this gestation period we began to experiment in the office with movement toward and away from me. Feeling like a baby, she tried crawling away and toward me. She reported crawling away made her sad and lonely; "staying put" made her mad, and that she "can't get and can't do without." Crawling toward me was awkward and hard at first, but resulted in her wanting to look at my face, and wanting me to see her.

Eventually, she worked her way up to standing and walking toward me and away from me, feeling her ability to choose her need for contact or her need for distance. She could now tolerate bioenergetic work on her tense musculature, and was able to release some of the second-skin formation to allow contact in without her fear of spilling out.

It seemed as if she had internalized our time together as a containing other, and could now tolerate some sense of relatedness without intense anxiety.

In the world outside of the therapy, Carla had left her job as a teacher and after some searching developed her own retail business selling educational toys and books. She began attending gay bars and found one that became a community for her. She uses these new relationships to study her movement toward connection and disconnection, and brings the results of her studies into the therapy.

Carla recently had a dream where she had an appointment with a priest and with me at nearly the same time. She tried to cancel the appointment with the priest by chasing him down with her bicycle but didn't reach him in time. Then she tried to get to my office but got lost in a construction site. She nearly had an accident but a construction worker helped her avoid it, and she ended up under a freeway where kids were everywhere. Now there were three people, Carla, a woman, and a priest. Together, they climbed out of this no-man's land. The woman and the priest got far ahead, and Carla was faced with a bridge with movable planks. She got up the courage and ran, almost falling off, but momentum kept her going across the bridge. She ended the report of the dream by writing, "Now that I think about it, it was Gayle and Father (the priest) who were with me. I missed both appointments, but somehow we were together walking back. I was planning to go back to the convent to get my gifts."

In this dream is her story of missed connections, the dangerousness of the new construction of her self, but how she is helped and joined by others. In the end, it is her courage that helps her cross the bridge of relatedness, and allows her to retrieve her gifts.

SUMMARY

Carla began her treatment with me searching for contact, and terrified of finding it. In the first years of the therapy, she existed in session in an autistic state, experiencing intense bodily sensations without any apparent sense that there was another human being in the room. Yet, it was important that I was there, that the room was there. The space was created to hold and contain the sensory experiences Carla was having. When contact threatened to penetrate, her fragile sense of sensory cohesion threatened to spill out into relational space, and she felt she would shatter or fall forever. She used second-skin formation and intense muscular tension to form a hard surface to hold herself together, and used the pain of muscular spasm to counter the threat of contact with me. Over time, Carla was able to internalize the holding and containing environment enough to create some psychic skin that allowed for a boundary between self and other. There was enough cohesion so that she could begin to experiment with contact with me without the terrible sense of disorganization that occurred in the early years. She could study the way that contact needed to be broken when her anxiety began to be intolerable. Carla developed an ability to move back and forth between connection and disconnection without being paralyzed by terror, and to use her awareness of her process to re-establish contact when needed. Her lifelong work will be around the terror of connection, but she has developed enough psychic skin to allow some contact to penetrate her internal world. As in the dream, she has attained in real life the courage and momentum to cross the moveable bridge of relatedness and receive her gifts.

$$* \quad * \quad * \quad * \quad *$$

Since the writing of this experience, Carla has been able to establish and maintain a relationship with a woman for two years. In the first six months of that relationship, she relived many of the terrors of connecting that she had experienced with me. Understanding them in her mind and body, she was able to move through her terrors and into relatedness with a significant other. She has begun a one-year termination process with me, feeling she has accomplished what she came to treatment to find: relatedness.

HEDGES' COMMENTS

In Gayle's and Carla's beautiful and moving story we see the power and danger of the ongoing drama that characterized the therapy process. It is easy to understand how such a fragile process could quickly be derailed—especially by a fluke outside occurrence. In cases where such a delicate working-through process has been accidentally interrupted by insurance or financial problems, job or marital failures, or chance encounters with unempathic or hostile forces such as survivors' support groups, media misinformation, or whatever—disasters have often ensued, with the therapists being accused of all sorts of misadventures. Here you can see how the perilous route between the Scylla of terrifying connections and the Charybdis of ruptured connections hurtles Carla along her way with restored mother and father figures supporting her gifts. Certainly courage and hard work are the essence of this process, but what makes the difference between a process that allows a new bridge to form and one that ends in disaster? Steve Shehorn, a Seattle psychologist, in reviewing his experience of processes that have made it and ones that have failed says, "In those few who have chosen to make the long and arduous road to transformation I can look back and see that at all points, no matter how bad, evil, destructive, or helpful I was being experienced in the transference moment, there was the sustained belief that somewhere inside of me—if he or she could just find it and hold on—was enough goodness that they could somehow learn to live and be in a new way" (personal communication, 1997).

7

Terror in the Dark Pit

Clinical Contribution by Jolyn Davidson

HEDGES' COMMENTS

Rarely do we have an opportunity to see and feel what lies beneath the archetypal reconstructions of satanic ritual abuse experiences. Davidson skillfully moves us past the memories, the dissociations, and the multiple self-states that serve as resistances to experiencing the here-and-now terrors of emotionally connecting in a personal relationship. Through a careful study of the nonverbal resistances and transferences, what emerges is a clear picture of a variety of kinds of infantile trauma that had found their initial expression in "memories" of cult abuse and incest.

"Therapy is difficult," says the client. *"If I accept that it is difficult, then paradoxically it will be more manageable than if I continue to expect or demand that it not be."* Nowhere is this a more important principle than in working with people who are dealing with transference issues related to the organizing level of their development.

Transference and countertransference issues are a central part of therapeutic work, but dealing with the terrifying transference adds another dimension. This dimension taps into the central core fears of both the client and the therapist. As such, the terror that gets evoked in the client can tap into the therapist's issues as well. This case presents a piece of the therapeutic journey through "the valley of the shadow of death" where these fears are encountered and relived, both by the client, Rachel, and myself, as her therapist.

Rachel was born into a large family that was quite poor. Her father died when she was an infant, and her mother remarried. Her mother left all the children except Rachel with foster families and moved with Rachel and the stepfather to a different state. She appears to have been a passive schizoid person who didn't know how to manage relationships or her life. The stepfather was schizophrenic and had been hospitalized in a state hospital several times. Rachel reported an extensive history of psychological and sexual abuse and neglect by her parents and others.

When Rachel began treatment, she presented with symptoms of depression, panic attacks, and suicidal behavior. She made frantic efforts to avoid what she called abandonment. She was compulsive in several areas, including bulimic behaviors, which had been a pattern for twenty years. Rachel had difficulty managing interpersonal relationships both at home and at work. She frequently developed enmeshed relationships with people who would ultimately overwhelm her with their intrusiveness or abusiveness. She attended multiple self-help groups and would conscientiously try to act according to everything she heard. She avidly read self-help books.

At first, the "symptoms" Rachel presented appeared to be more of a borderline style of relating. Even though her behaviors fit the *DSM-IV* (1987) diagnostic description of Borderline Personality Disorder, if I were to have responded to Rachel as functioning primarily at a symbiotic level of development I would have been misled. As treatment progressed, the underlying core organizing issues, crucial to understanding and treating Rachel, became more and more apparent. What she referred to as fears of abandonment seemed more like fears of the loss of attachment to others that she needed in order to keep herself intact but could not make consistent use of. The bingeing appeared to be a frantic effort to take the object in, but then an inability to hold onto the object, and hence the vomiting.

Rachel seemed arrested between the pre-symbiotic and symbiotic levels of development. A metaphor that seems to capture her dilemma and state of being can be drawn from a popular fantasy. It was as if Rachel were in a *Star Trek* episode, in the process of being transported from one space and time into another. In that transition, she was left fluctuating between one state of being and another, with one energy source trying to pull her back and another trying to move her forward. There was always the threat that the process would fail, and that her atoms would disintegrate somewhere between the two worlds. If that happened, she feared she would cease to be.

What was it like for Rachel to live in this psychological state created by a schizoid mother and schizophrenic father? Take a moment to imagine yourself being thrown into a time tunnel. You're being whirled back, back, back in time. Then abruptly, the tumult of wind stops. You are dropped into a deep, black hole. You are now the character—you have become the very little girl Rachel.

"I see faces of witches with hoods over their heads. They look down at me one at a time, then disappear. I am in a deep pit waiting, waiting. It's cold down here and my body is cramped. There isn't room to straighten my legs. I hear them all leave. They are leaving me here in this hole. I'm alone. It's dark and damp and cold. No one knows where I am. They aren't coming back. I can't get out. Please come and get me. I'll be good. Don't leave me here. Where is my mommy? Am I going to die? Get me out of here. Please, please don't leave without me. I'll do whatever you tell me.

"I hear them coming. They are passing by. Don't they remember I'm in here? Get me out. I'll do whatever you want. Someone is close now. If I hold my breath they'll get me out. Reach down here, please! Someone is here now. Their hands are bloody, covered with wet blood. I'm lifted out with those bloody hands.

"I see a fire that's used for light. There is a naked body of a woman stretched out and tied to a log next to the fire. I am taken in front of the group of women who are circled around the fire. The women are chanting in unison. The leader takes me to the body. With my hands in hers, she picks up a long sharp knife. Together, we lift the knife into the air and thrust it into the neck of the woman. I feel the knife plunge through the flesh. The blood spurts out like a fountain and splatters all over my face and hair. The head falls to the ground.

"Watching the blood and sacrifice sets in motion a frenzied, excited chanting in the whole group of women. The chanting intensifies and becomes shrill and screaming. The women are moving in a trance. I'm caught by one of them and undressed and bathed in the blood of the body of their victim. I am the central focus of this ceremony. I have a feeling of impending doom. The horror is indescribable. My naked body is covered with the blood of this naked, dying person. The leader forces me to drink that blood.

"The end of the ritual is evil. The leader places me back in the pit, this time naked. The women laugh as they look down into the pit, then turn around, squat over the pit, and urinate on me. The urine is in my hair and on my face. My body is motionless and numb. But my mind races, 'Let me out! No, this *can't* be happening.' Then I'm pulled out again. They make me put my clothes on over my sticky, bloody, smelly body. I am made to trail behind them like an outcast as we go back down the mountain. Somewhere, someone turns a water hose on me. The water is freezing cold. I don't know how I got back home. I just know that I am turned back into a little girl like nothing has happened.

"Back into being his little girl. I play with my friends. I go to school. I am good. None of the terror exists, or does it?

"I feel deserted. There's no one here to help me. I lie here in the middle of their bed. The adults I look to for nurturing are stretching my vagina with their fingers. My daddy tries to force his penis into that small opening without success. Little did I know the excruciating pain that would follow. Now, my mother is holding me down while Daddy spreads my legs and inserts a cold, metal device into me. I scream and fight while Daddy works to make the device get wider and wider. They know I am in excruciating pain yet they scream at me to hold still and be quiet—like I am the one doing something wrong by resisting. My mommy is right here watching as he penetrates me with his enormous penis. After it is over, I am embraced in order to make it all right. 'Endure the pain, then we'll hold you tight' seems to be the message.

"Now, they both prepare me to participate in sexual activities for the pleasure of the men and ceremonies of the cult. My daddy is the initiator. When he has penetrated me both anally and vaginally, he can give me to the others. Then, they will be able to use me. My mother watches him. She is part of it. She's there all the time. She prepares me before each encounter. She tells me to obey—to do what I have been taught to do so that the men will get what they paid for: 'Lick their penises like a soft, little kitten, make moaning noises, don't kick, don't bite.' Then she sends me off to the garage. She always waits in the house until after it is over. Waiting to hug me. If I perform well, I can go back to being a child. I can be hugged and loved. I can play.

"At one point, I lost all ability to fight. The life, the energy, the will to survive left me. My self was shattered into tiny fragments that seem to be irretrievable. Another part of me sank into a deep, dark hole from which I can't seem to get out. I think part of me died.

"I now believe this to be true: if I try to reach out to connect with others and to get nurturing, I will be violated, damaged, and die. It's not *just* that others will kill me, but that *I* will be forced to participate in that destruction. Yet a very real part of me is still alive crying out, 'Hang on to me—don't let me go.' I'll hang on for dear life, too.

"I constantly face a terrible dilemma: if I don't reach out to relate to others, I will be left alone in the pit, in fear and in danger of abandonment and ultimately of death. So, I try to be good and act like I'm supposed to. I read from others' body language what they want, so I can give it to them and survive. If I act like the others want, I will get some kind of connection with them. I keep hoping that I will get pulled out of the pit and get the nurturing I long for. But what I really get is more violation, denigration, and abuse. Others always hurt me in some way. Even if I protest it doesn't help. I have come to believe that I'm bad and that others will punish and damage me more if I don't cooperate. I believe that the only choice I have is to detach from my feelings and isolate myself from others or to be abused and violated. I'm left with an unbearable choice.

"I've spent years trying to find out how to act so that I could get a sense of connection and get my needs met. Constantly, I have sought out and longed for being nurtured and connected to someone. I've gone to three and four Twelve-Step groups at a time, and avidly read self-help books to find someone or some key to my pain. I've attended church and been on lots of committees in the community and at work. I have constantly gone to some meeting or other. I write frantically in my journal every day, hoping something will help. Even though I keep myself very busy, I haven't been close to anyone, really. I may look like I'm close to lots of people, but really, I haven't let anyone in to reach me. It's not safe, you know. Someone will die. And I think that someone will be me. I think that someone already *was* me.

"I started therapy awhile back, hoping to get some help and relief from my pain and terror. It's been a long journey—a journey down into that pit of darkness and despair and back into that bed of fright, pain, and helplessness. I now know Jolyn has been there all along this journey, though many times I couldn't feel her presence, or if I did, believed she was damaging me, too.

"At the beginning of treatment, I saw Jolyn twice, and then I wrote her a letter saying I wanted a different therapist and wouldn't come back to therapy, because I 'wanted more direction' than she would give. It was frightening to begin to tell my story and to begin trying to connect with someone. She called me up and reassured me we would keep working on helping me get my needs met. She acknowledged how frightening it is to begin reaching out to someone and to be afraid of being damaged. There was nothing in my experience that would give me the basis for believing that she would be there for me. But, something in me compelled me to tentatively reach toward the top of the hole I had been in. I went back."

Frequently during the first year of therapy with Rachel, she would cancel her appointments, claiming concerns about finances, even though she had excellent insurance coverage and I knew she could manage the fee. Each time I was able to re-engage her until the next cancellation. There was no particular pattern I could discern to indicate any external stimulus for the disconnections though it was apparent something was happening internally. My best guess at the time was that at some moments in treatment she could feel some inner reaching out, from both her and me, and it frightened her.

Internally, Rachel seemed to be re-experiencing a need to flee from what she experienced as a danger to her: a connection with me. According to Fraiberg (1982), this need to flee is one of the three almost biological reactions that she perceives the organism uses to control the stimulation received from the external world and to protect itself: aversion (flight), freezing, and fighting. Fraiberg sees these three reactions as mechanisms the body uses reflexively to protect itself from perceived threat to the integrity of the body system, both physically and psychologically. These mechanisms are considered as *pre-defense*, because they occur without organized or conscious thought.

Rachel would express other behaviors that appeared to be forms of fleeing in session. Though an adult, she would twirl her hair and talk in a childlike voice during sessions. She was markedly overweight, but would enter the room with movements that were also childlike. Her behavior was designed, as she put it, "to manipulate and control" me by being charming and entertaining in order to get her needs met and to be accepted by others—to be the "good, compliant girl" in order not to "be damaged." She even mentioned once that she was afraid I wouldn't keep her in therapy if she didn't "act like a patient was supposed to." In all of these behaviors, Rachel succeeded in moving away from me psychologically.

This style of relating seemed to be part of what Hedges (1994a,c) refers to as the "mimical" self: watch how others act and then enact those same behaviors. Then it will *seem* like you are functioning normally. Then, you will be safe or get some nurturing from others. It correlates, also, with the *as-if* concept Deutsch (1942) describes: act "as if" something is a certain way, then it will *seem* like you *are* that way. In neither of these modes, the mimical self or the "as-if" mode of relating, is an actual self developed. This is different from the conforming, *false self* described by Winnicott (1952), in which a person actually develops a "self" but it is formed by conforming to the other. In a way, this as-if way of interacting with the world seems to be a form of flight. It was psychologically protective for Rachel to be superficial, compliant, and charming. It kept a distance emotionally. Rachel believed she could avoid the terror of rejection and the resulting damage from the loss if she just acted in a way she perceived as normal and acceptable, even though this was like playing a role to her—to her, a life or death role.

At other times, Rachel would describe family dramas of fighting, chaos, and psychological abuse at home that reflected the mode Fraiberg (1982) described as "fight." Rachel would rage at others or endure their rage at her. There were multiple episodes of all the family members arguing and screaming at each other. There were even times when Rachel would angrily chase her teenage daughter, or the daughter, in turn, would attempt to terrorize Rachel. She seemed to be involved in the process of *participating* in "killing" them while at the same time being damaged herself. Her husband participated in the pattern also, by being verbally abusive to her. When he attacked and criticized her, Rachel would curl up, literally, in a ball of fright in the corner (Fraiberg's freeze response).

During or following rage episodes, Rachel would also relate to her daughter and husband in a regressive, childlike way. She would talk baby-talk, and act helpless and powerless. As she described going into the baby mode, the question emerged, was Rachel *re-experiencing* the childhood abuse during these fighting episodes or was she trying *to avoid being "killed"* through the regression?

It seemed inevitable that Rachel must experience this transference rage with me in therapy, as well. About the fifth month of therapy, she began sending letters to me between sessions expressing her rage at me. In one of these letters, she wrote,

> Today I felt very distant from you. You sat there with your arms folded, crossed, and closed to me. You listened, but you yawned. I can't hang on to you like before. You're really not there. I can't touch you. There might as well be a window of glass between us. I need you at least right now. But when I reach for you, you move away. I can't hang on to your skirt. It's not there anymore. You don't feel warm, cuddly, and concerned. You feel cold, indifferent, and analytical. I feel detached from you. The bond is broken. You seemed rather indifferent.

Through the rage directed at me, I began to understand how Rachel lived her entire life behind a metaphoric glass barrier. "I see you, but you're not available to me." The living part of her could not be seen, touched, or found, so that, in the transference, I became the cold, aloof, uncaring, and damaging parent.

During the sixth month of therapy, following one of these incidences of rage at both her family and me, Rachel overdosed on medications and had to be hospitalized. The hospitalization seemed to serve several possible functions. The hospital may have served as a retreat from the new sense of life she was cultivating in her direct experiences with me in therapy. It was as if she were experiencing a significant connection with me and her family, and it was too much presence for her to manage at home. Or Rachel may have needed to experience her rage and fears in a safe place. Also, it may have been that she found that piece of me that gave her the freedom to realize she was in an abusive home environment and to escape from the family pattern.

In the months following hospitalization, Rachel separated from the living situation with her husband and daughter in which she felt abused. Of course, I supported her in the idea of protecting herself from abuse. However, it was unclear to me to what extent she had participated unconsciously in creating and maintaining a self-abusive situation or to what degree her *experience* of abuse in deep transference was being stirred up by her therapy. Any contact with her family or even *thoughts* of contact with them elicited panic attacks. Much of the work of therapy for the next several months was spent just trying to be with her and to respond to concrete problem-solving issues. She seemed to be more guarded, concrete, and superficial.

During the second year of therapy, Rachel continued to fluctuate between these behavioral patterns of flight and rage. Frequently, she would make comments about being afraid of becoming attached to me but would fantasize about holding onto the back of my skirt. In these fantasies, she would report that I would not be aware of her clutching. Rachel would call me in panic when she was out of town for fear of losing the attachment to me. Between sessions, she would visualize me sitting in my chair in the office so that she wouldn't experience losing me.

Rachel came up with a plan for us to exchange scarves in order for her to have some tangible way to hang onto me between sessions. If she could hold onto a scarf of mine, she could remember me. If I were holding onto a scarf of hers, I would remember her. It was as though, in the "pit," not only did she have difficulty maintaining a sense of others, but she was afraid people didn't know where *she* was—they didn't remember *her*. She talked of her ambivalence about connections. She experienced a need to merge into a caring relationship but was terrified of engulfment. A sense of detachment accompanied these conflicting needs. During this time, Rachel began to talk more of her history of molestation experiences by her siblings and stepfather. She expressed her feeling and belief that they had "damaged the fabric of my person."

In deciding how to respond to Rachel's requests for a scarf and calls, I had to evaluate the nature of those requests. I had to determine if the use of the scarf would serve the function of *wish gratification* or if, in fact, there was a psychological *need* that required a supportive response from me. It was helpful to consider the factors as discussed by Hedges (1994c).

> Winnicott has pointed to the enormous difference between gratifying a wish and being responsive to a need. And, at the organizing level, once the disconnection is being worked, the need is for availability and potential contact. . . . Such is the case with these urgent requests for organizing contact. . . . the client's need is simply "to hear your voice and to know that you're there, that I can find you, and that we're connected so I can go on with my life. . . ." The client's reaching the therapist is not unlike the demand feeding of an infant, when *the act of finding mother organizes out of mother's response to the demand.* Without mother's understanding and willing response, the panic, the agitation, and the anxiety only intensify and create multiple problems. . . . When an infant is in contact with mother, his or her entire body and mind become immediately organized. [p. 220]

This was particularly significant, in that Rachel described having experienced her mother as being generally absent and unavailable emotionally, or actively threatening her if she expressed any emotion. Coming from this frame of reference, even my presence evoked her feelings of emotional trauma. This was despite her paradoxical need to hold onto my scarf in order to help her feel connected. In the transference, Rachel began expressing rage at me "because you are here." Rachel would follow these rage episodes *in* sessions with letters sent between sessions stating she wouldn't continue in therapy. She would write,

> I'm not coming back. You're cold and indifferent. You don't really care. It's just a job to you. I feel so afraid that if I let down, if I cry, if I fall apart, you'll just sit there like a bump on a log, analyzing me, figuring me out, but having no feelings, having no emotions. You're just like everyone else. I'm weird. I'm tainted. I can't figure out how to climb out of my hole.

She was re-experiencing with me the feeling of being left "in the pit or in the hands of the abusers." She was experiencing me, in the transference, as the detached, observing mother of the molest "memories" or the cult leader of the witch "memories."

Again, Rachel demonstrated her dilemma in the transference as reflected in the third of Fraiberg's (1982) pre-defense styles, freezing. In this style, Rachel expressed her frozen rage. She believed that I could provide more for her than I was giving during our interactions. She felt helpless to get what she needed from me. She believed I was withholding from her. She stated,

> I guess when I really share my anguish with you, I feel you move away emotionally. Your body language is pretty loud and clear. Because I take my cues from the response of others, I just don't realize that I listen so closely to voice intonation, body language, and subtle verbal responses. I'm trying hard to find a connection to someone who understands and who can help me walk through these feelings and experiences that I detach from. You *could* be there for me, but you're not. I have my guard up, though. I'm pulling away from intimacy from everyone. I spend lots of time sitting on the floor curled up between my bed and dresser, hugging a big stuffed bear. I turn inward and isolate myself as often as possible. My guard is up. I'm afraid to feel. I'm afraid to feel an empathetic response from you.

Naturally, I was concerned and perturbed that Rachel continued to read into my behavior a set of responses that I didn't believe I was giving to her or, at least I hoped I wasn't. But—transference or not—it was important to me that I at least evaluate the possibility of her experiencing me as cold and unavailable. But even upon reflection and consultation I was not able to discern any feelings of withdrawal in me. In my perusing these possibilities, I wondered if the function of Rachel's experiencing me withholding and withdrawing was to actually push me away, to actually *create* a sense of ruptured contact or unavailability.

A period of weeks went by in which Rachel seemed to alternate among the three pre-defensive styles: flight, rage, and freezing. First, she was detached and walled off. She had extreme difficulty being with me in the session. She described her fears, "Maybe I put up an invisible protective shield when I'm afraid of losing contact with you. Anyway, I often feel the shield. I can see you and hear you, but I don't feel a connection on an emotional level. That will hurt. I'll be naked, embarrassed, humiliated, and you will be obligated to respond. But what if you're clinical and cold?" Secondly, she continued to rage at me, both in session and between sessions, in her perception that I kept moving away from her psychologically as well as physically. Thirdly, she continued to believe and complain that there was more I that could give her, but that I was withholding from her. The situations varied over the weeks, but the pre-defensive patterns would continually emerge.

As the year progressed, Rachel made a decision to go ahead with a divorce. Though she made this decision, she would alternate between periods of feeling guilty and periods of feeling strong. She described the emotions following this decision: "I feel like I'm plunging into a black hole. On the other side is light, but I have to go through this dark period of grief—a terrible loss like a death. This time I'm not the victim, I'm the perpetrator. I'm damaging him [husband]. I'm destroying his dreams."

By this time, clearly, some rudimentary forms of connection between Rachel and me had begun. Rachel cried for the first time in therapy. Her voice tone and body language began to become more age-consistent more frequently. We were able to be together and deal with here-and-now issues of her relationships with her family and me more frequently.

It was at this point in treatment, as we were beginning to experience real moments of connection, that the trauma memories started emerging. Her letters written between sessions contained much of the bizarre abuse content described earlier in the chapter. Her handwriting in the letters was different in each paragraph, suggesting the potential for multiple self-states. Not so surprisingly, as the "memories" would emerge, she began having more frequent episodes of bingeing and purging. She also had more frequent dreams of impending disaster.

During this time, when Rachel would experience overwhelming episodes of intrusive "memories" of the satanic ritual abuse, she would panic. She would call me with an "emergency," usually very late at night on a weekend, to tell me the "memory" in graphic detail and for me to calm her. As much as I was empathic and served to contain her during this period, I found myself feeling pressed-in on with her anger, demands, and mood swings. During the calls, in some ways, I felt like *I* was being intruded upon. I experienced the intrusive abuse *myself* by just having to listen to the awful "memories." I didn't *want* to listen to the horror she recounted. I felt like pushing her away. On one level, part of me was engaged in keeping a connection, but, on another, part of me would detach in order not to be overwhelmed myself so that I could preserve myself and still respond to her.

How tempting it might have been to try to figure out the "meaning" of the abuse memories. But to do so would have been to miss what was happening. As long as Rachel was entrenched in archetypal symbols, she avoided dealing with me. I understood the resurgence of memories and the dissociative qualities as representations of fears emerging as a result of our growing relatedness. Therefore, I chose to be empathic to the memories and to the dissociated sense of self, but to keep our focus in therapy on relationship issues with her family and with me. In other words, *I understood the emergence of the memories and symptoms as a psychological resistance to Rachel's experiencing her transference terrors more directly with me.* Every time she tried to draw me into a memory story, it was an attempt to flee from a connection with me. Hedges (1994c) describes the character of the resistance at the organizing level: "At the organizing level, the resistance is to dealing with the psychotic mother transference structure, to dealing with the breaking of contact and the rupture in relating. The breaking of contact guards the door to keeping the person from re-experiencing primitive overwhelming trauma and breakdowns that once occurred when contact was sought and had to be painfully withdrawn from" (p. 192).

About this time, Rachel's images of her connection to me had begun to shift. The images were no longer ones of just hanging on to the hem of my skirt. Now, she fantasized sitting in my lap, and hanging on tight to my arms. She still reported little sense of me responding by holding on to her, however. We scheduled one regular five-minute call between sessions to help her contain her anxiety, which emerged when she wasn't able to maintain an internal sense of connection to me. She demanded I make her a cassette tape describing her progress, so she could hear my voice between sessions. And, I hoped, so she could experience my reaching out to her through the tape. She took a picture of me so that she could have it at home to remember me when she couldn't bring up my image mentally. Again, she requested that I give her a scarf of my own that she could hold onto as a concrete way to hold on to me, though she reported losing the scarf at times and then feeling depressed. She wrote of her experience between sessions with these objects. "I have your scarf in my fingers, near my face, I like to bury my face in it. I look at your picture to remind myself that you exist and of what you look like. There's a king-size pillow on my bed that I lean against or put my arms around and pretend is you. I just can't let you get away."

It was not altogether clear to me exactly what function these objects and contacts served for Rachel. It was as though she was using these concrete objects to express experience that is pre-relationship (Hedges 1994c). In part, she used them as a way to engage her senses of touch, sight, and hearing in order to help her maintain a sense of safety and of continuity with me between sessions. In part they may simply have served as sources of comfort and soothing. Tustin (1981) makes a distinction between the functions of safety and soothing. She refers to the objects used in early infancy as *autistic objects*. She describes the early autistic objects as ones that are *hard* and that serve to give the child a sense of safety. In contrast, in later development, the child uses *soft* objects to obtain a sense of soothing and comfort. Either of these uses of concrete objects as autistic objects differs from what Winnicott (1953) calls the yet later *transitional objects*, in which the child uses an object like the teddy bear to *symbolize* mother's presence when in fact she is absent. At times, Rachel seemed to be using these objects in *each* of these ways.

As the molest memories continued to multiply and intensify, Rachel began to press me for a brief hug at the end of sessions, like she experienced at the end of Twelve-Step meetings. Also, she began expressing thoughts of wanting to know more about me personally. Rachel began bringing in little gifts for me: a small inspirational book, a small wooden carving from a trip, a Christmas ornament. This increase in concrete objects seemed to be her way of ensuring that she was with me. She wanted me to not forget her between sessions, either. It was as though, by giving, she was searching for a way to bring "mother" toward her.

I felt somewhat uncomfortable with Rachel's requests for "Twelve-Step hugs" and her continued presentation of the little gifts that she insisted on bringing despite my protests, interpretations, and attempts to stop them. Obviously, her need to relate to me in these forms was very important to her. I was afraid that if I protested too strongly or tried to deflect these actions more actively, it would have disrupted seriously the sense of continuity we had worked so hard to attain. But her insistence and my discomfort also seemed to represent a certain kind of breach in connecting. In the intensification of requests and attempts to draw me closer, she had in fact succeeded in disrupting the connection *in me* by getting me to feel uncomfortable and so backing away slightly. That is, her insistences functioned to disrupt our emotional contact by unsettling *me* rather than by *her* holding back.

In trying to understand what was happening with Rachel and with my own countertransference feelings, I was reminded of Hedges's (1994c) description of the dilemma experienced in these therapeutic situations.

> In work with unorganized states, it is not uncommon for the therapist to feel that he or she is being manipulated, cajoled, forced, . . . and made to do various things against one's wishes. In looking carefully at the organizing experience, these countertransference feelings are generally inappropriate to what is actually going on. . . . That is, infants have a great many needs such as . . . to be held, . . . to be talked to for extended periods of time so that sounds can be enjoyed and so that the mind can organize auditory stimulation, . . . [and] to feel in possession of the maternal body and mind. . . . These are all necessary for the infant's mind to organize time and space with the body and mind of the maternal person . . . [p. 226]

Hedges (1994c) describes the paradox of a person protesting and demanding for the therapist to be closer but unconsciously using those behaviors as a way to create a disconnection.

> The deceptive thing to the listener is that often people living organizing experiences express the fear, "I won't be able to have you" or "You're going to leave me," when in fact the fear is that "We're going to connect." That is, fears of abandonment, dependency, or helplessness are so universal that anyone expressing them can feel somehow understood. But to an organizing experience these fears are resistance. A clamoring fear of abandonment expressed by a person working an organizing transference is more likely *another way to disconnect or not be fully present and engaged in the moment* so that the abandonment content per se can be disregarded and/or interpreted as resistance to sustaining connection. It is important for the analyst to differentiate the fear of abandonment from the fear of connection, which is terrifying and marks the appearance of the traumatizing psychotic mother. In organizing experiences it is always the connection that is feared. And without the assured presence of the other, the fear can lead to a negative therapeutic experience. [p. 215]

To help me gain more of a sense of how the traumatizing psychotic mother was internalized for Rachel, I tried to imagine what our interactions would look like in the early child interaction between Rachel and her mother. I could picture Rachel's mother as a person who was passive and withdrawn, and who didn't know how to respond to her baby's needs. The mother was either very detached or intrusive. The mother had a "mimical self," *acting* like what she thought mothers were *supposed* to be like. She would "go through the motions" of mothering. It was as if she were saying, "I don't have anything inside to connect to you with." Other times, she would move intrusively into the baby's space, demanding that the *baby* respond to the *mother's* needs or to act in a prescribed way. The message to Rachel was, "when I'm in a certain mode, *you're* supposed to give to *me*." The mother was not in tune with the interpersonal reality of infant and mother. Instead, she was clinging to the baby. Her clinging to the baby was, in a sense, abusive, in that it was not a mutual connection. Rachel persisted in clinging to me.

Extrapolating from my own experiences with Rachel, I could picture how Rachel's responses to the dilemma created by these mothering behaviors became part of the frame from which she experienced the world. "With mother being so detached, I have to second guess from her body language what she wants and needs. If I don't figure this out and participate, by giving mother what she wants or demands, she will become outraged, and either withdraw even more or actively punish me. Either way, I am cut off from my lifeline. If I protest in any way, mother tells me that I'm bad, which damages me even more. It's now my fault. So, I try to stay connected to her in any way I can. I reach out to her. I promise to be good and to do whatever she says. I live in fear of what might happen to me if I inadvertently hurt her by not giving her all she wants." This fear of what might happen is what Winnicott (1974) refers to as "the fear of dying" and that Rachel described graphically in her ritual and sexual abuse "memories" in which she gave a description of her ego shattering and her resulting experience of dying psychologically.

Hedges (1994c) describes the nature of this fear in more detail.

This means that in listening to organizing experiences, there will always be in the background the fear of the loss of the needed other upon whose presence life itself depends. . . . What is feared is the threat of death (in a myriad of forms) and experiencing the agonies associated with fearing death that lie beyond failed dependence. The fear of breakdown, death, and emptiness resulting from the breakdown of somatopsychic channels to survival sources is an ever-present (and often deeply repressed) memory of any person reliving an organizing state. In early experiences that blocked the path to further organization, the infant experienced an environment devoid of responsiveness. The formation that remains in psychic structure is emptiness, fear of breakdown, and/or the threat of death. [Winnicott 1974, cited in Hedges 1994c, pp. 112–113]

With this picture in my mind, I had no trouble understanding how Rachel could represent this nightmare of infancy through the archetype of satanic ritual abuse and of organized sexual abuse. Also, I then could empathize more with her symptoms of vomiting, dissociative states, anxiety, panic, depression, rage, and with her physical sensations of trembling, difficulty breathing, chest pains, and falling into a dark hole.

Despite my increased understanding and sensitivity to Rachel's internal experience and needs, I was still in a very real dilemma. I wanted to transition Rachel from physical to mental and emotional forms of connecting. I was feeling a need to set some firm boundaries about the hugs and gifts. But I knew she would experience this action on my part as rejection and damage, no matter how hard I might try to reassure her that I was not rejecting her, and no matter how hard I might try to frame the boundary in some type of interpretation. In the countertransference, I felt that I was under the threat "to be a good little girl, minding my p's and q's." If I were to be more "me," I feared she would be angry and leave me, just as her mother had done repeatedly with her.

When I spoke with her about the boundaries, Rachel, in fact, did become tearful, hurt, angry, and depressed as I had anticipated. She wanted to run away. We talked about how she experienced me, at that point, as giving her a message that said she was bad. We discussed how she *believed* she was bad because in her life, she was blamed for having needs. Through interpretation, I tried to clarify the issues. My words were like dust in the wind. The key to the therapeutic intervention at that point was that I had to be very active in reaching out to Rachel and in trying to maintain a connection. One day, I talked to her fervently about the fact that both of us needed to hang on at that moment—she must hang on, and I must hang on. We *both* needed to find ways to stay connected. I felt that at some level, she heard me.

That night, Rachel wrote me a letter that expressed the rage and damage she felt when I set the limits on physical contact and the gifts. She wrote,

> I always leave these two king-size pillows on my bed. Then, when I go to bed, I arrange them. I pretend you are there, and I can touch you. Tonight, I'm throwing them off my bed. I want to throw away your scarf and your voice on tape. I want to turn my back and walk away. I hate you . . . I hate you . . . Oh! I wish I didn't love you. I wish you weren't so important to me. Then, I wouldn't hurt so bad. I feel devalued. How can I sit in front of you and share my insides and be torn apart? So naked. So vulnerable. So alone. You can just sit with me and watch as I go through the drama of the past—the horror and degradation. I always had to hang on to you anyway. Now I don't want to hang on. I want to let go and kick you and bite you and scream at you. I want to keep it up—screaming, and screaming and screaming. I want to call you names and tell you that I'll never trust you again.

Rachel was re-experiencing and re-enacting with me the essence of the early trauma she had experienced with her mother. As painful as this place was, however, Rachel had to re-experience and work through the early trauma of infancy in a *here-and-now* relationship in order for her to develop different modes of relatedness and to move on in her psychological and emotional development. We had to work continually on finding ways to stay connected during this fragile and vulnerable time.

THE WORKING-THROUGH PERIOD

For many months, Rachel continued to struggle to work through her traumatic organizing experience over and over again. My task, for the working through phase of treatment, was to continue to serve as a container for Rachel—a consistent object, present and providing responsive holding. To refer back to the *Star Trek* metaphor at the beginning of the chapter, it was as though my function were to hold Rachel's atoms together while she was in the process of being transported from an unorganized self into an organized self. I needed to continually reach out to connect to her and to engage her in continuing to reach out to me, despite whatever threats or disruptions we encountered.

During the working-through phase, Rachel alternated between feeling a connection to me and feeling rage at me for her being in that terrible, traumatic emotional place. She kept coming to sessions, but she continued to express complaints of experiencing a chilly, cold distance from me. She reported that the scarf I had given her was worn to shreds and demanded a new object from me. I gave her a plain keyring with a piece of cloth sewn onto it, which she reported lost a few weeks later. During one of her prolonged international work assignments, we arranged to keep in contact through weekly five- to ten-minute phone calls, at her request. She continued to express fears that she would not be able to keep seeing me for therapy and looked to me for reassurance. As Rachel was going through this distress, she needed to be assisted by the use of antidepressants and antianxiety agents as well.

Rachel continued to attempt to escape the experience of the trauma of relating through various representations of her pre-defensive styles. Several patterns emerged in these representations. Frequently, her flight style took the form of various psychological and somatic disorders. Her rage fight style was reflected in both direct and indirect behavioral patterns that demonstrated her transference anger at me. The frozen rage was seen in frequent demands that I give her help that I was "obviously withholding." Sometimes, I just needed to "be there" with Rachel. Other times, over and over, we explored together what she was experiencing and how her behavioral patterns reflected her attempts to disconnect from me. Our discussions about that seemed to help contain her somewhat for a period of time.

During the working-through phase of treatment, Rachel demonstrated how she experienced the terror on a body level. On one occasion, Rachel had an incident of heart palpitations that caused her to be admitted to the hospital because of her fears of dying from a heart attack. The doctors determined that she had had a panic attack. We understood the panic as a means to move her away from feeling in her relationship with me and dealing with her anger.

Also, Rachel reported frequent bingeing and purging episodes and focused more on her "eating disorder." A pattern to the episodes emerged: she would experience an emotion, either positive or negative; then she would deny or discount her own feelings or experience others as discounting her; she was then left feeling angry at herself and others; and finally, from the place of anger, she would binge and vomit. It was as though she would take in resources desperately, but not be able to retain them. She would actively get rid of the food. Also, we saw the purging as a way she put her life in chaos. While there were some symbiotic qualities to the bulimia in that a dyadic interaction seemed involved, part of the function of this symptom also seemed to be to dip into the pre-symbiotic issues of breaking the connection to others.

Another way Rachel attempted to escape the experience of the trauma was reflected during a period in which she decided she had a multiple personality disorder. A friend had given her a book on MPD and convinced Rachel she probably had it. We discussed her experiences of dissociation under stress. She made a decision to attend an intensive two-week inpatient therapy group experience for victims of sexual and satanic ritual abuse who "had MPD." She talked of her plans to go in a way that seemed aimed at testing out my responses *and* expressing anger at me. Though I wasn't enthusiastically supportive of the idea, and tried to maintain neutrality, Rachel used this as a way to move away from me. She framed it by saying, "I have to make my own choices. . . . I feel like I'm being a teenager." She requested we maintain phone contact while she was in the program. Over the next few months following completion of the program, Rachel allowed me to direct her back on the track of dealing with relatedness issues instead of dissociation symptoms.

At times, Rachel expressed her rage at me more directly as well as indirectly. She reported that she was still angry that I had set a limit on the Twelve-Step hugs because the limit made me feel unsafe. She talked of having an increase in suicidal fantasies: "I have thoughts of putting a hair dryer in the bathtub, and calling you over to my house so that you can see my body turn rigid." She wanted me to feel the same guilt, fear, and helplessness that she experienced. We continued to work directly on the anger issues. Concurrently she began clinging to the scarf again.

By now, Rachel was divorced. She became involved in a series of intense sexual relationships with men she deemed inappropriate, though she compulsively sought them out. She described becoming close physically and enjoying the physical contact with them, but also reported feeling violated emotionally. She did not use any form of protection during the sexual encounters with high-risk men. The nature of Rachel's relationships with these men was one of moving close, then pulling away. When she broke off the relationship with one of them, she became extremely anxious, then went back with him. Hearing of unprotected sex, needless to say, did serve to disrupt and disconnect me from time to time.

Rachel seemed to use the telling of the sagas about her experiences with the men as a way of not relating to me directly. However, over time, she did explain her involvement with them as a way to express anger at me for what she experienced as my abandoning her during different points of time in her treatment. She offered the interpretation: "If my mother rejects me, I'll leave her and go to my stepfather, even though he abuses me." Also, she reported seeing the sexual behavior as a way to say "I'm not worth anything." After several unsuccessful attempts to disengage from these relationships, which put her at risk physically as well as psychologically, Rachel finally was able to stop the irresponsible relationships. She did report feeling a sense of loss and mourning after this. We explored the possibility that she was not looking for momentary nurturing in these interactions, as she supposed, but that she was looking for a way to disconnect from me by creating chaos in her life. Rachel's mood and stability improved after this for a period of time.

I had to continually call Rachel back into relatedness with me, in place of letting her sidetrack down paths of sexual abuse, MPD, eating disorders, suicidal ideations, and sexual encounters. For awhile she would venture into new modes of relating that she reported as being more positive and peaceful, but then she would retreat back into the problem behaviors. We were able to understand all of these "symptoms" as attempts to disrupt the growing connection between us.

Throughout the working-through process, Rachel and I continued to work together to understand some of the various themes that were interwoven in her life. We explored how her denial and detachment from past traumas ended up making her vulnerable to traumas being recreated in the present. Rachel began working on understanding the ways the violation and disconnection pattern was re-created each time she didn't allow herself to feel or to see the overwhelming distress she experienced in her relationships, or to set appropriate boundaries to protect herself. We looked at the way the compulsive symptoms fit into this pattern. Over time, Rachel began experiencing and expressing her feelings more directly and appropriately to her mother, stepfather, and other people whom she experienced as threatening in here-and-now interactions. She began setting boundaries and asserting herself in family, work, and social situations more effectively. She reported experiencing pleasure as well as fear and guilt in doing so.

Rachel began to talk of an increased awareness of another pattern she had of "using helplessness and dependency behavior to keep from dealing with the feelings from the incest." She saw attempts she made to get others to depend on her as a way to take care of her own dependency needs. She struggled with the tension of conflict between a pull toward isolation in order to avoid becoming overinvolved and enmeshed, and the desire to be a dependent little girl. Rachel described becoming aware that she compartmentalized things to keep safe, but that ultimately her relationships were sabotaged. She worked on disengaging from the child role she took with others.

Rachel also worked on her internal expectations that she should be able to handle anything, and that she should be perfect. We worked on her dualistic belief (and the resulting internal conflict) that she either had to be an expert, or if not, it meant that she was "the village idiot." She talked of trying to control everything so as not to *appear* to be "the village idiot." We explored how she attempted to be acceptable to others and to survive in the world by acting as if she were a certain way that she perceived as being the good or right way to act in order to be okay. Along with this, we worked on her belief that achievement meant a person was worthwhile. She began to report, over time, instances of feeling she was acceptable even though she was not "allknowing." She became more accepting of her strengths, limitations, and needs.

We also worked on how these expectations affected the therapeutic relationship. This was particularly important in helping Rachel learn to manage momentary breaches in empathy and availability of the therapist. Hedges (1994c) describes the importance of this issue.

> By nurturing the belief or fantasy that everything should be, nay must be, perfect, ideal, blissful, happy, or totally cured, these individuals insure ongoing and unending unhappiness, misery, suffering, and unrest. The ideal state of mind and being, like the ideal analyst who provides all that is necessary for comfort and safety, is a fantasy that is difficult to relinquish, especially if it is accompanied by an attitude of entitlement, the right to a perfect analyst, to a perfect analysis, and to a perfect and blissful outcome. Perfect trust in a perfect analyst is demanded so that "basic trust" (Erikson 1959) in an "optimally failing analyst" (Kohut 1971) cannot be achieved. [p. 167]

As Rachel and I continued to work on these various themes and resistances, she began to report more feelings of sadness—about life, losses, and her inability to change the past. We worked on how her denial of the past was a way to avoid loss feelings, but also kept her locked into re-experiencing past trauma in the present. We discussed her belief that if she expresses anger it will always cause rejection, which will lead to her feeling totally worthless, and eventually to her experiencing the world as if it were collapsing. We talked about this as a "feeling memory" based on what already had happened in the past (Winnicott 1974). We worked on how anger may result in rejection or nonrejection, but that the world doesn't have to collapse. We worked on learning to hold the feelings and to take action to understand and manage them more effectively.

As time went on, Rachel continued to develop an increased ability to internally maintain a connection with me. She gave back the scarf I had given her, though she asked me to save it, as she might need it again. She reported not needing the five-minute calls between sessions any longer. Her vomiting behaviors subsided. She lost significant weight. If she had a panic attack and was unable to reach me, she became able to calm herself or to use other resources such as friends to help her. She said she was trying to get out of co-dependent relationships and "always looking for a mother to care for me." She was trying to do more herself. She experienced some anxiety and struggled with this but was able to manage the distress more effectively. Rachel showed an increased ability to problem-solve on her own. She catastrophized less frequently. She began to see her pattern of trying to rescue as a way of trying to connect. She expressed more experiences of positive connected feelings, strength, energy, and comfort with setting boundaries for herself, and reported feeling much more stable, though she still felt fragile and vulnerable. We worked on Rachel's allowing herself to feel good and settle into good feelings and relationships without reverting to creating chaos.

We also continued to work through the pain and agony of her early trauma of infancy. As she continued to report longer periods of feeling more stable and happy, Rachel began to think about termination. Although we knew we had much more working through to do, I celebrated with Rachel the thought that someday she would be strong enough to be able to leave me.

While preparing this chapter, Rachel and I talked about her terrifying journey out of the "pit," and of all the work she has had to do—the "witches" and "molesters" she has had to face and stand against, past and present. At one point she said, "I was thinking about the past several years of going through this. I remember how terrible it has been. But then, I realized you went through it with me. It must have done something to you, too."

Yes, Rachel, our journey together *has* "done something to me." In order to be with you, to stay with you, and to "hold" you, I have had to face my own fears. In a sense, I had to find my own way of going into the "pit" and into "the bed of abuse" with you in order to try to understand better how terrifying the world has been for you and the rage that you have felt about the trauma you experienced. In doing so, I have had to face my own fears of anger, of engulfment, of abandonment, and of being damaged on a deeper level. In learning how to be a safe and reliable container for your overwhelming fears and anger, I have learned more about managing and dispelling my own. Faith has been described as "the substance of things hoped for, the evidence of things not [yet] seen" (Hebrews 11:1). It is very dark in the "pit." It is very difficult to "see" through the darkness, to maintain hope, and to believe that there is a way to bring healing to the traumatized parts of our infant selves. Our journey together has confirmed and fortified my faith and my belief that there *is* a way out of the "pit of terror."

HEDGES' COMMENTS

What better example could we ask for of how *not* to become carelessly involved in organizing level content! By not colluding with the content-resistant ploys, Jolyn safely moves her client toward fulfilling relationships.

PART III

ESTABLISHING SAFETY: THE FIRST VITAL STEP TOWARD CONTACT AND CONNECTION

8

Enveloped and Suffocated by Slime

Clinical Contribution by
Miguel Reyes and John Carter

HEDGES' COMMENTS

John Carter thought I might enjoy hearing about a strange countertransference reaction from one of his supervisees, Miguel Reyes. The
three of us met for the discussion that follows. The case is not far enough
along for us to have a full sense of the historical origins of the dynamic
registered in the emerging countertransference. But Miguel's reactions
are vivid and they illustrate how projective dynamics can be traced
through fathering experiences toward earlier mothering experiences.
Here Miguel is disturbed, disgusted, and frightened that his identity will
somehow be invaded, marred, or defaced. Many therapists have strong
and disturbing countertransference reactions that are as peculiar as this
one and have no idea where they come from. John and Miguel's work
points toward some ways of staying with such reactions and trying to
unravel their therapeutic relevance.

Sigmund Freud (1911), in his famed discussion of Judge Schreber's memoirs of psychosis, points out that any theory of psychotic experience must take into account the person's preoccupation with body sensations and parts. He took the position that hypochondriasis is to psychosis what anxiety is to neurosis—an indicator of the kinds of traumatic stress a person has had to endure in early life. Here the preoccupation will be with skin and disgust and how they relate to primitive terrors of invasion and somato-psychic damage.

> *Miguel:* This couple, Maria and Arturo, I've been working with is intriguing because although I had been working with them for over a year, I still had not been able to understand the particular transferences and countertransferences operating throughout that year. But the couple recently separated. And that's when I first got a glimmer of what had been going on. The best thing I can say to start with is that the transference felt splashy, gooey, and that it left me with a feeling of slime or filthiness. I know this is a strange description of transference and countertransference feelings but . . .
>
> *Larry:* It is strange . . .
>
> *Miguel:* It was like some kind of slimy feeling that I would clean myself from after sessions, but I could never quite understand what it was about. I would leave the session feeling like, well, the sexual image that comes to my mind is someone ejaculating all over me, smearing me with it, and my not liking it.
>
> *Larry:* This is strange.
>
> *Miguel:* That dirty, slimy feeling was disturbing and confounding to me, until recently when Maria separated from Arturo. It finally came out that he had been screwing other women behind her back. And it was almost as if she had been carrying his ejaculations, or his raging, or his rageful ejaculatory processes for a long time. And that the rageful, sexual sliming was being somehow transmitted to me, through her. That's the feeling of it.
>
> *John:* Can I ask you a question? Didn't you say at one time, and maybe I'm jumping ahead, that Arturo tried to act as a pimp and prostitute her in some way?
>
> *Miguel:* Yes he did.

Larry: This is an amazing beginning, because what you're saying is that the sexual processes here are being used really for . . .

Miguel: The primitive sexual processes.

Larry: . . . some kind of gruesome hostile purpose.

Miguel: Yes. Gruesome hostile purpose, exactly.

Larry: And that some of this primitive, hostile sexuality has been directed at you. That's the feeling that you've been having?

Miguel: I know it's strange, but yes. I went fifteen sessions with this couple until they divulged that when they first got married they had no money, so she went off and worked as a prostitute. He managed her, allowed her to do it, and sold her. But in retrospect I'm not so sure the pimping and prostitution was only for money. There was something really disgusting about it all. Behind it was driving rage and terror.

Larry: We might not always find prostitution disgusting. But there was something about it in this case that you found totally disgusting?

Miguel: It was degrading, that's why. It was forced upon her out of rage with humiliating intentions. And there was some deep unidentified element of terror.

Larry: I'm thinking, for example, that we might find someone raised in a barrio and living in desperate conditions finding some meaningful sense of self through prostitution. Or engaging in sex for money out of necessity of for some other important purpose.

Miguel: Yes.

Larry: So we could imagine many reasons for prostitution that might have some redeeming value to the self or to life—given certain circumstances. But that doesn't seem to be the case here. Here you're saying we have degradation, force, humiliation, rage, and fear.

Miguel: Yes, there was a degrading quality to all of their sex like it was done more out of anger and fear. It was like his saying "Fuck you," and "I will screw you over good." And her feeling some terror and a need to submit. It was that quality. But when Maria later separated from Arturo, that slimy quality stopped. It was almost as if she were a vehicle, a carrier of his rageful degrading transference, or whatever he was projecting. And it was landing on me.

Larry: The disgusting, degrading, dominating, slimy, transference was aimed at you. It had a "fuck you" quality, aimed squarely at you?

Miguel: Aimed at me, channeled through her.

Larry: Your body language shows us not only facial disgust but a sense of your skin crawling.

Miguel: Yes. Some sense of dirt, slime, ooze, splash—"get off me."

Larry: Yes. This continues to be strange.

Miguel: When much later Maria broke off the relationship with him, things were suddenly cleaner. I was suddenly cleaner. I didn't feel slimed on by a disgusting pimp.

Larry: An awesome beginning.

Miguel: I thought a description of those strange feelings might help clarify something of the nature of their relationship.

Larry: Yes.

Miguel: Arturo refused to continue therapy on a regular basis after that fifteenth session because he was angry at her. After their disclosure to me of their pimp–prostitute activities he became very mistrustful toward her. He felt that she was going to go out and continue using her body as a prostitute behind his back. That was his constant complaint. But though he stopped attending regular sessions, she continued to. That's when I really started sensing this slimy, gooey, repulsive feeling like someone was ejaculating all over me. But I couldn't define the feeling very well until she left him and then it was like I wasn't weighed down any more with trying to clean myself off all the time. It was like I didn't have to waste my energy dodging the slime. I was able to talk more freely. During the time when the oppressive transference projection was occurring, a lot of my energies were directed toward cleaning myself off, cleaning the mess up. I can't tell you how, it's just the feeling.

Larry: Well, here again, we can imagine a variety of circumstances in which we might think of sexual juices, ejaculation, and so forth, being on us in ways that could be interesting, exciting, and even beautiful.

Miguel: Yes.

Larry: And yet, there's something here about it—that is, the essence of love itself, is being used to smear you. That's the feeling. I'm really eager to hear how the imaginary sexual juices of these two accomplished this!

Miguel: That was the feeling. It was smearing, their juices being used to smear me. I was once working in a special school setting with a child who enjoyed smearing his feces over the bathroom wall. This had that over-the-edge quality to it.

Larry: There is a time and a place for body products. But in this case we have misuse of them.

Miguel: Yes, I was being smeared. Well, that's how I experienced it.

Larry: The hostility in it, the fringe of sanity quality.

Miguel: The hostile edge to it. In the case with the child he was very hostile, very angry, rageful toward his mom. It was almost as if he were smearing feces on the mom. Needless to say in my case Arturo did have rageful issues with his mom. Mom cruelly and repeatedly abandoned him. Given the dynamics that unfolded here, maybe she engaged in prostitution or had a pimp. He's like smearing the person, coloring, covering them over with his own body fluids, something like that. Something about coloring someone up or smearing somebody over with one's body fluids. Like there's some kind of perverse goal there. Like there's a gain in doing that.

John: I believe you once said "mar."

Miguel: You mar them, yes. "Slime them." It's like hand painting, body painting, and you're like sliming somebody, it was sort of like that. That's the image that comes to my mind. When I go back to the countertransference, it's like I was ejaculated upon, smeared upon, and in essence there was a distorting of my image. Marring of the image. Marring of her image, marring my image.

John: Is it envy that spoils the good? As you're talking I'm associating to about fifteen or so years ago. Some guy in Italy hit the Pietà, you know the Michelangelo statue.

Larry: Right.

John: The Michelangelo statue of Mary holding Jesus. He hit it, I think with a small hammer. He was trying to deface this symbol that is traditionally beautiful and significant. But he was trying to . . .

Larry: Deface it. Deface Maria.

John: Yes. Deface it. Deface her—Maria, exactly. Like you know, people who deface buildings, or whatever.

Miguel: Yes. It felt like a defacing. It's like spilling paint over a sacred statue. This particular man was originally from Argentina. And now that I think about it, if I'm not mistaken, it's by no means uncommon in that culture to deface symbols that represent authority you are disgusted with, that you do not like. You deface it by painting, you pour paint over it and discolor it, distort it, deface it, mar the image.

John: My mind went to just the word itself.

Larry: Deface. To wipe out the identity . . .

John: To change identity by distorting, defacing it.

Larry: Well, Miguel tell us about the case. How did it start? How did it go? How did all this awful feeling develop?

Miguel: The feeling emerged slowly after the fifteenth session when they both divulged this secret. Obviously there was a lot of shame around it. She had agreed to provide the money to pay for food and rent, and he had sold her, degraded her, defaced her. They both felt the shame. She felt the shame afterwards, in that she had done it. And he felt the shame for allowing her to do it. There had been a collusion, a shameful one. They both felt the shame, and they kept it inside for fifteen sessions. All of a sudden it came out, just before they ran off on a vacation. When they returned, she came in alone. She wanted to continue therapy, he didn't. She wasn't clear as to why he didn't want to come back. I had him come in once or twice and I did talk to him. He was very passive-aggressive. He couldn't exactly tell me why he didn't want to continue. But, strikingly, when she starting coming in on her own, she started dressing very provocatively.

Larry: Distinctly differently from the way she had dressed before?

Miguel: Oh yes. She came in with mini skirts more often, frilly blouses, short belly shirts. I felt like there was some sexualization of our process going on. As though perhaps she were prostituting again. Almost as if she were being sent in by the pimp. Like some aggressive intent was being lived out through her that was affecting not only her but me.

Larry: You had not felt the negative intent in the first fifteen sessions?

Miguel: No. There was actually a nice collaborative sense among the three of us. We worked well on communication issues.

Larry: So the feeling in the countertransference is slowly evolving as she provocatively comes in by herself.

Miguel: It's slowly evolving. It was hidden the first fifteen sessions.

Larry: Can you report any countertransference sensations in those first fifteen sessions? You haven't told us yet why they came, or how divulging the secret of the prostitution happened.

Miguel: Yes. Well, the presenting problem was that they were in warfare about communications, they both complained about not being able to communicate.

Larry: How long had they been together?

Miguel: Three or four years. They wanted to work on better communication. Specifically she complained about him being overly dependent on her. She felt very suffocated, engulfed by him, dominated by his dependency. He complained about feeling that she didn't care about his, um, what was the way he said it, *Ella no me hace sentir importante.* She doesn't help me feel important. She complained about feeling engulfed by his demands. But at the same time, it was as if she were inviting that engulfment. She wanted the mental-physical fusion. But then she complained about the stifling, suffocating effects of the fusion.

Larry: When you moved into Spanish, the implication becomes more passive than it is in English, doesn't it? We can say she doesn't make me feel important, but it doesn't quite carry the same passivity that it does in the Spanish?

Miguel: No it doesn't.

Larry: Spanish uses the reflexive. Like it's her job to make me or help me feel important.

Miguel: Yes. Maria complained about the fusion, but then she wanted, she invited the fusion. And then Arturo complained that she was making him feel unimportant. Much of this came through glimpses of their sex life. There was no problem with their sex life in the sense that it was active and alive.

Larry: They were together three or four years. Were they married during this time period?

Miguel: Three years married, the first year they lived together.

Larry: And the prostitution occurred during that first year?

Miguel: It occurred toward the end of that first year just before getting married.

Larry: Like the fulfillment of the engagement?

Miguel: Yes.

Larry: And how had their economic situation shifted by the time they started seeing you? There had been difficulties in the beginning?

Miguel: Arturo had received some kind of compensation, through a lawsuit or something to that effect. So they had a large sum of money, and they were able to use that. And Maria was working as a massage therapist.

Larry: Body work. Did he work at all?

Miguel: He was working in construction.

Larry: So, during this period of their marriage, they both had gotten to working steadily and they had this lump sum of money to help them through.

Miguel: Yes.

Larry: So they were doing much better economically at the time that they came to you?

Miguel: Right, yes. But physically there were problems. This is one couple that skin contact was very important to. Let me just tell you something about her. It's like she knows that she exists through some type of tactile sensory process. She needs the skin contact. He does too. Very much so. Both of them have some desperation for skin contact. I'm sure that's why sex was so frequent and so lively.

Larry: In the countertransference, your images are tactile about ejaculation, slime, dirt all over you. These are skin sensations. So it is almost like in the countertransference you felt the hostility being projected at the skin level.

Miguel: I hadn't thought of that, but it's true.

Larry: You didn't tell us, for example, that your stomach turned or your heart was racing, or your feet were cold . . .

Miguel: No. The feelings definitely had a tactile reference. Now, while she was still with him but coming to therapy by herself, she dressed provocatively. It was as if some sexualization of her surface were going on.

Larry: There again she is showing skin.

Miguel: Yes, she is showing plenty of skin, plenty of skin.

Larry: And, let's face it, invading your boundaries that way.

Miguel: Invading my boundaries?

Larry: Sure. A female client comes to a male therapist in a professional environment and gives him lots of skin. It is a kind of violation. You are not there to look at, to be entertained by her skin.

Miguel: That is true. She is bringing up my awareness of her skin, but she is not bringing up much about herself.

Larry: This is a professional relationship. She knows it, you know it; and she is provocatively intruding, violating it by showing plenty of skin.

Miguel: You're right.

Larry: This is different than somebody coming in their sweats or shorts from the gym. But even there you don't necessarily show skin. She is deliberately showing skin.

Miguel: It's out of context with the reality of why we're meeting.

Larry: Right.

Miguel: Then all of a sudden this is when we started experiencing troubles. It could be that he was disapproving of her coming to see me. On the one hand sending her alone, but on the other resenting her seeing me, provoking me. Like he was playing off the theme of feeling important. He wasn't feeling important by her coming to therapy on her own. But he didn't choose to come in with her.

Larry: He's either knowing that she wanted to seduce you. Or he's knowingly sending her to seduce you, to have a skin relationship with you—all the while feeling neglected or unimportant.

Miguel: Yes. So he gave her his rage, projecting it into her through their primitive skin, ejaculatory contact processes.

Larry: You're suggesting that in some perverse way a third party may be an essential aspect to their deeper, but disturbing sexual urges. That he's using her to express his hostility and sexuality toward you.

Miguel: Yes. So I continue probing, just continue to probe not being able to make much sense of anything that's going on of what I'm feeling. I don't think she knew what she was doing consciously. She may have sensed that she was a carrier of his rageful, defacing projective identification. Because surely there was a place in her that was compliant, that found this position somehow familiar. And, now that you mention it, it is interesting that I characterize my own activities at this point as probing.

Larry: Let me ask you a cross-cultural question here. I'm well aware that among Latinas there is a greater tendency to show skin in mini-skirts, belly shirts, and so forth—say, more than there might be in the Anglo culture. What is your feeling here?

Miguel: Good question. Because I have other female clients, Latinas who come in showing plenty of skin, but there isn't that sense of sexualization, of provocativeness, of seduction.

Larry: So her skin was highly eroticized and you felt it?

Miguel: Yes. I felt it, I certainly did. I mean, I've had other clients who come in wearing mini-shirts and belly shirts, but there isn't that energy of sexualization in it all.

John: Even I felt it that time I accidentally ran into her in the hall at our clinic.

Miguel: You even felt it, and you knew right away it was her.

Larry: You saw her?

John: Yes. I was coming back from the restroom one day when she was leaving the building. Afterward I ran into Miguel in the staff room and I said . . .

Miguel: He knew it was her from my description of my feelings.

John: I knew by the way her skin was eroticized. I didn't feel the seduction, but I felt the eroticization of the skin. What do you call what she was wearing?

Miguel: A belly blouse.

John: The belly blouse. And the way she walked. She looked over at me, not seductively. But her skin was alive, her skin was alive, vibrant, eroticized. I don't know how to describe it but it truly was.

Larry: So you do make a distinction between the way she carries herself and other Latinas who may also show skin as a part of a cultural feature.

Miguel: Right. When I meet with other Latinas who show skin, there isn't that charged quality. It seemed almost with her that I sense her skin trying to envelop me, trying to cover me, trying to reach out to me, to come upon me, to cover me over.

Larry: So it's an assault. A defacing of your identity.

Miguel: Yes. It's like coming upon me, covering me. With other women I don't feel that enveloping sense. Their skin, their beauty is just there—a part of them. That's who they are and they're retaining their skin. Keeping inside of their own bodies. Here she's giving away her skin. There is the distinction: other Latinas can retain their skin. With her it's different. It's like she—really both of them—are putting it on you for the purpose of knowing something about themselves or you. Funny image—not retaining your own skin but aggressively engulfing someone else with it.

Larry: Like some sort of an invasion.

Miguel: It is an invasion. And with it a quality of suffocation.

Larry: Suffocation?

Miguel: Yes. It's almost like putting saran wrap, cellophane wrap around your head and you are trying to breathe with it. The texture is over you. You're trying to breathe. Hmm. (As if he has just discovered something)

John: You're really getting into this, Miguel!

Group: (Laughter)

Miguel: I'm really going into this now because of what I'm sensing as we talk. I've been trying to understand these feelings for a long time and that's what I've been feeling. It's like a cellophane wrap being wrapped around me and it's a skin-to-skin pressure—a tactile, sensory process and it's suffocating to me because it's wrapped around my face.

Larry: There is face again.

John: Yes. There is face again, and perhaps even womb.

Miguel: But, prior to her breaking up with her boyfriend, her husband, that tactile quality of wrapping around me somehow involved his semen. Before the fifteenth session there was nothing, no discernible countertransference. There was just a couple struggling with communication problems that I was hoping to help straighten out. But after the fifteenth session . . . one or two sessions after the fifteenth session when he refused to come in with her, there was the skin, the sense of yuck, what I eventually came to call the skin with smeared semen.

Larry: Now the way you say it has a homosexual overtone.

Miguel: How?

Larry: In his dynamics, first the sense of his somehow putting his semen on you man-to-man, even though he uses the woman as a vehicle. Also, we hear that he has seduced other men to screw his girlfriend or wife. There is always a homosexual overtone in pimping—seducing a man to do it.

Miguel: Yes. There is. You're right.

Larry: But it may not be a particularly significant issue, so that's why I'm asking.

Miguel: Let me finish this other thought before I lose it.

Larry: Go ahead.

Miguel: Then I'll get back to the homosexual thread. Could it be that in his rage he smeared her skin with his rageful semen, and I picked up on that because of her trying to envelop me with her skin which was already smeared with his rageful semen? Like it was inevitable that I feel his rageful semen because of her process of always trying to envelop people with her skin?

Larry: So, once again you're saying that the feeling theme seems to be not his striving for direct contact with you, but your feeling contact with him and his rage through her.

Miguel: Right. I was picking up the rageful semen that he was ejaculating on her and smearing through my contact with her skin as she was seducing me, making me feel important to her.

Larry: It's a three-way somehow and you're feeling used, your presence is somehow important to who they are together . . .

Miguel: . . . making me important, yes.

Larry: We have to figure out "important" in what sense. As a third person, a love object, or as a fetish?

Miguel: Well, she is going to another guy for a relationship.

John: Yes, and it's intimate.

Miguel: For self-fulfillment. For a relationship, perhaps for orgasm. He complains she's prostituting herself with other guys but she denies it.

Larry: So he sends her, but then we feel his rage.

John: He doesn't show up himself, but he sends his rage.

Larry: So, Miguel, give us a feeling for what it's like when she's with you. You're giving us the countertransference feelings, but what did the sessions actually look like during this period?

Miguel: Okay. But we haven't addressed the homosexual thread yet. In the first fifteen sessions he expressed a deep appreciation for my help. I mean there was a level of genuineness in his expressions of appreciation.

Larry: There was help, he felt it, and he expressed his appreciation to you.

Miguel: Yes. There had been something upsetting that happened when they had visited her family in Colombia. He was deeply grateful for my help in sorting all of that out. It had been important. Because he really opened up. He cried. He let himself feel deeply in the short time we had together—which I found remarkable for a man who was very invested in machismo.

Larry: So the homosexual thread is really more of a deep maternal attachment?

Miguel: Yes. I would say it's a dependent maternal attachment.

Larry: So possibly mother's body is being assaulted with his body products? Yours is.

Miguel: Yes.

Larry: And there's your association to the little boy smearing feces who is angry with his mother.

Miguel: After the fifteenth session comes a month or so off, a vacation and few phone calls from her. She is eager to come in, to see me. I tell her I want her to come in. I want to see them both.

Larry: What were those sessions actually like?

Miguel: Okay. The sessions—well, on several occasions she would walk in and immediately shake my hand and kiss me on the cheek. An invasion. You're right, a skin invasion.

Larry: This is not just a friendly Latina greeting? This is more an invasion?

Miguel: It is an invasion.

Larry: Okay.

Miguel: During the first fifteen sessions she had greeted me with a Hispanic handshake and kiss twice but it was different. Now the greeting took on a different quality that made me feel uncomfortable. It was sexualized. It was excessive. It was more in tune with the skin. Suffocating. It was like the cellophane wrap on my head.

Larry: So she shakes your hand and kisses you on the cheek. But you want to pull back.

Miguel: And then she starts complaining. She did a lot of splitting—seeing her husband as all bad. In contrast, she was very solicitous toward me, always complimenting me on how nice I was, how I have helped her a lot, what a nice person I am, or how she liked a particular shirt I was wearing. I felt overidealized by her. She was putting me on a pedestal, all the while denigrating, devaluing Arturo. She was very childlike in her neediness as though she were very dependent on me. She would always say, "Oh, I don't think I could ever make it without you. You are the only one who listens to me." It was excessive and suffocating too.

Larry: One great way to ensure no real contact in a relationship is by excessively praising the other. It always alienates. "Praise to the face is shameful."

Miguel: Yes. All this verbiage on her part was suffocating. It was like, I didn't feel like I was Miguel. I didn't feel like she was relating to me. I thought, "Who is she relating to?" It was like I wasn't there at times in the session. You're right, it's like I was some sort of idealized fetish.

Larry: Was she using the sessions to solicit advice and help or more just to pour out her woes and seduce you?

Miguel: She was trying to use me to give her quick answers to her problems.

Larry: And how did that process go?

Miguel: I never gave her quick answers.

Larry: But she still idealized you?

Miguel: I kept trying to take her back to her pain. And, she would cry for a brief moment and then jump on the idealization track again.

Larry: So you really never had hold of her?

Miguel: No, I never had hold of her. She seemed to slip through my fingers—so to speak!

Larry: I have a question since we have here an erotic transference of sorts. We live in a day now where we are paranoid about sex in therapy and therapists being accused of sexual encounters. Was there ever any sense of her trying to engage you sexually or did this really stay more at the level of this deep, destructive slime and invasion?

Miguel: It stayed at the level of that deep, destructive slime, that invasion. Come to think of it though, there was a moment in which it was almost as if she were inviting me to go between her legs.

Larry: Can you tell us about that moment?

Miguel: I should have brought my case notes. There was a session where she started idealizing me. But the idealizing was such it was almost like she was inviting, "Have sex with me, come alongside of me, come inside."

Larry: Then and there.

Miguel: Yes. "Join with me." It was like "Be my pal outside of therapy."

Larry: Did she actually say that?

Miguel: That was the implication to the nature of our talk. The way she was idealizing me and how I get her to talk. Like it would be really great being intimate with me.

Larry: On the one hand she wants you to be her buddy or to have sex with her, but on the other hand she's idealizing you and in that way you are not Miguel. So there is a depersonalization of you, and yet she still wants friendship, intimacy, sex with you. Interesting that her husband complains that despite good sex she doesn't make him feel important. Her overtures didn't make you feel personally very important either.

Miguel: No. This goes back to her fusion with me, her wanting me close to her, next to her. There goes the tactile again, the skin. Maybe the "inside her, between her legs" is more my material in response to her. She was giving me skin, she wanted skin fusion with me, and there was a point in that process where she wanted fusion in a sexual sense, but a fusion that defaces, depersonalizes, suffocates me. Perhaps this all goes back to her father, if you look at her developmental history. She had a very close, fused but unsatisfactory relationship with her father.

Larry: Was it sexual too?

Miguel: She was emotionally incested.

Larry: But not, so far as you know, physically?

Miguel: Not so far as I know. She never acknowledged anything like that. But there was a lot of emotional incest. He used her as a surrogate spouse and as a source of emotional containment. It could have been skin again, closeness, sensual, sexual I suppose.

Larry: So this whole question of being given away to another to be used, which comes up in the relationship with her husband, is a long-standing theme for her as well. Her mother gave her away to her father who fused with her in some primitive, sensual, erotic way. And she is now being given away to you.

Miguel: Yes. There is a theme of her wanting to fuse with dad—but an unsatisfactory attachment with her father. It's as if she were somehow trying to accomplish that same sense with me in therapy. And with other men in general by giving away her skin. That's the way she knows she exists, that's the way she knows she's important. That's herself. Her identity involves her enveloping, containing a man—or someone. That's her source of existence—fusing with the other.

Larry: So go ahead, you saw her for this period and then we have a break-up in the relationship don't we?

Miguel: Yes. I told Maria that it would be best if we meet as a couple again because of the nature of the problem. Since it was relational, since we were talking about marital issues.

Larry: You're smiling a bit. Are you trying to tell us also that in the countertransference you felt some awkwardness with the seduction, or . . . ?

Miguel: Well, I started panicking.

Larry: Panicking, because?

Miguel: I felt panicky because I didn't want this to go anywhere, to get out of hand.

Larry: The sexual seduction?

Miguel: Right. Knowing her fundamental lack of reality testing, I felt that she could easily distort the therapeutic relationship to possibly mean something else in her need for intimate fusion and her overidealization of me. So I thought I'd better keep a check on this by seeing if her husband could be a part of the process too.

Larry: What were you afraid of?

Miguel: I was afraid of being accused of misleading her. I was afraid of her distorting the relationship. And I was afraid of her marring my image.

Larry: In front of him, the world, your wife, what?

Miguel: Yes. At all those levels I suppose, my wife, the world, as a professional, as an individual, and as a therapist. By getting him back into session I was trying to protect my image. To prevent it from being marred by her delusional process. I was trying to preserve myself.

Larry: From your physical discomfort here, it's like it hit a deep level, this fear.

Miguel: Yes. Let me give some background. They first came to know me through a workshop I conducted at a large local church. So I have a public and professional image at stake.

Larry: So in the broader community in which you live and practice, if Maria revives this incest experience from her childhood, transfers it to you, and somehow accuses you of some sort of impropriety, then you're not so much worried about him coming and killing you as you are about some sort of discrediting, defacing exposure in the community? A third party again is the source of danger somehow.

Miguel: Yes. I'm not as worried about Arturo as I'm worried about my image in the community being marred by her distortions of me.

Larry: His transferential violence is not so much murderous as marring, defacing, suffocating, degrading, damaging—all words that imply the third party. You have assessed that both of them have a reality-testing problem of sorts in their dependent fusing dynamics, so there is some sort of a psychotic process here in both members of the couple, and probably going on between them. So you have not only a countertransferential fear of close contact but a realistic one as well?

Miguel: Yes, I sensed there was a psychotic process operating in subtle ways and that's why I was even emphatic. I felt a need to firmly set the boundaries. I told her that I would continue seeing her in the context of marriage because the nature of the problem was essentially marital. I was firm in telling her that we needed to go back to the problem of communication.

Larry: But in holding the boundaries regarding the couples aspect, you were also implicitly refusing the seduction, the transference role being assigned you as the fetish object of the fusion, of the object of perverse hostile envelopment.

Miguel: Yes. So I finally got Arturo to come in for several sessions. He was accusing her of whoring around. Recall, she lived with her dad growing up, her mom wasn't around. I know little of the early mothering process. As you say, her mother gave her away to her father. There was an aunt who was basically her maternal figure. Her aunt repeatedly accused Maria of being a *puta* (a whore). And basically that is what he was doing to her in the session. You are becoming a *puta*, you are acting like a whore. She claimed that when she got married to her first husband she was a virgin and she never did whore around as an adolescent. I think she's sincere about that.

Larry: So the skin invasion that you felt so very clearly has been operating throughout her life. And her aunt picked up on it. Arturo is using it to abuse her in front of you.

Miguel: Oh yes. And come to think of it, it's a skin invasion designed to tantalize and tease.

John: I've been having this thought that in a sense that's what father did. Father invades with all his seductive treatment of her, his using her for whatever his merger needs were. He invaded her with his own emotional needs and with his verbal or emotional sexualizing during her growing-up years. So she married somebody who does a similar thing to her. And you feel endangered by that transference with an invasive, boundaryless, psychotic core.

Miguel: That seems right. Scary, isn't it?

Larry: Where else do you want to go with this, Miguel?

Miguel: Well, Arturo basically criticized her for being seductive. She likes to dance. But every time she invites him to dance his fear is that she will be too provocative with other men at the dance club. He laid out a lot of accusations that she was whoring around doing this, doing that. Ironically enough when they separated she discovered—they ran a small coffee shop to-gether—that he was having an affair with one of his employ-ees. She had long suspected it and he had denied it. But after they separated the woman told her, "Yeah, we've been screw-ing around." After that discovery she started coming again by herself. After the separation all the provocativeness, all the sexualization, all that skin contact, and all that slimy, gooey stuff stopped.

Larry: The acting out of the primitive three-way ceased. And she had gotten your message about professional boundaries. So what has this last round of therapy been like then?

Miguel: This last round of therapy has been the most productive. We're getting someplace now.

John: In what way?

Miguel: I don't feel invaded. She respects my space. I don't feel I need to protect my image, conserve my image, save face. There is not that concern about being marred, slimed upon, or defaced. The deep unnameable dread or terror has com-pletely disappeared.

Larry: What is she working on?

Miguel: She's working on defining what part of her true self is putting out that skin erotization, envelopment on other people because she has a deep need for contact. But she senses that her ways of going for it are somehow not working for her.

Larry: So the idea of her coming off like a whore is part of what she's trying to come to grips with?

Miguel: Yes. She's accepting that and seeing that it extends from an inner need.

Larry: And how does she formulate that need?

Miguel: Well, she's starting to connect that with her need for fathering. She's looking to attach to a father figure who will respect her body.

Larry: But we're a long way from getting back to the early mother skin contact?

Miguel: Yes. I have no idea about her mother.

Larry: Except that we have to assume the hostile fusing feelings, using transference–countertransference feelings, *are* early memories of maternal contact. You're saying that she's starting now in her therapy to get beneath the transference illusion to realize there is some desperate need at stake and she has gotten so far now as to relate it to her need for love from her father. We haven't yet moved to the place where she's able to trace that back to her early mother experiences.

We have only five minutes more. Let me test your intuition, Miguel. As you follow her in therapy, where do you predict this is going to go in terms of the maternal, the deep maternal? What is her need, her deepest need that she's going to be trying to work out?

Miguel: I think her deepest need is the opposite of what she's trying to do toward men.

Larry: Say it.

Miguel: She needs to be enveloped. She needs to be wrapped around. She needs to be held like a mother would a child. It's like she's rejecting the void, or the opposite, or the lack of envelopment by the other. She wants to be safely and enjoyably held.

John: She has been functioning on the object side of the self-object continuum. She can envelop others but she doesn't know how to be enveloped herself.

Larry: So in a way we might say that the reason that she's been able to slowly respond to you and to your efforts to contain her and to hold her is because the therapeutic offering really promises being held in that way, promises being safely and satisfyingly enveloped by care. You've been doing that to her.

Miguel: Yes. I have been. There is a strong texture to my holding. In fact, she's starting to see therapy as a home. She will say, "I am coming home now." Sometimes I greet her with, "*Bienvenida a tu casa*"—welcome to your home. The home she is looking to house herself in, to be held in. That's the track we are on now.

Larry: That's where you're going. That's a good place to stop. Thanks for sharing this peculiar reaction with us. I wish we knew more of the dynamics of where the hostility originated from and how it has gotten perversely merged with the erotic. But what we can say is that it was serving to alienate you through provoking panic and fear.

Miguel: Yes it certainly was.

HEDGES' COMMENTS

The complexity of this case and its yet early stage of development does not permit us a clear view of Maria's or Arturo's dynamics. But in studying organizing transferences we have learned to focus on body parts and sensations *as sources of disruption in contact and connection* (Hedges 1994c). Here the skin and possibly the disgust are involved in ways that we are told are somehow deeply frightening. The therapist feels the terror of being fused with, engulfed, suffocated, defaced, marred, slimed, and damaged. Maria's yearning for skin contact might be traceable to some problem in the enveloping womb, some tactile intrusion or deprivation in early maternal contact, or some infantile trauma in body bonding that left her desperately searching for fused togetherness but then traumatized by it.

I must say I am not altogether convinced with Miguel that Maria's ultimate search for consciousness of her personal meanings will lead simply to her being able to enjoy and make use of a good holding and containing environment—though in some sense he is surely right. Rather, I suspect that now with Arturo out of the picture and the dust settling, Maria does need to establish nonsexualized safety with her therapist. Then there will likely be a period of enjoying safety with him. I would then be ready for what I have called "the clamor," her making Miguel into the object who envelops too tightly or somehow hurts her in the holding process, or wants to mar her with fusion or to give her away. Then one or the other, or both of the participants will begin to manifest in a more clear and more useable way the emotional qualities that have already appeared—merger, hostility, degradation and, ultimately, a terror of contact that can then be worked through. *Buena suerte*, Miguel!

9

"Catch Me!"

Clinical Contribution by Linda Barnhurst

HEDGES' COMMENTS

More than once I have been asked the question, "Do you think psychotherapy maybe isn't good for this person?" Usually the question and the answer hinge on some issue involving expenditure of time, energy, and focus. Like, "Shouldn't this person's energy be used combating some physical disease rather than on struggling to regress to a new and deeper place?" With Linda and Lynne there was no realistic thought of death beforehand, but now there are lingering questions. Here Linda memorializes her client, the love and the process they shared together, and the important questions their work raises for us to consider.

Larry: You lost a patient.
Linda: Yes. In preparing to meet with you today I've been reading my notes and the outpouring of her writing and her pictures.

I am stunned that we were only together for a year and a half, because her impact on me was profound, as if we had been together for a very long time.

Larry: Lynne had attained a very special position with you.

Linda: Extraordinary.

Larry: The personal bond that evolved was deep.

Linda: Yes. The evidence is not only in the depth of my sadness and grief in having lost her, but in this shopping bag filled with her writings and her pictures, depicting both her despair and her deep and growing connection with me. Lynne was incredibly creative in the way she expressed these themes. Early on, she made a box filled with broken pieces of small colored objects and flowers and dirt. If you scratched your way through it, at the bottom was the word "alone." I remember one little green felt box that she brought filled with a bird's nest and three little eggs that she had painted. It was about reasons to live, each egg was a reason to live. One reason was grass between her toes, one was my eyes, and the other was laughter. The last time I saw Lynne she gave me another tiny box with two women's hands touching, like the Michelangelo painting of God and Adam, and inside was a little wooden heart with letters spelling out the word "HOPE." That was the piece she gave me just before she died.

This lady had a laugh and a charm and a vivaciousness that was always unnerving. There was a sense about her that I can only describe as electric, intense, burning. The MMPI, the Rorschach, and other psychological tests describe her with words like unconventional, disorganized, and impetuous. While they're true, I think such words have a slightly moral quality—they represent the observer's perspective. But when I sit in somebody's life with them I begin to lose those categories.

Lynne and I first met in a hospital program. I called her by name. She thought that was the most astonishing thing—that I called her by name. She was the seventh of eight children, and never felt she had a name of her own—there was this long list starting from the oldest and going to the youngest when all the kids would be called at once. So the fact that I called her out by name all the time astonished her.

Larry: "Here is this strange doctor in a strange setting and . . .

Linda: Yes, "She called me by my name." When we first met, I thought I was trying to contain her. But what she recalls is her putting her hand on my back and telling me to calm down. It makes me laugh because the rapidity of her thought and verbal delivery could be totally unnerving. No one has been as attacking as this lady was. The wattle under my arms, my need for continuing education, my insensitivity, my aggression, my lack of it.

Larry: A constant clamor?

Linda: A constant clamor. But she was also the most generous of my patients: poems, art creations, collages, painted plates, all these things that she would use to express herself and us. From them I knew where she was emotionally, what was coming. She wanted very much to live. I think my earlier work with you about the organizing experience was very helpful in understanding of her fear of connecting. Connecting felt like dying to her. It was amazing to me as I read over some of the material how often that was. . . . Unfortunately, I saw her fear of dying as a metaphor rather than a potential reality.

Larry: Say the themes as you're thinking about them now.

Linda: There were several. Lynne felt a sense of disgust about herself, that's one. She was born into an extremely large and poor family and her mother had little left to give her. Lynne was sick as a child and she was cross-eyed. She needed braces, and this was a very poor family. They ate cereal with water. She felt hideous. She had constant dreams about shit and evacuation. Her dad used to line up all the kids and give them enemas. They were eating such lousy food, it's not surprising. We also learned from her older sister that they were so poor that they couldn't wash the sheets with soap, so the bedding often smelled of feces. Here is this little girl, in some ways deformed—by the crossed eyes and the poor teeth—sleeping with the smell of shit all the time. Another theme was loss and violence. Her mother also died young, at age 49.

Larry: When Lynne was?

Linda: Nine. One brother hanged himself. One brother was mentally retarded. Another died of cancer. Another used to use her sexually in the basement when she was a child. I never saw a well-written history—the hospital, my own notes, the psychological tester—we all got the history wrong because it was too much and too overwhelming. I had to have her write it out with me—year by year of devastation. So, for this . . . I keep wanting to call her "lady," I want to give her dignity, it's not the right word, maybe I'll find another one. For her to bring herself to another person with all this chaos and rage could not help but be terrifying. Her sense was clearly that it was going to kill her. There was lots of acting out, and she recognized it as acting out. Lots of medication to bring her in and calm her down. She'd discontinue the Klonapin and drink on the weekends. One pattern that became clear was the weekends. That's when she would allow herself to most need me, feel most desperate, most have to be dying—in order for me to pay attention to her, which of course was when I was least able to.

The only time Lynne recalled getting her mom's attention was when she herself was dying as a child. She'd even had last rites. I don't know what it was—the whooping cough or what. She was 5 or 6 years old. They thought she was going to die, and she remembers feeling taken care of. Most of the times she remembered that her mother would send all the kids outside and lock the door from the inside. I saw pictures of her mother. She was beautiful, but like a very thin, pale mannequin. There was just nothing left of this lady with all these children and all the problems they presented. Nothing much that she had left to give to them.

Larry: Was this a rural family? I'm asking because of the continued enemas.

Linda: No. Not particularly rural. I don't think that was why. Partly cruelty perhaps, but mostly it was macaroni and cheese and cereal and water.

Larry: So they needed the enemas?

Linda: Yes, although there was something invasive and insulting about them certainly. I never got the feeling that it was simply cruelty or perversity. Humiliating, yes—this constant sense of humiliation. Lynne would want me to replicate the invasions in various ways. I was supposed to go in and cut out the feelings, blow her apart, make it happen, clean her out with violence. She was always furious with me that I would never be doing it fast enough. It's hard to talk about her, trying to read my notes. Like trying to grab hold of the wind, or get all of the stars in a little bag. She's just exploding with creativity, with pain, with distress, with need, with love.

Larry: Would an outside observer think of her as hyperactive or manic?

Linda: Yes. She had been diagnosed by a psychiatrist I work with as bipolar. She hated it.

Larry: But so she never tried lithium?

Linda: No.

Larry: Any antidepressants?

Linda: She was on Klonapin. She was determined in her feelings that being bipolar was not an organic condition, that it was a psychological condition. That mania was a flight from self. She didn't want to be medicated to the point where she wouldn't be able to do the work she needed to do. I felt helpless in facing this struggle. Having a little bit of education about people being bipolar and how seductive it is, there were times when I worried if it was unethical to continue seeing her without lithium or Depakote. But I was also challenged by her desire to do the work—really wanting to see if maybe she could.

Larry: She did have a psychiatrist. The medication is ultimately a psychiatric decision but nonetheless it made you feel uncomfortable.

Linda: Oh, big time. Some experts consider it unethical to treat bipolar people without medication. But ultimately the patient does have some say. I could have been tough and said, "If you don't take meds, I won't treat you." We did have conflicts like that . . .

Larry: So you did put some pressure on her?

Linda: Not so much about lithium, but about drinking and being on medication. I was always afraid of respiratory collapse. There was one brutal time where she came into a session a bit drunk. When she left, she left her keys, which was an indication that she wanted to stay, but also that she wasn't at all with it. We had a shoving match, I made her go back into my office and did my "you can't drive and drink" stuff. She was furious with me for pressuring her. I felt unprofessional and out of control. But it turned out to be a real healing moment for us.

Larry: She knew you wanted to protect her.

Linda: I didn't want to protect her from her pain, only from something stupid happening, or going too fast. She always knew that. All of my errors, all the things that I did wrong, she always had a sense that I wanted to protect her.

Larry: You were the one reaching out through all these things, and she is the one who was terrified of connecting. So she had to scream and clamor.

Linda: Yes. But maybe some of the screaming was her way of saying we were going too fast. Listen to her words of November 4. She says:

> I have some impending dread that I have some sort of stomach or colon cancer, some intuitive sense based in part on physical symptoms. Remembering my father and aunts that died of cancer. I have been terribly down fighting, drowning in my depression. My body aches from muscle tears, from overrunning. I have essentially no appetite and I feel horribly irresponsible.

Larry: This was November 4. When did she die?

Linda: November 19. Almost a year ago.

I just opened a sheet called "Wind of Dust." "Touching fingers, catching my thoughts as they spun through the moon. Your eyes waiting for me as I walk slowly to meet you . . . in the dust." I have a note from September, she asked me if I would be her mom. It was not a regressive request. She knew I had no children, she just thought that would be a good arrangement—that I would be her mom.

Larry: How did you respond?

Linda: "No."

Larry: Tell me about that.

Linda: I don't have any question that she made me her mom through all the crises, through all the holding. But I wanted so badly to be her therapist. I don't mean that in a rigid sense. I talked to her about wanting to be there for her as what I was— that I was afraid if I chose to be her mom she would lose that other part of me that she needed so much.

Larry: The therapist. She understood that?

Linda: Yes. The request was both an expression of liking and a defense against future loss. "Let's make this arrangement, we'll stop therapy and you can be my mom."

Larry: Great!

Linda: So it wasn't an injury in this case when I said no—I injured her plenty of times but this wasn't one of them.

Larry: It's interesting to me because when we're talking about doing therapy with people with deep damage or trauma, there is a question of are we reparenting or is it analytic? What is the nature of the therapy? It's interesting that the two of you stayed right on that line. She needed to be reparented so she would experience you in a variety of ways, as protecting her, containing her, holding her, mothering her. Yet you also let her know that there was something else that was real that you wanted to give her, provide her. She understood there was another part of you, busy taking apart the damage, undoing the trauma—an analytic function that is different from mothering.

Linda: You can see her understanding of the problem in her collages.

Larry: Describe the collage you're showing me.

Linda: This is a collage of fall leaves and babies' faces. A baby in a cage. A mother and daughter laughing, another baby sleeping, the words "see me." Another mother–daughter with the words "be with me." A montage of children's faces and birds with "teach me to fly." A crying child, "feel with me." Another child crying, "let me fall." More birds, "soar with me." "Don't forget me." Lastly, "Catch me."

Larry: Very expressive. Very colorful. All pictures taken from magazines or wherever she could find them.

Linda: Contrast it with this one, also very colorful. Always very colorful. The green and purplish-pink leaves are background.

Larry: Green—growing, growth? Purplish, pink, orange, do you understand anything about what those colors all meant to her?

Linda: I do. She used these green leaves to echo the green of her eyes. *The green of her eyes meant she had an identity.* This was part of who she was. It's not that it's a growing thing.

Larry: This is not symbolic. This is *expressive* of identity.

Linda: Yes. This is, "My name is Lynne." Here is a collage that represents the other side of her. The words are "All ripped and torn. If there were a public execution, would you go?" Then: "Seeing is deceiving, fear, hitting the abyss, hell, cold water, how to end dead, dead, dead." There is a head and a pair of legs caught in a mountain stream.

Larry: Do you have any thoughts about the head and legs in the mountain stream? I see it cascading, it's a beautiful mountain stream. It's as though, the way I'm looking at it, the legs are upside down in a cascade of rapids. So it's as though the body is below the water cascading. What is your thought?

Linda: I don't have a thought. I have to tell you I don't have a lot of thoughts, Larry, I have mountains of things.

Larry: But not a lot of thoughts.

Linda: No, it came too fast.

Larry: Thoughts also require that all of these different things, disparate elements have links, some kind of logical connection. That's the nature of a thought. A sentence has a beginning and an end, an actor doing. I think what you're saying is that Lynne was so vastly intruded on by a lot of circumstances throughout her growing-up years that part of why she needed a mother was to pull all these disparate experiences and expressions of herself into an identity, a person.

Linda: Into a thinking person. Right. There was lots of noise.

Larry: So for us to try to think of these as symbols or representations would distort what she is about. She is *expressing*, trying to say, "Here I am, this is what I am, these are elements that are me."

Linda: "Hold me."

Larry: "Hold me." But for us to try to grasp it or to put it all together, or try to make sense of it violates what she was trying to tell you—"I need to be held." "I need to find out and know who I am." "Catch me."

Linda: Whatever it is.

Larry: Yes.

Linda: Collage was a wonderful medium, because it could contain so much of her all at the same time.

Larry: What I see in the collages as I see you sorting through them is that there are a lot of words. Sometimes she would write on the collage, but many times she would choose the words and phrases from other places, cut them out and put them where they belong.

Linda: Here's a wonderful one. This is when she was mad at me. Can you read that?

Larry: It looks like the piece was taken from a magazine—a picture of a canyon, with some sort of orange or lava flow that says, "losing Lynne." and "strike three."

Linda: Right, I had failed her again.

Larry: The third try and now Lynne is out with the lava cascading down the red canyon rocks. "Please return my video and pictures of my mother and my pictures of me as a child."

Linda: Yes, at that point she had determined we were never going to see each other again.

Larry: Is it useful for us to know what her anger was about at that time?

Linda: I can probably find it here in my notes.

Larry: That's okay. What you're saying is that there were many times when she was very angry and needed to experience her anger and express it. Each time it ended in death or disconnection somehow.

Linda: Yes. You said something really important about not trying to see this material as symbolic. The need to express herself came out in so many ways: collage, painted pottery, and poems. There were times when there would be so much, and she would go so fast, that I would shout at her, "I can't do this anymore!" I remember the first time it happened, I was trying to hold it, trying to process it, think of it as symbol, trying to respond to something here. I thought I was going to lose it. I finally screamed at her, "I just can't do this anymore!" Expressions like that constituted a breaking out of my own vulnerabilities, and they were a treasure to her. Lynne was always forcing me to be real with her.

Larry: That was what she never had.

Linda: Yes. Yes. She was ruthless about insisting that I be real with her. She knew when I was the "therapist." And she loved it when I was real.

Larry: When you were "being the therapist" what would she say or do?

Linda: I'd get a memo about needing more continuing education, that I really did hate her, and that she wasn't important to me.

Larry: We might infer from the near death experience at age 6 that the only way Lynne felt herself real was when there was an intense experience. So when you were comfortable and happy in your role as a therapist, she knew you were skating on ego or adaptation or some such thing. She knew what she had lacked was real contact, so she sought after it. Although you said that as soon as she had it, it would be too overwhelming.

Linda: That's true. Feeling connected was overwhelming. But there's something else here I think. Real contact meant to her being raped, almost dying. I've already mentioned the molestations when she was a child, and the enemas that were in stark contrast to the absence of any meaningful positive contact. In high school her first couple of years she drank and acted out a lot. Her mother was gone and she was living with various members of the family—doing badly. She could do a lot with the smallest amount of encouragement. Someone told her she was smart at the end of her sophomore year, and she turned around and got all A's and went to college. She totally stopped acting out. But life continued to deal her difficult cards: the suicide of a brother, her father's death, the death of two dear friends. She was also brutally raped at 19—there were seven mistrials, but she eventually won.

Larry: Were the circumstances important to us?

Linda: She had been out running I think.

Larry: So, a stranger, not date-rape.

Linda: Yes, but she was always being hunted and haunted.

Larry: Why was she always hunted and haunted?

Linda: She was gorgeous.

Larry: Seductive?

Linda: Yes and no. She was very lean, no body fat. She had been in physical fitness for a very long time. She liked to run, that's one of the reasons her death was so shocking. She was 40 and training for a marathon. But people making comments to her about her looks, as people would, raised the terror of another rape, another invasion, another intrusion. Connection was dangerous. At other times it was clear that if she weren't getting attention, she would be seeking it with style and drama. When she was getting attention, it was the wrong kind, always.

What she needed to feel seen was to have someone acknowledge that in some way she was ugly, not that she was beautiful. Notwithstanding that this was a striking, trim, healthy looking, sophisticated, well-dressed woman that I couldn't take my eyes off not only because of her seductiveness, but because of her artistic and dramatic flair.

Larry: Drop-dead gorgeous?

Linda: Yes, but she could never see herself as gorgeous. She showed me her first-grade picture, a child in a little sweater with stains on it, crossed eyes, misshapen teeth, scraggly hair, not even combed. She had to know that I could understand that picture of her, of the inadequacy. The humiliation of not having breasts was another sign of how inadequate she felt, how empty she was really.

Larry: Would some diagnosticians call her anorexic?

Linda: No, she just never had breasts.

Larry: She was just that way?

Linda: She just never had them, she was always that way, even when she was heavier. No, I don't think anyone would call her anorexic. Not having breasts was another sign of her shame. I worked with her to take her body back, to enjoy her body, to embrace her physical being as she really was.

Larry: But to see *her*, you had to see the ugly child.

Linda: I had to see the ugly child. At some level she was terrified of changing her perception of herself. Perhaps she could change only if someone knew her as she perceived herself.

Larry: So she would only feel seen if you could see her as ugly, unwanted, and disgusting. She could only really know you were speaking the truth if you acknowledged that and spoke it.

Linda: Yes, and I knew that. I need to have spoken something, an honesty that was never spoken before. Here is this woman who is gorgeous and fascinating to me. I wanted to be able to see her as ugly! I couldn't. But I knew that was what she felt and that I could speak. I could hear it in those constant dreams of being covered with shit, and horror.

Larry: How was it like to have your own perceptions constantly invalidated? That is, you saw her as a beautiful person, not only physically, but beautifully full of life. You admired her, you loved her. And you connected deeply with her creativity, her aliveness, and her vibrance. How was it for you to struggle with how you saw her versus the piece of shit that she felt she was and her need for you to see that?

Linda: Early on, there was a lot of angry countertransference.

Larry: About?

Linda: Oh, she was just so damn provocative. She made fun of everything I said, mocked me, put me down, pushed me away. Later on (it sounds like five years), I would feel this incredible sense of sadness when she would push me away.

Larry: So you understood that the provocativeness was her desperation to not let you come near, to not let you see her, to not let you love her, or to connect with her. That made you angry. But later you could see how desperate and how hungry she was for the contact. Then it was sad that she wanted it so much but couldn't allow it?

Linda: Yes. Lynne's poems describe this too. She would bring them to me with incredible expectations. Am I going to hear this one, understand it, receive it? Am I going to make enough meaning of it and if I do make enough meaning of it, was it true? Or am I just doing it to make her feel like *I* had a sense of meaning and caring for her.

Larry: There's the bind. If you like it, or try to interpret it, or try to say that she's beautiful or that you like her—in some way or another you are violating her. She is simply putting green out there to say, "I am the color green, I am Lynne, I am these words." When you try to organize them into *your* picture—something you can make sense of—you are not with her.

Linda: Absolutely, absolutely. I'm sure there are at least ten poems in here that say just that. Sometimes Lynne would bring tapes with music. We would play the tapes.

Larry: Her music, or somebody else's?

Linda: Somebody else's.

Larry: But something that was meaningful?

Linda: Oh, absolutely. But I once mentioned some of my associations, and she saw this giving of myself, of my mind, as a violation—she was furious at me. I wasn't taking *her* in, just as you said.

Larry: In my book, *Working the Organizing Experience* [Hedges 1994c], in a chapter called "The Idiosyncratic Use of Symbols," I speak of our temptation to look for symbolic meaning or even representations of self or other or of the relationship in the seemingly chaotic material of the organizing experience. If we are really in tune with the organizing experience it is neither symbolic nor representational, it is simply *expressional—and there is a difference.* The expressional always stays in the concrete. "Here is a thought, or a phrase, or a fragment, or a word, or a picture, or a color. This expresses me now." If we, as therapists, try to represent or symbolize, or, as you said, respond to the expression by trying to decode the expression as we might a symbol, or by giving our mind, it is a violation of the expression. She simply needed to express and to have the expression acknowledged. We attempt to understand a symbol where we can only receive or acknowledge an expression. There is no "meaning" in such expressions in the ordinary sense of consensus, shared realities, metaphors. Often, something about connection and/or disconnection is *expressed* in this way.

Linda: The one thing she could accept from me, although not all the time, was tears.

Larry: Tell me about that.

Linda: Sometimes there would be a poem or a picture or a box she would bring—another gift of herself, to be heard, to be seen. I would be so moved by . . . if I say the sweetness of the gesture, I don't mean it was sweet always, but like the generosity when a baby gives of itself. Sometimes I just ached with how hard she was trying to tell me, ached with how much she had been through, and then she would see my tears.

Larry: You knew if you tried to put the tears into words or reflection, that would be a violation of her sense.

Linda: I didn't know. I was learning. But anyway the times when I was most right-on were when I just wept, had feelings that communicated she had had an impact on me.

Larry: She could feel that you were connected with her then.

Linda: Yes. There were times when we would sit shoulder to shoulder. Making contact, sitting on the floor. When I knew she was in enormous distress, she would say, "Can I come just sit next to you?" We wouldn't talk necessarily, just be there together frightened.

Larry: You sat on the floor side-by-side leaning against each other, frightened.

Linda: Shoulder to shoulder.

Larry: If we had to ruin the beauty of that by putting it into words, what words would you choose?

Linda: I guess knowing that there weren't any words for me. Allowing myself to not be able to heal. Not to be able to say anything. Allowing her to know my *witness*.

Larry: Witness. I am feeling the need to use my words and see how they set with you. When we think about the organizing experience, and the learned need to push away and to break away, we think of Bion (1977) who taught us about the breaking of emotion–thought links. In the primal mothering situation, thought arises because mother thinks first and is *with* the baby. Ministering with her thought. So the baby slowly learns thought through the mother's witness—a linking of two bodies, two affect states. As I heard you, I was thinking that this woman was bent on destroying every link she possibly could. But at the same time she knew that the only course to becoming human, to becoming something other than an unwanted creature, was to be effectively held *with*, linked *to*. That her cure was going to come through your saying to her, "We can link," but saying nothing else. Only being with. *And assuring her that she didn't have to run from that link.* That you could stay, that she could stay—through the physical contact of your shoulders touching, and the mental contact of the witness being present. It was your way of saying, "You do not have to destroy this link. I am here, you are here, I can be with, you can be with." How did I do?

Linda: You did well! There were times when sitting shoulder to shoulder was the best thing I could have possibly done, and she took it in that way. There were other times when I reached out to her, when it was the worst thing I could have done. Reaching out, even emotionally, felt violating. It took a long time for her to feel that I was not going to be sexually violating of her. That I could care about her in some other way than somebody else might.

Larry: That making contact mentally and physically could be beautiful and nonviolating.

Linda: Yes. But we would have to work through the sexual, then we would have to work through the projected revulsion—that surely I was disgusted with her. And there were moments of psychotic transference in which my face changed and all she could see was my loathing. Then there were those moments of grace when she let me be with her for a moment, then we would move back to another . . .

Larry: Disruption?

Linda: Yes.

Larry: You said "moments of grace"?

Linda: Yes. She was really struggling to allow herself to enjoy me hearing her. Enjoy me seeing her. Even though it was terrifying. She did much of that work away from me, through artistic production. It was safer to feel the closeness, and to anticipate that I would receive her when she was working it out through a creative medium. She used it as a transitional space, to experiment in fantasy with my tenderness when I wasn't there.

Larry: During those moments when you were sitting shoulder to shoulder or she would bring or say something that would move you to tears, the grace was that for a moment she would be able to link and be able to receive your gift of love?

Linda: Yes. But it was more mutual than that. Lynne would have to see *me* receive *her* gift of love.

Larry: Yes. Then she could receive your gift of love.

Linda: Yes. Classic Winnicott. When I look, I am seen, therefore I exist. So she would look, be waiting, watching, always, listening to see if I was seeing, hearing, receiving. If I was, then she could be!

Larry: What a strain it must have been on you to have to be absolutely quiet and set aside so much of yourself so that you could truly be there at those magical moments.

Linda: I didn't always succeed. I didn't always know how to be as quiet or as excited as she needed.

Larry: Some of those moments of grace might have been when you screamed at her? There is not a particular quality to it. It's the seeing and being seen and knowing that I exist that's the moment of grace?

Linda: Yes, and you're right, it wasn't always pretty.

Larry: I understand. I'm thinking of the research of Tronick and Cohn (1988) where they are looking at normal mother–baby combinations and discover that only 30 percent of the time when the baby searches does the baby feel found. I'm thinking that's the normal, expectable path. But with people who have had major infant trauma there is likely one chance in a hundred or a thousand that you could finally be there, oriented to her at exactly that moment where two could feel their identity confirmed in each other.

Linda: Yes. Let me read this to you. It's on painted paper, pale green, the color of her eyes. This is dated September 15, about two months before she died. Her poems suffer in a sense because she thinks she is being symbolic and yet they are more like her collages, simply expressive.

Larry: Yes. Collages can more easily be beautiful, expressive, and nonsymbolic. Poems can be beautiful but you would think a good poem also would rely on symbolism. If you are trying to be symbolic and you don't know how to be, it doesn't quite make it.

Linda: Exactly. This is another kind of word picture:

> Still you shed tears, and I continue to become. Inquisitive, I quietly search for meaning beyond your limited understanding, I can find no words, as I struggle to wonder, struggle my will, how long this place continues to breathe in me, I know not. Small whispers of molecules, more emerge, forming a more steady stream. Terror meets this falling as I become one with a strange new closeness. Singular, I learn to be part of another, forbidden fright engulfed embraces, erases me.

The poem seems to reflect what you said about a moment when identity in another could be confirmed. And here is a sample of the underside of the connecting moment, the disruption.

I feel I am a monster, and you are only doing your job, regretfully, and wiping, washing, cleaning, and sweeping me away the moment I leave. Some people clean portable toilets for a living, engaging themselves in shit, urine, and horrendous stench just to pay their bills. When you are with me I feel there is no difference between you and the toilet cleaner. I do not feel real or acceptable. I am repulsive, dirty, smelly, and not acceptable.

Larry: There she illustrates how internalized her belief is about being a disgusting piece of shit. When she is with you she knows she can only have you because you are so repulsed by her.

Linda: Yes. Here is another piece that shows how the moments of grace were gathering into constancy.

> In the midst
> of my
> rather ordinary day, this day,
> I thought of your face suddenly,
> without notice
> my eyes drew tears, quietly and unexpectedly
> I thought of missing you
> one day
> when our time has been completed
> I thought of how I now, missed you
> though you had not gone, nor I
> my sadness grew to more, realizing
> my life
> has been a series
> of losses,
> yet this, would be knowingly different
> when it came,
> for I know I have not ever experienced anything
> quite the same,
> nor will I expect to . . .
> in this same way,
> I want to thank you now

for your goodness, your truth, your spirit
but mostly your soul,
thank you
for experiencing me in a way
I've not yet known
hearing me,
feeling with me
being with me
and seeing me,
allowing me
to see back.

Larry: This is a beautiful memorial you have created for Lynne today. What else belongs?

Linda: One of the gifts she brought me was this picture of a girl holding a bunch of roses. A longish white dress with bare feet, sitting in front of a picket fence. Brown and green and purplish orange leaves. She is a really beautiful child. I know Lynne wanted to give me this part of her.

Larry: A beautiful and free 6-year-old child.

Linda: A 6-year-old child, beautiful child. Filled with flowers. Pretty. I have it in my office and behind it is a little thing that she had made that looks kind of like a dead mouse, a hand-sewn, misshapen little thing that she called her inner child. She had had a baby picture printed on fabric and sewed it into a tiny sac.

Larry: Her inner child.

Linda: When she died, I went to this very intimate gathering of her friends and family. A dear friend gave it to me saying he knew she would have wanted me to have that. I keep it and the picture with little box with the word "HOPE" in it on my bookcase. Every now and then, I will look at that box and say, there is hope here. It's my own private, concrete joke that Lynne left me with. Even when I'm not feeling any hope, I know there is "hope" here.

Her oldest sister also needs to be in this memorial. She wants to be a psychotherapist. It was she who got Lynne to go to the hospital program of which I was a part. I feel that she is going to take this death, and all the deaths in the family and keep on trying.

Larry: Lynne's life as a memorial will sustain her.

Linda: Partly. I know that she took all the artwork, the plates, the drawings, the computer files, Lord knows what Lynne said about therapy that I don't know about. Let me be still a moment and see what else comes . . .

(Silence)

Linda: Tears. Lynne didn't want to be forgotten. I promise I won't forget.

Larry: She won't be forgotten. Is it time to tell us about her death?

Linda: I had gotten a page and answered it at 6:50 P.M. The same dear friend who gave me her "inner child" told me Lynne had died. In my sensitive, psychotherapeutic manner, I said, "You *are* kidding!?" I stammered for the next five minutes, and at last I knew that he was not. I hung up knowing I had another client waiting for me. Lynne and this client knew each other in passing because they were the only people I saw on Saturday mornings. Because of what she was working on I couldn't turn her away. I asked her to walk with me and I told her that Lynne had died. She held me and I cried and screamed.

That Saturday there was a small memorial held for Lynne in her apartment. I went. Her sister had all the poems, the collages, and the boxes displayed on the walls. A wonderful apartment, she had adored it—her own place at last, with all of her touches, her uniqueness. People shared. It was sad to me that most everyone there knew a piece of her, but hardly anybody there knew the depths of Lynne.

Larry: But you did.

Linda: Yes, and maybe her sister as well. But I think I knew her.

Larry: Yes.

Linda: This memorial began over a dialogue between you and me as to whether or not I killed her. I'm not any closer to an answer to that than I was ten months ago. I know there was a respiratory collapse. I know that she said to people at work, "Don't leave me." There was no alcohol in her house, so it doesn't seem to be a drug infraction. We had thought about that just a couple of weeks before and she promised me she wouldn't risk that again. In truth, I don't know if it was a stroke or heart failure that took her. She was afraid she was going to die. I wonder, would some other clinician have sent her to get a checkup, to see if there was something wrong? Another bipolar patient once said to me, "In the past four years I have burned up energy that belonged to the next twenty years, and I don't know if I can keep on going." Lynne, too, was on fire. I wonder if this period of time that I knew her was in part so terrorizing for her because she had always had somebody to help hold her together, to help contain her, to organize her external life. At nineteen she met a guy and eventually got married to him. Not long after that ended she met the fellow who called me on that Tuesday night. He provided an environment for her. They were lovers for a while, but that wasn't the key. He got her lawyers when she needed lawyers, he got her a place to stay, he bought her things, he mothered her physically, enveloped her. It was when she finally couldn't stand it anymore and had to rip out of this suffocating envelopment that she went into this incredible manic phase.

Larry: Burning very brightly. Coming out of a relationship that hadn't held real possibilities of connecting.

Linda: Yes, which landed her in the hospital. She didn't sleep for two weeks. She had ripped the covers off herself. She didn't want those covers anymore. But without the covers . . .

Larry: She was terrified.

Linda: Absolutely terrified. So, then she attached to me, grabbed hold of me. Called me almost daily. We were scheduled for three times a week. The woman is getting a master's degree, working a full-time job, driving almost two hours to sessions, and still needing or grabbing for more. Terrified, because she was at last in touch with everything internal.

Larry: Her truth.

Linda: Yes, but not a singular truth. It's too simple to say truth, her truths.

Larry: Being enveloped for so long had served to protect her, but at some point she knew she wasn't alive. So she chose life, landed in the hospital, and that's when she met you. Again and again, she wanted you to be her mother, to envelop her, to protect her from her truths. But another part of her knew better, you knew better.

Linda: She really knew better.

Larry: So when you refused the mothering and enveloping role she knew that you wanted *her*. You didn't want her to feel you as just mother. You didn't want her to only feel your good milk. You wanted *her*. That allowed her to burn very brightly, to feel her terror very deeply. So of course, you worry—did you, did this therapy, did this process kill her?

Linda: Someone asked me that. She said, "maybe when there is that much trauma, to invite people to change, to go to the depths, is too much for the body to bear." I don't know, do you know?

Larry: No. But what's coming to my mind are some of the last words of Heinz Kohut [1984]. He writes about this experience. He said basically, "I don't know how to help someone recover from such trauma. Maybe it is the limitations of traditional psychoanalysis. Maybe it is the limitations of my personality and technique. But I do believe that in principle, it should be possible for someone to go deeply, to find this trauma, and to form a *self de novo* as a baby does in early life. But in order to do it the person must be willing to be totally dependent upon the borrowed ego of the therapist for a period of time—to stay with the deep terror of moving into pre-psychological chaos." Then he says, "I don't know why anyone would ever want to do that."[1] He was considering the same question. Why would any person want to risk experiencing such chaos and terror?

Linda: Lynne is why.

Larry: Yes. You didn't just go to her and ask her if she wanted to have this heavy-duty experience. She landed in your life, begging. She had searched a lifetime for someone who could help her open up this place of depth. We don't know what biological time bomb she had possibly been carrying with her that led to sudden death. The probable answer, of course, is a coronary artery occlusion. Undoubtedly there is enormous strain on the body in this type of work. But I can't say I believe that you or the therapy killed her. I can say, with you, that this was a strain.

---

1. Paraphrase from Kohut (1984, pp. 8–9).

That Lynne took it on and that you went with her. At that point, we had a fluke, a shock, and the thing that she had feared all along happened. We don't know if she feared death because she knew that there was this condition in her that could cause sudden death. That seems unlikely. More likely, her death fear was, as it with so many organizing personalities, her expression of her knowledge that, "If I ever really connect, the self that I have always known, the being that I have always been will surely die." I must say that in every piece of therapy I have seen focused at this level the person at one point or another expresses a fear of going crazy, being an empty shell, or dying. Of course that experience of primal self is terrifying. Every time she did connect, she experienced it, expressed it as death. Flying through the universe.

Linda: Falling.

Larry: Falling, yes. "Catch me," she said.

One last thing. You mentioned that you fear that you might have let yourself get too close to her. What about that?

Linda: Yes. I believe in loving with all my heart, not sentimentally but with connection. I believe in the need for extraordinary gestures sometimes. Allowing the ego to be solely dependent on somebody else is an important human experience. If somebody does allow that, then you have to be ready to extend yourself to catch. This was not a game. But, I feel fear, fear of the condemnation of others—that I may have gotten overinvolved, that I was fusing, that I was acting out the countertransference. There must be a hundred morally tinged psychotherapeutic words that we could condemn me with, they haunt me. So, I try to be secret about how much I loved being wholly with her.

Larry: At the family gathering, they knew that you had loved Lynne.

Linda: Yes.

Larry: They knew it was that love for her that gave her the hope. It was your love that was searching to catch her when she fell.

Linda: Her oldest brother whispered, "Thank you." They all knew something crucial had happened to Lynne in the last year and a half.

Larry: Of course they did.

Linda: You always use the words, "something happened" to describe glitches in the organizing experience. In a different sense they were all seeing that something had happened. She was so ready for something new to happen. She had spent five, six, seven years of therapy with someone in Beverly Hills in which there were no feelings, nothing happening—at least according to her report.

Larry: She came very prepared knowing about therapy, knowing how to make use of the safety, the rules, knowing how to talk, knowing how to watch herself, knowing how to express herself. So the seven years had served her well in that regard.

Linda: Yes, and I think it had helped contain her.

Larry: She came very well prepared and started off dramatically with the hospitalization, the bright burning, breaking through the old self-protective envelope. What I hear you saying is that as a human being, you felt you were being called upon to receive lovingly what Lynne was offering. To have done anything less than that would have been less than human.

Linda: I had an image as you were talking, that when she came to the hospital, the eggshell had cracked, and I was trying to hold this . . . (Gestures with hands, trying to hold, to catch, to contain)

Larry: Lynne finally slipped between your fingers. I'm sorry for her. Sorry for you. I won't forget Lynne, ever. Thank you, Linda, for allowing this glimpse into a very special and private place.

HEDGES' COMMENTS

Rarely do we find a therapist who is as prepared and willing to catch, to contain, and to love as Linda was. More rare is finding a therapist brave enough and honest enough to share her work in this deeply moving manner. Lynne finally found an opening to be seen, to be known, but a different fate caught up with her in an untimely way. Could any of us really have done less than Linda did? Could any of us really have done more?

10

Murder in the Motel Room

Clinical Contribution by Shirley Cox

HEDGES' COMMENTS

Often enough relationships come to an abrupt end that puzzles us. Often too we are hurt or dismayed by the other's leaving us without an explanation. Therapists frequently experience such sudden cessations of relationship and seek to understand their underlying dynamics, their precipitating causes. We always want to know if we somehow missed something.

Good murder mysteries create questions to be solved. But a murdered client leaves us with many unsolved questions—especially when the murder seems vaguely suicidal. What body terrors did Julie suffer on that awful night? What unspeakable body terrors had she suffered in the past? Was the countertransference suffering, the fear and uncertainty that developed from the beginning, reminiscent of what Julie had suffered? And the denial? If Julie had been brutally violated in the primeval past or even the not too distant past, how could she pass on from suffering and uncertainty so quickly, so blithely, so nonchalantly? Julie's terrors lived on at a body level and were finally acted out in a motel room. Her therapist, her group leader, colleagues at the clinic, friends and family all want to know, "Julie, why did you have to leave us? Was there nothing we could have done or said to hold on to you? Why did you do this to us, to yourself? How did we fail you?"

The first call came in the middle of the night. The detective told me that Julie's abandoned car had been found. I wrestled with speculations until the light of dawn gave me permission to get up and get going.

The next call came two days later. Local police found a body that had no identity except a business card from our center. The race and size were a match for Julie. "Damn," I thought, "suicide."

I told the officer that I believed I knew whom he had found. Did it appear to be a suicide? "No," he responded, "we believe we have a homicide."

The next week was chaotic. As Julie's group therapist, but primarily as a human being unable to do otherwise, I handled many of the unsavory tasks created by her tragic death. I talked with family members, and persuaded the police to filter details of the brutal murder through me, at least temporarily, to soften the impact on Julie's brother and sisters. The rest of the members of Julie's group, shocked by her death, also needed to be heard and supported.

The time I had between the inevitable tasks for the living that death creates, I was lost in the reworking of my two years with Julie. Had I missed something? Was I guilty of acts of omission or commission? Did I pull back my compassion because of her inability to respond?

I clearly remember the first time Julie showed up to our eating disorders group. Her primary therapist, Jennie, had asked me to add Julie to the ongoing group, though she wasn't sure if Julie could function in such a setting. The group met the next night. Jennie's request had a certain urgency. I set aside the usual pre-participation interview, and okayed Julie's inclusion. Maybe I was being hasty, but I wanted to support Jennie.

It seemed a low-risk gamble that Julie would be inappropriate. The group already had some psychologically unsophisticated members, and others who lacked interaction skills. But all were good-hearted women with strong maternal instincts.

There were five of us that evening. We sat comfortably, on couches and in armchairs. I invited Julie to join us. Instead, she chose a folding chair, and placed it in the circle apart from the rest of us. She sat, head down, arms enfolding her body, feet locked behind the crossbar of her chair, and gently rocked herself. She said nothing. I explained our format to the top of her head, a mass of unruly curls. Again, no response. We checked in and began.

Our normal process is to first listen to somebody's dream, then go around the group with each person sharing a feeling level response, and then an association. Finally, the dreamer, having heard a huge assortment of responses, associates to her own dream. The underlying belief is that eating disorders indicate early psychological connection failures. The pressure to self-soothe with food or starvation has a massive unconscious component that no amount of conscious regimentation or knowledge, characteristic of most food-management programs, can reach. Sharing dreams, feelings, and associations gives members a chance to find commonalities as well as to access the conflicts for which the eating, starving, or purging serve as defenses. The women in the group grew very close. I believed they were picking up missing pieces of connection from one another. We didn't do interpretations of the dreams; it's too easy and too habitual for eating-disordered women, the world's self-appointed caretakers, to delve into realities other than their own. Each is keenly aware of somatic difficulties, and each has felt the sting of insensitive others. Beyond those awarenesses, self-insights are limited.

We have a clear rule in group that anybody may "pass" on any round. When I told Julie the format, I asked her if she understood the pass option. She nodded. The first two dreams, she opted to pass by lifting one hand and waving to us. Suddenly, about halfway through the third dream, Julie got up and left, quietly closing the door behind her.

Immediately, all eyes were on me. I was mentally running my options. Ignore her, send somebody after her, throw a soothing sentence or two out to the group and proceed, stop the process and discuss it, pray, wait for somebody else to comment, page Jennie. And as suddenly as she left, Julie walked back in. She had an apple in each hand. She sat down, head up, attentive, and began eating. I had no doubt that she was now with us. On the next dream, she added her own associations. Her speech was slurred and muffled, but her comments were intriguing. Group members strained to hear. I could tell that Julie was processing the dream, her own reactions, and the comments of others. She'd be okay in group. I needn't have worried. The other members were already responding positively to Julie's adorable, childlike presentation. They'd protect her and tolerate her eccentricities. Even to the point, I noted mentally, that they'd soon be colluding with her practiced patterns of avoidance.

Julie came regularly to group for several months. She was verbal, animated at times, and laughed often. At check-ins, she'd put forth her current life situation with its multitude of difficulties, and then challenge us, passionately, to solve her problems. "I can't stand the way I'm treated at work; the others blame me. I think they hate me. I don't know why. What should I do?" I could easily see in round one endless repetitions of "yes, but" being set up. Julie was most alive, most appealing, most difficult to deny when she was troubled. My group was rushing to the rescue. I decided to let them bounce off the wall a few times, to take the heat off their crusade-like efforts, before winding Julie down by agreeing with her. She wanted an opponent, not a partner. She lost interest quickly.

Stopping Julie in this manner always left me in conflict. If I let her run with her sad tales, we'd lose our dream time. The group work was going wonderfully. I didn't believe that I could change the format so that it would better accommodate Julie and still maintain the magical effect I was witnessing. And yet I could see how desperate she was. To assuage my guilt, I kept telling myself that it was Jesus's job to go after the one lost sheep, my job was to stay with the other ninety-nine.

As Julie shared dreams and associations, we began to learn how she experienced life. Her focus was often on loss. She dreamed of the people who had abandoned her, and in the dreams, they often didn't see or hear her. Julie cried as she talked of past therapists and the painful breakup of relationships. The other pattern that I began to see besides the obsession with lost beloveds was an inability to possess anything. Julie stopped two courses short of a bachelor's degree, denying herself a diploma. She worked sixty- or eighty-hour weeks but never held a job for more than a month. She moved frequently, often living in her car. At times she considered giving that away too. She was in great debt, but would either lose her money gambling, or hand it outright to the first needy person, preferably somebody whom she didn't know or somebody she was sure couldn't pay her back. When Julie began to talk of anything with fondness, such as one of her jobs where she supervised children, I knew she would soon let go of it. Her life had the same feel as her gambling. Acquire, and then be crushed by loss. Hope, and then be devastated by disappointment.

Julie couldn't find satisfactory containment, even in the group. Often, she'd leave. Sometimes she'd disappear for weeks. At other times, she'd refuse to leave, or to adhere to the necessary structure of therapy. One evening at 11:00 P.M. I found Julie standing in the bushes outside the office. Another time, we had to threaten to call a psychiatric assessment team when she would neither leave nor talk. During that standoff, she got phone numbers and addresses of therapists from a staff list. We began to get late-night calls. Nobody would be on the line. Julie admitted making the calls, but said she couldn't stop herself. Jennie, her primary therapist, had to change phone numbers. Julie could also describe our homes in great detail; she was obviously including our neighborhoods on her late-night cruises.

Whenever she was in the waiting room, she began studying staff members who happened to come through, talking with clients or talking with one another. She learned staff names and greeted each cordially. I soon began hearing stories from various center therapists of late-night, emergency break-through calls from the exchange. Julie had been the caller; she had asked for each person specifically by name. She'd start the conversations with a suicide threat, telling the dazed clinician that she couldn't reach Jennie or me. Of course, she was taken seriously by each listener. Usually, according to her self-report, she was calling from a phone booth in an unsafe area. She'd offer vague self-devaluative comments. "I'm really bad. I've done bad things. I can't tell anybody what I've done. I'm very, very bad."

Each clinician handled these late-night calls in almost the same manner, though styles varied. First, Julie was asked for a promise not to harm herself. She'd respond, challengingly, trying to trap the clinician. "What difference does it make to you? Why should I believe you care?" A few predictable back-and-forths later, Julie would agree not to harm herself. The second issue was finding a safe place. "Is there a friend with whom you can stay, Julie?" Again, a debate ensued. Julie would assure the listener that she had burned all her bridges. There wasn't anybody available. After a long problem-solving effort, all options including hospitalization explored, Julie would suddenly remember where there was an available place.

The final part of the late-night dialogue would be the solicitation of a promise from Julie to leave a message for Jennie or me to call. She readily agreed, though she had no intention of contacting either of us. A few of the late night listeners would also ask Julie to call again if she needed to. Some didn't give that permission. All felt wearied by the encounter with Julie. *It was as if she had temporarily shed herself of her chaotic world, and now the clinician was buried by it. The listener could be Julie for awhile, frustrated, angry, restless, and uncontained.*

I was beginning to get uneasy around Julie. I could control her, but I couldn't connect with her and I couldn't trust her. One night, shortly before her final disappearance, as she left the office, she saw a car hit a pedestrian. She curled into a fetal position in the parking lot. Jennie finally coaxed Julie to come to the porch and sit. Julie remained unresponsive for some time, and as Jennie and I sat with her, talking gently, we shared a look that said neither of us had a clue how to love this woman.

The police came and left. They assessed Julie as not dangerous to herself or others. Jennie and I continued to sit with her. Julie began talking to deceased relatives in a very childlike voice. I had the sense that we were now witnessing a performance rather than a regression. Jennie's eyes told me that she shared my discernment. But a performed regression is as significant as a spontaneous one, so we waited. Julie finally told us of hanging by a halter in the garage with a car repeatedly running into her swinging body.

We had both heard such horror stories from Julie before. The theme was always the same: damaging, insensitive, ruthless parenting. We never tried to sort fact from fiction. It wasn't important. These perceptions were Julie's reality, her tormentors. They were important.

Julie finally evidenced to us that she was clear-headed, and we allowed her to drive home that night. I would never see her again in group, and Jennie would only work with her for two more months. Then Julie hospitalized herself again, for the last time. She was planning to disappear after being released. Jennie elicited from her a promise not to harm herself. Julie agreed, and said that she'd pay her bill before leaving. Because of this commitment to settle financially, Jennie asked for a second promise. Would Julie agree to acquire the money legally? Julie would not.

The story beyond the last phone call is secondhand. Julie met a man in the mental institution and they planned some Bonnie and Clyde-type bank robberies. Julie wanted to pay her debts, party on cruise lines for awhile, and then suicide. He wanted to gather enough money to go to Mexico, steal back his children, and murder his wife.

They met after Julie's last hospitalization, went to a casino to gamble, and then checked into a motel. During a night of arguing and lovemaking, Julie and the man planned their capers. Julie was impatient to get started. Her accomplice insisted that they proceed slowly. She threatened to call the police if he wouldn't follow her timeline. When he heard this, he announced that he could no longer trust her. He bound her with ropes and duct tape, and in the morning brutally murdered her. Her body was undiscovered for ten days. Her isolation in life was duplicated in death.

Two weeks later, services were held in a nondescript funeral home in an undistinguished area. Over a hundred assorted friends, acquaintances, relatives, and mental health professionals gathered to say goodbye to Julie. Many of us spoke that day, trying to share our little piece of this untrackable, ungatherable woman's life. Each of us, I believe, wanted a last chance to find a key to Julie, hoping we might discover information from the collected group which none of us could find individually.

HEDGES' COMMENTS

The long period of safety-formation that is a prerequisite to transformational therapy with organizing experiences was never completed with Julie, though Shirley and her colleagues were off to a good start. Many people damaged in infancy are compelled to live chaotic and dangerous lives in accordance with the only patterns they know. Therapists do their best to encourage sense and sensibility during the period until connections can safely begin. It is tragic when someone gets lost along the way. And we are always haunted with the question of what else we might have done. But finally we are faced with the fact that we are not in control of many forces in this world—and that throws us into our own special kind of organizing experiences.

11

From Ritual Abuse to Making Connections

Clinical Contribution by Cynthia Wygal

HEDGES' COMMENTS

In the late 1980s it had become popular among many psychotherapists to direct trauma work toward recovering "memories" of childhood abuse, past lives, satanic ritual abuse, alien abductions, and altered states such as multiple personality. In time it became clear that while much childhood abuse has occurred in our society, infant trauma leaves emotional scars that are difficult to revive for therapeutic study in the transference (Hedges 1994b). It seems therapists were afraid of drawing the primitive transference terrors toward themselves where they could be worked with in the here-and-now relationship. Instead, therapists were inadvertently participating in resistance to transference remembering by encouraging people to "remember, be validated, and confront the perpetrator." Many people later had to recant their false accusations as they got to deeper levels of self-realization. The people presented here represent the incompletion of those "memory work" times, as Cynthia

Wygal struggles to get them back on the track of working on building the possibility of relationship. Cindy and I got together one day to review her cases to see which one she might write up for this book. The following wonderful session occurred. I'm glad we put the tape recorder on because we captured some incredible glimpses into deep terror.

> *Cindy:* I want to talk about three clients that other therapists have worked with extensively. The earlier work had stirred up all sorts of "repressed memories," but the therapists hadn't known how to complete the process. The referring therapists have said, "this is as far as I can go with them, they're not getting better, and I don't know what else to do." So they sent them to me.
>
> Michelle is in her mid- to late twenties and was referred from a board-and-care home where she was sent after her previous therapist gave up. She's one of the scariest people I have ever seen. I haven't been working with her very long—about ten months.
>
> *Larry:* What's scary about her?
>
> *Cindy:* She still has hallucinations. She will all of a sudden look at somebody and say their eyes are scary. Like, "He wants to take me out and rape me and make me have a baby." That's her fear. She doesn't tell me a lot of what her memories are. But she will say, "I did a lot of repressed memory work."
>
> *Larry:* Satanic ritual abuse memories?
>
> *Cindy:* Yes, that's a part of it.
>
> *Larry:* So the scary thing here is that the psychotic transference is clearly present, wide open and available, but you have no way to turn it toward you in a useable way?
>
> *Cindy:* She can turn it on strangers easily. Even in an empty house she will feel like there's someone, something, or some evil thing lurking. Or she'll turn it on her mother. She has been known to suddenly throw things at people, apparently trying to fend off an invisible or anticipated attack.
>
> *Larry:* So the transference even occurs in the context of a total stranger, in the lack of a deep relationship.
>
> *Cindy:* I do my best to front load—I'll say, "You know at some point you may feel some of these fears toward me. When that happens we need to be able to work through them together."

Larry: Has there been much countertransference other than the fear that at any moment the transference could overtake you?

Cindy: That's mostly it—watching what she does, trying to decipher her patterns of fear. For example, if she gets scared in her house she doesn't simply get out of it. She calls 911 and has them take her to the hospital. The other night she said her body just went numb. She lives with her mom right now and they called 911. The paramedics came and sat with her to make sure everything was all right. Her heart rate, breathing, and other vital signs checked out okay.

Larry: So she called her fear a medical emergency. She thought she was dying or something?

Cindy: She was totally physically numb. It wasn't like an ordinary anxiety attack or terror. When she and her mom get into a disagreement, she believes she needs to move back to the board-and-care home where she had been before. She has fantasy pictures about a lady serving juice and cookies, and someone to watch TV with during the day. It's not like that, of course, and her sane self knows it.

Larry: Her reality sense suffers during these moments?

Cindy: I have to remind her, "The board-and-care home is not the way you think it is." Her mom then comes in and says that *she* doesn't need her to go, but it may be what Michelle needs—trying not to stop her, but also trying not to make her go. The last time she was in for twenty-four hours and then back home.

Larry: Why did she stop therapy with her previous therapist?

Cindy: Her previous therapist said she didn't know where to go with her. So few therapists understand psychotic transference and fewer know how to work with it. Therapists throw their hands up with the Michelles of the world.

Larry: What about the other three people you mentioned?

Cindy: One is a 52-year-old woman, Korelan. She has recovered memories of satanic ritual abuse and some of it may be real. She has checked records in her home town, and people she thought had died really did. But how to interpret her memories is another problem. She had terrible damage internally that has been medically verified. She had several miscarriages before finally having a baby. Then she had a hysterectomy. When she had the hysterectomy the doctors said, "No wonder carrying a baby was so hard, there was so much scar tissue that you had only one little spot on the uterus that a baby could attach to."

Larry: So without question there was a lot of damage, though its cause remains unverified?

Cindy: There is definitely physical damage.

Larry: She did her recovered memory work with another therapist?

Cindy: Yes. I didn't actually do any memory work with any of these people. They each had already pursued that route as far as they could. Their therapists felt stuck and exhausted, saw little improvement, and so I got them for further work. Korelan is just now getting to the place where she's recognizing that emotional connection to people is the difficulty. She's been coming to me for more than two years.

Larry: How do you and she work with the problem of interpersonal connection?

Cindy: When our sense of togetherness increases she wants to work in the sand tray—making dioramas of places and events that seem to her like memories.[1] But in fact her sand-tray work takes us away from each other for a while. Most adults who use the sand tray use it like a meditation or free association session that serves to connect their deeper selves to me and to their more conscious side. That is, I usually find the sand-tray technique helps people represent deeper feelings and patterns. But it doesn't feel like it works that way with Korelan. She is the one person I work with whom I think the sand tray disconnects. Because she does something like dissociated "memory" work that way. Her work is like someone who goes into a dissociation trance or an alter personality to avoid the present connection.

---

1. The sand tray technique is a widely used method that allows children and adults a way of communicating nonverbally. Small toys, objects, and symbols can be taken from a shelf and arranged in a tray of dry or wet sand to represent thoughts or feelings, like a fantasy or dream.

Larry: Does she actually go into altered states or have personalities appear in the room with you?

Cindy: Sometimes. She has control of them, she says—because she's been in therapy for so many years.

Larry: How do you manage the altered states and personalities?

Cindy: I just let her do it. Then we talk about it. I encourage her not to forget there are parts of her that she has pretty good control of. After the personality dissociations she'll sometimes report missing time. Or she'll have physical symptoms and sensations that seem to her expressive of deep movement, but in fact serve to disconnect her from here-and-now communication.

Larry: Why, when she's working with the sand tray, does it seem to you that she's disconnecting?

Cindy: I think because she goes into an altered state almost like a trance.

Larry: In the sand tray, like a child or something?

Cindy: Yes. Usually a child-part, attempting to show something that once happened to her. But, you know, it's like she leaves the room emotionally. She leaves any sense of connection with me when she goes into these dissociations. But one time recently, she stayed connected to herself and to me when she did "dream work" in the sand tray. That was the day it finally dawned on her that she has no sense of connection to anyone all the time. It was an important realization for her that had been a long time in coming.

Larry: Tell me about that.

Cindy: This was not Korelan's usual way of simply getting lost in playing out her altered states in the sand tray. She wanted to work on a dream. Korelan had an upsetting dream and decided to work on it with me using the sand tray. In the dream she was a bear, not a human being. She could remember that in the last part of the dream she was trying desperately to get back across a street to her home in a woodsy-looking place so she could be safe. She was scared because there were too many cars coming. She figured out her lack of connection to the human world that day because as a bear she knew she looked different. She knew she didn't fit in with the world of people.

Larry: She's playing out this dream in the sand tray?

Cindy: Yes. She knew the dream had immensely upset her. But she didn't understand exactly what was so upsetting. She begins as a little bear coming from the woods. Somehow there is a path to get into the world where she is, but there is no path to get back home to where she lives in the woods. And no way to stop the cars. She sneaks around, she has laundry to do . . .

Larry: Dissociation and dirty laundry!

Cindy: Yes, dirty laundry to do in the human world, and she knows there are people walking around. But she knows she's different, so she hopes they won't notice that she's a bear. When she is ready to cross back over to her world, she has this laundry. She knows there are other bears in the bear family over there. But there is no way to stop the cars, to get back across. She realized that getting help from any people on this side was never like, "Oh, I could just ask someone." She could watch people and see what they did and imitate them, but she didn't have any sense of being one of them or of people being available to help. When I said that to her she cried and realized that she never has any sense of being able to relate to a real person who could really connect and help her.

Larry: "I'm not a human being, I come from a nonhuman family. I can occasionally cross over and move around in a human world to do dirty laundry. I can imitate human life and somehow pass, but I have to hope they don't notice that I'm not human. There is no one who understands or who can help me."

Cindy: ". . . I have to watch them and see what they do, how they act—what real people are like!"

Larry: She gets along on the basis of her mimical self.[2] What was the aftermath of that dream connection with you? I'm assuming that with the crying in response to your comment she was more connected with you at that moment than usual.

Cindy: Yes, she stayed more connected with me through that. I had talked with her about connection and disconnection often

---

2. Hedges (1994a,c) speaks of the "mimical self" as a more primitive formation akin to primate *imitation* than to Winnicott's (1952) "false self" based on *conformity* to maternal demand.

before, but she hadn't ever really understood it. She would say, "Well, I have friends," and, "I have an ex-husband—before he became abusive, I had a connection . . ." But, of course, she never really connects to anyone. She just didn't understand the concept of mutual interconnection at an emotional level until she shared that dream and heard my response.

Larry: Had she done her dirty laundry?

Cindy: In the dream? Yes, she had done it and was ready to return but she couldn't.

Larry: So, she went into the world of humans with her dirty laundry, she did get it cleaned . . . something like being in therapy maybe . . . ?

Cindy: Yes. But when she wanted back to her world she was worried she was going to drop it, or that she couldn't get the laundry back there. She was concerned that she would be in trouble, be rejected, if she didn't get back.

Larry: Therapy is a one-way path, isn't it? Once you've started seeing the world in a different way you can't quite return to your former safety. You can't simply clean up your dirty laundry and go back. It doesn't work! How long ago was that dream?

Cindy: About a month.

Larry: So we haven't had much follow-up. Did her sharing the dream with you seem like a genuine breakthrough or more like a random event?

Cindy: It hasn't changed things dynamically yet, so that she can consistently work in a more connected way. But it certainly was a breakthrough moment. We were both aware of a different quality of relatedness that we've come back to talk about several times. Her eyes have been opened. It was both wonderful and terrifying for her. But for the first time she does have a clear sense of the direction our work is headed. She used to think recovering memories was the goal. Now she senses that relating is where we are going. But she's clear that relating is scary.

Larry: What about your third person?

Cindy: Joselyn is in her mid- to late forties. She worked for five years with a therapist who did hypnosis and relaxation exercises to enhance the recovered memory process. So she has plenty of

recovered memories—babysitters, neighbors, and relatives, including her father and her sister. But not of satanic or ritual
abuse—at least not yet. Although when she talked to another
person she met in a recovery group who has satanic rituals,
Joselyn said, "Do you think I have satanic ritual abuse too because I have some of the same feelings?" I'm sure she could go
that way if someone just leaned on her a little! This "memory
recovery" process is amazing—how a little suggestion can generate a host of images.

Larry: How did she find you?

Cindy: She had been seeing her previous therapist for five years.
About the time of the Ramona case against therapists doing recovered memory work both Joselyn and Korelan had therapists
who abruptly terminated them because they didn't know how
to take them further. Joselyn's therapist simply said, "That's all,
that's as far as I can take you, we have to stop now."

Larry: You said, she has incest memories with her sister and father?

Cindy: Yes, some incest memories. It seems that one of her sisters was in therapy and had recovered memories about their dad
molesting her, but now she's recanted and said she was a victim of the false memory syndrome.

Larry: The sister?

Cindy: Yes. Joselyn is married and has three little kids. She has
sexual problems. She doesn't really enjoy sex. Or for that matter any forms of physical or emotional intimacy. Her sister with
the false memory syndrome has never married, never dated, and
never had a relationship with anyone. Another sister is now a
lesbian.

Larry: Joselyn feels like one or both of her sisters molested her?

Cindy: Not exactly. The really bad recovered memories are not
of the sisters. She does remember when she used to run to one
of her sisters with nightmares all the time and crawl into bed
with her. Maybe there was some holding and fondling but that's
not the big thing. The main memories burst out in therapy when
all of a sudden everyone molested her. The father molested her,
her uncle molested her, and there were others. She went
through all of those memories with her other therapist under
hypnosis and in dreams.

Larry: Did she make any attempt to go back and confront or talk to anyone?

Cindy: She never did with her dad. I think she wrote a letter to the neighbor next door, the one that she's almost sure it really did happen with. She hasn't confronted her dad.

Larry: Did she get a response from the neighbor?

Cindy: No, I don't think she wanted a response. She just wanted to scare him, like, "I know what you did, don't do it anymore." It was early in her therapy with the other therapist. I'm not exactly sure what the letter said. She's the one who really questions the memories all the time. Was it real, did it really happen, could I have imagined it?

Larry: How have you and she worked together?

Cindy: I remind her that she had no memories of molest before her hypnosis. I tell her that we have no proof of these things ever actually happening, and that hypnosis can make things seem very real. "Possibly these things really happened or possibly other things happened that made you feel like you were getting hurt by everyone around you. It could be a picture of how things felt to you. The memories could be like dream-images— that is, the best picture your mind can give us of what really happened—which may have been earlier and/or quite different." I tell her I believe that she has suffered some early traumas, but that we can't be too sure about their nature on the basis of memories.

Larry: She goes along with that okay?

Cindy: She doesn't like it.

Larry: What doesn't she like about it?

Cindy: That makes her feel confused. She doesn't know if she's right or wrong in her memories. I tell her that whether the molests did or didn't actually happen the way she remembers them, what really matters is the way she relates to her dad and other people. I think that does make a difference to her. If she thought the molest really happened, then what does she do with her dad?

Larry: So as it stands now, the "truth" of the memories is all still up in the air? You're working on the relationship?

Cindy: Yes, Joselyn has started working on our relationship. I've seen her in a group at a clinic for three years. After her therapist quit on her, there was a hospitalization. So I started to see her through the hospitalization and we began to work individually as well as in group. Now it's difficult to see her often because she moved to San Diego, nearly two hours away. When she comes to individual therapy, she has a tendency to lie back and go into this trance state. That is, at the beginning of sessions she's so agitated and anxious inside she'll say, "I feel like I'm going to disassociate." Then she'll lean back and she'll still talk, but in a sort of trance state. Then she's like gone. In that state she wants me to hold her hand, and she says, "Can you sit by me?"

Larry: Have you been inclined to do so?

Cindy: Yes, and I talk to her about it. I ask what the physical closeness brings up for her because it's important for us to know what that feels like. Today I asked her why she feels like she needs to go into that trance state in order to ask me to sit next to her and hold her hand. Does she feel embarrassed to ask when she first walks in? I'm trying to show her that when she goes into that trance-like state it really disconnects us. I think the trance is where her previous therapist wanted her to go.

Larry: But from your standpoint she's disassociating?

Cindy: Yes, disassociating, disconnecting, going away.

Larry: So while you have been willing to accommodate Joselyn in order to hear her and to try to connect with her, she is slowly allowing you to question why she really needs to go into this trance state in order to avoid connecting?

Cindy: Yes. I have had to really struggle several times to get her back out of the trance state because she never really learned how to go in and come back out by herself.

Larry: How do you get her out of it?

Cindy: I make her open her eyes, put her feet on the floor, look around, and stand up. Sometimes I have to be really firm with her.

Larry: The picture I'm getting is that Joselyn has chosen to see a therapist a long drive away so that she can't see her very often, and so that the contact is necessarily somewhat minimal.

Cindy: She comes up twice a week, once for group. I see her individually after group and she spends the night here with friends and comes back for a session in the morning.

Larry: So you're pulling her in as close to contact as you can. But the picture is that she's very anxious actually coming to make a connection to you. Then she breaks the connection by going into a trance. In the trance she can ask you to hold her hand and to sit next to her. So what you're working on now is basically "We can be here together, so let's try that." That's taking a long time to accomplish.

Cindy: Yes. She's an intelligent woman. But she acts like she doesn't know what she feels. I say acts because I'm not sure. She seems to use the trance to obscure things. She feels bad because she doesn't know how to tell me what she feels. She is very concerned about "doing it right."

Larry: This is characteristic of a number of people who may be quite intelligent, and who may even function very well in the world because they have enough ego strength to do so, but when it comes to integrating emotional relationships they just can't do it.

Cindy: She has a total blank—she says when she was a little girl she doesn't remember ever thinking about how things were. Her mother was an alcoholic who died in her early adult years. She still has a real grieving feeling about her mom. She feels her mom was a really good one, although she was an alcoholic and not very affectionate.

Larry: She hasn't grieved mom yet?

Cindy: No, she's now realizing that mom never came to her and offered to take care of her. But if Joselyn went to her mother and asked for a hug, then she would reciprocate, sort of. But she never really initiated closeness. So can I come to her, can she come to me, how can we be together?

Larry: For whatever it's worth, I recently heard a very interesting example from a woman who is psychoanalytically trained and therefore not inclined to have any physical contact with her clients. But she does understand that many of these people with primitive transferences need very direct contact. The direction I have suggested [Hedges 1994, pp. 151–160] is token interpretive touch that allows for moments of connection when the client is in a concrete disconnecting thought mode. Instead, she has asked the person to sit up, rather than to allow him or her to lie on the couch. She has decided that face-to-face is better during this type of working-through period. She also insists that the client look into her eyes and talk directly to her. Then the disconnecting fear can be studied in response to the firm insistence on direct personal facial, vocal, and visual contact.

Cindy: That's what I feel like doing with Joselyn when she goes into the trance. It feels strange to have her so absent, yet talking.

Larry: She's pretending that you're there when for her you're not. She's pretending to relate to you when in fact she is not allowing your presence. She's talking but not to you, not engaging you. It seems that the previous therapist went along with that. The psychoanalyst I'm referring to is very aware of the same disconnecting transference that we've been aware of as we've evolved the interpretive touching method of holding the person in contact while the transference fears are being processed. Somehow we must draw the person's attention to the concrete here and now, to the actual interpersonal relationship, in order to study the fear of connecting and the body reactions that accompany the fear.

Cindy: Keeping her there, emotionally present in the room . . .

Larry: Yes, and insisting that she stay here, not letting her look away. Holding the person in contact is a very strong technique and the analyst I'm speaking of uses it only at the same kind of moments that we would use it, that is, when we believe that the client does want to be present and when she's developed enough trust and safety so that some presence and interaction can be tolerated. At that point we put direct pressure on her to look at us, "stay here, don't look away, talk to me, listen to my voice, tell me what you're feeling, where are these sensations in your body, would it help to hold my hand?" I was impressed that this other analyst is doing the same thing that we're doing, but without using actual physical contact. Intuitively she has discovered the importance of this kind of direct framing of the psychotic transference. It's taken our group years working on these cases to evolve our technique. She had some training with me many years ago, but long before we learned to work in this particular way. She intuitively found her own way, but without actual concrete touch. She feels she is getting good results. And she's a very well-trained analyst, so she knows when to insist on active here-and-now contact and for what purpose.

Cindy: Joselyn will go off on this wild emotional thing. It starts off sort of okay, and then all of a sudden it's like going on a roller-coaster. So I told her, "If you feel like you're going on a roller-coaster ride, then let's get you back here so we can be together and talk!"

Larry: I would be inclined when you're calling her back, to ask "Would it help you to hold my hand, would that help you to stay present?" It was interesting for me to hear this other very skilled analyst say that she was accomplishing the same thing in a direct mode, by saying "Look at me and do not look away, listen to my voice, tell me what you hear, tell me what you feel." She is also going after transference elements, because then the patient can say "I'm scared," or "Your voice is harsh or mean." The therapist can then ask, "Where is it in your body?" So this analyst appears to be doing the same that we're doing. And so we may not actually have to use physical touch. That is what James Grotstein says in the introduction to *Working the Organizing Experience* (Hedges 1994c). That was the one objection he had to the general framing technique, that there must be other ways of holding the person than using actual physical contact. He didn't suggest directly what those ways might be, but he mentioned that his own analyst, Wilfred Bion, talked about "dreaming" the patient—that the analyst, by staying in a near-trance state, at that time could maintain mental contact. I find however, that the moment of the organizing experience is very concrete and quite limited in interpersonal reality testing, so that some kind of direct, active, and concrete contact is required. Some insistence that "You must look at me, listen to my voice, and tell me what you are feeling in your body." Bion himself may have been able to achieve such strong linking contact in the experiences he spoke of as "dreaming the patient." But can the rest of us achieve contact at such moments without somehow introducing the concrete?

Larry: Is there someone else you are thinking of presenting?

Cindy: I've seen Kelly for five years. Her mother committed suicide when Kelly was 6. She has almost no memories of her childhood until she was 9 or 10 years old. We're flying by the seat of our pants on what may have happened to her because there is no real memory at all. Whatever ways of relating to people she's tried haven't worked very well. She has a pastor at her church toward whom she has intense transference reactions. She also responds to two women at her church with intense transference emotions, one positive and one negative. I recently did a sand tray with her, which she doesn't usually like to do because she's very proper—playing in sand is usually a little too much. I've been trying to get her to be more spontaneous, you know, to take a risk. She did, and she had a "dream," not like a sleep dream. She occasionally will have a sort of vision, a picture of something, that feels like a dream, but she's awake. In the vision the pastor she so idealizes came and stood in the pulpit and announced that he was leaving the church. She was devastated. This is one of her greatest fears, that he will get a job somewhere else and leave her. She said that in the dream-vision she wanted to stand up and stomp out. But she wanted her husband to stay so she wouldn't miss anything! She wanted to tell him to stay and to get a ride home, and she would stomp right down the middle aisle so that the pastor would know she was angry and leaving. She would take her car and go. There's a woman that she's afraid of in the church. The woman has no boundaries and often demands things of her and will actually poke at her at times. Whenever they sit next to each other in church they disturb other people, so she is really scared of this lady. But the lady loves her and wants her to be her best friend. So in the sand tray, this woman was like a monster, and the pastor was the most handsome man in a tuxedo. There is another lady (represented as a gypsy) she knows who works in the nursery at church and she gets a hug from her.

Larry: Wow! Sort of like a reenactment of the death of mother!

Cindy: You guessed it! This fantasied loss of him hit her so hard, she wonders, "How must my mother's death have hit me as a child?"

Larry: Any mother who dies when her child is only 6 leaves a major impact—a hole, a gap, an emptiness. But if I recall correctly from our talking about her before, it seems like we've suspected that, whatever the issues of loss of contact, they have to point back as far as the first years or months of her life. Is that so?

Cindy: Her mother was severely depressed in her early years, she's been told. The mother's mother had died when she herself was very young.

Larry: I was thinking about this sand tray in light of the possibility of superimposing the image onto it of an infant needing to be connected to a depressed mother. Mother in effect is saying "I can't or won't be there for you." The infant rage, the temper tantrums, the kicking of the feet, the storming out—however the infant might physically do it. Then there being somebody trying to comfort her who felt like a monster. But then someone in the nursery who could hug her. Do you think somewhere in her past there was someone who could hug her, or is that an emergence of who you are?

Cindy: No one that she can identify. The aunt who raised her mother is her great aunt. Kelly went to her great aunt's house for a couple weeks after her mother's death and she remembers her as kind, but not really affectionate.

Larry: Let's think about the images there. The handsome but abandoning pastor. The intrusive monster who tries to comfort, and the gypsy woman in the nursery who tries to give her a hug but is preoccupied with other babies. Not quite a story but quite a set of relational images.

Cindy: In the vision she knows there are babies in the nursery to take care of. It's funny, the baby she got out of the sand tray was bigger than the woman who gave her a hug.

Larry: The baby the woman had to take care of was big, so there is competition even in the nursery. We might think of all three of those images as transference images. She's afraid that you will abandon her. That in your trying to console her you will be a monster. She is also afraid that you may be there to comfort her but that you've got other bigger babies—you are an itinerate gypsy. What a spot! Are you working with her around the issue of connection?

Cindy: Yes.

Larry: How has that gone?

Cindy: We talk about connection, she has moments of connection . . .

Larry: What do those look like?

Cindy: Usually, she'll get tearful. When we do connect the focus is generally on something that's legitimately an issue between us.

Larry: Give me an example.

Cindy: One time she had been talking about different people in her life who had affected her recovery and her growth. She either didn't mention me at all, or she left me out or something. I asked her . . .

Larry: "What about me?"

Cindy: Yes! Next week she said, "I realized that you might be angry," that I might be angry about her leaving me out. I said I didn't feel angry, but my feelings were hurt a little bit. At that point, the tears welled up in her eyes, and there was some realization that our relationship is real.

Larry: So in failing to acknowledge to herself and to you that a connection was forming she could see that she had hurt you. Winnicott [1975] talks about a critical element in the development and recognition of otherness in infancy when the baby realizes that "I have the power to hurt mother." In the wake of mother's hurt and withdrawal is guilt, and then the attempt to repair. The normal cycle, he says, begins with some type of assertion of self or self-expression. The child experiences hurt from the mother and then a bit of withdrawal. Then the child feels guilt and an urge to repair the break. In his paper, "Reparation in Respect of Mother's Organized Defense Against Depression" [1975], he points out that if you have a depressed mother the full cycle fails to develop and the child is stuck in an endless set of reparations, kind of an external co-dependency—running around the world trying to do everything for everybody so nobody will be able to withdraw. The suggestion here is that as an infant she blamed herself for mother's depression and later for mother's death.

Cindy: She does and she's constantly repairing! Especially with those three people in the scenario. The pastor she works really hard to patch things up with. He wants to be okay with her and he tries, but then he gets upset. I think that may be his issue, not hers.

Larry: She works very hard to repair that relationship.

Cindy: Yes. To bring him back.

Larry: But in the sand tray she finally can't bring him back.

Cindy: No, she can't get him back. The one she sees like a monster, she's faithful in repairing, but that one goes off again.

Larry: How about the one in the nursery?

Cindy: They have a pretty warm, legitimate connection. They can tell each other when they're in pain, but she's not always available. She actually does have a young baby.

Larry: Preoccupied. But even though she has other babies, in the therapy group perhaps, there is something there. As you begin to focus on the therapeutic relationship instead of encouraging her to remember her traumatic childhood, we can move back well beyond the age of 6, when we know that she actually lost her mother, back to the original situation with the depressed and basically unavailable mother. The suggestion here is that there was a part of mother that she could connect with and her relationship with you may begin there—though you too may have to look after competing babies! The work of connecting for her has to let her begin to realize that it's possible to connect and that she does matter to you, which she never fully learned with her mother.

Cindy: Several times lately she has come back and let me know that she is upset about something I said. Like one day I talked to her about the pastor, and that—given who she perceives him to be—it's not likely that she's going to get what she really wants from him. She took it really hard. She came back and cried and cried. She thought I was trying to take away her hope. She believed that he was her only hope of connecting. Then she came back and said, "I know that when you show me things you really are available and I know I'm afraid of that."

Larry: We might conceptualize her dilemma in terms of Melanie Klein's [1957] depressive position. Klein places this issue as early as the third or fourth month of life, when it begins to dawn on the child that she does not have the power to bring mother back.

Klein is hoping for therapy to promote the full realization of the depressive position, which I believe takes years—if not a lifetime—to accomplish. Working through to "I can be okay, and my love objects can be okay without total merger. I don't have to have that total connection, I can be separate, and separateness means that I don't control the breast, the other, the mother." When we talk about working thorough the depressive position, that's the way life is: "I may not be able to hold totally onto the minister, I may not be able to hold totally onto you, I may not be able to hold totally this other woman! But I know I can get some good things from all of you. I know that I can feel good some of the time, but I don't have to have absolute control." Whereas in the pre-depressive position, the child believes she is in control of the mother's body, of the mother's breast, of the mother's mind, but fears persecution by the mother body–mind. What Kelly never had an opportunity to work through in the earliest months and years with mother was the gradual loss of or disillusionment with the maternal presence in a way that was tolerable and manageable so that she could go ahead and build her separate and satisfactory psychic structure. She hopes for absolute trust in a never-failing mother but she must learn to live satisfactorily with "good-enough" trust. So that's what she's trying to do with you. On the one hand she doesn't want to need you or to acknowledge your importance to her. But on the other, she is fearful and frightened when she sees that she has an impact on you and that a real relationship is starting to build. She wants and needs connection, a trusting relation to you, but is terrified of it.

Cindy: That's where we are.

HEDGES' COMMENTS

The flurry of "recovered memories" in therapy during the 1980s followed in the wake of a cultural realization of how much child abuse really exists. Infantile trauma is not necessarily a result of abuse, but it leaves emotional scars that can be brought to consciousness through archetypal images of abuse that, like dreams, serve to condense a series of experiences into a single narrative or set of abusive dream scenes. You have just witnessed Cindy struggling to stay connected with a series of people whose previous therapists had found it more sensible or convenient to do such "recovered memory" work. Experience shows that as the connection begins to develop and as the primordial fears are brought into the here-and-now transference of the therapy session, the frequency and intensity of recovered memories diminishes and finally gives way to real relationships.

In the last example, Kelly, we see how the two are struggling to evolve a workable connection amidst a fear of abandonment and disconnection. But most profitably for us, Cindy's report highlights *the long period of safety development that is the necessary prerequisite to the process of beginning connections. And then the terrifying tentative contacts that we know gradually lead toward meaningful connections.*

PART IV

MOVING TENTATIVE CONTACTS TOWARD MEANINGFUL CONNECTIONS

12

"I Am Going to Die"

Clinical Contribution by
Audrey E. Seaton-Bacon[1]

HEDGES' COMMENTS

Large numbers of clients who need to experience terrifying transferences are seen in public clinics and training centers by student therapists or by newly licensed therapists who are willing to work cheaply for short-term managed care facilities. Unfortunately, this means that many such clients are never allowed to explore their deepest experiences because of the severe limitations that usually prevail in such treatment settings.

1. I would like to thank Dr. Larry Hedges and my case consultation group for their support, without which I would not have been able to respond to the needs of this client. I would like to thank my supervisor, Dr. Jack Pascoe, for his support in allowing me to sharpen my skills in a climate where there is widespread terror in working with individuals at this developmental level. Most important, I would like to thank Anne Marie for her courage and dedication to her own growth in our process together.

But I learned something else many years ago. New therapists, if they are not unduly hampered by their early working conditions or straitjacketed by their training experiences, are sometimes absolutely the best possible people to work with clients presenting early developmental issues. The reason is simple. The most important tool we have as therapists is our own intuitive self. And the best way we can use ourselves is to be natural, honest, and spontaneous. We also have to be aware that no matter what kinds of life experiences we bring to being a therapist, we must be able to turn freely to colleagues for reflection and resonance about our work.

You are about to read a piece of the most astounding work I have ever witnessed, done by a therapist-in-training who clearly knows how to drop into the depths of her soul for intuitive understanding, and how to turn to colleagues *and to her client* for help in understanding and surviving the extremely difficult situation handed to her by Anne Marie.

"Will you sit by me?" "Will you hold my hand?" "Can I lean on you?" "Will you hold me?" "Please don't hurt me!" "Help me!" "I can't find you!" "I'm scared!" "What's happening to me?" "I can't make it!" "I have to hit myself." "I am going to die."

These statements and questions expressed the need and the terror that Anne Marie felt as we immersed ourselves in her organizing experience. Nothing in my previous training had prepared me for this. Her demands for physical contact and total emotional presence created terror in me. She needed me to be near, "empathy near," and this was not my usual way of working. Her need for closeness frightened me. It felt as if she would crawl right into me. At times I felt lost with the newness of this approach, as well as with the intensity of my own experiences of Anne Marie. I feared the loss of my practice due to malpractice concerns. But most important, I feared the loss of the work that I so love to do. I struggled. My thoughts raced: "How could I communicate this experience to others? How could I share this with my supervisor who at the time seemed preoccupied with malpractice issues and questioned this new, more intensive, therapeutic approach? How could I explain this when, like Anne Marie, I struggled to find the words that would put meaning to our experience?"

For Anne Marie, the terror came in her reaching out for connection. She had not been emotionally connected with anyone for much, if not most, of her life. She struggled to be emotionally present. Physical contact was the only way she knew how to, and could, stay present. She regressed back into what seemed to be her first month of life. With wide-eyed innocence and intensity, she searched for the other—me. Her reaching out produced fears of being hurt, abandoned, dropped, and dying. Her body betrayed her with memories she could not identify and memories of being sexually abused. She recoiled. She reached. She recoiled and reached until, several months into the process, we made contact. The connection we finally achieved was immensely satisfying to both of us. It was intense with aliveness. All our senses betrayed us. We giggled. We watched each other. We imitated each other. We played. We found each other. We disconnected.

When asked to present this case, I found myself spoiling—minimizing, destroying, and ignoring—the request. I feared exposing my own struggles in the depth of this approach to transference analysis. I distracted myself as the anxiety and terror of the connection and disconnection continued to be a daily reality in our work together. We are currently steeped in the working-through phase of this process and the transferences are just as intense as when we began.

It has been just over two years since Anne Marie and I began our work together. After a failed attempt at marital therapy, Anne Marie decided to continue therapy individually to address her history of childhood sexual abuse, anorexia, and bulimia. Several attempts at individual therapy failed, according to Anne Marie, because of her becoming locked into a power struggle with her therapists. But now she was ready for therapy and took off like a horse at the Preakness. I restrained her because we needed the time to bond, to know each other, and to allow her to develop an intrapsychic world that would become a part of our experience. In addition, I was concerned that she would violate her own limits, replicating abuse by forcing herself to do what she was not yet able to do. More basically, I feared the loss of control, of being dragged by a runaway horse that I was not certain I could control. My insecurities as a young therapist mocked and ridiculed me. Eventually, I matched Anne Marie's commitment and determination and we began the process of relating. As I reflect over the past two years, I have become acutely aware of Anne Marie's courage and commitment from the onset of treatment. In the early months of our work together, Anne Marie talked of "feeling shaky inside," her fear of being hurt, and her feelings of being empty. Her emotions were split off—disconnected from her daily experience of relating. Anne Marie related intellectually, but not affectively, with others in her life. When she began to experience emotions, they were ambitendent—alternating good and bad feelings of equal intensity. For example, her ambitendency was seen in her longing for intimate relationships—for connection—and her equally intense resistance to and destruction of relationships. She reported feeling that she does not belong anywhere. As we continued our work together, she began to experience the intensity of her own neediness and grew more dependent on me. Her struggle with anorexia and bulimia, which she had felt was under her control, reasserted itself. She fought her dependence and was very self-critical. I interpreted her harsh and critical behavior as her internalized parent's response to her neediness, and as an overall attempt to prevent or break any connection she made with me. She accepted the interpretation and allowed herself to become more dependent on me. Issues of trust became critical. She feared abandonment. Shame and rejection were experienced within the limits of our relating process, and the boundaries established in it.

As Anne Marie regressed, she demanded more of me. There were times that she struggled to find me. Sitting across from her seemed too far out of reach. She asked me to sit beside her. She needed me closer, but the closeness triggered memories from her past. She struggled to stay present. She reached her hand out for me to hold in a desperate attempt to stay present. I held on feeling helpless and conflicted. She flinched. The body memories were present. She cried. She wanted me to make it stop. I couldn't. I reminded her that they were memories of an earlier attempt to reach out. She kept reaching until the body memories subsided. At first she just looked intensely around the room and at me. Emotionally, she did not recognize me. I just sat. Any outside noise or voice startled her, and some frightened her away. At this point in the process, Anne Marie needed more frequent contact. Weekly sessions were increased from one to three, and daily five-minute phone contacts were added.

Anne Marie grew more aware of the other—me. In a preverbal state, she appeared to have studied everything about my office and me: She noticed when I removed a family photo from my desk. She noticed everything about me—facial expression, changes in my voice, my body posture and energy level—and responded to the changes she found.

Changes terrified her as the transference of unpredictable, abandoning mom and abusive dad became a part of our relationship. She looked for evidence of my not being present, of abandonment. Often, I reminded her that I was there and would not leave. As she grew able to speak, she asked me why I was there for her. I told her that I chose to stay. Hearing my reply, she settled for the moment only to ask the same question again and again over a period of several weeks, until I responded to her unspoken question. I told her that I cared about her and chose to stay until she did not need me. Sensing it was true, Ann Marie settled with that response and has not asked that question since. She then became very playful in the sessions and brought in children's storybooks for me to read to her. I read the stories and bonding began to crystallize.

A BRIEF HISTORY

Anne Marie is the oldest of four girls. She was born in the western United States. At the age of 5 months, she moved with her parents to another state. The move, Anne Marie was later told, was very traumatic for her as she cried and screamed in terror during the three-day journey. She had been told that she had intractable vertigo and was inconsolable.

As an infant, Anne Marie could not be held. Her mother stated, "She would not let me hold her." Consequently, Anne Marie appeared to have been left without comfort. She was fed using a bottle or spoon while sitting in a bassinet or high chair. One year later, her sister was born. Rivalry between the two girls began immediately. Her sister could be held and seemed to receive all the parental love that Anne Marie desperately wanted but pushed away. Two other sisters followed and Anne Marie's wish for parental acceptance, love, recognition, and presence became more faint. As she grew, Anne Marie struggled to find safety in the parental messages that she perceived to be ambiguous, confusing, and conflicting. Verbal messages were contradictory; "I am here for you, but I can't be" and "You can count on me, but I am too busy." In addition, she found the physical contacts abusive and violating. Although she was uncertain as to its onset and frequency, Anne Marie reported being sexually abused by her father until the age of 13. When she became aware of what was happening to her, she would lie anxiously in bed at night waiting for him to come to her bedroom and fondle her. His intrusions grew unpredictable and impudent as he began to fondle her during the days, regardless of whether or not her mother was at home. His intrusions came at any time and any place.

The abuse brought a pseudo-representation of the longed-for contact. Greeted initially by terror and betrayal, contact with her father became the only vestige of love, and was later pursued. Finally, when she was 13, the anguish and pain drove her to confront her father. He stopped. Years later, during her hospitalization for anorexia, around age 20, she told her mother. Her mother verified her story with dad but nothing further was said or done. No one heard her isolation, her pain, or her struggle, which was expressed mainly in her conflict with food. Her emotional battle, reflected in her anorexia and bulimia, began to show itself when she was in her early teens and continued into her early twenties. She wanted the emptiness to stop, but could not bear to let anything inside her. Her attempts to control her world—her emotional environment—almost cost her her life. The treatment in the hospital helped contain the symptoms, and she returned home alive but emotionally void.

At the age of 23, she met someone who finally noticed her (at least this is what she thought). At 26 she married, believing this to be her salvation from a life of inner isolation. Such was not the case. Immediately after the wedding, Anne Marie reported experiencing a recapitulation of the emotional abandonment and abuse of her parent–child relationship. Once again she was alone. She had no real friendships. She stated, "Everyone I let myself get close to, reach out to, leaves . . . hurts me." So she resigned herself to never letting anyone in. At 29 Anne Marie gave birth to a little girl. The birth of their daughter seemed to deepen the wedge between Anne Marie and her husband. Her focus centered on the care and well-being of her daughter and her marriage became nothing more than a legal tie. Her husband immersed himself in work and other outside activities. He was rarely at home. When Anne Marie was 32, the couple came to my office for therapy as a final attempt to salvage their marriage. Unfortunately, Anne Marie's husband was resistant to engage in the process and the marital therapy ended after seven sessions. Anne Marie decided to continue therapy on an individual basis to address her internal experience of isolation, as well as to improve her overall quality of life.

THE THERAPEUTIC ENCOUNTER

Trained in object relations psychodynamic therapy, I began to examine Anne Marie's internal and external object relations. This modality seeks to understand the nature of an individual's internal representational or symbolic world of self and others, and how these inner representations affect current intrapsychic and interpersonal relations. Initially, Anne Marie's object world seemed harsh, abusive, unpredictable, withholding, and abandoning. From her experiences in relationships, her perception and understanding of herself was that she "is inherently bad," and that "something is wrong with me." She perceived herself alone both internally and externally. Her internal realities thrust her into a world that was experientially isolated, numb, and deceptively safe. She was split off from her affect, not being able to experience her emotions, and she displayed all-or-none thinking. Socially, she had developed a mimical or false self that lacked the depth and richness of genuine relatedness.

Anne Marie quickly replicated the duality of her parental relationship with me. Specifically, she voiced her need for relationship, but consistently destroyed me inside herself, or emotionally distanced herself. This process was particularly apparent during moments of silence. When confronted about her ambitendency, she reported fears of being hurt. At this point in the process, Anne Marie also reported feeling "shaky inside." The shaky feelings first emerged when she was instructed to lie on the couch during one of our sessions. The instruction to lie on the couch was an attempt to reduce her anxiety through a series of relaxation techniques, as well as to observe the changes, if any, when there was no direct eye contact. Some time later, she shared that lying on the couch, as well as her awareness that the office used for that session belonged to my male supervisor, intensified her feelings of vulnerability and triggered her body memories. Although we have been consistently meeting in my office since that initial experience, she has not chosen to, nor have I asked her to lie on the couch. In addition, emotions relating to the sexual trauma were evoked when she attempted to complete some of the exercises in a workbook for victims of sexual abuse. She struggled to control her emerging emotions. She cried, "I don't belong anywhere." And she reported feeling very young, "like an infant." She stopped talking. She had no words.

Not fully recognizing the extent of her regressed state, I explored her silence. She stated that she did not like it when I sat across from her in my chair. It frightened her as she perceived me as an authority figure who could (and would) control her. She became extremely critical and verbally harsh with herself. She coiled her adult body into a small ball—a fetal position—and cried. Anne Marie's silent sobs came from deep within her, a place unfamiliar to both of us at the time. Between sessions, she phoned feeling "panicked, trapped, and in terror." Her anxiety grew as she came to the office. She was afraid of the unknown and so was I, but for different reasons. She did not know what to do with the infusion of emotions she was having or how to make sense of her regressed state, and I was intensely afraid of the parental transference that was being established. At this point in the process, I became cognizant that we were working with psychotic or organizing elements in the transference that were unpredictable. Was I safe? Was she safe?

THE BEGINNING OF TERROR

No matter how many times one reads about the complexity, intensity, and utility of the transference relationship, words fail to communicate the power of the moment, the nuances, and the impact when it is successfully mobilized in therapy—especially when it contains psychotic elements. Words also fail to fully describe the terror experienced by both parties in the primitive transference–countertransference relationship. Nevertheless, I will attempt to put into words some of my, and Anne Marie's, terrifying transference–countertransference experiences on our journey to relatedness.

Anne Marie's initial anxiety in coming to my office was intense. My attempts to contain her anxiety through deep breathing and making herself comfortable on the couch resulted in an influx of strong emotions and a regression. Anne Marie grew aware of these unidentified, fused emotions, and attempted to get away from them—to detach. She described feelings of numbness in her hands and an intense need to get away. This, she said, was the way she felt when her father had come into her room at night. "No body (referring to her physical body) there, mind only . . . turned off my hands, didn't recognize them." Now she wanted to get away from me, but it was not me. Instead, it was the father she had needed to get away from but could not who had been revived in the transference relationship. She had many body memories. She felt physical pain. "Audrey, what's happening to me?" She became totally numb physically and reported being mentally lost. I sat helpless. In my naiveté I simply told her repeatedly that the abuse was not actually happening at that moment. It seemed critical to me that she know that the abuse was not happening again. I needed her to know it was me and not her father in the room with her. But headlines raced across my mind. "Client Accuses Therapist of Sexual Abuse." I was acutely aware of how easily blurred the boundary between the memories of the past and the present transference reality can become. Although I understood it was important for her to contact the abusive father who lived within, and through the transference to experience me as him, I did not want to be confused with her father. It was terrifying for me. It felt awful to watch and experience Anne Marie's pain, and to feel like the perpetrator. I was relieved at the end of the session. I was emotionally drained. I needed consultation. Anne Marie was also emotionally drained. Unable to move or drive, she lay in the next office for about two hours before leaving.

The above episode opened the door to a whole new way of doing therapy. Anne Marie grew relentless in her challenges and demands as she felt certain that she was on the right track. In the next session she reported feeling "broken, alone, isolated, and physically cold." She asked me to sit beside her on the couch and to hold her. Again, my thoughts raced. "What does she really want?" "It's much more comfortable in my chair across from you." "What you need and what is comfortable for me in my professional posture are not the same." After clarifying her request, I realized that she was asking me to be near, to be real, to be present. She needed me to be a real person to connect with and not simply a distant professional. While I understood the need therapeutically, it felt as if she had asked me to step out on a plank that dangled over a bottomless pool of gurgling lava. I sat next to her and she appeared to have moments of what I thought at the time seemed to be dissociation. I later came to understand these times as moments of interpersonal disconnection which were brought about by her longing for and/or achieving intimacy. My physical presence during her disconnections helped to ground Anne Marie to the present, but triggered my childhood asthmatic condition. I struggled to breathe. I wanted to get away. She was too close. *The more she reached out for me, the more difficult it was for her and for me to stay emotionally present. We were both terrified of connecting.*

Before continuing, I must add a clarifying note. When it became clear that Anne Marie was needing more in-depth analytical work, she and I talked about my ability to work with her at this level. She agreed to continue her process with me, knowing that there were uncharted waters ahead for both of us to deal with, and that I would seek ongoing consultation in her treatment. She was also informed that she could seek consultation if our difficulties became too intense. In addition, I wondered what impact, if any, ethnic, cross-racial, and cross-cultural issues would have on our work together. Generally, during the initial interview, I inform clients that I am Jamaican, and that although I have lost most of my accent, they may occasionally hear an accent or expression that may be unfamiliar. Also, once a potential client comes to my office, he or she becomes aware that I am of Negroid descent. Historically, my cultural, racial, and ethnic origins have not been a significant issue in therapy. However, as this level of relatedness demands a greater level of intimacy, I am never quite sure what to expect. Despite Anne Marie's report of her husband's racism, my racial and ethnic origin has been considered, but it does not appear to have had any particular impact thus far in our process. Instead, as I will explain later, I have noticed a childlike curiosity and a treasuring of any personal information learned about me.

It has been my experience that children who are untainted by racism seem to approach racial differences with curiosity instead of fear, dread, or hatred. In one particular session, from a regressed but connected place, Anne Marie looked at my hand as she held it, looked at hers, then back at mine, brushed the top of my hand with the fingertips of her other hand, then looked up at me and smiled. While a similar pattern of relating has occurred at other times, this was qualitatively different from other attempts at relating. This was not her typical attempt to ground herself using me—the other. Instead, it was filled will wonder, curiosity, and relatedness.

Anne Marie also seemed to treasure any personal information she learned about me. Initially, I was concerned and felt uncomfortable about disclosing personal information. This was not my usual mode of operating. However, as she and I moved toward connection, I realized that, as with any healthy relationship, her questions developed out of genuine interest and a need to know rather than entitlement. One question was about my birthday. She remembered the month as a result of leftover items from a staff celebration last year, but did not know the day. Initially, when she asked, I declined to tell her. She accepted my choice but could not hide the hurt. She gave me a birthday card and a little flowerpot (quite symbolic in our work) for my desk. She wanted to celebrate my birthday as it was important to her—I was important to her. Eventually, I shared my birth date and took in her care for me. I took her in and became more vulnerable to her. She, in turn, was able to take me in and connect with me at a much deeper level of relatedness.

As we moved toward more relatedness, Anne Marie continued to regress. She emotionally and verbally reached for me, then pushed me away. I observed this with her and interpreted her terror in making the connection. Sometimes she sat curled up on the couch with her head buried in a blanket that she wrapped protectively around herself. At other times she placed the pillows around herself to form a barricade. As memories of her father plagued her, incidents of bingeing and purging became a therapeutic issue. Her regressions initially took the form of an angry teen, a helpless child, and then a terrified infant. I sat next to her to help her stay present. Eventually, her regressions became so complete that only touch would help to ground her.

Her request for physical contact, for hugs at the end of the sessions and/or to be held, was another crisis point in our work. Throughout my training, I have taken a conservative position about touch. My position grew out of my desire to stay far away from anything that could be misconstrued by a client. However, the more I learned about individuals in the organizing and borderline levels of development, the more I learned about the potential therapeutic value of touch. My hesitation and cautions, although well-founded and appropriate, slowed her regression work. Anne Marie responded to my hesitation with anger. She felt rejected. She and I had many talks about the therapeutic purpose of touch, which was solely to help her stay present. She read, signed, and discussed an informed consent contract regarding the use of touch in the therapeutic process (see Hedges 1994c, and Appendices D and E of this book). Overall, she felt that touch helped her to stay present, to know that she was not alone, and that someone cared. In retrospect, it seems that much of the time spent discussing the issues involved in touch was a way for both of us to distance from the intensity of her regressions and her transference intensity that I *experienced as terrorizing*.

Anne Marie was not allowed to be angry or to express her anger as a child. Expressing her anger brought the anxiety that, like mom, I would withdraw and not be there for her. As I struggled to maintain my personhood, she found it difficult to trust my words or to sense my emotional presence. Holding her hand, allowing her to rest her head on a pillow in my lap, allowing her to lean on me, holding her and/or giving her a hug during or at the end of our sessions, would convey my presence more than my words. Quite often, she returned, when she knew I would be between sessions or had a break, and asked for a hug. She needed to know that I was still there. On one occasion, I denied her a hug as it seemed that her desire was less to stay in contact and more to soothe bad feelings that arose in the session. I wanted her to know that I was still there, but that she did not have to get rid of her bad feelings. However, this response left her feeling abandoned, alone, and bad. She withdrew emotionally into a place she identified as "strange." Anne Marie was not yet able to know that I was still there, irrespective of her bad feelings. Jealousy for my attention surfaced in group, much the same way it did with her mother after her sister was born. We had successfully recreated her early parent–child relationship with its traumas as well as with the intense longing for someone to be there for her.

Anne Marie wrote in her journal:

> Once upon a time, there was a little girl—who knew that she was searching for "something." But that "something" was not something she could find. She searched and searched but wasn't able to find her "something" that she was missing. She felt incomplete—that she lacked the things that others had found—would she ever find that part of her that was so deeply hidden—so bruised and battered, so scarred—the trust that was so injured so long ago—she can't even remember what that innocence

was like—it was ripped from her—as an infant she learned to survive—
to make it on her own—to not let *anyone* inside—they would hurt her
again and again—so she went inside herself—so no one could ever hurt
her like she was hurting—<u>never again! Trust—NO ONE!</u> The little girl
grew. She didn't like herself—and the person she'd become—but to undo
that would mean certain death—she didn't want to die, so kept it all
inside—but still knowing that something very dear to her was missing—
But she blocked it out of her mind, she went on with her life—But her
soul—her heart—oh how it ached—she wanted—searched for more . . .

REGRESSION TO DEPENDENCY

Over time, Anne Marie became more aware that her longings and
needs were not bad, but that the perceived or actual injuries that she
experienced in her initial reaching out to satisfy her needs caused her
to recoil and emotionally split off, and to detach her emotional self. She
moved further toward connecting with me. Once again she talked about
having "strange feelings." Initially, the strange feelings were thought
to be her fear of reaching, but later she realized that they were the needy,
dependent longings inside her. As she reached, body memories became
more painful. She would scream, most often without sound and sometimes with screeching cries, whimpering, and intense sobbing. She
would twist and turn her body, pushing an unseen something from her
face, wiping her face, kicking or recoiling into a ball, barricading herself with the pillows on the couch, pulling the blanket tight around
her—covering every inch, and then end suddenly in a frozen state. She
was unable to move, breathe, or swallow. When her eyes would open,
they were empty. She was gone.

Once I realized that these body memories were mocking her past
traumas and *serving the internalized psychotic mother who kept her from
connections*, I would talk more to her during these times and/or hold her
hand so that she knew I was there. The internalized psychotic mother
is described by Hedges (1994c) as the internalized representation of the
traumatizing other experienced during early attempts to connect. I
talked, in part because I felt helpless and wanted her to know that I was
there, and also because Anne Marie, when she was able, asked me to
keep talking. Talking and holding her hands or her, she reported later,
helped her to maintain her awareness of me and facilitated brief mo-

ments of connection. During this phase of work together, touch was an essential part of our work. However, it was not until I talked with my consultation group and supervisor about touch that I became more willing and present enough to be therapeutically effective with it. I am still anxious about physical touching in therapy, but not because I see it as inherently bad. On the contrary, I now know its place when used appropriately in and outside the therapeutic setting. My anxiety remains because I know how easily touch can be misunderstood and/or misinterpreted, and that there are still many therapists who believe physical contact is inappropriate.

Sessions were doubled as the process slowed to meet the depth of her regression. Then she began to recall "familiar feelings" as a range of emotions was returning. This phase, the working-through phase, continued intensely for quite some time. We both became exhausted, and I believe welcomed the times of disruption and disconnection in the process. Finally, in one session, the terror in the connection stopped for a few minutes. Anne Marie had asked for and had been granted permission to lean on my shoulder. She exhaled and settled. She had allowed herself to be emotionally held. We both knew it. She felt small—an infant. It was peaceful. It felt wonderful. She left the office that day with a borrowed teddy bear as she attempted to hold on to that place in which she found the other—me.

The following are excerpts from Anne Marie's journal about her experiences in the process:

> The helplessness, the vulnerability, the small, small child, no, the infant—wanting to be loved, cared for, and cared about—weeping—waiting—holding on—but only there's nothing to hold on to. But still waiting—waiting for that "something" to occur. It's always there—that fear—the terror, that skull crushing—body wrenching terror—nowhere to go, nowhere to hide—it's there—lurking in the shadows—waiting—waiting to crush the infant—beat her to death with its curse . . . Run—run to the safe place—the peaceful comfort, safe—secure—but where??? It's here—right next to you—in front of you—waiting for you to come inside to be safe—to find that secure, comfortable place—to rest—oh, how you need to rest—exhausted no, totally exhausted from your hiding, running, freezing—fighting—rest little one—rest—for you only need to open your eyes—yes it's right here—next to you—let it in!!!

The last several lines seem to represent a beginning internalization of a maternal presence. Regarding touch, she wrote:

> Touch, touch is something that happens to the heart when you let another person inside. Like the infant exploring her world—her universe—she uses the sense of touch, hearing, sight, smell—to feel—to take it all in—her world. She explores slowly at first—hesitantly—carefully, so carefully. Is that really happening to her—does she dare to explore further—to reach, reach out and feel, to touch. She first notices her hands, and face, and others' hands—she takes it all inside her—she relates to her world and to those special people around her—she trusts them with her whole heart—she knows of other 'things' outside because she has experienced things a little child shouldn't ever have had to experience, but she did—they scarred her—she wears that scar, those scars—but they are healing—slowly, so slowly—she doesn't want to re-injure herself, so she goes slowly—touches slowly, explores with terror at times—afraid of what's to come—the feelings, the hurt? Her past haunts her—it follows her—like the scar, it's there to remind her of where she's been—but the touch is where she is now and her heart tells her that, that this touch, genuine touch that she can trust and depend on—this touch will not hurt—it will <u>HEAL</u>! . . .

Predictably, our connection was short-lived. As we became more accustomed to tracking the connections followed by disconnection, the process of reconnecting became the focus of our sessions. Although there were intermittent abusive, withholding, and abandoning father transferences to me, the transference relationship of the rejecting mother was at the forefront and would remain so for quite some time.

On one occasion, Anne Marie discussed the abandonment she felt in group when I attended to other group members. As she processed the feelings involved, she discovered they were similar to those she had as a child when her mother attended to her siblings. The transference relationship with mother also included feelings of betrayal, distance, unpredictability, and "never being there" or "being there but not there." In addressing these issues inherent in the transference, I observed her resistance to taking in the good and in allowing herself to be emotionally comforted by it. I began to use infant analogies more frequently in our sessions. I described her as a colicky baby who was fussing and kicking so much that she was unaware of mother's presence, or that she was being held. Given this picture of herself, she would attempt to settle herself. It is important to note here that Anne Marie has had frequent exposure to infants and children and so such metaphors have special meaning for her. Subsequently, she was actively involved in the process of understanding some of the infant-like behaviors that she exhibited during sessions.

As she settled herself and moved once again toward connection, Anne Marie again began to experience what she termed as "strange feelings." Somatic memories intensified. She reported being scared and feeling frozen. The predefensive reactions, flight or freeze, were present in her relationship with her parents and were being recapitulated in our relationship. Her emotions were very frightening to her. She feared being dependent. After an extraordinary internal battle with the vulnerable, infant self, she allowed herself to regress.

This was the first time that I had observed such a complete infantile regression. She connected with me in a very dependent, needy place. She sat on the couch and her adult body behaved in ways characteristic of an infant. She sat with her face turned into the couch, or against my arm, with movements that resembled rooting. During this phase, her use of the teddy bear was critical in maintaining the connection we made in that vulnerable place. Periodically, she asked me to spray the teddy bear with my perfume. She had connected with me though touch, hearing, and now smelling—infant senses. Following my experience of such a complete regression, I spoke with a colleague who is familiar with these types of regressions, as well as with my consultation group. I was quite relieved to hear that infantile body reactions during the regressive working-through phases of therapy are not an uncommon experience with individuals who have sustained deep infant trauma.

The intensity of this place was unparalleled. Sitting beside her, at times, I felt vulnerable. In the earlier moments of connection, I felt that Anne Marie would crawl right into me if that were possible. She would look at me intently, as if studying and taking in every expression, every movement, every sound I made. The sessions that followed were filled with her repeated playful checking to see that I was still there. I would catch her looking at me with mischief in her eyes. She would giggle and play with the stuffed animals. She would take my hand and put hers next to mine as if matching them in size. She perceived and reported that her hands seemed smaller than mine. When the sessions ended in this silly, playful place, invariably she would return a few minutes later for a hug. This place of connection was short-lived. It ended when I informed Anne Marie that I would be unavailable during an upcoming weekend.

THE WEEKEND ABSENCE

My announcement was met with rage. Anne Marie repeatedly banged her head on her knees and hit herself with her palms on her head, arms, thighs, and legs in angry episodes, broken only by some moments of calm. She felt she had done something wrong and/or was bad. Consequently, she believed it was her fault that I was leaving. In a very small voice from somewhere deep inside her, she pleaded, "Don't leave me." I assured her that I was not abandoning her, but that I would only be gone for the weekend, and would be at our regular appointment on Monday. She heard me and reached out her hand, touching my fore-arm, as if to validate the reality of my presence in the room with her. Although we discussed my absence for several sessions prior to the date I would leave, its timing was unavoidable and unfortunately it came right after a time of connection. She was enraged that she had allowed herself to embrace me and felt responsible for my leaving. The badness she ascribed to herself was relentless and she was plagued with suicidal thoughts. I explored the content of these thoughts and assessed them for intent. She had no immediate plan to harm herself, so we verbally contracted that she would not act on the thoughts, should they return, but would discuss them in our sessions. She agreed.

At this point in the process, Anne Marie did everything possible to push me away. She projected the badness she felt into me. For a while I identified with the projection and felt awful. In my narcissism, I did not want to be this bad mother, I wanted to be a good mother, but she would not let me. I felt stuck—trapped. She continued to beat herself up physically and verbally. She began to push the limits with five-minute phone calls. I colluded with the breach in the five-minute limit because I wanted to make it better. I wanted to be the good mother at all costs, but I found myself getting lost in my thoughts. I was irritated and did not understand why. I felt confused. In the sessions, I felt light-headed, dizzy, and sleepy. I did not want to be with her, and emotion-ally I fought myself to stay as present as I could. I was relieved to talk

to my consultation group, which helped me to see that she was successful in recreating her irritated mother with me, and that she was setting
me up to reject her. Feeling battered and bruised, but more enlightened
and focused, I interpreted her terror in connecting with me and feelings of being abandoned, as well her attempts to irritate me enough so
that I would leave her. She took in the interpretation and calmed. But
as she moved toward connection again, the body memories returned.
This time they seemed even more intense than before. Now we had to
work through the transference of the abusive father. The physical
thrashing, the stiffening of her body and curling up into a ball were
accompanied with chilling but controlled screams—"No," then she
became limp—not moving a muscle. Throughout this experience I
talked to her. "I am here." "It's not happening now." "You seem to be
experiencing a memory. You are safe with me. I won't hurt you." Hearing me talk helped her to stay grounded until I said "It's okay. I won't
hurt you." I later discovered that those statements brought up memories of broken promises and betrayal by her father.

Anne Marie expressed happiness in my frustration with her. The
more we moved toward regaining the connection, the more she pushed
away and looked for anything to use to destroy any connection we made.
Everything was wrong. She scolded me for making observations and for
using her words in an empathic response to her. Nothing I did mattered.
In almost every session the transference relationship of either an abusive or abandoning parent played itself out through a role reversal in
which she tortured me. It grew emotionally and physically exhausting
to keep up with her. I was tired and it showed. Anne Marie recognized
my exhaustion and was afraid that she would lose me. The phone contacts, teddy bear, lullaby, or story tapes were not helpful to her in maintaining the contact with me. She would stop by the office between sessions to see me briefly or to ask for a hug. When we were able to process
her reactions to my exhaustion, she talked of her memory of a time
when her mother was seriously ill and everyone told her that her mother
was fine. She later grew distrustful of what she was told and as a result
seem to look for hidden meanings and/or unspoken thoughts in every
interaction. She was quite perceptive, as I had an ongoing medical condition that contributed to my exhaustion.

Anne Marie's constant search for anything that she could use to
disconnect or withdraw from me was crazy-making. I was initially un-

comfortable with her intense study of me. At times I wanted to break the silence and ease the tension that came from her consuming stare. Other times, her search was replaced by unspoken needs. As Anne Marie began to allow herself to grow dependent on me so that her organizing issues could be exposed, she struggled to verbalize her feelings and needs. In one session as we sat side by side, she had her head in her hands and on her lap. Then she allowed her head to fall, resting on my right thigh. Resting her head on my thigh felt uncomfortable. I felt as though she had taken something from me without my consent. I was hesitant to say anything too quickly, but according to Anne Marie later, "You let me know it." It pushed me further from her and disrupted any movement toward connection. I explored this behavior with her, and then with my consultation group. I came to understand that resting her head on my thigh was not a manipulative act. Instead, she was attempting to get a need met. *She needed to be in that small and vulnerable place with me where I was stimulated to the point of discomfort.* In later sessions, I was able to grant her request to rest her head on a pillow in my lap. Resting her head on a pillow in my lap helped her to reestablish an emotional connection. She settled in a place she described as safe and peaceful.

As Anne Marie and I continued to work toward maintaining emotional presence and connection, I was aware that my therapeutic approach was also changing. As I shared these changes with my supervisor, he expressed concern. He observed the changes, noting that this was not my usual way of doing therapy. In sessions, I had become more real, less distant, and more open to working with regressions than I was before. Also, I was quite excited about this new level of process, and communicated my excitement verbally and behaviorally. I agreed with him, my therapeutic approach was changing, reflecting my professional growth, and so was I. Not surprisingly, he was concerned that I felt solid in what I was doing and had support from my consultation group.

Although I saw the positive changes in Anne Marie as a result of being empathic and emotionally present, I could not help internalizing my supervisor's anxiety. My own anxiety in learning a new approach was compounded by his anxiety and found its way into the therapeutic process. I obtained consultation. In the ensuing session, however, Anne Marie sensed my anxiety and began to respond by becoming anxious herself. She perceived me as more withdrawn and became fearful. She coiled physically into a ball, barricading herself once again in the blanket on the couch. I told her about my consultation and she became more relaxed. I also relaxed. We talked more about the purpose of touch and the role it played in her process. Anne Marie seemed frustrated with me and my struggle with her need for touch. For her, touch was necessary to stay present and to establish contact. Later in her process, she shared that the therapeutic touch she experienced gave her the needed physical contact that she did not have growing up. Overall, she was able to experience my concerns and conflicts as positive indicators of my ongoing commitment and involvement in this process. She came to know that I would "be there" and it frightened her. We made contact and she cried. From deep inside her, she sobbed: "I always wanted my mother to reach for me but she never did." We had another moment of connection. We had also learned, by now, to anticipate some ensuing form of disconnection, and we began to watch for it on a regular basis.

As Anne Marie experienced more times of connection, her disconnections became more discernible. Ambitendent feelings expressed themselves emotionally, cognitively, and physically (hot and cold body temperatures). She became more aware of her own process. She began to dream again. Her journal entries became more descriptive, intensely reflecting her search and desire for connectedness, and her questions about trust.

Another journal entry:

> She opens her heart and her soul to let the other person inside . . . she doesn't allow herself to feel, to get close because it will hurt—others are not to be trusted. Stay within yourself little one then you'll be safe—yet very alone—isolated, on your own island—but people are all around you—but you don't let them near you, nor touch you—touch your heart, your soul—betrayal, shame, hurt, your fault because you allowed them inside, . . . it's all you've known—you accept it, but something isn't right, something is missing—there's an ache—a longing—a wanting to belong, to be you! To trust again, . . . you are precious—God's creation—you matter, you're valuable—trust/innocence—is so easily given and taken away—shattering the person inside.

She clung more to me, both in the sessions and on the phone. She began to express a deep sadness and missing me when she was not able to hold on to the connection. She was successful in working through much of her mother transference and began to internalize a more nurturing mother. This was an exciting place to come to in the process, but it was also the beginning of a different kind of terror for both of us. The transference of the abusive, abandoning, withholding dad made itself known once again. The body memories returned but more intensely. Anne Marie reported feeling an indescribable terror along with feelings of neediness or longing. She reported familiar feelings of "fighting and giving up" that she had experienced with her father. She noticed that the closer she allowed herself to get to me, the more she would emotionally and physically hold her breath.

In one session, she reached her hand out for mine. I hesitated, wanting to fully understand the current need for touch. She struggled with her own feelings of fear—intense longing, rage, being bad, and being trapped—all associated with her father transference. Once again, I feared accusations of abuse as the boundary between reality and psychosis can become blurred during these times. She noticed my hesitation, emotionally withdrew, and began to detach. My anxiety at the terror associated with her father transference prompted this disconnection. Fortunately, we were able to talk about it and that prevented a complete disconnection. During the next session we discussed my hesitation as well as the necessity of always exploring her need for touch. She got angry with me and physically turned away, verbally scolded me, and threw two pillows from the couch toward me. She admitted wanting to hurt me, "like [she] was hurting inside," because I did not hear that she felt lost and was having difficulty staying present. I observed how difficult it was for her to need me and not to have what she wanted, as well as her fear of being abandoned. She calmed and we were able to further examine her responses—withdrawal, disconnection, struggle with food, and suicidal ideation—to the phone limits as well as to my hesitation regarding touch.

THE UPCOMING VACATION

Anne Marie continued to become more present and began to sustain connection for longer periods of time. We moved from experiencing only moments of connection to her being able to stay connected and hold on to me for a day at a time. She talked about the good feelings she had in finding and being able to sustain connection. At one point she described her feeling as "joy." It seemed that the more present she became the more difficult it was for her to tolerate any breaks in the process. At one point, shortly before I went on vacation, she became frozen with fear. She told me that she felt as if she were left out for a truck to run over. In her terror, she asked me not to leave. The body memories, the physical coldness, the all-bad self, and the suicidal ideation returned in full force. (I note here that her suicidal ideation was assessed for lethality each time it was presented.) This was a very difficult time for me as I fought being identified with the all-bad mother who abandoned her child when she was needed. The professional and personal support system I had established helped me to navigate my way through this arduous place.

Anne Marie exhibited ambitendent feelings toward me both before and after my vacation. Eventually, she made me all-bad in order to communicate the hurt she felt when I left to go on vacation. Once again she was angry at me. She withdrew emotionally from both her individual and group therapy, and challenged me verbally about everything. Initially, she minimized the items given to her as aids to maintain connection with me, as well as a phone call I made and a postcard I sent while I was on vacation. Later, she talked of the importance of the items in my absence, but spoiled her care and need for me through creating a good-bad split between me and the good-bad therapist she worked with during my absence. I was all-bad, and she continued to perceive me as all-bad until I reflected how awful it was for her while I was away. She cried, validating the scared, frightened feelings she had. It was at this point that I realized that her anger was not really about me, but about the needy, vulnerable, dependent infant self that she had projected onto me.

For a short while she reassumed ownership of her infant self, but hated the way she felt. So she projected her infant self onto the teddy bear, and then directed her anger at it. She was not allowed to direct her anger at herself (hitting herself with her hand) as she had in the past, but now began to abuse and destroy the teddy bear. I took it away, verbalizing that it was not acceptable for her to abuse the vulnerable, needy, dependent part of herself. She got very quiet and reported feeling as if she had no arms, the same feelings she had with her father.

She was helpless and did not know how to take care of this small part of her.

I verbalized my sadness and anger at her abusive behavior (her internalized parent) toward the teddy bear, which was interpreted as the vulnerable part of herself. I modeled protection by refusing to return the teddy bear until she agreed not to harm it herself. In agreeing not to harm herself, she stopped projecting her vulnerable/infant parts onto me or the teddy bear, and reintegrated them back into herself. Her projection was a defense against her own helplessness, vulnerability, dependency, and the overall neediness she felt with me. It was terrifying to be so needy and vulnerable because it took her back to the trauma with father. Once again, she was troubled by her "badness," which I now understood as her neediness. She became more abusive toward herself, that is, hitting her head, legs, and/or arms with a fist or open palm. I stopped her. I interpreted her self-inflicting of physical abuse as her attempt to destroy the needy parts that she blamed for the pain she experienced with her father. She expressed a deep desire to run away, to get away from it all. It was very chaotic. Attempts to communicate seemed more arduous due to misunderstandings. Limits were challenged. Then came the ultimate attempt to stop the process and destroy the connection that was there.

THE BREACH

Anne Marie violated her verbal agreement not to leave her daughter at her parents' home. We had agreed that as a state mandated reporter, I would have to report any behavior that would place a child at risk for abuse, particularly with a known offender. Consequently, we had agreed that she would not leave her daughter at her parents' home for babysitting or any other purpose.

At first, it seemed that Anne Marie's violation of our agreement was a careless act. But as we explored her behavior it was apparent that she was quite aware of the risk involved. Her behavior was inconsistent with the responsible, conscientious adult that I otherwise observed throughout our work together. Anne Marie lamented, "This is not like me." I agreed. As we questioned this particular behavior, and why it occurred at this point in the process, it became clear that this was an all-out attempt to destroy the connection I had with her infant self. Anne Marie—the infant self—was connecting with me, and the internalized psychotic parent was summoned to stop it at any cost as the memories and trauma associated with father were being relived in the transference.

I somewhat reluctantly filed the required abuse report and Anne Marie and I continued to process the terror she felt in connecting that very vulnerable, needy part of herself with me. This seemed to have been a very significant period in our work together. It was the turning point to a deeper level of processing.

As a result of changes that she was experiencing, Anne Marie's dreaming became more regular and reflected her internal life—her searching, her struggle, her needs, her fears, and her truth. The following is an excerpt from one of her dreams:

> I want to bathe but don't want to take off my clothes or towel—they are staring and I can tell they mean me harm—appear nice but the comments and body language tell me to stay away. . . . Then a door opens and a pregnant woman comes out, the women are mean and threaten her—tell her to go back and do what they tell her if she doesn't want to get hurt—she goes back and continues to wipe the shower down with paper towels—comes back to them—it's not good enough, then they want something else done—nothing is ever going to please them—I can feel they aren't going to let her go—suddenly she balks—doesn't do what they want and they grab her and take a long broom-like stick and shove it inside her—I'm terrified—I know she'll lose her baby.
>
> Then I am in another place with others around and there is a woman having a baby—but it's too young—it's too small—I know it is—I hear someone say "We can try to save it"—but I know it's too little—could hold it in one hand—the mother—something is happening with her—her mouth—surgery? repairing it? The baby is held up and then gone . . .

Anne Marie's dream, an internalization of her childhood realities, reflected the lack of safety in her internal world. It identified a world marked by threats, penetration, and a life-and-death struggle. She feared that the self that she is giving birth to, that vulnerable part of herself, was too small—too young to survive. *She lived in constant and terrifying dread that she was going to die.*

CONCLUDING THOUGHTS

Anne Marie's struggle for life and for connection is evident. And while we have a great deal of work ahead of us, there is much to be gleaned from our journey thus far. My work with Anne Marie reminded me of several things. First, that our clients will do the therapeutic work they need to do only when they are ready. Second, she has reinforced in me a healthy respect for the courage it takes to begin and sustain such an intense therapeutic process. Third, I see that I, as well as all clinicians wanting to undertake this level of processing, must be prepared to discard the traditional clinical distance in favor of being emotionally present and vulnerable when working with organizing and borderline levels of pathology. Fourth, this process sealed in me the heretofore not fully understood statement: "countertransference is the royal road to the merger experience" (Hedges 1992). Last, and in a quite humbling way, Anne Marie taught me that she is the master of her ship, the creator of her future, and I, much like a parent, simply provide and maintain a healthy and safe environment for her to grow in—to metamorphose into the fully functioning being that she was meant to be.

HEDGES' COMMENTS

We are indeed fortunate to observe these trying scenes between Audrey and Anne Marie. They graphically portray the kind of struggle that I believe regularly accompanies the relinquishing of the early schizoid defense against or resistance to experiencing the terrifying transferences from infantile trauma sustained during the early organizing level of development. The road to establishing a mutual cueing process or a set of symbiotic scenarios is necessarily paved with a series of disruptive breaches in connection as primitive somato-psychic memories from infant experiences of deprivation, neglect, abuse, and trauma are revived for transference re-experiencing. Audrey is absolutely right: traditional therapeutic techniques based on experience-distant objective frames of reference will not do for this kind of therapeutic transformation. Only an intensely personal and affect-laden intersubjective frame will allow the requisite analytic understanding and working-through process. And Audrey is right about something else—such a process is terrifying and taxing for both participants. The ongoing avail-ability of an outside, third-party consultant or case monitor is essen-tial to give both the courage to move forward in this arduous task.[2]

As our book goes to press Audrey has just received her California psychology license. And well she deserves it. I told her only a few weeks ago that work of this quality often takes us twenty or more years to ac-complish. She clearly saw the challenge, rolled up her sleeves, made clear to everyone that she was willing but inexperienced and scared, and then rose to the occasion. She was lucky to have Anne Marie show up in her office, lucky to have a supervisor who didn't get in her way, and resourceful enough to seek out other supervisory experiences to help her on her way. Recently Anne Marie has made some significant break-throughs in relating and Audrey's consultation group is spellbound at what is happening. But more than simply a fine piece of work, this re-port illustrates with exquisite clarity the deep and mutual sensitivity that contact with terrifying organizing transferences necessarily entails. Congratulations Audrey! We are eager to hear what else you have to teach us!

---

2. Case management practicalities are discussed in detail in Hedges (1994c), and informed consents for this type of therapy are found in Appendices D and E of this book.

13

The Delusion:
"With Touch I'll Be Okay"

Clinical Contribution by Sean Stewart

HEDGES' COMMENTS

We often speak of stalking, of obsessions, of mental preoccupations, of fascinating, tantalizing, psychotic objects—all without quite knowing what we are talking about. The only thing that is clear is that people sometimes get stuck endlessly repeating an idea, an act, a ritual, or an enactment that makes no logical or social sense.

In psychotherapy we study at length these compulsive enactments, these endless obsessions, these frantic and compelling rituals, pleas, and activities until, if we're lucky, they dissipate in intensity or frequency or seem to disappear.

But we can't honestly say we know what caused the particular obsessional thoughts, demands, or activities or exactly why they left. We can only believe that some form of agony was being expressed by the obsession or the enactment and that the agony has somehow subsided. We hope it has resolved itself permanently, but experience tells

us that old obsessions and rituals have a way of popping up in later agonizing contexts, almost as if they are some primitive, inexplicable, or
abortive form of coping with interpersonal stress.

Studying the organizing experience and the organizing transference has given us a slightly new angle on how to think about and work
with the obsessional thoughts, compulsive acts, and seemingly endless
pleas and demands. Earlier in this book we spoke about "the clamor"
that is characteristic of psychotherapy work with the organizing experience. The clamor takes an infinite variety of forms, including persistent and perturbing silence. The clamor is a way of describing some
feature of the person's approach to relating that cannot be satisfactorily responded to given the nature of the demand, the personalities or
capabilities of the people involved, or the realities of the interpersonal
situation. The person often expresses a sense of being victimized by the
other, the realities of the situation, or the limitations of the self. "The
clamor" as a descriptive term highlights the demand quality as well as
the *expectable perturbation* that it creates in the person to whom the
clamor is addressed.

The particular way that a person raises an impossible clamor appears to evolve over a lifetime and repeatedly alters its forms to accommodate the shifting demands of new interpersonal situations. But two
features seem consistent and somewhat clear: (1) that whatever is demanded, desired, or sought after is a valid expression of some desperate need of infancy that was not adequately responded to at the time,
and (2) that since the request as constructed is unfulfillable, given the
current relatedness situation, it serves as a perturbation in the relationship—as something to limit, rupture, spoil, or to make impossible a
mutually satisfying interpersonal connection.

But why is the clamor by its very nature unfulfillable? The answer
seems to lie in some early conditioning experience of infancy. The best
generalization is that early connections with significant caregivers were
repeatedly strained or traumatically interrupted in such a way as to leave
the person with a terror of experiencing reciprocal, rhythmical, body-
and-soul-vibrating kinds of contact, stimulation, and connection. Put
a different way, the frantic clamor expresses what was once an unmet
vital need. Moreover, the plea for the need to be met was addressed to
early caretakers within a traumatic context, so that *the very act of extending* came to be experienced as terrifying. By almost classical condi-

tioning the mind-shattering or life-threatening experience is associated with the infant's active, reaching-out connection to caregivers that prevailed at the traumatic moment. The message left in the body, imprinted on the reaching neurological system, was, "Never reach in that way again. Never go for connections like that again because they are bound to be shattering." The memory of shattering stands to guard the avenue to reaching.

What remains in the aftermath of infant trauma is a desperate unmet somato-psychic need for interpersonal connection of a certain type that *must be pursued obsessionally and endlessly*—often in nonsensical or enigmatic ways—and a traumatically conditioned terror of the very interpersonal connection process that might allow a fulfillment of that need, almost as if one were permanently suspended in an approach–avoidance gradient. The clamor then exists as an *endlessly repeated memory* that simultaneously serves both purposes: (1) to express an intense need that was at one time phenomenologically valid, and (2) to fend off the very interpersonal connections that might have the power to respond to the fulfillment of and/or transformation of that need—because connecting itself is believed to be traumatic.

Every mammal somehow knows it must "find the warm body or die." But if the rhythmical, reciprocal connections of sucking, rocking, and emotional interconnection are feared, then one can only approach in desperate need and then let out a clamor that alienates the other so that the need cannot be responded to. *The clamor stands as a memorial to primordial psychic conflict.*

The conflict that prevents reciprocally meaningful connection leaves a deep developmental scar, a profound deficit in the relating capacity. Why? Because the organizing experience occurs in the months immediately preceding and following birth. The infant's primary occupation during that period is figuring out how to organize channels to the physical and psychological environments in order to be nurtured, soothed, stimulated, and enlivened. When these earliest of channelings are traumatically cut off so that reaching in various ways and directions is forever after forbidden by the internal signal cry of "Danger! Danger!" then subsequent interpersonal reaching and relational development is tragically limited, thwarted, and stunted. Then the later symbiotic relatedness period is destined to become systematically limited and/or negatively colored by the prior conditioned inhibitions in the reaching and connecting process. Thus *the very capacity—reaching and connecting—that allows human relatedness intelligence to grow and relational consciousness to expand is systematically stunted for people who have experienced greater or lesser traumas in infancy.* Whole areas of relatedness ego, of smooth interpersonal relatedness flow, of spontaneous, joyful, and trusting play are made impossible or at best left with troubling turbulence. Yes, the person may still have good gray matter to work with and may still develop good cognitive intelligence based on imitation and conformity. But serious deficits remain in the capacity for smooth, satisfying, stimulating, and safe relating that is fulfilling and reciprocal. A psychosis of a kind remains, though it may be encapsulated or even quite limited in its nature and scope. An organizing or psychotic pocket remains that does not allow the person to participate freely, spontaneously, automatically, and unconsciously in the consensual relational realities of the surrounding social milieu.

The case conference you are about to read highlights a therapist's struggle to stay attuned to the clamoring need of his client for satisfying visual and tactile contact. But you will see how her clamor makes impossible the very thing she really needs in order to grow—warm, empathic interpersonal engagement.

> *Sean:* Trula follows me around. She drives to the tract where I live. She needs to know where I am twenty-four hours a day. Sometimes she calls ten to twenty times a day to see if I am in or out of the office. I've thought of every stalking dynamic I know. I've been forced to set some limits for her that she has been able to bear and to respect. But clearly her stalking goes deeper. The desperation for any kind of contact—which, of course, makes me very uncomfortable—stems from somewhere. She has a deep psychotic core but I don't know how to show her what's going on.
>
> Trula is 29 years old. We are in our fourth year of work. We've had three solid years, three times a week. I started off seeing her as borderline, but it later became clear that in critical ways she's operating at a fundamentally organizing level. Trula started off expressing fear of abandonment issues in the way she described herself. It soon became clear, especially after consultation, that she had very little interpersonal contact in her early object relations, and much less as an adult.

I'm going to read a letter that she wrote to me that summarizes much of her history. As I said, we meet three times a week, but one of the sessions is usually with her husband as a couples session. I realize this is an unorthodox technique, but the reasons for it will become clear as I talk. Trula has a young child. She will also soon be graduating from a university in the area and begin graduate school, studying to become a professional woman. Her major struggle is that training programs put her into groups and situations where she has to—even if it means faking it—relate and talk to people. This is a lot of pressure on her social life that she finds very difficult. In a lot of sessions the struggle for her to talk, to tell me what's going on inside of her, is difficult. I've always felt good about her because I can feel her in the struggle, and therefore I give her an "A" for effort. But she just can't get it out. She's been talking a lot more. In the last year the whole focus for her has been on wanting to touch me, wanting some sort of physical contact. We've been talking about touch now for a year, so it pretty much consumes her mind. I have always given her the idea that I agree that she needs physical contact and that she should be getting it from her husband and her child in appropriate ways. As far as her organizing issues go, and the way we've been viewing it, at some point in time I think "interpretive touch" is going to be necessary for her.

Larry: Recently I had three wonderful hours with Hedda Bolgar, who is 86 now.[1] She had read *In Search of the Lost Mother of Infancy* and loved it! Hedda told a story of how years ago there was a woman who was wanting this type of contact or touch, and Hedda sensed that it was somehow very important for her. The woman was being seen in some sort of facility. Finally the woman was able to say, "I just want to sit in your lap and nurse." Hedda brought her a nursing bottle and milk and gave it to the nurse to warm (the nurse then thought Hedda was crazy!). As

---

1. Dr. Bolgar is a psychoanalytic psychologist trained in Vienna. She worked closely with Franz Alexander after they moved to Chicago and Los Angeles. She has informed, inspired, and critiqued my writing for more than twenty years.

per the request, Hedda held her and let her nurse on the bottle. The woman was very happy. I believe this happened just once. The next day, she didn't need to be held, but still wanted to suck on the bottle. The following day, she said, "There is still something else that I want, but I don't know what it is." Hedda said, "I think you want me to promise that I will never leave you." That's what's behind so much of the yearning, that's what we all want. I had never heard that said so clearly and cleanly. In that instance, by giving her what she thought she wanted, the woman was able to express what she really wanted—never to be abandoned. I sometimes wonder if the incessant demand for physical contact isn't about just this.

Sean: If I could get her to that type of statement that would be nice. I do think that is what this woman is wanting. Not long ago I actually read to her the informed consent for physical contact form, which explains what interpretive touch is, compared to other forms of touch that you can get elsewhere.[2] Her husband is very jealous of her desires to have me touch her. That meant getting the husband in on all of this from the very beginning.

Larry: You can say, "I think you really want contact from him."

Sean: I think she does.

Larry: "There are things holding you back. You've been with him a long time and I think there is an accumulation of inhibition. With me you are trying to get to the bottom of what it is that you really want, and what you really want is to be able to be intimate with the person you love."

Sean: I'm trying so hard to make that clear.

Larry: When spouses begin to sense that what you're doing is opening the person up to be more available to them, they usually support the therapist.

Sean: This man has been coming weekly for three years. He also understands that if he doesn't want to show up that's fine. It will be an individual session for her. But he keeps showing up to support her. She is willing to do whatever it takes to get touch

---

2. The Informed Consent for Physical Contact form appears in Appendix D.

from me. She read your false accusations article [see Hedges 1995 and Appendix B], and became furious with me. She said, "You think I'm going to sue you, and accuse you of raping me? That just sends me through the ceiling. Why does this have to be such a big fucking deal? I just want touch now." She wants to sit in my lap and to have me hold her and I'm not willing to do that. I told her having her sit on my lap won't work.

Larry: No, first of all, it's now against the law. When Hedda did it, it wasn't. But buttocks are now considered a sexual part under California law.

Sean: Good, I didn't know it was illegal, but I'll throw that in.

(Group laughs.)

Sean: I began to ask her to think about ways in which we could have some form of acceptable touch but her response is "Bullshit." I put my young daughter in my lap. Since Trula follows me around she's seen it. In her fantasy, that is what she would love to do with me. The issue for us, since it's so consuming for her, is how are her husband and I, how are the three of us going to get to a place where I can provide for her some limited contact that's going to be therapeutic for her? I've given her the idea that touch may make things more difficult rather than easier. She has this fantasy that if I allow her physical contact with me everything will magically change. Any thoughts before I read the letter?

Larry: We all know there is something magical about touch, but we can also bet that whatever touch you may provide will not give her what she wants. She has to come to grips with her desperation. Simply touching her will not help.

Sean: But will it move us closer in terms of helping her come to grips with it?

Larry: I don't think so. Not the way you describe her. She's saying, "I'm missing something." You're saying, "I want you to have what you need, and I'll be glad to give it to you, if it's in the right way." That's misleading her.

Sean: I'm very clear on the idea that touch is not the end of the road here.

Larry: Nor the promise that "I'll love you forever and never leave you."

Sean: Which brings her more into desperation.

Larry: Right, but it does bring her closer to the organizing experience.

Sean: Right. Touch isn't going to be soothing like she thought it would be, it's going to throw her into the black pit of her organizing core.

Larry: So then, there's no point in touching her.

Sean: But isn't the black pit where we want to go?

Larry: Right. But she needs to go there on her own volition and in her own time—not because your touch pushes her there.

Sean: But touch is the way to get there, isn't it? I'm open for other ways to go.

Larry: Your thinking is, "If I can find some way that's safe and not misleading, I can give her touch, and that will prove to her that touch isn't what she wants. And then she will fall into the black hole." Instead you can say to her, "Touch is what you believe you need from me. If we found some way where touch would be satisfactory, I think you would then find that it isn't what you want. And then whatever experience you're avoiding, you would not be able to avoid any longer. But I don't think you have to have comforting touch from me to get there. What you are needing is to experience the terror of not being able to have what you need when you need it. And to experience me being with you in your sense of horrible desperation."

Sean: How do we do it without the touch?

Larry: Keep withholding the touch. Not to torture her—but because touch won't help and it may be misleading.

Sean: I am withholding it, I'm not gratifying this person!

(Group laughter)

Larry: The difference between touch for comfort and what I have called *interpretive touch* is very great.[3]

Sean: When I've talked about touch with this person I've only talked about interpretive touch in terms of her and me. I've suggested she go out and get the other kinds of touch elsewhere.

---

3. See "Transformation through Connections" (Hedges 1994c, pp. 151–160).

Larry: The only place that interpretive touch is effective is when she is actually in the process of falling into the black pit and she is withdrawing *at the moment.* She is withdrawing because she feels that you and nobody else will ever be with her. You are trying to stay with her, saying that's not true: "Just because I will not hold you and suckle you doesn't mean that you cannot have me in other ways. If you take hold of my hand, maybe that will allow you to realize that you can have me, that you can stay present, that you don't have to withdraw again." That's why I keep emphasizing that the value of touch when it's well-timed is interpretive, as opposed to the "magic" of touch. The way you're thinking about it suggests that you may be misleading her. You are saying to her implicitly, "I'll find some way to give you some touch so you can have what you need or so you can learn that it won't work."

Sean: If I came across that way, it's not what I meant. I've been thinking about it as, "I'll find some way to give you what you think you need, interpretive touch, so we can go forward." I do agree though, I've been thinking that there are elements in the interpretive touch that she would like.

Larry: Whether in her mind or in your mind, so long as there is a thought that giving her touch will help her, then you rely on the magic of touch. She will continue to think, "If I can just have it, then I'll be okay." *Interpretation—verbal or nonverbal—is a communication that has the power to reveal how some aspect of transference or resistance from the past is operating in the here-and-now present.* Comfort serves to gratify, to lower anxiety. But it simply plays into the resistance. So magical touch for the sake of helping the person feel better colludes with resistance. Touch for comfort supports her delusion. Her delusion is that "If you just touch me, I'll be okay." But of course she won't. We all want the warmth, reassurance, and comfort of being touched—but that isn't how analysis proceeds.

Sean: I've said it a million ways, but she's hanging on to her delusion. In my opinion, the touch might have some elements of joy, at least momentarily.

Larry: I've never seen anybody joyous with interpretive touch. I've seen them terrified and shaking, convulsing and barely able to react. And the moment the touch is there they go into a thousand fragments that fly terrifyingly through the universe. Interpretive touch is terrifying because it's contact at a key moment when contact is desired but greatly feared. Babies physiologically need to be held. They need a lot of stimulation. Certain babies, because the holding and putting down was done in such ways as to tantalize them, continue to think, "I've got to have it, I've got to have it." They work their whole life just to get back there, just to feel what they believe they have to have. An ordinary baby at some point learns to relinquish the incessant demand to be comforted by being physically held. The baby discovers that there are other competing things in the world that are more interesting and that can also be comforting. There are other ways to have stimulating access to mother's mind. In utero, contact is absolutely essential for the growing fetus. In the first four months after birth there is a slow giving up of skin contact in favor of smell, sound, sight, taste, and movement. This is because the child begins to realize that stimulation and comfort comes, in many different ways. In utero, mother is mainly known through physical contact, through touch. But in the first four months after birth the child begins to realize that being in touch with mother is more than physical contact. Mother is mind. It is her mind that I need now. Your woman didn't learn that. So in her delusion she keeps saying, "I know I'll have my mother forever if I can just touch you." Your job is to keep pointing out to her that it won't work! To point out that her insistence on physical contact is because she fears mental contact. Learning to connect to mind when you've been conditioned to fear it is a terrifying business.

Sean: I've told her that touch is going to make it more difficult, not easier for her. She's insisting on hanging onto her delusion. I don't think there is anything I could say to her to make her give up on this delusion.

Larry: The flaw in your thinking is that you believe you must prove it to her. You think that if you can just find a way to demonstrate that it won't work then the delusion will stop. You're thinking of delivering some kind of token touch that's safe. You believe that that token touch will prove to her that it isn't what she needs. It's like trying to prove there aren't little green men. You can't do it! A delusion is supported by deep psychotic anxieties and cannot be undermined by cognitive or even realistic proof. That's not the way people give up delusions. You can't get people to give up little green men. You simply can't!

Sean: The interpretive touch will show her.

Larry: I don't believe it for a minute! *The only function of interpretive touch is to hold the person momentarily emotionally present when the regressive transference is actually and actively pulling them away. Or to bring the person back into contact when they are losing it. In these circumstances concrete touch can stand as a nonverbal interpretation of the resistance to establishing and/or sustaining contact. Interpretive touch says, "You can stay present even though you are afraid and believe you must flee."* Over time, the therapeutic action is that, through a series of such experiences the person, almost by classical conditioning, learns that "I can stay safely in the room without having to leave. It's okay for me to be frightened of you. It's okay for me to be afraid of your mind. The shaking, trembling, stomach jitters, or whatever *are* my fear responses long ago conditioned to human contact." People believe they fear abandonment. But people living out organizing transferences fear connection. People living out borderline or symbiotic scenarios fear abandonment and then split when they don't get what they want. *Organizing people shatter when they do get the connection they clamor for.* Yes, we all desire the eternal peace of Eden. And yes, we tend to believe that being held will put us there. But it isn't so, and the clamor for Eden forecloses the possibility of any real relating.

Sean: I've got three years of solid work with this person. We've spent a lot of time studying the breaks in contact and restoration through empathy in the room.

Larry: It sounds like you're doing great!

Sean: For example, I'll say something to her. She'll come back later on and repeat what I said. But not quite what I said. Sometimes she does it to tick me off, sometimes she knows it's not what I said.

Larry: At a time when she does something like that to tick you off, I would definitely interpret it as her trying to break the contact by provoking you to be perturbed by her misunderstanding.

Sean: She writes me letters. She has such a hard time talking in the sessions that I told her to start writing me letters. Then I read them aloud and we go over them together in sessions.

Larry: Can you get her to read them to you in a way that fosters contact?

Sean: That's what we're working toward. But for now when it's in writing and she hears me say it, it pulls more of her out. She'll comment on what she wrote and we can talk about it. So here is some of the letter: "I have these intense feelings to be held by you, and it gets more intense when I am with you. I had no problems fantasizing about touch until you asked me *how* I want to start touching you." Now that's a distortion; I did not say to her, "How would you like to touch me?" I said that touch was in the realm of the possible, but we have to be in the right place.

Larry: But you can see what she does with it. She's living the delusion. The reason I think you're supporting the delusion is that somehow in your mind you think, "I will touch her and then she will discover it doesn't work." She is thinking, "If I can finally get him to touch me, then I'll be okay." Both of you are delusional!

Sean: I know it's going to upset her so much if she ever gets the sense that I'm not going to give her touch that feels good. She does long for Eden. We really need to have all the hatches battened down on this one. Back to the letter: "Every way I try to imagine it, making touch is scary, making touch really makes me nervous, but the fantasy of it is becoming very frustrating, because it's not real. If that makes any sense, you are one up on me." I can see that in her mind, in order to get to the right place where we can touch, all we really need to do is to sign the informed consent form for interpretive touch, and then we need to get her husband's jealousy managed—all this so she can touch my finger!

Larry: Well I like it all! Work is getting done on every front.

Sean: Right—so many hurdles! It's provoking a rage within her and a desperation too.

Larry: So that's where she has to go? She has to feel the desperation? She has to feel you tantalizing her?

Sean: The obstacles are putting her there. Continuing the letter: "The only time touch feels okay with Dustin (her husband) anymore is when I'm wasted." This means intoxicated on vodka. She's not an alcoholic, but she deals with her frustration in two ways. The primary way is to get high on alcohol. The other is to cut herself on her ankles very lightly until blood emerges to relieve frustration temporarily. "Any other time touch feels irritating or empty. Dustin says it's because I think about it too much."

Larry: Let me be sure I understand what she's saying. "When my mind is put out of commission by the vodka, then my body can enjoy touch." You're saying, "We are going with you and your husband to where you can feel your mind and your body together without the vodka. Our goal is for what you already know to be pleasurable at the body level to also be pleasurable at the mind level."

Sean: Yes. For her not just to be physically connected but psychically connected.

Larry: We can see with this one comment where the gap is. When her mind is out of commission she can enjoy physical contact. We can infer that the moment mind is operating again, she is terrified.

Sean: Back to the letter: "Maybe I just expect too much from it, but whatever it is, it's becoming frustrating to me. It doesn't seem worth ever having any type of touch with my husband. Sex feels frustrating because I don't feel close to him when we have it. It just feels like an orgasm. And I can do that without my husband. At least with masturbation, I can feel the pleasure of the orgasm. I want to feel closer to people, but it just isn't happening." That, by the way is false. It is happening. She is getting closer to people. That's one of the things that ticks me off. She wants to say that our therapy isn't working and that's bullshit. She's closer to people now than she's ever been and we both know it!

Larry: There's a breach. When she says such things, that allows you and her not to feel close. The devaluing accusation drives a wedge between you. You can take her up on that. On how she keeps a disconnecting tension going.

Sean: "I am worried that touch with you is going to be as irritating and empty as it is with my husband. The closeness we (talking about me now) do have just isn't enough. Maybe touch for me just isn't going to feel comforting and good. Besides, comfort isn't what you want to give me anyway." She's getting that. But it started to tick me off here because once again she's implying, "You don't want to help me." "And this is really what I want, comfort and closeness. You know I never saw my parents touch each other." This is amazing because what she's recorded here I believe to be absolutely true—touch was never used to soothe and comfort her. Her mother was home for the first two years. She changed diapers, held her, and breast-fed her. But her mother did it because the baby needed it, because it had to be done, not because mother enjoyed the mental and physical contact.

Larry: This points us toward the genetics of her problem. Physical touch from mothers ordinarily originates from their sense of mental connection with the baby. Baby knows that the search is for mother's mind, not simply for her touch. Trula's mother's touch came from somewhere else—from duty, obligation, ritual. Even as an infant she knew it was mother's mind that she wanted.

Sean: She did get bits of mind when her older brother would come into the room. It was her older brother who was mentally present intermittently, not mother. But he was sadistically present. He was cruel. The whole family was sadistic.

You know I never saw my parents touch each other, until, I think, I was a senior in high school. We were walking back to the car from some banquet, and I saw them actually holding hands, I was shocked! I knew that they had to have had sex at least three times in their lives, because they have three kids. But other than that I really didn't think they touched each other. I imagined that when my brother, my sister, and I were young they did at least have to touch us. As babies you have to touch them in order to take care of them—to feed them, change them, and carry them from place to place until they're old enough to do all those things for themselves.

Of course, I don't have any memory of this with my brother or myself, but with my sister I know they did these things.

She knows mother's touch, but the mind of mother is not there. "What I don't understand is how they could live without much touch themselves. I'm going crazy without the touch I want. I was brought up with no hugging or touching except for kidding. I think affection was considered weak and pathetic in my family. You're not allowed to need people for comfort." By the way, the more she's gone into wanting touch, wanting closeness with people, wanting psychical and physical connection, the greater has become her sense of being pathetic and weak. I have to deal with this too, because the message from her parents was that if you need comfort or touch, if you need people, you are pathetic and weak. The healthier she is becoming, the more she understands that she needs people, that she needs physical and psychic connection.

Larry: So we could say, "You think what you need is touch, and as a baby you did need that. What you need now is genuine interpersonal contact. Meaningful contact is first and foremost mental. Mental contact often manifests itself in two people actually touching, like with your husband in bed. But you have physical touch and mental contact so confused that personal contact is terrifying and you can't allow the physical touching unless you're inebriated."

Sean: She's got that down, and it angers her to know. I really have to do more work on distinguishing for her the idea of mental and emotional contact and physical touching. "I remember having this craving to be held since about sixth grade. I started fantasizing about being held by my teacher in school."

Larry: "At puberty there was a chemical shift in your body, a shift toward wanting more contact. Most sixth graders realize that what they are needing is not just physical but mental contact with someone. The body is driving them to want a boyfriend or girlfriend. With you it was the desperation to be touched that manifested itself, not so much a hunger for a boyfriend." One of the things I was interested in watching with my own daughter (and you'll see it with yours) is that when sixth grade hits, the social scene changes. It suddenly becomes very complex. Boys are in competition for girls and girls are in competition for boys. Notes, phone calls, cliques, hatreds, loves—all of this incredible network evolves. The sexual juices enliven the wish to touch and to be touched. But it's not just the wish to be touched, it's mental and emotional contact *with* touch that is sought. The additional chemistry makes relationships feel alive in a new way. She says that in the sixth grade she became more aware of her need to be touched. She wanted to be held by one of her teachers. The chemistry mainly excited the need to be touched, because she hadn't developed the capacity for relationships. It's not like she had the fantasy of an affair with him, or of competing with his wife or finding a boyfriend of her own. People who have developed normally to the sixth grade know that the complex gratification they're seeking comes through relationships with each other. She didn't know how to relate. All she was aware of was the heightened chemistry and the desperation to be touched. By puberty she was actually aware of the same problem she brings to you—a desperation to be enlivened by touch.

Sean: "I know I could never get the touch I wanted from my parents. To them I was a bother. They didn't want to touch me. If they had been given the chance they would have gotten rid of me. They didn't want me. Maybe the nervousness I feel with you is because . . ."

Larry: I sure would watch that one, because that's what she's saying about you. "You don't want me. When you refuse to touch me, that proves you don't want to give me comfort, that you don't care about me. That you don't want me. If you could, you would get rid of me." Thick transference material.

Sean: She saw a patient walk out of my office one day with one of my teddy bears. She became enraged. Trula must be the most important person in my practice. Everything is interpreted as I don't want her.

Larry: As transference this sounds key. "My parents didn't want me. They would have done anything to get rid of me." What you say is, "Your belief is that I don't want you either. You believe that I'm looking for any way not to give you comfort, to push you away. You believe that if you can't get me to touch you you'll die." And you see, she did die in a way—the infant who yearned for stimulating, enlivening human connection and relationship died. She has not the slightest idea how to relate. She only knows this isolation is horrible.

Sean: The minute I ask her to sign an informed consent for physical contact or I say perhaps we're not quite ready for touch, it's like "See, I told you so. You don't want me. You don't care."

Larry: You could say, "What you believe is not true. I want you here, I want you to be mentally and emotionally alive with me. I want us to have an emotionally alive and stimulating relationship. But I know you don't believe that because you have physical contact confused with mental and emotional contact."

Sean: (continuing the letter): "Maybe the nervousness I feel with you is because you want to touch me. But to be held makes me feel weak and pathetic. A strong person, a person who could handle life, wouldn't need to be held and comforted. I don't know. I want to be able to be touched, you say I can get this, but that's bullshit." What I'm doing is trying to tell her the distinction between touching people on the shoulder, shaking hands, that is, reassuring touch, and interpretive touch. I told her she can get that other kind of comforting, reassuring touch anywhere in the world.

Larry: She thinks what she needs is physical touch. She's looking for the wrong thing. By the fourth month of life we already know that we're looking for mental and emotional contact. She is right when she senses that a simple drive for touch is not normal. Most of us grew up in a world where there was a lot of inhibition about touching, hugging, kissing, and other forms of physical intimacy. What a relief it is for all of us to let the shackles off and be able, in a close relationship, to put your arms around somebody and enjoy a big hug! But that emotional part of us can be engaged in nonphysical relationships as well. When you say that the time may come that you will give her some interpretive touch, I think she is still hearing that as you're holding out until you finally give her what she needs. Interpretive touch may or may not ever come. But I don't think it's going to be what she needs to comfort her at the time, it's going to be very scary. What she needs is a series of experiences with you in which she feels the yearning for physical touch but realizes that she's getting emotional contact that feels satisfying. Mental contact is complex. We don't know what will happen next, we don't know what will happen in the relationship. If you're touching people and the focus is on concrete physical touch, you can to a certain extent either anticipate what's going to happen next or deal with what's there now. Because simple physical touch alone is concrete it's relatively easy. But in mental contact when there are two minds engaged you never know what will happen next. And, let's face it—in human life it's normally not possible to simply have physical touch without psychic touch. Even with our pets there is rudimentary psychic touch.

Sean: She'll sit in the chair so nervously. "I want to be able to get the touch I need from other people. You say I can do this, but that's bullshit. The only person I can get touch from is my husband, and it feels irritating and empty. If I could get this touch from others, I sure as hell wouldn't be begging you for it."

Larry: In your own mind, Sean, I think you need to treat her touch talk like little green men talk. If somebody comes in with little green men, you ask them, "What are they doing now? What is it like? There's a pink man in the crowd too? Oh, how interesting." You talk with them about what they bring because that's all they can talk about. But never once do you assume that talking about little green men is going to help. The little green men, the psychotic symptoms, go on and on as long as mental contact is not possible. *In your own mind the emphasis always needs to be on how we are going to accomplish some kind of genuine interpersonal engagement today. And what reactions you both will have when you do feel the connection.* With increased contact the little green men slowly drop away.

In contrast, Trula believes that touch is the critical dimension here. "If we just get all these little green men straightened out, then I'll be okay." Your meta-message, which you don't necessarily need to speak, is, "I know that's how you think, but that's a delusion. Those little green men will not trouble you anymore when you have learned how to sustain a mental connection that nourishes you." The psychotic material reappears when people lose or cannot sustain contact, or are terrified of threatening contact. But when people finally are able to receive and use the nourishing interpersonal mental contact they need, there is no need for the psychotic symptoms. Obsessing with her about touch or her cutting behavior will not cure her of anything. I know you have to do a certain amount of little green men talk, *but in your own mind* you need to realize that talking about touch will lead you nowhere with her. For Trula touch talk is a psychotic symptom, an obsession that prevents what she actually wants!

Sean: It's all she thinks about.

Larry: Little green men, satanic ritual abuse, molest memories, past lives, or alien abductions are all some people think about too. It's tricky business. They come in and talk about little green men the whole hour. About all you can legitimately focus on that is interpersonal is, "Your clothes are neater today than usual. Perhaps you gave some special attention to your appearance before our session today, hoping I would enjoy you more." Or some such interpersonal indicator that allows you to transcend the little green men content. And that is the sole interpretation of the hour, while the little green men go on. Because you're working on ways of making object relations interpretations. That's where your own mind must stay with her—regardless of the little green men chatter.

Sean: Tolerating her rage is hard. She wants touch so desperately.

Larry: Remember in the Sandy case [Hedges 1994a, pp. 305–333], she was finally able to say, "Every minute raging at you is a minute that I don't get to be with you."

Sean: That's exactly what I'm going to say to her. All this person coming into my office wants to know is how close or far are we from having touch. All this touch talk makes connection totally impossible. And, of course, it's all my fault because I won't give her what she wants and needs.

Larry: If it weren't touch, believe me, you would be failing, or hurting, or depriving her for some other reason. She has to keep the emotional gap open. And this obsessional talk is Trula's clamor. When she says, "touch," you can think, "little green men," and you'll know there's nothing you can do about it. Defenses take so long to relax.

Sean: As far as touch goes, she asks, "Touch, is this ever going to be something I'm going to have? What's the answer?"

Larry: "Your belief that when conditions are somehow just right and we do finally touch each other and then you'll be okay—is just not going to happen. *You are going to continue to be frustrated, angry, and hurt until you fall into the despair that you felt as an infant, and your body is going to feel like you are totally falling apart. You need to know that despite the intense pain of not getting what you want in the way you want it, nevertheless I am with you. I know this is frustrating and painful but if you can achieve this deep self-knowledge, it will sustain you the rest of your life through many important relationships.* Not the touch. Our holding hands at a moment like that, when your body is in pain and your mind is swimming, feeling that we are losing contact, may help you remember that I am present with you. But it's not my touch that's critical, it may be that through touch at a critical moment you will be able to recall that I'm here with you and for you. And that you don't have to flee from our relationship. We're a long way from that now."

Sean: Thanks, I got what I needed. It hangs together for me now.

POSTSCRIPT: TWO YEARS LATER

As the analytic process continued, Trula and I marched forward into the next six months, meeting three times a week but with one significant change. Her husband decided to stop coming to therapy, thus leaving Trula and me faced with the potential of more contact, as well as the inevitable transferential rupture of that contact. Trula soon seized the opportunity by reaching out ever so carefully with her mind and affect, flirting with contact, while continuing to maintain her subjectively safe state, a disconnected (psychotic) clamor for touch. Despite the now more ideal frame in which to work the organizing transference, and Trula's increased ability to extend herself relationally, the moments of contact were too terrifying and still could not be intercepted and sustained. I sought additional consultation, whereupon it was decided that interpretive touch (the holding of her hand) at this juncture in her treatment might be a beneficial technique. After much explanation as to the specific purpose of interpretive touch to Trula and to her husband, a case manager was arranged, and appropriate releases signed (see Appendices D and E).

Trula felt an additional sense of terror knowing that *I* could now reach out physically and hold her hand as a means of keeping her connected, as opposed to her simply transferentially fleeing the contact moment. It was not long before I had my first opportunity to intercept and sustain a connection through the use of interpretive touch. The experience was powerful for both of us. As Trula was in session sitting silently, I noticed and felt her intensely reaching out for contact, yet she was too terrified to latch on to me. It was at that instant I asked her if I could hold her hand. With a real tear running down her face, she reached her hand toward me, and for the first time Trula and I had contact accompanied by a sustained connection. From here, at the point of interception through the use of interpretative touch, we began sustaining a dynamically alive physical and mental connection by discussing what it felt like to hold hands and be so appropriately close and connected.

In the months that followed, Trula and I vacillated from a sustainable connection, to breaks in the connection, and back to an even longer sustainable connection. We were gradually able to develop a true relational bond in order to analyze the transferential ruptures or breaks in the connection. This new style of relating brought forth an associative plethora of rich genetic material, partnered with an ability to verbalize her feelings of wanting all of me. This working-through process eliminated the acting out of stalking types of behavior and her desperate need and clamor for touch. Presently, Trula and I use interpretive touch as one of an arsenal of techniques to sustain contact in the midst of her pulling away. Therefore, interpretive touch is a luxury to analyze breaks and to enhance bonding, rather than a hard-and-fast necessity or a reality that merely helps or supports her.

Trula and I are now in our eighth year of treatment, meeting for sessions twice a week, and we continue to work the organizing experience at a higher developmental level. Though her life is far from perfect, Trula works hard at consciously creating more intimacy with her husband, myself, her family, her friends, and others whom she encounters. She no longer cuts herself or uses alcohol as a means to anesthetize the terror of human contact. She is growing tremendously in her chosen profession, both careerwise and socially. Trula has a newfound confidence and connection with herself, with her relationships, and with the world around her.

HEDGES' COMMENTS

We are able to analyze early psychic structures by frustrating them, thereby bringing them out into the open. The organizing or psychotic structure here that needs frustrating is Trula's incessant pushing away from the interpersonal contact—by withdrawal, by cutting, by alcohol, by pleading for touch, by raging at her needs not being met. All of these are the "little green men symptoms" of her terror of being in contact. Sean must be persistent in showing her he has complex mental and relational capacities that she longs to know about, to understand, and to interact with. Her safety and well-being as a human being depend upon her finding ways of tolerating her terror of encountering other minds. Trula has been totally invested in that never happening. Sean's interpretive message pushes her to give up a whole way of being, an entire lifetime of fighting and fleeing in favor of tolerating mutually engaged presence.

14

Terrified by Disconnecting Rage

Clinical Contribution by Sean Stewart

HEDGES' COMMENTS

A regular aspect of countertransference in response to organizing transference is the arousal or revival in the therapist of a fragmenting fear that *we* are not being heard, responded to, or being acknowledged as a real and present person in the therapeutic relationship. Our own deepest fears date back to infancy when we reached out hoping or needing to connect to our own (m)others. And either no one was there or we were somehow painfully rebuffed. When the organizing transference is operating, we therapists find ourselves reaching out, struggling to be responded to, and collapsing or fragmenting in our own sense of despair and/or terror. The following is a transcript of a case conference that had everyone in the room on the edge of their chairs as the client created an episode of full-blown psychotic rage. It is a rare portrayal of two people living together in terror.

Sean: Eddie and I are in our eighth year together now. When "Playing Peek-A-Boo With Sunglasses" was written we were in our fourth year, and I later wrote a postscript (see Hedges 1994a, pp. 75–107). Today I want to report an amazing encounter we recently had. For those not familiar with the earlier work I'll fill you in as we go. Eddie and I set up a week when we were going to meet three times—on Monday, Wednesday, and Friday—and also have five-minute phone contact every night. The regular contact calls we've been having for some time now give us a sense of connection, even if they're just a couple of minutes. Eddie has seemed to use the calls to help him with creating a frame to bring into our relationship the organizing or psychotic transference. In his own way Eddie can describe the theory of the organizing transference—he puts it in terms of his reaching out for contact with mother and encountering some type of violent intrusion that breaks the contact, and then the pulling back of the reaching tendril with the resolution to never go there again.

Jeanne: How did you start talking to him about that?

Sean: Let me work into that question, because that leads into our last session on Friday.

Gary: Could you say that again, Sean?

Sean: Basically, Eddie now understands the sense of violent intrusion he often feels when he is with me as being replicated from much earlier in his life. He now understands experienced intrusions as sometimes very real and at other times as transferred representations of his life's earliest intrusions. Usually the associations start with something present and take us back in time. Eddie has come to believe that the violent intrusions started for him before he was born, when his mother's not wanting to be pregnant affected him. She was schizophrenic. He believes that her body was biologically pulling away from his even while he was a fetus. As he was reaching out to stay biologically connected he was feeling her pulling away. That is, Eddie now believes that somehow her mind–body was actively thwarting, intruding into his life space and supplies even before birth.

As I speak about this I am not trying to say this is the way it was. I have no way of knowing how it really was for Eddie originally. I only know that the way Eddie and I talk about it seems to be transformational for him and that's important in itself. This narrative of a crazy, withdrawing mother who comes forth from time to time to attack him has become a way of speaking for us.

Larry: You say you're increasing your time together?

Sean: It was one month ago last Friday when we decided to meet three times a week with additional phone contacts. We have had a lot of phone contact—once to twice a week, depending on how . . . life is hard for Eddie. Things break down in his life so much, from his car to everything else.

Larry: Why did you decide now to increase the contact time?

Sean: Because Eddie and I had not been able to get together enough the previous month in our usual twice-a-week way. I thought it was because he was having troubles at the homeless shelter that he now manages. He has a separate apartment from the homeless psychotic people now instead of being housed with them, which is his way of differentiating himself from them concretely. His car was breaking down. There was rain that flooded the streets. He's been having some problems with his teeth so he was going through a period of a lot of pain. We just weren't able to meet as often as usual. So we had to spend more time on the phone. Phone time is different than being with him. After missing him for so long I found myself saying, "You know we haven't seen each other much lately, Eddie. Your car is working now. Who knows what's going to happen next week? We really need more time together. Let's get it on, come on in." I gently pushed and he was up for it. So we decided on three times weekly for awhile. We've done that occasionally, even if things were going fairly well. (Sean now begins going over his process notes from the session—partly reading, partly recounting.) The first Monday on our new time schedule Eddie comes in feeling very good, with his dentures in.

Mary: That's a sign he's feeling good?

Sean: That's a sign, because his dentures often hurt him and he can't or doesn't wear them. He's looking great! He's very color coordinated. He's well dressed, which is a sign. There's a connection to social consensus for him by how well things are put

together. And he's laughing. He's feeling good. The first thing
he notices in that session is Mullon handing me my coffee.
(Note: Sean is in a wheelchair; Mullon is his assistant who helps
him start the day.) Eddie had come in early, and I'm still setting things up. I just let him come in. He doesn't usually talk
to Mullon. Mullon's bringing my coffee over to my desk. Eddie's
engaging Mullon saying, "Why don't you let me do that?" And
I'm saying, "No, no, Eddie, it's okay, just relax. Mullon can do
it." Then Mullon's just kind of looking at both of us and Eddie's
looking at me and then at Mullon saying, "No, I'll do it. It's
okay." I realized later that this was perhaps my first three-way
interaction with Eddie. He's been with other people and me on
occasion before, but this time he's relating to both of us as an
interacting triangle.

Larry: It's the first time he's taken in the fact that Mullon or another one of your attendants was there. That he's actually relating to him as a person and he's wanting to participate . . .

Sean: And he's connecting him to me and me to him as a person.
Before there have been secretaries or other people present. But
there's never been any of this three-way consideration. If there's
been anything it's been conflict with them because he found
them in the way, not an embracing of a triangular relationship
with his wanting to participate. Before it's been more like wanting to get father or brother out of the way. Like, "Go away, you,
let me have Mom all to myself." So on Monday I have an exchange that includes both Eddie and Mullon. Mullon doesn't
say much, but that's okay, he's the father figure here. But he is
somewhat surprised to be acknowledged and nicely spoken to.
Historically Eddie can't handle a triangle. He's just not developmentally that advanced.

Larry: If we're going to watch an interesting week develop now,
it's important that the kickoff is with Sean noticing that they're
relating to the third. And that Eddie's wanting to relate in the
triangle. He's never done that. So as we consider what follows
during this week of expanded relating, it's important to notice
how it begins. Our psychoanalytic theory says that when children reach for the Oedipus situation, for triangular relating, and
they run into problems with it, there's likely to be a regression

to a preoedipal phase, which is more familiar or secure. When a child attempts to relate in triangles instead of the established symbiotic dyad, we can anticipate that frustration will lead to the so-called castration feeling—meaning the loss of the sense of power, or the painful sense of injury that results when the symbiotic at-oneness is relinquished in favor of more differentiated, but interpersonally less powerful self-and-other relatedness. In this case Sean actually cuts him off by saying, "Let Mullon take care of me," thinking at the time that he was just managing the circumstance well. But, not to be dissuaded, Eddie persists! It's a seemingly small piece of business but as a kickoff to a week in which both participants have made a renewal of commitment it may be critical in understanding the events of the rest of the week. The other thing present at this time is budding narcissism, in terms of his dress and prideful demeanor. You said he was dressed better than usual and seemed proud of it. Recall how bad his hygiene and dress had been in the past.

Sean: Yes. As a matter of fact he was color coordinated and feeling pretty dapper—quite a feat for someone who has been so socially inept for so many years. When we started, anyone would have seen him as a "burnt-out schizophrenic," a total emotional and social wreck.

Larry: Did he elicit a comment from you?

Sean: (Smiling) Yes. He came in smiling with his glasses on. He knows he looks good. I say, "Eddie you look wonderful today! This is the best I've ever seen you look." I was sincere and I really was thinking that I wouldn't mind having a shirt like that! He was able to take my compliment in and laugh, to tell me "thank you," and to feel good about it. Mullon was still present and was allowed to be a part of the jovial interaction.

Larry: So we have two higher levels of development being activated at the beginning of this week, which you tell us is significant. We have a touch of body narcissism and enjoyment with the selfobject function of feeling good about being admired. And we have an ambivalent emotional triangulation—small but significantly new emotional indicators, presumably in response to your invitation to have more committed time together.

Sean: You're right. It's like intuitively we both already know—because of the beginning contact, because of the way things are being set up, and because we haven't been together without interruptions for a while—we both sense we're going to have an encounter at the wall, at the interface of who we are. *We have spent years creating a frame where we can have an encounter with the barrier that keeps us apart and be able to work with it productively.* So this is what we're intuitively setting up at the beginning of the week. Now with hindsight, I can see it so clearly.

We have a wonderful first session on Monday. Eddie's talking about how he's going to get his car working again, and about his clients, as he calls the people at the homeless shelter where he works. One of the reasons we didn't meet for so long is because he was having problems with a person at a day treatment center who was saying bad things about him to his psychotic clients. Eddie was wanting to go get a lawyer, spend all kinds of money, and sue this guy. It takes a certain level of self-esteem to feel offense and to want to do something about it—something that in the past wouldn't have dawned on him. Part of what we did in these sessions was to process the idea of suing this person. I'm saying, "Eddie, you can't go hire a lawyer. You can't pay. You're in a bad financial situation. And besides it's a lot of hassle you don't need." Lately, I've been able to get irritated or in small ways to be angry with him. Not like you might get irritated or impatient with an infant who has just exasperated you, but more like you would get angry with a 24-month-old who perhaps did something he knew he should not have done, and you respond in an appropriate chastising or oppositional way. You might communicate your frustration to that 18- to 24-month-old knowing he could tolerate it and knowing he's going to fight you back a bit. We had done this a short while back on some other issues where he allowed me to be in opposition to him.

In the Monday session we were kind of bouncing back and forth, somewhat playfully, about his hiring a lawyer, why he can't afford it, and why it is or isn't a good idea. He's able to engage with me and to tolerate my being irritated with him. We're able to do this for fifteen to twenty minutes without either of us backing off or breaking down. And without his going into a psychotic part of him or hearing voices. The spontaneity and repartee were fun for both of us. By the way, no voices at all this day. He often still hears murmuring of some sort or another. But no murmuring today. He's able to engage me playfully today. I can be angry with him and say, "You can't do that." And Eddie is able to respond, "I can very well do what I want." It feels like this exchange is consolidating for him. Part of his growing sense of consolidation is that he's realizing he's able to take me on a bit—to stay with the conflict and no demon comes in and says, "You're a piece of shit," which used to happen to him quite frequently. He's getting built up in this moment. So this is the essence of Monday.

Larry: You're characterizing the interaction as with a 2-year-old as a separation movement. In that phase mothers call "the terrible twos" we feel aggression, playful opposition in the service of individuation.

Sean: Yes. We are definitely in a separation-type process.

Larry: That's what the fighting is about.

Sean: Yes.

Larry: "I have my own mind."

Sean: Absolutely. That's why I characterized him in the 18- to 24-month-old phase, because in his own way he's separating and individuating.

Larry: So you've got three higher-level functions all operating in this hour—a touch of the oedipal, a touch of the narcissistic, and some separation-individuation material.

Sean: With a previous month of his just being very absent—physically withdrawn, and with everything breaking down in his life. This one worker at the day treatment was saying horrible things about him to his clients, who would come back and tell him. Then he would go tell his boss. It was quite disturbing and he had a hard time separating reality from paranoid delusions.

Cindy: Did he confront that person?

Sean: He's confronted that person. Although this person, I have a feeling is also pretty disturbed. So his engaging the other person is not solving anything. But I did encourage him to confront his boss more. I'm saying, "Eddie, your boss knows you. You've been managing this place for three years. She just got you your own place to live. The owner loves you." These are the people who own the place and know him. I say, "If you're going to confront anybody, go confront *them* with the issue. Why don't we just erase this man out of your life? He's nothing to you anyway." It's counterproductive for Eddie to engage the worker because it just activates his paranoia and everything's back to the old days of our first year. And it does him no good. He can then relapse to a day of what it was like when we first met. I hate to see him when he falls into the old patterns again. He becomes very disorganized and miserable.

Cindy: I would think that it's progress for him to be able to go to this person and say straight out . . .

Sean: Yes. It is progress that he can do that. But it's not productive for him to engage over weeks with this other psychotic man. It just pulls them both deeper into a paranoid place. Initially the idea of, "I'm going to go confront this guy," was very helpful. But he's heard that this other man has a history of violence. So following through on it very much not only disorganizes him but is unnecessary and potentially dangerous. Good reality testing means knowing when to confront, when not to confront, and when you personally need to avoid various kinds of overstimulating circumstances.

Cindy: The fact that he didn't turn it into his usual self-blaming "you're a pile of shit," but he was able to go to somebody and say . . .

Sean: Yes. That he came to me with it and that he went to his bosses, who validated him, saying, "Look, we know this person is misinterpreting you and we are on your side"—that was all useful to him. He never used to be able to have realistic thoughts like this, to see things outside himself before. We worked long and hard for things like that. That's Monday basically. We talked briefly on the phone that night. We talked briefly again on Tuesday.

Wednesday's session was similar. He's well-dressed, doing good. But I'm noticing that it's not quite as good. Where Monday was a 10, Wednesday was a 7. We're doing the same thing, but I'm also noticing it's in me as well, in the countertransference. I'm not feeling as good about him, about us. We talked

again Wednesday night. We had made solid interpersonal contact Monday. And predictably, by Thursday he's breaking down.
He's not feeling good, he has headaches. The voices are beginning to speak to him—the murmuring started late Wednesday
night. Murmuring meaning audible hallucinations that he can't
quite make out. But by Thursday he's hearing the voices again,
and he's feeling strange things. There are a couple of problems
at the shelter with clients. Things aren't going right in his life.
There are many little details that are going sour on him. He's
deteriorating in the wake of the great Monday session and a good
Wednesday session—both of which were containing and solid
interactions with real personal contact occurring between us.

Larry: So watch out now! Connection has been made and felt.

Sean: Eddie wakes up Friday morning. This is going to be our third
session this week. He's noticing early in the morning that there's
a police officer patrolling the area where he lives. He had a bad
encounter in the early seventies where he had a problem with
a cop. It was so bad he actually got a settlement from the city.
Eddie is Hispanic so there was not only violence but racial overtones. By Friday morning he's really in a psychotic place. So in
his mind the police officer is not merely patrolling the neighborhood (which so far as I can tell he's doing). But the cop is
experienced as actually watching Eddie, spying on him, and out
to get him. The cop is waiting for an opportunity to attack
him—just as he was attacked in the early seventies, and beaten
up badly. By Friday morning his body is in all kinds of hypochon-
driacal pain. He's hearing the voices saying, "You're a piece of
shit, the Man's gonna get you." He's having all kinds of physical problems. He can't put his dentures in because he hurts so
much. So he comes in with bare gums. I think that's important
because that's a 4-month-old infant quality. And his teeth—his
aggressive potential—are removed. He gets to my office safely.
He was all right driving. But he felt that the policeman was following him. He felt that the policeman was talking to other
cops, that they were monitoring him with their radios. He's
looking in his rear-view mirror feeling very scared. The terror
is intensifying the closer he gets to my office . . . it's a strange
thing as he expresses it. On one level he feels like he's fleeing

the cop and at another level he feels like he's coming to some type of even worse terror as he gets near my office and our time together. He walks in and I'm not doing my best that day either. So the countertransference is exquisitely responsive to the transference psychosis! He's not dressed nearly as spiffy as he has been lately. His hygiene isn't as good. He hasn't showered. He doesn't have his teeth in. He's got his sunglasses on again. On Wednesday he came in and took his sunglasses off, set them on the table, and we laughed together as we reflected back to the days his sunglasses were used to shield him from contact with me. This is always in our minds now. When we think about the old days of his always hiding behind his sunglasses we laugh. Because it was wonderful working through that. So Friday when he comes in he doesn't take his glasses off, he's feeling paranoid and angry. A bystander might again say, "You have a paranoid schizophrenic in your office right now. He's very unstable and he's probably dangerous." He was so visibly agitated that I was feeling scared. This was only the second time I have ever felt scared with Eddie. As I talked to him he was breathing heavily and irregularly.

Jeanne: His breathing is important here.

Sean: When your diaphragm is paralyzed it's even more important. I didn't really have to ask him much. I said, "Tell me what's happened." Right away he knows why he's there. He knows he's there to tell me what's happened. So he sits down and he begins to just go off into a tirade about how this police officer, this motherfucker cop, is patrolling him, out to get him, and "God damn it, if he comes near me, God damn it, he's gonna have to draw his gun, 'cause I'm gonna get him." He's saying this with intensity, sunglasses on. He's furious. He starts off talking about the cop, about the situation, but he is talking wildly *at* me. He's raging at me telling me all this. It's so intense and his controls seem so tenuous that I'm feeling scared.

But Eddie and I have worked long and hard to get to this moment. So I allow myself to feel scared. It's a way of seeing where he's at. But while I'm feeling frightened by this madman in front of me I also feel strangely very safe. I think, "We've spent a lot of years structuring a safe frame for this to occur in. There are people in the office, secretaries and others whom I can call on in a moment's notice. I've got my phone at hand with 911 buttons I can hit. So right now I'm safe, just like he knows he's safe here. And what I'm doing is I'm allowing him to go into it. I say, "I want you to be able to feel my presence." And I just let him go. He heard me, but of course he didn't say, "Okay, Sean, it won't be a problem." He's gummy like an infant because of his teeth. The voices in his head are very loud for him. He is convinced at this moment that these are demons and that they're outside of him, screaming at him. He's talking about this cop, his face is grimacing—almost as if to say, "Let yourself experience me." It almost looks like his face moves closer to me. All of a sudden the full-blown rage is directed right *at* me. Like I'm the motherfucker cop. He's calling the cop a motherfucker, but he's shouting and glaring at me. It's as though he's shouting at another invisible person by talking to me. I feel the emotional force of it directed fully at me. I'm feeling as scared as I've ever felt. This is intense. I'm letting myself feel scared. Deep terror is a strange thing—it vibrates through your entire body. But another part of me is saying, "I don't care what anybody says, I know I'm safe. I know this man is not going to get up and hit me, or do any damage to my furniture, and he knows it too." He's allowing himself to be in a very scared place—a feeling that he reported either at the end of this session or later on when we processed this session.

During his tirade it slipped out that he had forgotten to take his antipsychotic medication today. This is important because forgetting for Eddie now functions very differently than it did for him in his first year. Now there is "purpose" in his forgetting. He doesn't simply "forget" or lose track of things any more. I realize he is unconsciously saying, "We've made a frame where we can experience my psychosis together. I can hang onto Sean while I'm feeling quite crazy. The medication is going to get in the way of my having the experience I need to have so I'm not going to take it." I think unconsciously that's how he thought about it. Maybe even consciously. That's how I thought about it consciously. I also thought, "We need to just experience this now. Later on I'll give interpretations."

Cindy: I'm really impressed. This is very helpful to me to see how present you are with yourself, and how present you are with him as this fear surfaces. I know you've worked hard to get to this place.

Sean: That's a welcome comment because I know you've followed this work with Eddie for a long time. I've struggled for years trying to stay present during our sessions, not to be bored or irritated, not to daydream. I've struggled to get him to be present, not to wander off in his delusions or little green men. It's a function of our work together to be able to stay present with each other. We don't daydream any more. And I'm not daydreaming in this session! (Group laughter)

Sean: I feel good that I've developed the ability to stay present and to focus this psychotic transference onto me, in what I believe is a contained way. When I heard he had "forgotten" to take his medication, which he never does, I knew for sure we were where we needed to be. But I will admit, even though I feel I'm safe, I'm using my countertransference to assess his fear. It seems you can't deal with this level of transference terror without really feeling on the edge of danger. Terror is an experience you can only know, not intellectualize about.

Larry: I'm hearing you say there are two things going on in the room simultaneously. On the one hand, you know and it also seems like Eddie knows that there's a frame or a "setup" that you've both spent a long time working on so that a certain quality of interpersonal experience can occur. You both feel the setup is essentially safe. But the experience that needs to occur within that frame is of a frightening, terrifying, or dangerous nature. So both of you are allowing it. He didn't take his medication. And as you're feeling closer and more scared, he's allowing himself to move toward being more out of control. You're feeling the fear he's lived with since infancy with his raging psychotic mother. But neither goes into a panic. You both know this situation must be lived out. You've both certainly rehearsed it many times together in miniature forms before you now actually try to live it out together so vividly.

Sean: Yes. And as he gets out-of-control . . . his out-of-control is being *carefully focused* on me. So there is a control in his "out-of-control" and both are directed at me. *That's the interesting paradox here; he's in charge of this out-of-control experience. He wants and intends to get me to be with him, to know, to share in his lifelong terrifying experiences. He needs to know that I know, to see that I see him and that I know him!*

Larry: Right. It takes a long time to reach such a mutual understanding, a consensus, such a delicate balance in the working alliance.

Sean: It's not merely directed out to the universe. Most psychotic episodes are diffuse, chaotic, fragmented, and basically undirected or uncontrolled. This is an intense and interactional communication and both of us are feeling our parts.

Larry: Exactly. This is so very important to understand in order to be able to assess your and his safety.

Sean: We were living in a controlled "out-of-control."

Larry: There's no question he's in the room with you, that he *intends* for you to share his experience, to feel his demons talking to you. He knows he's scaring you and that you must *feel* this to understand him, and for him to come to understand this part of himself.

Sean: That's what I've gotten so much of from being this group. An understanding of how we can follow these primitive states.

Gary: So Eddie's now able to bring all the paranoia into the session.

Larry: You've finally got the psychotic transference active in the here and now and you judge that its expression is safe. At the level of the intended communication the reality testing is functioning. But at the level of the interpersonal contact he has lost the reality testing function. Interesting and significant.

Sean: The paranoia isn't about the little green men he used to literally see on the wall. Now the little green man is coming out of my mouth and my eyes. It starts off in a diffuse way with his talking about the cop but as we hone in on it we focus on me and I'm allowing it. Feeling the fear, assessing the safety . . .

Larry: It's "*You're* a son-of-a-bitch, and *you're* out to get me."

Sean: Right. There's something to say about feeling on the edge here. Because if he ever did haul off and hit me I'm sure he would be surprised. I know I would be.

Larry: There's always a sense when exploring psychotic anxiety that you're on the edge. This is why Kohut [1984], when talking about this, basically said he didnt know why anybody would want to revive this primitive and chaotic pre-self experience for analysis. He believed that in principle this work could be done. But he knew he couldn't personally do it—the tools were not available then. But he knew the strain it would have to be on both speaker and listener and he wondered why anyone would be willing to put themselves through it. Eddie is, of course, the reason.

Jeanne: I have a question. Is there any sense that if he were to physically act out these feelings it would actually be directed toward you? Or would they just be acted out—like he might pick up something and throw it at the wall?

Sean: My sense is that during this session my ego is split in two. One part knows I'm safe and with the other part I'm letting myself feel the fear of this man. The split allows me to assess and to hypothesize about the nature of the psychotic transference arising from an early developmental experience. The experience to be remembered cannot be recalled directly but has to be analyzed by allowing this type of emotional reliving experience. Because of the strength of our relationship, if this man were really on the edge and we were to fall off the edge because I've misjudged, I believe he would protect me and hit the lamp and not me. That's him protecting me. I would also be more afraid if there was a history of violence.

Larry: Here's the way I believe we have to think about it: This therapeutic relationship has taken eight years to develop. Sean has been saying in many ways "Let me be your psychotic mother, let's have an experience here between you and me. I know you're afraid of it. And perhaps I will be afraid too. But let's see how much of the early experience that has damaged you so much can be remembered by our living it out together." Eddie has done everything possible not to be present during a month when his psychotic core has been realistically activated. But finally Sean says to him "Get yourself in here, we're going to really look at this now." And so we start off with a high-level triangle. We see the narcissistic urge for respect. We see the terrible two's— the growing independence of separation-individuation. And it's all directed at his therapist. It's all carefully structured. The dare is on, the ego nets are in place. So now we're going to drop into the psychotic place. And, as we see, it's structured too. Winnicott understood the structured qualities of the psychotic transference when he made his patients "line up" and take turns to experience therapeutic regressions with him. He knew they could wait and he knew the regression they needed to experience could begin on cue! He also knew that he could only handle working through one psychotic transference at a time!

Jeanne: But don't 2-year-olds sometimes hit their moms?

Sean: Yes. They do hit their mothers sometimes. But that's not Eddie's personal style, based on the past and on a lot of other variables. In-your-face rage has been the historical mechanism operating, not physical violence. And most 2-year-olds who hit Mom don't calculate and aim to really hurt her.

Larry: If Sean were harassing or carelessly approaching Eddie, he might conceivably get hit. But the point of this experience is that Sean is allowing a transference experience to be present. We have to trust the structuring effect of having worked for many years on the organizing transference so that Eddie can finally and safely direct his primitive rage at Sean in full force. And he's doing it right after this very nice set of connections for the week has been made. Which is exactly what we would predict—a terrified response to real interpersonal contact. Then, on cue, "You're trying to damage me, you're out to get me." And, "If you get near me you're going to have to use your gun." So *within the context of the transference development*, it's a highly structured response. We don't quite have to think of this the way we would if we were walking through a ward of unknown psychotic people who might impulsively hit you or who might be suddenly provoked by a hallucination to hit you. *To be sure, therapists who do not respect psychosis, who are not properly afraid, do get hurt!* But Eddie is not an infant. Nor is he 2 years old. He's a streetwise man who lives a peaceful, responsible life. We have

the presence here of considerable structure—relationship structure and transference structure—so that what we can anticipate
is the presence of intense rage, fragmentation, and terror, but
not likely the presence of realistic violence or danger. The distinction is crucial and the ongoing and careful assessment of
safety is critical. I have often enough seen therapists in denial
who foolishly believe that "this person would never hurt me."
We have numerous records of therapists who were not careful
and who have been badly hurt and even killed. But Sean does
not seem to be in denial here. They are both afraid but they are
both engaged in working to know and understand the fear. Our
anxiety is appropriate. But we have to trust these two and their
process together.

Sean: There's been a lot of thought in preparation for having a
moment like this. This is not our first month or year together—
"Well, let's give it a try," you know. When we finally drop into
the organizing level it does start off slowly as we both get ready.
We become attuned to each other over time as Eddie waits for
me to get ready for this. As I become more prepared, he begins
to focus in on me. And now suddenly—but not really so suddenly at all—I'm being called a motherfucker. I'm being called
a bastard. I haven't asked him to take off his sunglasses because
I'm too scared. I'm feeling very frightened. I'm backing up in my
wheelchair. He's leaning forward. He's in a very tense stance.
All kinds of things are happening—go down the list of what a
paranoid schizophrenic is for a diagnostic litany, and they're all
there.

Now the real question is, how long am I going to be able to
tolerate this. (Group laughter) I'm giving him ego support that
says, "You need to experience this . . . this has to be focused on
me. We need to keep this going and contained. You have to be
experiencing and assessing—we'll be processing this later. Part
of you must also be noticing how you're experiencing me." So
now Eddie's ready and he's really giving it to me. But it's rough
on me and the question is how long I can take it. Now my own
primitive psychotic part is being provoked internally, which I
won't go into now because that's for my own therapy. (Group
laughs) But in a moment like this I have to deal with my own

internal psychotic mother abandoning and raging at me. I become frightened, in some sense immobilized by terror, and I want to back off or flee.

Larry: Because at this moment you're afraid you can't reach him like you once couldn't reach her?

Sean: Right. And everything else that connects or fails to connect gets replicated. I let him run on intensely for at least a half hour with the thought, "It's just Eddie, you're safe." I'm wanting to get more information out of our experience. It's getting more intense. As he's sitting forward in the chair it's escalating. I have to back up. At that point it's more than that the voices are louder. Demons are now everywhere around us. And the demons are coming from me. I'm becoming a demon for him and he's raging at me. Finally, I'm too scared, too overwhelmed. And here's where I know that I'm safe. I finally say, "Eddie, you've got to calm down. You've got to stop now." And he instantly went from looking like this to looking like this (demonstrates threatening to contrite).

Gary: You touched him?

Sean: No. I didn't touch him. I simply told him, "Eddie, I'm too scared now. I've had enough of your psychotic mother. We have to stop now." And when I told him to do that he instantly shut it off. But there was an immediate sense of depletion. It's like he has some kind of container for his psychotic mother in his body. He released her to fill his body, to fill the room, and to be directed at me. Then when I asked him to stop he pulled it all back in—let it all go back into that depressed and depleted container. Then he's exhausted, spent, and empty. And so am I. I notice myself going, "Whew! I really am in control here, thank you God!" (Group expressions of relief) That's evidence that I am. And now I'm asking Eddie to relax. I'm asking myself to relax. "Why don't we just be quiet for a moment and just be together. This has been intense for both of us." This is toward the end of the session. I give him very little in this depleted place . . . I'm saying it more for myself. I say, "Eddie we've had some really meaningful personal contact this week that provoked something very intense in you. This is what happens when we get this close and we have this much good time together. We're going to spend some time looking at this. How should we end?" He wants to pray. And that's something we've done before. He just reaches out and holds my hand. This is interpretive touch, in that this is concrete touch that fills him back up, that he has learned allows him to stay present for a while longer. He regains vitality through my containment, our touch, and our silent prayer together. I'm feeling relieved. We can touch and we can have a true connection that he isn't terrified of. The silent interpretation is that we can weather this and be together. Now he's able to pray to Jesus and not be pulled into a psychotic dimension. The session ends not quite as nonpsychotic as I'd like it to be, but enough for now. I say, "We're going to have to be talking on the phone this weekend. I want you to go home and take a Trilafon. I want you to go home and listen to your music. I want you to take care of business and do only what feels good." Then we say goodbye and he leaves. So this was our week.

Larry: We only have a few minutes remaining. Do you have a summary or a follow-up?

Sean: We had set up an experience of the psychotic transference that we were able to analyze in the following two meetings in a phenomenal way. That's about all I can say right now. I would love to say how the analysis of that transference has brought him into better ego function, created more ego space, and brought us closer together via more connection with others in his life. Everything about Eddie is vastly more functional than when we began. His teeth are back in now, he's feeling better than ever, and he's physiologically much better. It's clear we reached a core experience.

Jeanne: Can I ask you a question? Did he come back and apologize for what he said to you or for screaming at you?

Sean: What's there to apologize for? No, he didn't apologize, because I had invited the expression and he gave it to me.

Larry: "We both knew that this was what we've been trying to do. So there's no reason to apologize." They both knew the experience was transference expression and not real.

Jeanne: Does he acknowledge that "I did it," or "We did it?"

Sean: Yes.

Larry: It's not that he did anything to Sean. It's that "We did something together."

Jeanne: That's acknowledged by him?

Sean: Right. I'm being used. He's using me for transference experiencing.

Larry: Your experience is very moving to hear about, Sean.

Sean: I'm very excited. As I think about the next two sessions that followed and how we analyzed the transference, Eddie said many important things to me about his past, his mother, and the demons. He was alert, thinking, and intact. He could have been here with us today dressed normally, feeling like us, and being able to read in the book about how he appeared on his first session eight years ago. This is not to say that if something were to hit him broadside tomorrow he wouldn't regress. Nor is it to say that our transference experiencing is over. I don't know about these. But I do know we finally got to a place in his infancy where he experienced monstrous terror and rage. Some of what he expressed was an infant raging at his mother for coming too close, for traumatically intruding. Some of it seemed to be identification with the aggressor—his raging at me and frightening me the way his psychotic mother did him. He needed to relate his infant needs to her, but she found them intolerable and tried to frighten him away by raging intrusiveness. He knows that I have a personal need to relate to him and he must attempt to frighten me away. I feel good about our work.

Group: Good! You should! Congratulations! Great work! Thank you for sharing this. It's been very insightful.

TWO-WEEK FOLLOW-UP

Larry: Today is an update of where your work with Eddie is?

Sean: Yes. In order to bring you up to last Friday's session, Eddie's recovery from an encounter with his "internalized psychotic mother" is incredible. It's important to know how he's benefiting from the effects of interpretive touch, and from analyzing that critical moment that we shared together. This form of analysis is what is giving him the ability, in my opinion, to recover and to be in a better place internally—being more aware, thinking about himself, and having his whole life in a much more functional place. I believe it's systematic analysis of his organizing structure, not just anything that's supportive, that's making a real difference in Eddie's life.

Three weeks ago, Eddie comes into the room very well dressed. This is the beginning of our setting up a week in which we're going to be together for three sessions and we're going to have phone contact every night. In our minds, we've set up the idea that we're really going to be together. He and I both know in our own ways that we're setting up a context for a regressive episode to emerge in a managed way where we're both safe, so the event can be understood later on. To me, analysis is living through an emotionally re-created experience and then finding ways to understand it.

Larry: How did you set up this new format with three hours of contact and nightly phone calls? The two of you have done a lot of work to get there, so that he realizes that something important is going to happen in the middle of this. How did you two get there?

Sean: Through years of coming at it from different angles. And from failing miserably to succeeding a little bit and giving him the idea in the most concrete ways possible. Especially in the last two years through his reaching out and touching my hand at the end of the session to pray—that we are here not just to be together as doctor and patient or as friends. But here to contrive an environment to understand a part of himself that needs to be analyzed in order for his life to be transformed. So literally, two years of saying it to him nonverbally. And verbally giving him the theory as directly as I would give it to you, to see what I could get away with. And even though much of the theory goes over his head, every now and then he surprises me and says, "Okay, you mean . . ." and he rephrases it quite accurately to me. I was prepared through caring about this man—I really love this man—and being persistent. I get ten percent of his limited income—I get as much as he can give me. It really puts him in a difficult place when he pays me. But you know the money is really down on the list as far as a reason to deal with this person. I'm learning tremendous amounts from this man. I find myself caring about him deeply and wanting to be very persistent with him.

Cindy: He's moving toward the spiritual. His need to pray is one thing, but when this all comes to a head, you two will have achieved a spiritual union that he will be able to move from alone. This is symbiosis and individuation happening live as Searles teaches us about.

Sean: That's a good comment. Because one of the things we've been trying to do more consciously in the last two years is give him the ability to connect together with himself, with his deeper personal and spiritual dimensions without being pulled into the psychosis. It's very difficult for him to do. Typically, what will happen is the minute he begins to talk about anything remotely spiritual there are demons in the room, and he's lost. And all of a sudden things are different—he's lost the spiritual in favor of dropping into the psychotic.

Larry: There is a difference between being spiritual as in being tuned in to one's self and others in the universe and in the symptomatic experience of religiosity.

Jeanne: Does this "spiritual" have any reference to any type of religion?

Sean: No. It's spiritual in the broadest possible sense.

Gary: From the way you talk it seems like you know where you're going and that you've prepared him for where you're going. I wondered if perhaps he was going to be surprised? Does he know that you're taking him to a place where he's crazy, where he's psychotic?

Sean: He now has a clear, if not intuitive, idea of what we're doing. He's able to conceptualize it at times and to talk about it and to see it. So in a sense he knows what we're doing, although that sense can easily get lost.

To summarize, three weeks ago Eddie came in color coordinated and well dressed and I complimented him on it and he takes the compliment. Right away he's off to a good start and he knows that we've got this week ahead of us where we're going to be together. Additionally, Eddie is able to see my attendant hand me some coffee at the beginning of the session. As I was setting my office up first thing that morning he was noticing it. He wanted to help my attendant and we had our first three-way interaction, a little dispute among us, and a little laugh and enjoyment. As we go into the second session of the week—Wednesday—he's able to come in and feel good about himself. Again, color coordinated and talking about his struggles in his world and at home. Recently he moved. His homeless shelter moved. He used to live within the homeless shelter with the homeless people and the psychotic people. The new place he moved to has an apartment for him off to the side of where the clients stay. That concrete separation is very important because it seemed to differentiate him a bit from a crazy part of himself. He can go into the craziness of the shelter and come out of it with his own separate place where he can be sane. He's able to grasp this internally because it has concretely happened in his external life. It helps him to differentiate this. On the third session of that week, Friday, Eddie comes in very paranoid. There was a policeman patrolling his area that morning, and he began to think that the cop was after him, was going to intrude upon him, arrest him, beat him up. He has in the past had a lot of bad experiences with policemen. But this morning was delusional because as I listened to the story it seemed clear the policeman was only patrolling. So as Eddie is coming to our session he's looking in his rearview mirror, thinking the policeman is following him. By the time he's in my office the voices are there. I'm sensing there are visual hallucinations, although I don't ask. At first it feels as though he's talking about a third party, the cop. All of a sudden it begins to feel as though the rage is being directed at me. Then he's yelling at me saying, "You motherfucker! You cops! You fucking bastards aren't going to hurt me! Do you hear me!" I start to feel scared. We're on a rare edge here with him being so present in the room and so intense. So I determine to stay with it as long as I can. I reassure myself that this man is not going to get up and hit me, this man's not going to do any damage. He's feeling something very deep and very intense. He's in a psychotic place. I'm feeling scared, but I'm gauging when I may need to shut this down. I say in effect, "Go ahead. See if you can stay present with me and tell me about it." As he does so he's drawn into directing his anger, his rage, his delusional thinking right at me, where "Those mother-fuckers are trying to hurt me. I'm not going to let them hurt me!" But it has an insinuation that it's me that's trying to hurt him. That's what I'm feeling. I was able to stay with Eddie raging nearly a half hour until I became too scared and backed off. I ask Eddie to calm down. He calms right down—which I take as indicative of a lot of control we've gained through connection over our eight years together.

Gary: Before you go on, are you saying that he was paranoid, and that the paranoia was really directed at you? And your sense that it was directed at you has something to do with your knowing that you were going to take him to this transference place where he was going to get psychotic? And that he intuitively knew that this is where you were taking him?

Sean: Exactly. At that moment it was intuitive. He would not have been able to conceptualize it in his mind then. In better places he would have been able to conceptualize that and talk about it. We've both known that for some time now we've been creating a frame in which Eddie could do just that—direct something at me, this paranoia, this psychosis—in such a way that we could simultaneously both be safe and as intense as possible.

Larry: So that whatever he's working to experience, to break loose of, can be safely contained.

Sean: Right. I knew he would need the weekend to recover from the intensity of it. But Eddie missed most of his sessions for the next two weeks! And I also noticed for myself that I was ready for a bit of a break to recoup. And to think about our week and about that session in particular!

Finally Eddie comes in last Friday, two weeks later. We had talked fifteen minutes three times each week between. I called him up to let him know I'm here, to ask him how we're doing, and to do some chit-chat. I can feel his mind slowly recovering from this intense experience we had—so that he can come in and we can analyze what happened. That's what he seems to be doing. He had experienced with me a controlled breakdown of reality testing and he was shaken and exhausted. There are moments when he would be able to say in more concrete, less sophisticated ways exactly what I'm telling you now. I felt like I needed a bit of time too. The recovery time is important because we each needed time to think about it, to process the experience inside ourselves.

Gary: Can you in one sentence tell me what you were scared of?

Sean: I was afraid he was going to punch me. My higher self that knew we had worked years to frame this moment was working hard to evaluate and rule out the possibility of real violence. But I'm allowing myself to feel the fear because it's giving me information about him and about the terrifying transference.

Larry: The violent nature of the transference?

Sean: Right. Even though I know it's not going to really happen, it touches something in me and it's scary. A half hour is a long time to go with the intensity of it.

Larry: You may also be picking up his temper while being in that state.

Sean: I think I am.

Larry: Your sense of needing to contain him—not just for you, but also for him.

Sean: Right. This man does not want to hit me. And this man is terrified and in the hot seat this month. He is so afraid. He also "forgot" to take his medication that morning. Four years ago that would have just been an organizing slip. But these days, the way Eddie is thinking and processing, he forgot, and forgetting has a different meaning. You see, that's him saying, "Let's take it to the edge." Forgetting is different now from our first years together. He's got more ego functioning now. He can forget with purpose.

Cindy: During this recovery period he can't take in any comfort from coming to be with you?

Sean: He's not able to come to my office and take any comforting from me. It takes a tremendous amount of effort to even be able to talk to me on the phone. He's able to repair his car, to help the psychotic people in the homeless shelter, to clean up his apartment, to have contact calls with me, and he's able to repair himself. So he's able to comfort himself, which is another ego function that he didn't always have. But he could not, or did not, or chose not to take comfort by actually coming to be with me during his recovery time.

Last Friday Eddie comes in. He is well dressed again, feeling good, and his dentures are in and fitting right. Looking as good as I've ever seen him, and I told him that too. He's thinking clearly, no delusions, no hallucinations, no pain in his body. The first thing I notice is how he comes in and how good I feel about that. Immediately I'm able to move closer to him. I'm able to feel a sense of contact with him, and he with me that feels again at a deeper level. And now what we get to do, now that we've reached this place, is to *talk* about what's happened! And that's what we do.

Gary: All right!

Sean: Here's how you all have taught me to help him to talk about that moment. Because, you see, now he's coming here to talk with me about that place. So how have I shown him, how has he learned it? We've learned a connecting-disconnecting set of interactions, through just operationally doing them over and over. With me getting away with any words I can think of to say at the time. But we're going to do it again now and talk about it too. We're in a kind of reciprocal rhythm. We're in a kind of symbiotic rhythm where we're going to analyze that one session—not only through action, containment, and touch, but through putting words to it. And exchanging emotionally. We're in a process of learning connections that's gradually being stretched out further and further, slowly lengthened, conditioned together. When we do have moments of the internalized psychotic mother transference appearing it's intense, but there's a rhythm to our ways of dealing with it all—now, here. I think there's a developing symbiosis in our structure and in our process that this man has never had before.

Larry: Kohut often talked of periodic sessions containing "summarizing reflections." Times when two people struggle to put into words the nonverbal processes and resonances they had been experiencing over several weeks or months. A set of events happens that the two live through together. Every few weeks there comes a session in which two people reflect and summarize what's been going on.

Sean: Not only did the internal psychotic mother appear, but everything in Eddie's life broke down that week afterward and he had to repair himself. So these are now summarizing reflections from repairing his car, his clients, his room, to his life, to what in the hell happened in that session. So, he's got his glasses on, and he had his dark sunglasses this time, not just his dark prescription glasses. Once again showing me he doesn't need his prescription glasses to see because he drove. He's got those big dark sunglasses on again and a big smile on his face. And he's waiting for me to ask him . . .

Cindy: He's really screened off again, but he's teasing you?

Sean: I said, "Eddie take off those sunglasses!" He lets out his big laugh and he takes them off and he sets them aside. Right away we were off to a good start, because we were both humorously transported back to that early period we went through playing peek-a-boo together and how we each understand the sunglasses. He's able now to take them off and laugh. We look into each other's eyes and we laugh together. And he's feeling good and I'm feeling good. It's sunny out after the rains and green—just a beautiful day. And so right away we're set up in a good place. I'm wanting him to begin the talk about the session because it always feels more productive than if I prompt him. I don't like to do much prompting. So, I'm playing around. I'm asking around a bit, waiting to see if he's going to lead in first so I don't have to. He brings it up first by saying, "Remember, that day I forgot to take the medication?" I say to him, "You know Eddie, it's interesting how forgetting these days is clearer than it was in our early days." He laughs, because he remembers his psyche being a collage, a mishmash with no order. So right away he's bringing up Friday by indicating to me that he "forgot" to take his medication. I said to him, "Well, what do you think that was about?" His response was, "I wasn't feeling as though I needed it that day or that I wanted it that day." This is Trilafon, which he takes daily. The dosage he takes varies but it's come down quite a bit. He takes another medication for side effects. I ask him what he remembers about the session. He remembers sitting in the chair. He remembers feeling the chair and feeling as though not only was he being attacked, but that he was attacking. And he felt as though he was going to go crazy. He felt the room was spinning. He felt very angry. And he felt very confused at the time. And so I'm listening to him talk. I pointed out to him, "You know it seems like, Eddie, whenever we meet a lot, whenever we have more phone calls, it seems like that's always a time when you have this kind of experience." And he goes, "Yes," realizing it. And then I go, "Eddie, why don't you give me your thoughts about that." He laughs, he thinks for a bit, and he begins to talk about how he's longing to be very close. He talks about it in the context of women. He talks about how he wants closeness with women, but how it's terrifying for him. How, whenever he gets close, the women always turn on him. He's referring to girlfriends and his ex-wife. He says he doesn't know how to get close in a safe way. We agree that we're somehow learning about why he can't have a rewarding relationship with a woman.

All the time we're talking about his needs for closeness and how women turn on him, there's moments of laughter, there's a flow to the conversation. I'm feeling very focused because I'm very interested in how he experienced that session and how he contextualized it. I asked, "How did you experience me in that session?" He said he felt me as far away, and he felt me as attacking. And yet he felt as though he were going to attack me—all at once.

Jeanne: Confused.

Sean: In that session he was confused. I then asked, "When you were here, the way we were in our last session—tell me about the times when you've experienced that before." I was cautious with that question because I didn't just want him to get off into listing psychotic experiences he's had all his life. I wanted something more fine-tuned, more relevant to our context and earlier—more etiological. I was trying to go for that. Eddie begins to talk about his mother and how his mother was. This is where I found out that his brother was three years younger, not nine months younger. And how his mother was always taking care of all of his cousins, all of her sister's and brother's kids, so she was never around for him. And then he begins to talk about how as he grew up he had to take care of his older sister's kids. And how he offered to take care of her kids because she really wasn't able to and how he spent a lot of time raising these kids. Then in the end when he wanted to go off on his own Lupe was very angry with him. "You can't leave me. How could you do this to me?" She was attacking and very angry, and he was very angry back at her. "I've spent all my teenage years helping you out and now that it's time for me to move on you're angry with me. For that I'm angry with you."

Gary: Which fits with the same rage you experienced with him in the session.

Sean: Yes, so all three of those components are there.

Larry: It's interesting that he's associated this directly with when it's time for him to move on, to experience some separateness, some oppositional energy.

Gary: He's doing so well at this point in time, I wonder if he's having thoughts about moving on, ending therapy. He's wondering if you're going to get mad at him.

Larry: Yes. It may well have occurred to Eddie by now that there may be a world for him without Sean, life after therapy!

Sean: Yes. That's a possibility. Up until now our relationship has always been framed like we're just going to be around forever.

Gary: Maybe it's easier for him to deal with it that way—you being angry with him, than for him to experience something different like maybe positive feelings. Maybe it's easier to be angry than to feel separate or sad.

Larry: The possibility comes up that somewhere it's dawned on him that he may be able to live without you some day. And that sense allows these associations to go back to leaving his sister.

Sean: When he moved out on his own he got a lot of resistance from the family for doing it.

Larry: When he was 3, he moved away from mother. We had learned before that he felt her distant attacking around the birth and care of his brother. Now the attack is linked with separation.

Sean: I noticed in the two sessions leading up to that Friday session where he was very psychotic that we were having a good time. We were jostling personally and humorously back and forth over the issue of his hiring a lawyer.

Larry: So part of it was you having an "I–Thou" confrontation with him on actually growing up?

Sean: Right. I was being angry with him saying, "Eddie, you can't do this. You don't have five hundred bucks." And he was able to get angry back with me, but see . . . he said, "Sean, I can do what I want to do." It went back and forth, but the opposition was done in a way we could stay connected to each other. I never could relate to him this way earlier. He can now tolerate me saying, "No Eddie, you should not do this. It's not good for you."

Larry: We're seeing that the two of you are establishing a certain degree of separateness. He is living out separateness with you by fighting in this way.

Sean: And I'm able to tolerate his anger very easily, but he's very persistent.

Larry: The new question all of this raises is, "Do some of Eddie's traumas have to do with when as a child he turned away from mother?" Beginning with birth, there's the ever-present problem of being with mother and then of turning away from her—even in terms of early connections—looking at mother's eyes and then turning away. So, you see, by giving this Lupe association, and then the association of when he lost his mother to his brother when he was 3, is Eddie trying to show us that the disruption has something to do with separateness?

The paradigm that may help us here is the one we see in videotapes of mother–child interactions—half the screen has the mother and half the screen the child, so you can watch their interaction. You see a lively interaction and then the child averts his or her eyes, almost as if to process. And you can see the empathic mothers allow that processing and wait until the child turns back and then pick up the play again. The intrusive mothers go after the child, or get discouraged, angry, or turn away. From the very beginning children have an awareness of the maternal presence and a turning from it. In early infancy we can't talk meaningfully about separation in a psychological sense, but simply of achieving some degree of momentary togetherness and separateness. Is this material pointing to some very early traumatogenic event? When infant Eddie turned away to process something, or when mother turned away while he still needed her . . . What happened? I don't think we know yet. But the suggestion is that in-your-face rage is involved.

I witnessed an incredible scene in an airport some years ago. It was the year when we first had to go through security checks. My wife and I were headed off for Christmas vacation. The airport was in pandemonium. Planes were late, lobbies were full, people were angry and impatient and nobody knew what was happening—a regular mob scene. We were all checked in at the gate. The air conditioning wasn't handling the crowds well. We were literally sitting all over the floor, with bags, Christmas packages, and children everywhere. And there's this incredible scene. This little 3-year-old kid was running out of control around and all over through this—the mounds of suitcases, packages, and people. He's moving right up into people's faces and talking to them loudly, insistently, angrily, and anxiously. I don't know quite how you can tell at 3 but everyone could see the kid was obviously crazy. People were wondering, where is his mother? I'd never seen such odd, bold, intrusive behavior like this in a child so young. Finally, he goes back to touch base with mother. You won't be surprised to hear that she moves right into his face in the same forceful way! He tries to turn away to avoid her and she *forcefully turns his head back toward her* in-the-face rage. She's obviously and overtly crazy. She's holding that poor child in connection with her hand on his face, in captivity when he wants to escape. Of course he's identified with the aggressor, turned the abuse around, and does the same intrusive thing to everybody else. I thought, "We've got the makings of schizophrenia here," in the sense that there's angry forced connection accompanied by terrified withdrawal and disconnection. There's an intrusion into the child's cause-and-effect processes. Mother demands to be seen, to be heard—in times and ways that do not make sense to the child's natural reality processes. But he turns passive trauma into active victory in order to learn the crazy interaction. His reality testing will be as bad as hers!

Sean: The child is disconnected internally from the forced connection.

Jeanne: I remember doing that!

Group: (Laughter)

Larry: I don't think we know yet from the material, but the screen memory with Lupe is interesting in that it points to-

ward the original trauma being associated with a sense of separateness. The transference episode starts off with a three-way
interaction and then your achieving separateness by being on
his case with him fighting back. There is the possibility that
someday there will be a world without Sean, without therapy!
Please review for us that three-way interaction with Mullon
in this light.

Sean: My attendant was helping me with my coffee to place it
where I could drink it. And Eddie was looking on, saying, "No,
no, I can do that." And interacting with him *wanting* to do that.

Larry: So, whether that's the brother, the third party, or the
mother's preoccupation, that situation opens the three-session
week in which we have a psychotic regression. It's a touch of a
three-way interaction. Then several days of jovial opposition
between you two.

Sean: The first thing that actually happens is the triangle that
leads us into Friday—we regress from the three-way, through
narcissistic, to the symbiotic-oppositional, and finally to the
psychotic-delusional.

Larry: Yes. Following it all, you allowed the craziness to reach
violent proportions and then you called for containment of it.
And he quickly allowed it to be contained.

Sean: I said, "Eddie, you've got to calm down." He went from acute
tension to a drooping. It stopped. And I felt immediately relieved. I had it in control again.

Cindy: Wow, that's like a burst in the balloon.

Sean: He was deflated.

Larry: What seems important to me is that the regression after the
growth was demonstrated and then the regression followed by
the containment, which he allowed. The *ego flexibility* is the
impressive thing. Sean was able to reach out firmly with his
voice, "I need you to calm down now," which is what we do with
babies when they become agitated.

Beth: I was just sitting here thinking that we all function with all
of these things hidden in us. It's our ability to move back and
forth, our flexibility, that really counts.

Larry: Yes. Isn't it amazing! Because we all in our own ways have
this disconnecting part in us too.

Sean: I'm in my own therapy now and it makes it more difficult in some ways and easier in others to be with Eddie, because I'm aware that I'm struggling with the same issues he is but in my own way.

Larry: You can have more empathy for what Eddie's going through.

Sean: You bet! Hats off to Eddie!

Group: Hats off to Eddie!

HEDGES' COMMENTS

Again, we are treated to a rare moment in the therapy with an organizing transference—a moment when paranoid delusion and rage is aimed squarely at the therapist in a carefully framed, "out-of-control" expression or episode. At such moments the safety of both parties must be assessed and actively monitored *by both parties.*

I want at this point to take the opportunity to comment on an essential aspect of psychoanalytically oriented psychotherapy—the "as if" quality, or the mutually agreed upon game that speaker and listener engage in for a therapeutic or analytic purpose. This aspect of therapeutic processing is distinctly different from any realistic "holding," "containing," and/or "re-parenting" aspects of the therapeutic relationship. I and many others have attempted to distinguish re-parenting, ego-building, and *constructive* "educational" relationship-building processes that sometimes go on in psychotherapy from the more crucial dismantling, taking apart, destructive, "analytic" processes that have always essentially characterized psychoanalysis but are sometimes difficult to conceptualize apart from the ego enhancement or psychological growth aspects of therapy.

Freud's original psychoanalytic formulations centered on the 4- to 6-year-old psychic structures he named the *Oedipus complex*, which were understood to be accessible to verbal-symbolic interpretations. That is, since the repression of once conscious impulses was originally accomplished by the symbolizing mind of an older child, the analysis or breakdown of these inhibitory structures can be accomplished by verbal-symbolic means. The chess-styled game required for the classical analysis of oedipal structures can be accomplished with words, symbolic gestures, and silence. But earlier developmental structures cited as narcissistic and borderline by writers such as Kohut, Stolorow, Winnicott, and Bollas require a certain preverbal or paraverbal living-out in the here-and-now therapeutic relationship before they can be secured for the breakdown process that has always characterized psychoanalytic therapy. This is essentially because the early developmental structures targeted to be broken down by the analytic process were established before words and symbols were developed or fully useable and are therefore embedded instead in established patterns of affectively laden interactions that show up in a person's daily ways of relating to people. Writers such as Searles, Giovacchini, Grotstein, Tustin, and Hedges have targeted for the analytic breakdown process the earliest psychic structures that formed as the first psychological bridges between the developing mind of the child and her or his mothering partner were organized. Therefore, the subject of this book, *Terrifying Transferences*, could refer to psychic structures established at any developmental level, but are most likely going to be the product of the earlier developmental modes before the child began to establish reliable relational and verbal skills to deal with intense and overwhelming fears.

The "as if" or game quality of the psychoanalytic encounter necessarily persists in the analysis of structures built at all levels, although the encounter seems more "realistic" when working on developmentally earlier levels where the issues are farther removed from symbolization. That is, at all developmental levels of psychic structure brought for analysis, two people engage in a real relationship for a purpose—the purpose of bringing into the relationship for both to see and to know about, long-standing emotional relatedness habits and patterns so that they can be known, talked about, and lived with together. And in the process of living and talking they are giving a new symbolic place and perspective in both peoples' lives—the very meaning of "consciousness." (See Appendix A for a discussion of this essential aspect of duality in the therapeutic relationship as contrasted with other forms of damaging and exploitative duality.)

While this process of bringing forth from the "unthought known" (Bollas 1987) or putting words and symbols on heretofore unrepresented, unreflected, and unsymbolized psychological habits may require different kinds of techniques for different developmental levels in differently structured people, the aims of the psychoanalytic process remains the same. The subject of *Strategic Emotional Involvement* (Hedges 1996) is the contrast of different developmental structures and their differential accessibility through various kinds of emotional strategies that serve to bring transference and countertransference material into the known of the here-and-now therapeutic setting and relationship. Through representation and symbolization of heretofore unavailable, unknown, and unconscious psychological habits or psychic structures in the therapeutic relationship, both participants develop more *flexibility* in their ways of knowing about, processing, and participating in relationships.

In Sean's intense encounter with Eddie we can see how long it took to build safety in the relationship and how many years it took for the two to develop a language and a style of experiencing and talking about the deepest transference aspects of their relationship. At the moment of the encounter Sean tells us that he is clearly experiencing an ego split, that there is a part of him committed to experiencing the fear that Eddie has come today to show him. And there is a part of him that is observing, reviewing the safety nets, remembering their purposes, chuckling to himself when he finds that Eddie has "forgotten" to take his meds today, and conversing with his supervision group in his head, being sure that everything is in order and reassuring himself that this is a "focused, intentional, and controlled out-of-control" experience. For Eddie's part, he checks out the relationship on Monday and Wednesday to be sure everything is in place between himself and Sean. Then Wednesday night and Thursday he allows the regression to develop and cues Sean in over the telephone, so that by Friday morning Eddie is flying on the wings of his lifelong persecutory madness. The two meet in an emotionally intense encounter, Eddie using his sunglasses as a device to alert them both to the break in realistic contact that this episode entails. He even slips Sean the information that he is winging it today without his anti-psychotic meds. The in-your-face rage that has tormented Eddie a lifetime and from which he has been forced by the world to retreat is now to be given full reign and they both know it and live it fully for thirty minutes. Finally Sean says he can't take it any more, asks Eddie to stop, and Eddie collapses, totally depleted, the message from the depths of his soul at last fully expressed, fully heard and responded to.

There are many ways to understand such an intense interaction, but I am at this moment most fascinated by the "as if" quality, the analytic game of discovery and how these two play it. We see in the follow-up the memories that emerge and the new representations that develop between Sean and Eddie with the later expectable relief on both sides, and notably better functioning for Eddie—and for Sean as well. We cannot fail to be transformed by such deeply involving experiences.

In thinking about this complex communication situation, I want to cite a previously published vignette that I have used to illustrate the "freezing" quality of the organizing transference (Hedges 1994c and in Appendix F). Midway in the analysis of a woman with deep "organizing pockets," she would lapse into prolonged periods of silence that I had no way of understanding. There was no ideation that she associated with these silences but she noticed that it seemed important to keep her body absolutely still and rigid, to remain totally immobile on the couch, and to make no noise whatsoever. Then she began to notice that her ears were riveted on any sounds that I might be making—breathing, moving, sniffling—I was appalled at how many different noises I could make during a silent period! On days when I was restless inside, or "slightly off," or mentally preoccupied she sensed it all. Then she remembered having been told that her terribly quiet and shy mother was terrified to pick up her new baby for fear of "breaking it." And soon came a cascade of fantasies and memories of what she had been told and even seemed to vividly recall of long days lying in the crib tracking mother's activities through the house with her ears, trying to be quiet so mother would be encouraged to approach, then pretending to be dozing so mother would sit nearby, then absolutely not moving a muscle so mother wouldn't be frightened and go away. What agony it must have been for this infant to learn how to be all those ways so that some rudimentary connection could be experienced. And how painful were the various ways those relational habits had colored all of her relationships throughout her life and were being experienced in the analytic transference. But what I want to bring out here is the contrived, false, manipulative qualities of the silences that I first began to experience in the transference and the impatience I felt in the countertransference with what seemed like a contrivance I thought I was supposed to be patient with. It was only when I was able to address the forced quality of her silences and how oppressive they seemed for her (and for me) that her awareness of what they were expressing began to expand.

That is, just as Eddie the client is sincere in his expressions and must revive infantile states in the here and now that both he and Sean know are not fully authentic at present, the woman who was frozen in impotent rage *had to introduce a contrivance developed and practiced by her infant self in order to bring her childhood reality* into the interpersonal reality of the analytic situation to make it known. Likewise, Sandy (Hedges 1994a,b) in "The Development of a Transference Psychosis" forces eye contact and hugs at the end of the hour that serve to rupture contact with her analyst but that she later sees were originally manipulations designed by the baby to get what she legitimately needed and was deprived of.

In another instance a woman gradually made clear she was sensing that considerable physical contact was going to be required for some yet unknown expressive reason, but her male analyst proceeded slowly and cautiously. The client all but gave up the hope of more than token physical contact, trying to respect the analyst's personal preferences and professional boundaries. The analyst did not want to engage in comforting or gratifying physical behaviors that might intrude into or obstruct the analytic process. Nor did he want to engage in physical contact that could conceivably be misleading or misunderstood by a woman seeking to explore a very vulnerable state. At one point when she went into an extended and severe deep shaking, her male analyst came forward with a physical holding response that lasted for more than an hour and even necessitated his sending his next client, a supervisee, away. In the aftermath discussion two things emerged: (1) both were aware of the analyst's not really wanting to engage in the holding and how that countertransference response replicated for her in several important and painful ways the loathing her mother experienced with this unwanted child and how the mother's hatred escalated the child's distress and desperation for maternal contact; (2) during the prolonged holding with the ebb and flow of shaking and clinging and brief periods of some calming, the rise and fall of stress and calm the analyst observed and responded to did not follow an expectable pattern. That is, as the analyst lived through this extremely stressful and physically intimate holding experience with her, something peculiar, manipulative, and seemingly inauthentic was noted. In most infant stress states there are expectable waves of tension and traumatic shaking followed by slow calming and, in time, an overall diminution of the stress. Here the pattern seemed different and the analyst reported to her his sense of the difference and the inauthentic quality during the following session. She was able to make immediate use of that information, even to say that in moments during the emotional crisis she had flashed on the fear that she didn't dare give up the shaking or she would be left alone—the terrifying image of a baby left alone in a dark room on a cold, stainless steel table (to die) came up for her. What slowly became clear was that as a baby she had to generate, fabricate, and prolong an extreme state of stress in order to get her mother to hold her at all and not to put her down. The stress pattern observed in the analytic holding hour took on this inauthentic and manipulative quality, but neither client nor analyst would have ever guessed such a thing if they hadn't somehow lived through it together. She experienced an immediate and enormous sense of relief and a searching of fantasy and body contractions to see in how many ways her body had learned to produce inauthentic stress in order to ensure survival and some semblance of connection.

I have seen therapists while attempting to be responsive to deep traumatic states get caught for long periods of time in various kinds of physical holding of the client that seemed to go nowhere and made the therapist and consultant very nervous. The client demands the holding and urgently fears death without it. The therapist grasps the urgency of the demand and responds. But without the two processing the hesitations, the loathing, the comfort, the mutual desire, the burden of the whole sequence, third party views or whatever, no interpretation of what the experience is about is possible. At such junctures the therapist does need to examine what countertransference feelings of her or his own may be sustaining this stalemate. *A strong capacity on the therapist's part for deep empathy or for maternal or paternal care can truly get in the way of the analytic process here. Or a strong insistence on the part of the client that she or he must now have what has always been missing in order to be cured can also get in the way of analyzing the terror.* This is where re-parenting, attempting to fill in the gap with curative experiences, and trying to provide for the client the love that has been so long needed are truly anti-therapeutic. This is where therapists get lost, unwittingly overstepping critical boundaries, forgetting that the client is not a baby, or failing to realize that the sensuous needs of an infant translate quickly into an adult body as sexual feelings. How much processing of anything is enough or too much is a fine line that therapists must tread, hopefully with some good third party consultations and not critical blurring of boundaries.

The important point Sean's work and these vignettes bring out is that at the earliest level of making contact with the mothering person many babies have had to learn to read a complex and traumatizing emotional situation and to warp their physical and mental responsiveness in an attempt to hold on to their perceived sources of survival. Thus, early organizing experiences often take on a quality of coerciveness, manipulativeness, and inauthenticity. How such early warped learning sets up vicious cycles with caregivers that persist into later relationships to alienate others is the subject of much current psychoanalytic study.

It seems that several important lessons are to be gained from these observations: (1) therapists need to be exquisitely tuned in to countertransference feelings as vital sources of information (Hedges 1992, 1994c, 1996); (2) when working organizing experiences the connecting/disconnecting dimension must at all times be in the forefront of the analyst's mind so that every detail of relatedness can be scrutinized with this lens; (3) *various aversive reactions that analysts often have to organizing states must not be carelessly overlooked,* either for their connecting/disconnecting potential or for their manipulative, coercive/inauthenticity qualities. The wisdom that every baby is born with is how to track, adapt to, and connect with the available essential source of nurturance, comfort, and survival. When, for whatever reason, there is a deficient or faulty baby–environment meeting, the infant must do whatever she/he can to ensure survival. Being forced to react, to search, to think, to respond before she or he is ready is inevitably traumatic—whether visible at the time or not—and leaves deep organizing scars. It is these scars, like the ones Eddie's schizophrenic mother left him with, that must be brought to light in analysis. Working with these early scars is always a significant strain on the analyst.

15

"Bess, Bess, Why Didn't You Call Me?"

Clinical Contribution by Virginia Hunter

HEDGES' COMMENT

Over the years I have had occasion to hear about many suicides, but none more perplexing than the one you are about to read. After many years I decided to ask Virginia Hunter to review her 1970s work with Bess for us. In the final analysis Virginia still asks herself, "Why did Bess do it? Wasn't there something else I could have known, interpreted, said, and enabled her to put into words? Was there something else I could have done?" Virginia remains haunted with feelings of betrayal, loss, and anger that Bess didn't call, dismay that Bess couldn't seem to hold on longer, and deep pain that Bess didn't give her a chance to help her when she really needed it. But the truly terrifying thing about what you are about to read is the fated, almost foreordained quality of it all—to the very end. And the emotional scar suicide always leaves on those intimates who survive.

Virginia: Larry Hedges was one of the first friends I chose to see after learning of Bess's suicide. Larry and I go back to our shared time as postgraduate fellows at the Reiss-Davis Child Study Center. He was helpful to me in getting my book [Hunter 1994] to press. He is someone with whom I have shared a lifetime of professional experiences.

Bess became my patient in her late twenties at a time when she was deeply depressed. She was also scared because she had been arrested a number of times for drunk driving and was in danger of losing her license. The attorney whom she had hired to help her deal with these events had become her lover. He had just broken it off with her, and she was having fantasies of "getting him back" by reporting their sexual activity to his wife. She was lonesome and frustrated that he was no longer involved, and furious that she felt he had all the control.

She had a history of going into the scuzziest parts of town or down by the docks and getting drunk in beer bars. She would pick a man up, then go home and have sex with him no matter what color, financial situation, degree of cleanliness, or emotional or physical diseasedness.

Larry: The meaning of going down to the bars and docks, pre-AIDS, is very different from how we might think about it now.

Virginia: Definitely. She had been treated for lice, herpes, and a number of venereal diseases. She came from a dysfunctional armed services family. Her father was an alcoholic. He could sometimes be fun when he was sober, but was always abusive when he was drunk. He was a tyrant with his wife and with his children, and he would often physically and verbally attack them. Bess described her mother as being basically a wispy, passive, not-there, nonconnecting, nonrelating, not aware, out-to-lunch person. Bess had an older brother who, though he did not complete college, ended up doing well in a major retail chain. There was a younger sister, born when Bess was 8, whom Bess hated from the time of her birth. Bess felt the sister took all the mother "that was there" away. She hated that sister. The fact that her sister at age 21 ended up in a mental institution and stayed there for the rest of her life did not lessen Bess's hate for her. She had no empathy for her sister. She saw herself as a tough, clever, funny, intelligent, unlovable "bitch."

Bess began her sessions trying to explain her life to me in a matter-of-fact way, letting me know almost immediately about her anger. She was checking me out. Could I contain and tolerate her anger? She wanted me to know she was a very violent, nasty, sarcastic person, and that she could be outrageously verbally attacking and biting. Would I be able to contain the angry transference? Would I be comfortable with such a "bitch"? Right toward the end of the first hour, I knew it was about time for us to stop and I glanced at the clock to make sure. She felt she had "caught" me. The whole hour then came unraveled, in terms of "You're not going to care. You're afraid you're going to give me one minute too much. You shouldn't do this to patients. You're an incompetent therapist. You probably charge so much so you can afford those fancy clothes you're wearing." Then she teared. This is the first session! In tears, she said, "You won't want a patient who starts off by attacking you. I should have behaved myself." In truth, I was relatively calm. I was concerned, though, with her timing. At that point I said to her, "I think we can manage to understand the attacks, but it's going to be awfully hard on you if you really feel I'm incompetent and a money-grubber. I am willing to help you find another therapist where you might feel a better fit. I, myself, am more concerned about how you will manage our time. I question if our work would survive if you ended hour after hour and went away feeling alienated and feeling that you had attacked me. I'm uncomfortable with our first hour ending this way." She became very calm and very intellectual. She said, "No, I think I can fix that. I think I can time it better. I could have attacked you right when I came in, because you didn't shake my hand. I could have jumped on you right away about how rude that was. I was already thinking, 'Oh she looks fancy, and she didn't even shake my hand. She's probably thinking she's better than me.' I could have jumped on you at the beginning of the hour." It was funny the way she observed the two of us in the situation in terms of, "I'll try to do better about saying what's on my mind and attacking you earlier in the hours."

Larry: It's remarkable that she was so clear about how alienating she could be. And that she could so quickly articulate it.

Virginia: Absolutely. She spent many sessions crying about her lack of friends due to the fact that she felt somehow justified in alienating everybody. She used her giftedness skillfully to accurately find the flaws in others. We started off once a week but soon moved to twice a week. Within four months we moved to four times a week, with a flat monthly fee. She had a biting nasty anger. She had a sort of flamboyance with language that was often brilliant and extraordinarily intuitive. She had come from an uneducated family, but she managed to get a scholarship to a good Eastern school. She had graduated with honors but she was misbehaving all over the place. After completing college, she went off to Africa to work in the Peace Corps. While there, she developed a relationship with an African black man who mistreated her and who later ditched her. That was the crisis that brought her home. She had been raised part of her life in the South and had developed mixed feelings about people of color. She felt his ditching her was a double insult. He was her first ever boyfriend. The fact that a *black* man could reject her made her furious. She had apparently caused such a ruckus with him, hitting him and causing public displays, that she was almost thrown out of the Peace Corps. She was on disciplinary watch because she was expressing her anger at him verbally and physically in public. The Peace Corps was not at all happy with her behavior.

Larry: So from their perspective she was kind of going crazy, getting out of hand?

Virginia: Yes. She was definitely enraged about "How dare he?" She wanted him to say he was wrong, stop his other affairs, and make them up to her. The name calling quickly accelerated to physical hitting.

Where she truly engaged me, though, was in terms of the number of reckless drunken driving episodes she had. She always paid me what she agreed she would pay me, never missed a single session, and always did exactly what she said she was going to do. It amazed me she could drive around drunk endangering herself and others and think nothing of it. She was aware she was going to lose her license and also her job if she continued this behavior. She never drank alone. She wasn't a secret alcoholic. When she felt empty or unconnected, she would go out, get drunk, and pick up men with whom there was no emotional connection, no tenderness, no pretext of even liking each other, and no foreplay. It was just this brutal, "We will connect with each other physically, and soothe and abuse each other, and then we will drop each other." It had a definite quality of reviving all of her aggression in some sort of a sadomasochistic way. She never chose passive men. They were always men who ended up roughing her up somehow. So it was like some "masochistic" part of her that was struggling with an aggressive part of her somehow. She went to these bars and tied up with these guys who were aggressive, who hurt her, and who didn't even pretend that there was anything else except they wanted to "knock off a piece" to soothe or relieve themselves and/or abuse someone else. She described these encounters with ironic humor. It was an interesting way of behaving that of course left her in fear a lot, because if her supervisors or bosses or any of those more upright people had gotten any hint of all this she worried that she would have been fired. She said she was a good dancer.

Larry: So, given the rest of who she was, this was truly a double life—not unlike the Africa episode?

Virginia: A very double life. She also verbally bit at a lot of people at work. She was always having some kind of tadoodle with somebody. And it could be over something she took as a slight, or something she felt was unfair, or something she took as my not having understood. We were in one of these relatedness dyads in the transference almost constantly. I would be accused of being two minutes late. "I think last week you let me go three seconds early." There were constant complaints that she wasn't getting enough or that I wasn't really seeing her. The endless chain of complaints went on for probably three years. She accused me of liking and giving to all my other patients more than to her. In the meantime she began to copy my clothing. She started therapy with one of those shaved up the back of your neck bobs, but eventually, as her hair started to grow out, she began to copy my hairstyle. She was quite comfortable saying, "I think I've matched the polish on your fingernails exactly."

Larry: She knew she was aping you. Why?

Virginia: Why was she? I don't think it was that she didn't have an identity entirely, Larry. I think it was more that she did partly idealize me in some ways and that she envied what she could see of my lifestyle. She was very clear when she said, "I don't have the right people inside of me." She even used that language. She was very comfortable talking about her wish to have someone she could identify with inside her.

Larry: So she just wanted to take you in and she sometimes liked it.

Virginia: Yes . . . but then she could bite me, chew me up, and spit me out just as fast.

Larry: Of course (laughter).

Virginia: She was quite comfortable saying, "I've got 'shit' people inside of me." Very often if she thought I had said something that was terribly clever or wonderful or right in tune, she would say, "That one I'm going to swallow," and she would make a gulping sound.

Larry: (Laughter) She would gulp you right down?

Virginia: She would do it as a joke. She could be quite amusing and open.

Larry: But she also knew there was truth to her need to take you in.

Virginia: Yes. She didn't have that "Oh I can't possibly let you know I'm taking you in." It was, "Give me more so I can take it in."

Larry: She was terribly bright and she had certain levels of psychological sophistication, so she could make a joke rather than feeling phobic about the dependency need.

Virginia: She handled that well. But her attacks when she felt I had made myself unadmirable in her eyes were outrageous. She really kept me on the straight and narrow. She was very fussy about exact wording.

No, it was much more than that. If she created a metaphor about herself or me or our dyad, I was not allowed to initiate its use in our work. I had to find a new metaphor that she judged "good enough," but not hers. This created great difficulty in our attunement, in sharing, in communication, and in mirroring. At times, I had the fantasy that I was engaged in a chess game of language with the mad Queen of Hearts from *Alice in Wonderland*. She could make any rule and change it regarding our connecting with language. At the time it was extraordinarily difficult to work in and with. It had the quality of trying to understand the language of someone who was totally psychotic. It made maintaining, connecting, and emanating with her hard work. I had trouble getting her to sort this out. It seemed clear that she could only tolerate connecting if she had all the power whenever she wanted or needed to have it. It frustrated and annoyed me. It seems to me that it was only when I accepted her rules and could verbalize and appreciate their use did she relinquish the need to make and use them. Describing this would require another paper.

Larry: Would it be correct to say that she wanted to take in the all-good mother and she wanted to spit out any bit of bad mother?

Virginia: Absolutely. She wanted to beat up, confuse, disorientate, and cause chaos for the bad mother or father. She was a linguist who was always accurately finding me mispronouncing words that she would then try to correct for me. I would say, "You are trying to heal me. . . ." That part was sort of funny actually.

Larry: Trying to heal the bad mother?

Virginia: Yes. Trying to teach the bad mother–father how to be a good mother–father. Trying to improve the pronunciation of the imperfect dyslexic object. Two years into treatment she had a severe depression when her application for graduate school was turned down. At that point she blamed me for her having ever applied and having been set up for rejection. She claimed it was my wish for her to go to graduate school and not hers. Then she would back off and say, "No, I always knew I wanted to go on, it wasn't really you." It was a terrible narcissistic injury to get turned down. In truth, that year many people were applying for entry into her field and many highly qualified people were turned down. That narcissistic injury set her back to some acting out with the men again—and a lot more abuse of me.

Larry: So the masochism and the anger are linked to depression, to not feeling chosen?

Virginia: Yes, in part. Around that time she started asking about what I was reading. I have a chair near the door in my office that often has what I'm taking home on it and she would see papers and books and she would comment. Then she starting asking if she could borrow literature. She never disrupted her hours with it. It was interesting, she never came back and simply said, "I was reading about the false self." She would bring in her transference reactions, like "I was reading Winnicott (1949), and I know sometimes I make you hate me and sometimes I hate you." She would associate for many hours about such a subject. She was able to help herself by bringing ideas to therapy that she knew I would be aware of.

Larry: The readings she borrowed from you are psychological readings as opposed to novels?

Virginia: Yes. She would occasionally bring me a flower to say "Thank you." She almost always brought me changes in the laws from the journals or the newspaper that related to my profession. She tried to connect and give back in her own way. She was good at trying to repair the damage she felt she had caused. Even that first session, trying to repair. She eventually did get accepted to graduate school. Her income was not greatly affected because of arrangements to return to her employer for two years after school. She could continue with her analysis. I hardly even heard about school the whole time she was in school. Apparently there was no problem with scholastic work, she just zipped through. It didn't seem to throw her like it does some people. She had some fun wanting to involve me in debating behavioral versus psychodynamic therapies.

Larry: She was studying to be a therapist?

Virginia: Yes. She did fine and she got placed at a large training hospital for her field work. She did well there, they liked her. She had a certain street wiseness. She didn't alienate supervisors or get doctors to hate her like I thought she might. She talked about anger but she didn't act it out. But she still didn't make any deep personal friends.

At some point Bess began a correspondence with a man in India, an East Indian. Eventually we had a serious misattunement over him. She wanted to finance bringing him over—a man whom she had never even met! I questioned, "Why don't you go there and visit him first?" She was very annoyed with me when she sensed that I didn't think she should just sponsor and import him, and marry him so he could become a citizen, without ever meeting him. She was correct that I had an opinion about that. I felt that it might be self-destructive. She would have to vouch for him financially if she brought him over here. He wrote poems to her and she wrote poems back.

On Christmas or a birthday she would bring me her own original poems, mostly poems of gratitude or love. She finished graduate school. She had two episodes where she had taken medication for depression. During the second one, she said to the Indian man that she would come and visit him, and he said, "Bye-bye." He only wanted to see her if she would sponsor him to come here.

Larry: He was willing to have her bring him here and marry her but . . .

Virginia: Yes. She saw that as a victory I had had. She was very angry at me. She said I had ruined her fantasy, and I had in some ways. Because I did think he was a potential danger to her. I thought some of the poetry he claimed as his own was from Kahlil Gibran's *The Prophet* [1923]. When I raised the question that it seemed to me I had read this before she went and looked. And sure enough some of it was copied from *The Prophet*. That was a terrible to-do between us. I had destroyed this for her by raising questions, by having opinions. What did it matter if he had copied some of the poems and represented them as his? Strange too in a special way since I had not been allowed to copy or use "her" metaphors. Until this she claimed she was sure that he was not deceiving her. Now he wasn't the way he represented himself to her. She hated that whole thing.

Larry: Another disillusionment.

Virginia: Yes, and it too was seen as my fault for quite awhile.

Larry: It seems like you're saying that her reality testing was intact enough so she could eventually get a perspective and see that you had been being protective, that you had been pointing things out to her that she didn't want to see. That you had been correct in certain ways. She could see that. But at the level of the deep battle with mother who wrecked everything that she had, she hated you.

Virginia: Yes. That was really tough.

Larry: Any countertransference to report here?

Virginia: I was frustrated with her idea that she could just bring somebody over—a total stranger—and it would work out. It seemed naive. I thought she could do better. She was overweight, but she was a bright gal, and she could be a fun lady in many ways. She was good natured enough that she never had trouble picking up people. But she couldn't maintain connections with them. I thought if she wanted to connect with just any old man she should find one she could get to know before she was on the financial hook. She was right that I was annoyed with her. I felt it was not good reality testing on her part. What she did do was explode. "Why can't I buy a man? I bought you! How else do you get a person? You're the only person I ever felt was connected to me!" She was just abusing me. Despite her rage and hate toward me at that time, she was quite sincere in her questions. Her feeling of not knowing "how to get a person" was sincere. It was a tough phase for us to work through. I would handle this kind of thing differently now. I was lucky she didn't break off her treatment.

Bess then took a couple of cruises to singles' places with Club Med. She went on several and had a good time. She would go to bed with somebody. She would hear from the guys a few times afterwards. Nothing ever really clicked. Eventually she wanted to be in one of my groups. We reduced her analytic hours to three times a week, and she entered an intact group. Both of us felt it was a good idea and that it would hasten her ability to understand herself in relationship to others. Retrospectively I wonder if it was a good decision. But before her death I believed the group was helpful to her. They had occasional activities outside the group. I heard things about her from the other patients that I might not have known otherwise. Things like if they said, "Bring a covered dish, we're having a party," she would be totally in the dark about what to bring. She hadn't a clue how to relate. Not even the idea of going to Kentucky Fried Chicken and getting something. For a very bright person, it was fascinating. She didn't seem to have a concept of how to nourish or provide—even a simple thing like make a salad for other people. This brought up the memory that her mother ate and fed others almost nothing but canned foods. So there was a strange pattern of eating in her family of origin. It makes you wonder if she wasn't right that her mother was a little stupid—not just wispy or out of touch. Both the mother and father died when she was in her early twenties—the father of alcoholism and the mother of cancer. They were young, they went early. She wanted to know what some of my favorite party recipes were. Both I and the group shared with her. She told some very funny stories about her efforts at cooking. One of the other things that came out in group that she never mentioned to me was that she played guitar. She could play well enough that people could dance to it. She had taught herself to play. She had never said a thing to me about it.

Larry: Amazing.

Virginia: I did not attend the group's limited social get-togethers. Bess was a wonderful dancer. She always had more partners than anybody because she was a fabulous dancer and had lots of fun with it. She could be outrageous and funny. Members of the group described her prancing and jigging and shaking her breasts at people while gesturing with her hands for someone to join her.

Larry: What's coming through to me is that she had all sorts of talents and skills that she had evolved and that she was brilliant. But when it came down to the actual nitty-gritty of how to take care of, or be taken care of, or how to have a relationship or a friendship, she couldn't. One way she managed to avoid connecting is with that instant bite.

Virginia: I can tell you another story. I had the only illness I've ever had in my adult life. I was in the hospital for a week with pneumonia, and then I went home on a rainy day to recover. My patients had all been notified that I was out of the hospital. "She is home and will be back to work next week." I had a six-foot wall with a double door with locks in front of my house by the street. You had to walk through an open garden to get from the house to that locked gate. It's pouring down rain. There is this insistent increasing pounding at the outside gate. There had been no phone call prior to the knocking. Eventually, annoyed at the increasing noise, I threw some clothes on and I went out to see who it is. Bess had come to bring flowers. Afterward she spent several sessions raising havoc because I hadn't come immediately, because I hadn't invited her in to visit, because I hadn't been available to her.

Larry: As a sample of social interaction, here is the inappropriateness of her coming to your house and the timing of it. Then there is her not grasping where on earth you were coming from at the time. And then the raging.

Virginia: She was totally unable to see at the time that she had really come to get something for herself more than to give to me. Even her rage wasn't a tip-off to her.

Larry: Did she ever get it?

Virginia: She did. She saw it pretty quickly. The group was helpful to us. The group saw it right away, then sort of jollied her about it. "Don't you think that since it was raining, you hadn't telephoned, and she was recovering from pneumonia, that since they had just let her out of the hospital that day, that she probably wasn't dressed for company, had no makeup on, and didn't feel up to entertaining you . . . ?" That was interesting. That was while she was still in graduate school. Later, I attended her graduation and took her to lunch and the group had a party for her.

Now, two years later, we come to a series of truly unbelievable events. Bess's belief was that when she got out of school and continued to work for two years she would be provided with supervision that would enable her to apply for her license. Later, when it came time to apply to get her license and the state board asked for verification of her hours, her supervisor said she wasn't going to give them to her. We did not have time left to figure all that out. The supervisor said that the work she did wasn't clinical and could not count toward her license. Everybody else had previously gotten their hours counted. So whether Bess had alienated this person so much that she finally "just got" her, or whether, as the supervisor claimed, a policy in the department had changed regarding supervision of graduate students and she had failed to inform Bess, or Bess failed to hear her, I have no idea. Bess's anger did not help her this time. Instead she fell into a deep depression. She suddenly plummeted to flat affect, slow walk, slow talk—it was scary. She began getting deader and deader—there was no life. No life. Suddenly all the life just drained out of her—totally. I referred her back to the psychiatrist. He put her on the same medicine that had helped her before. I saw her every day.

Larry: A major disillusionment. He prescribed antidepressants?

Virginia: Yes. But of course it was going to take a few weeks for the medication to have an effect. Those were the days of the tricyclic antidepressants. In the meantime, Bess continued to collapse—said she just could not go on. She had a flat, flat, dead voice. She had become so flat I couldn't even get her to talk anymore.

Larry: Let me try to process this. She had been at this particular job for a while, believing that the supervision hours were going to count toward her state licensure?

Virginia: Yes. But when it came time to submit the paperwork, her supervisor said the policy had changed and she could not certify the clinical hours.

Larry: Other people did, indeed, get these hours?

Virginia: Not at that particular time period apparently, but in the past they had. The policy had apparently been changed but there was no written record to refer to either way. It wasn't a totally unrealistic expectation on Bess's part. It may have been a misunderstanding or the cruelty of her supervisor. I never knew for sure.

Larry: So she runs up against this woman who says, "No, I will not give you what you want."

Virginia: So in Bess's view she has lost two years of collecting supervision hours toward her professional license.

Larry: But you're also saying that she keeled over relatively easily.

Virginia: Yes. It was astounding. She was basically not getting a response from the department other than verbally that the policy had changed. She didn't have their promise in writing. They sponsored her through two years of school and she was obligated then to work for the agency for two years. She understood that during those two additional years she would get her hours certified. It had been the procedure in the past. She believed her hours would be signed off.

She may have been caught in an ongoing battle in my field. Many social workers feel that social workers, even those with advanced clinical training and degrees, should remain totally committed to only the downtrodden. It was known that Bess had other aspirations for herself.

Larry: What is your bet on why she didn't find some effective way to right that wrong?

Virginia: Because she killed herself.

Larry: But she doesn't sound like an ineffective woman. Why did she fail?

Virginia: Larry, I don't know why she failed. I really don't know. I don't think she knew why she failed either. The psychiatrist couldn't understand. None of us understood why. She had found another job that defined the giving of the supervision hours in a contract. It would take another two years, but she would do it. Somewhere, right in the middle of this decision, when she was going to start a new job in thirty days, the new job got cut. Now she has to stay in her old job since she has nowhere else to go yet. She was a single person who had to support herself. So she felt she had to stay where she was while she was trying to find another job. Her plan had been to take a vacation before starting the new job. She had accumulated sick leave, so she could have taken her vacation and sick leave to recover.

Larry: But she had to take this humiliating step back instead.

Virginia: She felt there was a good bit of unkindness toward her about it. She had antagonized some people who she felt seemed glad she had been given a good "whack," so to speak. It was a year after the Indian guy had said clearly, "You can't come here to see me. Only send money, and I will come there, you can't come here." He wouldn't even agree to meet her in Europe if she paid the airfare. It was a strange thing—"Send me the money, pay for me to come to America, and marry, or nothing!"

Before all this, she had been talking about thoughts of termination with me.

Larry: How far into the therapy are we now, roughly?

Virginia: We're roughly into seven years. She was thinking about a gradual termination. She had already stopped the group and we were down to twice-a-week therapy. We increased our time when she got so badly depressed. She knew there was no need for us to terminate her treatment until she was ready.

Larry: Is there anything we need to cover about why she left the group, or how that didn't work out?

Virginia: I thought it did work out, it was very helpful for her. She had been in that group for three years. She wanted to go on a trip. She had written her first professional paper. She was also writing poems. She felt ready to leave the group. She had terminated with the group satisfactorily. We had cut back in the previous six months to twice a week. She was thinking that she was no longer on medication or depressed. She wasn't acting out sexually. She was going forward professionally. When she went on vacations, she was sending me poems of gratitude and remembrance. She had accomplished much and we had estimated that in about three more months we would begin to talk more about terminating formal therapy. She knew and trusted we could meet when and if she needed or wanted to.

When she didn't get her hours of supervision certified and felt trapped there, she just plummeted, she couldn't even make eye contact with me. She was like a dishrag. She said she wouldn't go on. The medication didn't help, when in the past it had. I increased her visits up to four, five, and six times a week. She was listless about this, she did it more to please me than because she thought it would help.

Larry: You were reminding her that "we don't have to terminate until you are ready."

Virginia: Of course. At some point when I was questioning her thoughts about suicide—she was ruminating a lot about suicide—she said she really was going to. At that point, after great pressure from me, she went to her health plan and asked them to hospitalize her. The pressure from me involved my verbalized, genuine, and tearful fears for her and of losing her. Somehow that got through, and she finally agreed to seek hospital-ization voluntarily. I made contact with the doctor she would see, explaining that I had been working with her seven years, that she had already seen a psychiatrist and been on medica-tion for four weeks which hadn't helped a bit, that she was speaking seriously and directly of suicide, and that I felt she absolutely must be hospitalized. During her appointment, she told him that she was intent on suicide. But with the psychia-trist she also cracked jokes. He said they could not hospital-ize her except by sending her back to the same hospital where she had done her field placement. She feared being humiliated. She refused to go back as a patient to the place where she had done her placement.

Larry: They couldn't hospitalize her elsewhere because?

Virginia: The psychiatrist said they didn't have another psychiat-ric unit, and he would not put her in a medical bed. I begged him to put her in a medical bed for a few days. He wouldn't do it. She would not go to the hospital that held her medical plan's psychiatric unit where she had done her field placement. There were many people there who knew her, many professional col-leagues—she would not consider it. The medical plan's psychia-trist would only send her to that one hospital.

Larry: She would have to go there because of the requirements of her managed care insurance?

Virginia: So he said. She wasn't given an alternative choice. When I talked to the psychiatrist at that point, he said, "She is saying she's suicidal, but I don't really think that she is. Because she cracked jokes." I said, "Yes, she is suicidal. That's her usual way to save face." He was very dismissing. "The only thing we can do is send her to that hospital. If she wants to go there we will arrange for it." I couldn't get her to go there. He wouldn't hold her on a 72-hour hold.

The next day, which was the last time I saw Bess, she left my office taking an embroidered cross-stitched pillow that my mother had made me. I have written about using concrete ob-jects in the countertransference [Hunter 1996]. Bess made me a promise that if she felt she was really going to act to commit suicide, she would call me and we could meet. I believed her, I truly believed that she would call me first. She had always done what she had said she would. Bess's word was golden. What was I going to do if she called me? In truth, I didn't know. I would certainly see her at my office. We had some things I could consider. Maybe I could have talked her into asking some member of the group to stay with her for a few days after work and weekends. I knew I had to preserve myself as her analyst. She felt she had no backup family in this crisis and refused to avail herself of the one possibility of hospitalization. She would not call her brother. The public sector would have placed her at the same facility that her medical plan offered.

Larry: Both her parents have died. Her sister is permanently hospitalized, her brother lives in a distant state, she had a few friends, but there is no solid support system really.

Virginia: I last saw Bess on Thursday, which was her last appointment. She was still talking suicide. No way—she would not go to the hospital where they were willing to hospitalize her. I was very concerned. I was ready to spring into forcing a 72-hour hold if all else failed. She had always kept her word and she had promised to call me if she needed to, before she did anything to hurt herself. It came time for her Monday appointment, and Bess wasn't there. She had never, in all those years, missed a single appointment or been late for a single appointment. After twenty minutes I called her work and home. At work they had not heard from her all day and were puzzled. I had a terrible, sinking feeling that if she wasn't at work and she wasn't at my office, something really bad had happened to her. It wasn't like Bess not to let me know, totally uncharacteristic. I immediately called the police. I asked them to go check her apartment to see if she was safe. When they got there, the door was unlocked. There was a note to me, saying "thank you" for all I had tried to do for her, that she loved me, and that she hoped I would forgive her. Saying, "The will is in the drawer." It turns out that three years before, quite unknown to me, she had made me an heir to her estate. Three years before she had written a will and never mentioned it to me. Her brother, who was living, was also named. Three years before—it was a bizarre thing! It was like for all this time she was really potentially suicidal. She had

brought me this neat sealed envelope before she went on a
cruise. "Inside," she said, "are my keys, my brother's address, my
sister's hospital address, my doctors. Here is the person who does
my taxes, the person who does my legal stuff." She had a "how
to contact everybody" envelope made up for me. She said it was
just in case she was killed in an accident.

Larry: Three years before?

Virginia: Three years before, which she had discussed with me.

Larry: Everything is there in that envelope, dated?

Virginia: No dates—more a list of who should be notified at her
death. I gave the envelope and its contents to her brother at the
time of her death.

Larry: It came up also at other times when she was thinking of
suicide or going away?

Virginia: Yes. She never asked for the envelope back and I just put
it in her file unopened. In truth, I didn't really pay that much
attention to it. We talked about its various meanings. Sometimes I saw it as a call for my attention. That "You need to be
really worried and upset about me" . . . and I was, I was upset.
But I wasn't that upset because I knew we'd get through it then,
and we both knew it. One time was when she didn't get accepted
to graduate school. That was really tough on her. Sometimes the
envelope came up for her to say I was the closest, dearest person she had had in all her life.

Back to her death. The police called me and said she had
taken all the pills that she had and was dead. She had the cross-
stitched pillow my mother made under her arm.

Larry: Sleeping pills?

Virginia: Sleeping pills, anti-depressants—she took everything she
had. I think she took some Tylenol with it too. To tell you the
truth, I didn't even inquire much, except to learn that it was
an overdose. She had broken her word to me. I was in shock that
she would say she would call me if she needed me, and then she
didn't. I was terribly upset.

Larry: So you were also angry?

Virginia: Yes, later I was angry. I was flabbergasted, devastated,
horribly distressed. What did I do wrong? I sent her to her psychiatrist for medication. I sent her to her medical plan for hos-

pitalization. I'm seeing her four, five, six days a week. She promised she would call me. She didn't. I was grief-stricken, guilty, ashamed, self-questioning, and introspective.

Her brother called me from out of state saying when he would arrive in California. I debated about offering to pick him up at the airport and take him to her apartment. I decided I needed to keep a greater distance. He got in, rented a car, and called me and asked me if I would go with him to the apartment. I said I would. I was worried that he would hold me responsible for her death. The police found the note and told him. He had also heard about me from Bess.

Larry: There is not a lot of property or money?

Virginia: No. Although actually she had taken out a nice annuity insurance policy that had a cash value.

Larry: When?

Virginia: I'm not sure. I believe when she got back from the Peace Corps. When she started her first job they had options. She made me the heir of that sometime during her treatment without telling me. Once she went to her brother's family for Christmas. She felt they were all very distant and unconnected. I believe she may have made me a beneficiary after that visit. I declined everything, of course. The brother took care of the legal stuff and I signed off on any claim anyone might feel I had. The brother wanted me to take something. I took a small drop-leaf writing desk with one small baby drawer and a chair. Symbolically, I think I had the feeling that some day I would be reading there or writing there and something would float into my mind that would let me know what I could have done differently. I have some fantasy still that she is sitting out there on the tree somewhere saying, "Well I hope you'll figure it out eventually, Hunter."

Larry: The writing table also goes back to what you said earlier about words and her correcting you?

Virginia: Yes. Also I knew that it was a simple thing, a token I could put into my car easily and take it with me. It was something the brother wasn't going to take back East with him. He offered neighbors, co-workers, and members of the group whatever they wanted to have to remember her by. He disposed of most of her things locally. There wasn't a great deal besides what the insurance paid. She had a red car that she had been excited about. I had thought she was ready to go off into the world and have a good life.

I still don't know why all of her strengths and her internalization of me failed. She was like a dead limp baby. It just had that quality that she couldn't mold, she couldn't make eye contact, she couldn't cling. No good internalized objects. It was as though she had suddenly lost all substance. Have you ever played with an octopus?

Larry: I've seen them.

Virginia: If you take a little octopus out of the water, it wraps around your arm, and it will make red, sucky spots on you. But if you keep holding it out of the water, it loses all ability to do that and it becomes like limp string. It loses all feeling of substance. It can no longer suck or cling. You could put it however you wanted it and it would stay there and die. It's still painful to think of her choice. Very painful.

Larry: This is over twenty years later.

Virginia: Yes. I still feel, "Bess, Bess, why didn't you call me? You promised you would. I don't know for sure what I would have done, but I would have been with you."

Larry: She knew that.

Virginia: I think she had known that. It no longer mattered to her and yet her last written words were saying she loved me and asking my forgiveness. What irony!

Larry: That makes her choice all that much more puzzling. She knew that you could be there for her. That you would be there for her. That you would help her in whatever way was required because you always had.

Virginia: And she knew that the psychiatrist I share a suite with would do all he could too. He had before!

Larry: What's the pain like now?

Virginia: I think about her rather frequently. I liked her, loved her—I miss her, especially her irony, her honesty, and her cleverness and generousness with her words. I have to pass by her old apartment complex going from my office to the ocean. I still pass that apartment with a little salute to her. When I'm at her writing desk and I'm messing with a sentence that I can't get out right I'll think, "Bess, if you were just here you could write this easier than I can." Because she could. She could clean up text and edit well. She did it for a lot of people who were struggling with their theses or dissertations and she was very good at it. I feel regret. I feel a lot of regret and sadness. And I still have a hard time understanding her choice. She was not ill physically, her cognitive functioning was relatively good—superior in many ways. She was better than ever, with good prospects for the future. It remains puzzling to me.

Larry: When you and I talked about her over twenty years ago, you were in grief. Two things stand out in my mind that I want to ask you about now. I recall that in this relationship with the supervisor at work there were some reality problems with that woman. I believe you felt Bess described her as very distant, unrelated, erratic, and severe—a woman who seemed unreasonably distant to Bess. You had felt there was something about Bess's feeling that cruelty, that frustration, that deprivation, that refusal to recognize and relate to her that replicated an early mothering experience in the face of which Bess collapsed.

Virginia: Yes. Bess had done a lot of work over a considerable period of time in containing her rage. She had worked a lot at recognizing when she was "transferring." That was one of our major pieces of work, trying to help her feel that she could deal with her rage and that she could self-correct, self-soothe, self-protect, become self-aware, self-reflect, and self-organize. It had not been easy, but my theory was that in the rage at that supervisor and her feeling that the supervisor didn't care, Bess regressed and destroyed herself. I tried everything to get her to talk. I tried all kinds of things to try to get at her anger, her despair. Nothing worked! At the time it was easy to want to blame someone—to scapegoat the supervisor.

Larry: But, somehow in there, it seems like Bess also didn't really give it her all—that she gave up.

Virginia: It seemed like she couldn't. It didn't have that oppositional "I'm not going to" quality I had seen in the past. I felt she was unreachable and she may have felt I was too. She didn't seem to care about herself. For sure she felt the supervisor and administration were unreachable.

Larry: What does that potentially tell us about her early encounters with mother—that when she finally re-met her mother, she gave up?

Virginia: This was not something that I thought of at the time. She adjusted well to the group, after a while, though she had tremendous problems in that group that were difficult for all of us at times. There was a young woman in that group. She was a little, petite, wispy person whose father had humiliated her about many things, including saying she was ugly. She'd had an abusive father who verbally attacked her looks. Her mother was unable to protect either one of them. She had a phobia about anybody seeing her without her heavy makeup. The group had been trying to help her explore that. At some point, she decided that the next week she would come without makeup so we could see "her." What happened was that I had opened the door and gone back to my chair. She came late, so the group was assembled as she came into the room. I am probably twice as big as she is, literally. She made a dive for my lap, landed in my lap, buried her head in my bosom, put her arms around herself, and then turned her face where the group could see her. It took me totally by surprise, no prediction of that happening! Eventually she got out of my lap and was able to stand up and sit in a chair. We talked about her memories of attack. Bess came out with a raging attack in terms of "How dare you get in her lap, how dare you get so much attention. How much attention she wanted . . ." And then railed at me, "You'd never let me do that, you would have held me to a higher standard than jumping in your lap!" It was probably true but also an outrageous attack. I tried to contain it—to interpret it. I pointed out that she was really beating up on the "baby duck." Beating a "baby duck" had been words I could use to help contain her in the past. She just kept on, "Your baby duck is inappropriate." Then the patient who has just discarded her disguise starts to cry. Even with that I couldn't get Bess contained or introspective at all. The little person was getting more and more upset. None of us could get Bess to stop or introspect. At that point I ended the group. It is the only time I ever terminated a group early, out of failure to be able to contain somebody's abusive rage. I just said, "We are not having good luck understanding and introspecting about this tonight. I feel now it is not productive. We will continue trying to understand anew next week." I got up and left the room saying, "I will see you all next week." I terminated that group ten minutes early. It was so destructive I felt I had to stop it the only way I could. I tried to protect them both but also not attack the attacker. There was some caution of Bess in the group at times. But at times, people were also helpful in containing for her. They would help her, sort of jolly her: "That's not fair, come on you're doing your 'like your father or mother' thing again." The group often made interpretations that were helpful to her.

Larry: But they were scared of her.

Virginia: They were scared of her use of words, but they also tried to help and contain her. They also enjoyed her. She really did come along. She had a terrific sense of the ridiculous and could put it into wonderful, precise words. She could make people laugh at her or themselves.

Larry: But they also knew there was this really scary side to her?

Virginia: Yes, sharp as a razor. But she also showed the reparative side of herself. She would write poems. There were a couple of years where at Christmas and Valentine's Day, she made a unique poem for every single person in the group. She had them wrapped up with bows. Little four-line poems! So she did things with the group to say, "I'm sorry I rave." The poem would say something special about the person but also be an acknowledgment of what she had done that had injured them. It was both a gift and an attempt to make reparation, to ask for forgiveness.

Larry: So Bess learned with you, from the first session and later with the group, that at a reality level, reparation was possible. I believe at an internal level she continued to hold the belief that it is not possible to bring the mother/other back, and so the self withered and died. She was never quite able to take what she had learned from you and the group and transform the inner delusion of helplessness and despair she learned from her unavailable mother.

Virginia: It still puzzles me though, because I really felt she had taken me in.

Larry: It sounds like at the level of reality she did internalize you. That doesn't mean that the new internalization completely wipes out the first one.

Virginia: It obviously didn't. Though I would expect it to have been "good enough" to sustain intelligent life, Larry. After all these years, I still don't understand it. I still want to say, "Bess, by next month we will be farther along through this. Talk, free associate. Give it a little time. Don't act—float. It will pass."

Larry: She was 8 when her sister was born. She already had a "dead mother"[1] before 8, from infancy on. But it was acted out throughout her childhood, the rage at mother for having a baby duck. I couldn't help but wonder in what ways her rage contributed to her sister's emotional demise. And your therapy was at eight years. I also keep coming back to this supervisor, because my memory is that when I first heard about this, when you were still grieving, there was something really awful about what happened at work or between them. Like the supervisor was legally out of line on more than one occasion in unreasonable and cruel ways and that you hoped she would lose her job because of Bess's suicide.

Virginia: I fantasized suing her. I was distraught and it was easy to want to blame someone else. The supervisor was absent at the funeral, and other workers were aware of her absence. I went and I took a vase of roses and gave everybody a rose. I just wanted to do something. But retrospectively I'm not sure that I wasn't partly trying to get the focus off me as a bad object. The supervisor may have been as stricken as I was.

Larry: Do I remember correctly that this supervisor had been with this agency for a long period of time? And that in fact the supervisor had given these coveted hours to many people in the past? But what came up was, now she is not going to give them to Bess?

---

1. Andre Green (1986) speaks of the internalization of a "dead mother" as a blank, empty, silent space inside that records at a sensory level where the mother experience once was and then was not.

Virginia: Reality-wise, it was also at a time when this department, statewide, was having increased numbers, dramatically increased numbers. Less and less time was being given for supervision. Bess was not the only one who got shortchanged. A lot of people who were supposed to be having supervision were not. Still aren't, really.

Larry: You would certainly think, given that there was a past policy, she could at least get an attorney and go after them.

Virginia: She was unable to organize her thoughts or emotions to consider it. She hardly had enough energy to get up. I conferred privately with an attorney. When he heard the story he thought she had a legitimate case. Bess, at that time, was emotionally unavailable and unreachable.

Larry: When there is a policy that has been going on, she could have claimed bad will and been somehow compensated. But what we are looking at, I believe, is a replication of the death of a mother, a mother's availability in life-giving ways in infancy. Then of the baby having to lie down and die herself. All of the withering, the life going out of her, is what we see with an infant in marasmus. And a similar replication going on with her Indian man, and the specter of losing you.

Virginia: My sense of withering absence was so bad that a couple of times I literally went over, knelt beside her, touched her shoulder, and said, "Can you look me in the eyes? I want you to know and feel I am here with you." She would look, but the look was dead.

Larry: She was already dead inside.

Virginia: All of my efforts wouldn't connect with her.

Larry: So we have the resurrection of a dead mother.

Virginia: At that point, we have a mother, we have a therapist who is just beside herself, as though her infant is dying. "Wake up, look at me!"

Larry: When she hits the dead mother internalization, she cannot make use of reality because she is really in a psychotic place.

Virginia: It had a feeling of catatonia, it really did. Total dysfunction.

Larry: Hopelessness. Beyond despair. So we are reaching the terror of the case, that the group intuitively knew about somehow or other. On the surface it would seem like the terror is because she is so unpredictable—she bites so much. But it also seems like there was an intuition that you and everybody else around her had that said that at some point, when the biting stops, she is going to be desperate. The group tried but they knew that at some level she was not accessible as a person, not reachable. That at some level there was a total withering of personhood.

Virginia: When the biting and the sexual acting out stopped, there was an awful setback personally and professionally and vice versa.

Larry: So the sexual acting out had a self-preserving quality too.

Virginia: Yes, but there had been times when the biting and acting out stopped when her creativity had grown and been realized. She got to where the biting usually contained a good bit of humor.

Larry: Perhaps in her early history there were other people in the family, other friends, sitters, nannies, whoever, that could be turned to for momentary sensual soothing. So she later sought physical contact when she felt desperate. We don't know how to account for the survival tactics of first biting and then seeking random physical contact and soothing to prevent total annihilation of the sense of self. The other thing I recall from the period when you were in acute grief, the devastation that you felt centered around the obvious question: "What more could I have done? Did I do anything wrong? Why did she leave me? I am devastated and puzzled that she left."

Virginia: "How could Bess break her word? Her word was always golden."

Larry: Yes, but beyond that obvious part, I recall your communicating to me something beyond, which was, "How will I ever recover from this?"

Virginia: I still feel that, Larry.

Larry: Tell me about that.

Virginia: I wish I had at least learned something more from her death. Maybe Bess could have gotten some help from members of her old group or her brother. But I could not get her permission—I felt I could not violate her confidentiality except in legally accepted avenues. I wish I had done something more to insist she obtain a temporary caretaker.

Larry: But, of course, you didn't have full-on cues to do that. She wasn't making her sense of dying psychologically totally clear— and she had a history of honoring her promises. But the question I have now is not so much what else you might have done. It's about your sense of, "How will I ever recover from this?"

Virginia: I don't think I ever will.

Larry: Go with that.

Virginia: I've got a case now where there is frequently the possibility of suicide. When she feels that, a full alert goes on. She is given no mercy from me in terms of . . .

Larry: "You straighten out or I will take you home with me?"

Virginia: No. Early in treatment, when it was clear such enactments, threats, plans, or feelings would occur over and over, I prepared the patient and the spouse that if and when such serious feelings occur, she and her husband must agree to arrange to have somebody to be there with her, when I can't be. "We will try to protect and hold you until you can trust yourself again to be a 'good-enough' protector to yourself. The intensity of these feelings will fluctuate even if it feels like they will not." I insisted the husband notify me when he, too, was feeling imminent danger for her. Of course, not all patients would consent to such involvement early on of the husband. This case, too, had problems with money and insurance.

Larry: "No monkey business."

Virginia: "I know only you can choose to live. You must agree to have a 'good-enough' caregiver around the clock, until you are past these feelings, or you will have to go to a hospital. We must agree to this now. You must have a care person come and stay with you or go to the hospital. Because though you may feel helpless and angry and destructive, we want you to feel our love and protection." We found that it was not even necessary that the caregiver know why they were invited to visit. I believe this current patient would not kill herself with a guest in the house.

Larry: We do need to treat these things very seriously and firmly, but you did the first time, too. And you did not have the full-on cues that a prior internalization was about to kill her. Hindsight is great but you had no real way to know. *She couldn't tell you. She didn't herself actually know.* And it's almost an accident that she had unmonitored access to those sleeping pills at a time like that. That wasn't part of the treatment plan.

Virginia: No, it wasn't . . . I guess the other thing is it diminished my optimism. I felt she had betrayed me and the treatment process because I really thought she should have held on. She could have been okay. I believe there was hope for her. Time helps most things, if you give it a chance.

Larry: How did she ding your optimism?

Virginia: I didn't really believe that there were people functioning well in most areas that you couldn't help rearrange themselves. I have always believed that if you work hard enough and long enough . . . I still believe that.

Larry: But she dinged it.

Virginia: She really dinged it. I felt she owed it to me to stay alive to get through this and keep her word. We were on a journey together. The road got rough. You go over it. It was all our good work she trashed. She gave up. I don't know any different language or technique I would use with her even now, if I had it to do over. I have thought about her a lot. If I have another person going through something similar, what language will I use to try and connect with those kinds of total giving-up, despairing feelings? It was like all narcissism had gone, no self-love was even there. It was reminiscent of Freud's death instinct theory. But I don't believe in the death instinct.

Eigen [1992] talks about "The Thing That Does Not Change." He felt Freud's death instinct was his way of expressing his awareness of the persistence of a negative therapeutic reaction.

You're seeing it as a replication of the dead mother. And perhaps it is, but it also had the feeling of . . . her appearance dramatically changed, her kemptness changed, it was like somebody had pulled the plug out of her. Every bit of self-love just went "shhhhhhhhh," like a balloon deflating. All her good object internalizations seemed gone.

Larry: The really scary thing that Bess teaches us is that when you have had a dead mother in infancy, and you have had to go into a marasmic, catatonic state because nobody could be there for you—that the nightmare lives on. Despite whatever good, positive, warm, loving, and growth-producing experiences one has later, there is the danger that the dead mother and that marasmic child will rise again. Worse, we might even say that when we do succeed in mobilizing those internal objects, in promoting a full-blown "regression to dependence,"[2] it's awful to think of the grim picture that emerges. I find it very scary. Terrifying.

Virginia: Regression to dependence is difficult for some therapists. For me, regression to deadness is much harder to treat. I sometimes had the fantasy when I was thinking about the plug coming out, of whopping her good with a big yellow envelope, it wouldn't hurt her.

Larry: No, but you wanted to just whop her, "Come to life girl!"

Virginia: "Come back to life girl! Plug up, we'll put life back together." Yes! I probably did whop her with some words occasionally, trying to get some reaction from her at that time. I know I did try to provoke her and love her and connect with her and help her out of her stupor. I had some thoughts that I should try and engage her in some kind of physical connection or combat. I even raised the question with her whether some physical contact or combat might be helpful. I got no response.

Larry: "I am not going to let you leave me this way . . ."

Virginia: Right, "If I sit on you, then would you fight?"

Larry: "Fight for your life!"

Virginia: "I am going to *make* you stay alive, I am going to throw some water on you, or hit you with this pillow over your head. I am going to do something so outrageous that you have to fight." I seriously debated about what outrageous things I could do—to get her attention, to get her life force working. That's scary just thinking about it.

Larry: I recall that in her indiscriminate sexual contacts she would first lose some cognitive functioning with drink, then find a man who would rough her up. Did that seemingly masochistic, self-destructive, maneuver serve to bring her back to life? Might her

---

2. Robert Van Sweden (1995) has provided a penetrating study of Winnicott's concept.

early withering scenario have required a sensual form of near-abuse to make contact with her?

Virginia: Maybe . . . but I'm not sure that would have helped her. I verbalized a number of acting-out fantasies and got no response cues to help me. I am still not sure that I couldn't have connected to some fragile little part of her, that in order to reach her I would have had to have done something more delicate, sweet, and intuitive. But in my fantasy, the physical combat part would be so outrageous, and so likely to get you sued. Endangering me, if it didn't work, and if she decided to . . . who knows. She was a wonderful writer, she could have easily written the whole story up as abusive and left it with whomever.

Larry: That would have been the end of you? As I listen to your countertransference, at that moment, I am thinking of the countertransference that has been reported often by people who work with catatonic patients. At some point you have this fantasy that, "If I just start beating on them, forcing them to come to life . . ." A few have actually dared to do such a thing. But it violates our humanitarianism.

Virginia: My couch was upholstered with down pillows. I had another fantasy that I would take scissors and rip open the upholstery and just let all these feathers fall on her. She knew I liked my furniture.

Larry: Beat her up with feathers!

Virginia: Surely, my desperation or my willingness to violate my wonderful new furniture for her would connect to her humor and me if she was still inside herself at all. We would have "soft, white, baby ducks" everywhere. I verbalized that fantasy, too. No response. I could bring my baby duck in soft down so she could have a "good sleep." I wanted something to connect to her mind and heart.

Larry: The truly terrifying thing is that no matter what you might have tried, there is a possibility that nothing would have done it. That is scary! That you would have invested all this time. Really when your relationship with her was at a zenith. You were even imagining that she didn't have to have you. She was imagining terminating. For a moment now let's think of this in terms of how she had gone through a long dark tunnel, she still hadn't

really learned how to socialize well, although she had some experience with you, at school, with the group, and at work. She
had enough social skills to where some friendships could be built
and in a way were . . . There are a lot of people in the world—
demanding or not, friendships can develop. The basic skills to
live a good life were in place. The relationship with you was
in place. She was doing remarkably well. You are her second
mother, her second and good internalization. You finally made
it essentially to the place of the good object. She gives you grief
from time to time, but you became essentially the good object.
But there is a danger now that the good object is going to have
to be let go of for termination. There is no rush, termination
is not even a necessity. But for the first time it has seriously
dawned on Bess that she is going to let you go sooner or later.
That dawning has come.

At the level of reality, you are going to be there for her. We
don't know how precariously internalized, but she has made very
good use of you, as an object. As a reality object, and perhaps
as an internal object. But no matter how much use she has made
of you there remains the possibility that she knew the dead
mother was still there waiting for her. At the dawning thought
of losing you, the dead mother and the dead child begin haunt-
ing her. Termination thoughts, on no matter what reality basis,
remind her that she has an appointment she has been running
from her entire life.

Virginia: It is possible. I don't believe total cessation of the
real relationship and termination is essential to all cases. A
life with an acquired and secured base, even a hired one, can
be a life worth having. If you're going to bleed, it's good if you
know how and where to get a band-aid and be secure that it's
available.

Larry: Then, when this dead mother scenario was acted out at the
agency, with a woman who she felt could damn well have done
better by her, even if we had to go for a full-on Sacramento appeal to the governor for a release, could she overcome the dead
mother and the slumping child?

Virginia: A dying child cannot advocate for itself. Some infants
have faulty cuing and cannot help their mothers.

Larry: It's almost like the concepts don't help. Words don't help. It's almost like, *while it wasn't known until it was lived out,* the internalized baby had to be left for dead. There were so many things that she never told you, that you had to discover by accident. We could almost say that a part of her was intent on dying. In some sense she clearly intended to do what she did. In some other sense, there is almost an accidental, fated quality about it. Like, couldn't somebody have come into the house while her mother lay dying, and she lay dying, and have revived the baby? Maybe someone did, shook the baby, soothed the baby like her lovers did. But there was no way. Probably the first time around was just like the second time around. Part of the replication finally was that there was no one to revive her, not then, not now.

Virginia: I fantasized requiring her to come home. I have empty extra bedrooms at my house. Of course, I knew that if she had stayed in that state it would be more than I really would be able to handle. I wouldn't have been able to go to work and leave her because I would be just as afraid, while I was at work, of leaving her. She would have lost me as her analyst.

Larry: We also have a fluke here—an outside and unforseen factor that intervenes to tip the scale toward disaster. I have seen and written about so many of these psychotic transferences that end up in some sort of disaster because of a total fluke. A lawsuit, a death, lost insurance money, a divorce, or something like that occurs that was not predictable. Here we have several accidental factors. One, we have this awful thing with the agency. The other fluke we have is the managed care plan, the grim fact that the only hospital her medical insurance would send her to was the one where she had studied. I remember at the time you protested that loud and clear. You called doctors and insurance plans and everything to try to get a reasonable hospitalization that would have protected her. And the county would have sent her to the same place. This kind of fluke is even more prevalent now as managed care is expanding. It was in its early days then, but as managed care has expanded and people are pinned into these narrow choices . . . we have that additional risk of accident. You are saying, "Since she couldn't possibly go where her insurance would send her, and the doctor couldn't see her psychosis, I could imagine being pressed into actually taking her home. But realistically I wasn't sure I could have contained her and it would have meant giving up my own life and my need to work." She didn't fully signal that she needed that. So we have the marasmus acted out. I wonder if her mother was in a similar psychological place—"I can't reasonably give up myself to rescue a wilting baby who should be okay if we just wait a little."

Virginia: In asking what this has done to me, I think I am usually a "soft" object. Bess taught me how to work, I thought, in the negative transference. I had gotten relatively comfortable, I thought, with all of her negative material. I felt I had really learned a lot about containing her, containing and neutralizing her aggression. I thought I had learned to work with very negative and destructive attacks on myself, my language, my words—with everything. I could live with it. I felt that she'd been a piece of my learning and healing. I'd never had anybody quite that biting, that constantly biting. I felt like she had helped me learn how to work with really negative transferences and countertransferences. I felt this was a good treatment, we were on our way to saying, "Goodbye, go be a therapist, have a good life, keep in touch, I'll come hear you present your work." When she graduated, I went to see her graduate, took her to lunch for her graduation. I did things I don't ordinarily feel I should do. To me, it was like, "How could this happen?" I hear you, that you think the dead mother revival controls.

Larry: And the dying baby controls.

Virginia: She was quite careful as to which pillow she took out of my office. That symbolic enactment had been helpful to her in the past.

Larry: She wanted the one that your mother made.

Virginia: There were several that my mother made. But she took the one that was the softest, the palest—it was blues, very soft. She had taken it before and brought it back.

Larry: There, again, you had every reason to believe that the pillow would get her through the weekend. Your paper on "Symbolic Enactments in Countertransference" [Hunter 1996] comes to mind.

Virginia: Often, when severely distressed, she had been able to create poems, and she suddenly could not find any words.

Larry: She lost her speech.

Virginia: No voice for what she was feeling.

Larry: She lost her words, she lost her speech.

Virginia: Blood pressure went up.

Larry: She lost her body tone, her blood pressure went up trying to react to the loss of body tone. She went limp, she went marasmic. The final destruction, the final attack on links. Go to sleep forever.

Virginia: There is such a paradox to her having done it, time-wise, when she knew I would be the person who would first miss her, and that I would know immediately in my heart what had happened. It was predictable that I would guess immediately.

Larry: What did you do with that?

Virginia: One of the more painful thoughts is what if I had called the police twenty minutes earlier? Was she fantasizing that if I had a deep and loving connection I would use the keys she had already given me to find her and save her? She sometimes praised or criticized me for having uncanny intuition. I had been thinking about her a great deal over that last weekend. I almost called her. I agonized over what, if anything, I should do. But a therapist cannot become a policeman or an invader of privacy without a more immediate call from the patient.

It felt like she said, "I will leave the dead baby to you, you will at least take care of this dead baby, you will bury this baby, you will see to it that there is a ceremony, that there is some departure. You will grieve." And I did. I helped plan her funeral, based upon some information about what songs she liked. She left the last mother to bury the dead baby, literally. Or, perhaps, she died believing I would arrive or call the paramedics before she was dead.

Larry: Didn't her mother want her dead?

Virginia: She thought so, yes. She sometimes wanted mother dead. The sister was killed psychologically. The brother, when I met him, was . . . he would easily have done well as a mortician. He had that solid look of powerful, still posture with pale, pale skin and a very low voice. It was like, whatever I wanted would be fine with him, and I would never hear another peep from him. We agreed he would contact a local attorney who would prepare documents for my signature turning everything material and legal over to him. Members of the group and other friends helped plan the funeral, which he took care of. When it was all settled, he sent me a thank-you note. He never blamed me, he was very careful to say to me, "I think she really wanted you to have everything, you were the most important person in her life, we all saw the change. She loved you." I thought, "There is a dead baby and I am being told what a good job I did. This is full of irony and paradox." It still makes me feel tearful.

Larry: Try this on for size. I have been talking for awhile about how, when the organizing experience is transferred, we clinically see a great deal of clamor. When I talk about clamor, I am thinking of the clamor as, "You don't do it right, you are not giving me enough." Or, "I'll endanger whomever I want to. I will endanger myself however I want to. Leave me alone." Whatever the clamor is about I have to assume that in some way or another it expresses a primal need that the child has. It is a piece of history. But I call it clamor so as to pick up on a second quality, the alienating aspect of it. Whether it is another tale of satanic ritual abuse or the content is about being stranded on Mars with aliens, or incest, obsessive-compulsive rituals—whatever the psychotic content finally is—in some way or another it is always an effort to keep from reconnecting. Because when one reconnects, one re-experiences the primal trauma.

Virginia: You're leaving out the somatic ones, Larry. You're leaving out those that are experienced by some patients in deadened, deadly, and dying symptoms in the physical body.

Larry: You're absolutely right. Add those, because that is what came here. You had seen the depressive symptoms before. The draining, the wasting, the withering, the eyes not being able to make contact, the loss of body tone, the heart's hard work to revive her.

Virginia: Never that intense.

Larry: How long?

Virginia: Two or three months. She had time to see the psychiatrist, give the medicine a chance, and still hold on.

Larry: Let's talk about the marasmus, about the clamor, about the replication. We understand how well she was doing. And that in order to negotiate a termination, whether it was long-term, short-term, or agreeing to meet again . . .

Virginia: We knew and agreed we weren't going to terminate, completely, our real relationship.

Larry: There is something new here. There is the requirement of a real, honest-to-God negotiation now that cannot be avoided with you, my therapist. I think we often feel that in termination processes there is a real meeting of hearts and souls and eyes that has never occurred before. It's not the facts of your being, it is the *reality* of the negotiation. The "I–thou" aspect of the contact. She now had all the skills in place. She had everything it took to really do an "I–thou," Virginia and me, but she never had totally been nose-to-nose, soul-to-soul with you. Here is a possibility of a real, honest-to-God relationship. The first one in her life, since her mother died for her in infancy. So, I am wondering if we think about the paradox of it. The paradox of it is: if I relate to you, you must die or I must die. Or as a part of my relating to you, I must die and leave you to bury me.

Virginia: There's another piece in there. That is, when all this happened to her with the supervisor and the doctor, her fantasy was that *I* had never been treated in such a bad way. She was right, I haven't.

Larry: That you personally had never received such bad treatment.

Virginia: And that I couldn't empathize with it. Perhaps that I couldn't even imagine her state! She believed I had never felt the degree of despair she had. Earlier in her treatment she was angry and envious with her belief that I had not had that type of bad luck.

Larry: Because she certainly had, from the time she first died as an infant.

Virginia: There was some complaint in terms of what hadn't I given her of my luck. As though she had some fantasy that I had withheld my luck for myself, had not given it to her. Yet my feeling was that I was always trying to help her create a fate for herself, by preparing, planning, articulating, and narrating.

Twenty years later I know more about how to help the patient achieve discovery of awareness of the symbolization of resting on the couch as though she was the infant in the mother's lap—of going through the anxiety, fear, resistance, and sometimes the surrender to the peace, joy, and mysticness of feeling the discovery of true safety that can be achieved alone and also with another who is separate. This is a different, more silent, more separate reverie that can sometimes occur and be very helpful. But I didn't know that two decades ago. Then I was only profoundly aware of the inability to grieve the mother she never had.

Larry: I'm stretching here, back to the primal death. What had mother given her as an infant, when she was marasmic and mother was still alive? "Surely, my mother could have given me some of the luck she has."

Virginia: I had the feeling that if the supervisor's word or the department's word had been good, Bess would still be alive. I still really feel that. I'm not saying the supervisor killed her, it was Bess's responsibility to have enough to go on.

Larry: With the doctor too. And the Indian man.

Virginia: Yes. I think it was "unlucky." I don't know how psychoanalysts define luck.

Larry: In this case it is "some magical something that will keep me alive."

Virginia: Something that can say, "I will go on, I will make this work out somewhere down the road. I will find a way to make it work out somehow."

Larry: But at some point when we have her there in her apartment by herself, facing the pill bottles, her reality testing wasn't operating.

Virginia: She did have to work at it. She got turned down the first time she applied to graduate school. She got turned down one time when she applied for undergraduate school.

Larry: One would think these would be strengthening experiences.

Virginia: They were. She had managed to keep on going, but nevertheless, it *felt* to her that it was all bad luck she encountered or created.

Larry: Let's also think about striking out with every friendship.

Virginia: A lot of that, you can see how she created it. I don't know what I think about bad luck. The question is how can you be the new object, transcend the old? Obviously I didn't. But how could I have? I will always be searching for that.

Larry: But that isn't your job.

Virginia: I think it *is* my job. I believe being a transformational object is part of my work.

Larry: As therapists, we want to be the new object, we want to transcend, we want to be internalized in a way that is transcending. But we are not in control of all of the internalizations. We are only in control of who we are and how we present ourselves. Our object presentation, we are somewhat in control of that. In a newborn baby, careful and well-timed object presentation of ourselves and the world allows the baby to become whole. If we are dealing with somebody who is not newborn and fresh, but rather has learned to die before we ever began our object presentation . . . I think that the truly terrifying thing here is to think that no matter how we present ourselves as an available, good object to be internalized, there is the danger that the previously existing destruction of links from the first object can take over. Maybe "luck" is critical here—because maybe what we are saying is, she was so close, and maybe with a few more positive experiences, she would have overcome it. But whether we talk in terms of a fluke outside influence, bad luck, or good fortune . . .

Virginia: What happens when the person begins to make a connection and loses that connection? You struggle together to re-make it!

Larry: What does it take to transcend that early trauma? To what extent is that earliest attack on linking so internalized that, regardless of what other links are made, or what reality is available, the primal destructive attack is always at some risk of rising again? In my view, this organizing experience to one degree or another is universal—that is, that all of us once reached out to a human object at critical times and couldn't find it. There is at our deepest core this dynamic in its own peculiar form, such that at times we don't dare reach into a place where we were once hurt or left to wither. I am now talking about the organizing experience in terms of two types of primal experience—the withering because I am not contacted, and the pulling back because I am hurt. They are both ways of reaching and learning to withdraw. What does it take to allow us to drop into that pre-psychological space again and to form a relationship with a new object that can have precedence over the old? I'd be prepared to say that in some sense it may never fully happen for any of us. This missing piece that we see acted out by your client with you left holding the body, is this not present everywhere? People are certainly willing to give up their lives for a lot of very stupid things.

Virginia: Our society is so ill-prepared to help people deal with these life and death matters.

Larry: I'm asking if one aspect of why we are ill-prepared is because we have never really been willing or able to look at this deepest and universal internalization of a destroyed link in the face and realize that Bess is us.

Virginia: I think a lot about learning difficulties. With dyslexia. I know, Larry, that as a child I had no way to talk about my dyslexia; the dyslexic connection has no way to express itself. You cannot explain, a child has no words to explain the broken links, the unheard phonics, and the reversed symbols.

Larry: No, the broken links and reversed symbols are things that appear even later in the child's development. They seem to me to be a direct reflection or recapitulation of the broken link of infancy.

Virginia: Many children with learning difficulties of all sorts have no way to express them in language, which is one of the things that keeps them so powerful and so difficult to treat.

Larry: Just as Bess had no way to express this to you. It is so easy to say, "Why didn't I take her home, why didn't I send someone . . ." If you had had a clear communication from her . . . She said she promised, but taking the pillow was like an underline to the contract. She had been so good with her word forever—but this is before words. And marasmus happens before words.

Virginia: Scary stuff.

Larry: I really appreciate your being able to dig deep into your soul and bring Bess back to life for me and for the others who are working on this type of transference and who will be reading this book.

Virginia: I feel pleased that we're trying to do something with her life and death that will be helpful to therapists. I believe Bess would be pleased, too.

Larry: I want you to remind all of our readers that as you go over our transcript and rework this chapter, you will be doing it on Bess's small writing table—the one with the little baby drawer.

Virginia: I will. And then I will be ready to pass it on to one of my students who has a new home in the inner city of Compton and works with many hopeless children.

HEDGES' COMMENT

However clear hindsight reasoning may be, in the clinical moment therapists are too often left guessing, as Virginia was—trying to preserve the human dignity of her client by trusting her word and having nothing better to go on than past history—and Bess had always found a way to hang on, to get through despairing situations safely. Who among us can truly imagine a personality inscription so deep and morbid that it could only be read by dying?

And yet, as Virginia's and my discussion suggests, isn't such an inscription much more widespread among us than we would care to imagine? How exactly can we think of people with diagnosed heart conditions continuing to smoke or eat salt or red meat? Or people continuing to have unprotected sexual encounters when a known lethal virus is ravaging the planet? And who among us truly takes care of him- or herself the way we know we should? Our lifestyles are almost universally unhealthy—physically and mentally—in one way or another, and we know it. And do we not throw our hands up in the same way Bess did? Do we not run ourselves ragged, blow up, deny, and finally wither, wilt, and despair—all over struggling with better management of ourselves in the very same way? It seems to me it is only a question of degree, of kind, and of how we get caught in the consequences. We all know what it means to hit an obstacle and to wilt in defeat and despair. At these moments our relational history wells up before our eyes and in our bodies. To the extent that our earliest infantile experiences of frustrated reaching were overwhelming or traumatic, we can be sure that the current replay will be more intense and enigmatic. And are we not impatient with ourselves for caving in to our despair, just as we are impatient with Bess? We all know something of Bess's experience of needed connections being unavailable, ruptured, or lost. We all hope to make better choices for ourselves.

We now have in place from the series of case studies thus far presented all of the essential ingredients needed to conceptualize a long-term, ongoing, working-through process that the following case study of Paul will illustrate.

PART V

WORKING THROUGH
TERRIFYING
TRANSFERENCES

16

Paul: Working the
Organizing Transference and
Countertransference

IDENTIFYING INFORMATION

Presenting confidential analytic material to colleagues for research and training purposes necessitates disguise in order to protect the privacy of the client. Since my purpose in presenting this material is to illustrate a certain type of *transference and countertransference development*, I have chosen to omit virtually all family history and life information that does not directly bear on the transference–countertransference material. Much of my material is taken from my notes and so is in the present tense.

Paul, a good-looking man in his mid-thirties, brought some journal notes that his mother had kept of her observations of him during his first two years. What was most striking in the notes was how detached Louise felt from her child and how cruel that detachment felt to the boy who wanted very badly to relate to his mother but who was constantly thwarted in his attempts to reach her. She, apparently not having the slightest idea how to relate to a child, would at every juncture when he approached her, find some way of shutting him down, cutting him off, or frightening him away, thereby chronically prohibiting a connection to her from developing. Paul's frequent telephone conversations with his father, Leonard, have a quality of banging loudly and angrily on a door that will not or cannot be opened, though there is an occasional sense of a stirring within and a good-will or token attempt by his father to offer a more satisfying response. Leonard admits that in Paul's earliest childhood he knew that Louise was emotionally limited and unable to adequately attend to the needs of their children. Paul maintains that his father did have the ability to be more supportive of her efforts and at the same time to reach out to rescue Paul from her inadequacies and inadvertent cruelties, but that Leonard failed to do either. Defensively, Leonard claims that he had his work to do outside the home and that Louise's job was to take care of the children. It wasn't his fault she was such a poor mother. Paul is invariably enraged at what he perceives as his father's shifting the blame to Louise. Leonard defends himself from these harsh attacks by reminding Paul of the ping-pong games they used to play and other father–son activities he used to engage in with Paul. Paul acknowledges that his father did some ritualistic activities with him but never related to him caringly or emotionally. He bitterly complains that his father never let him know that he was worthwhile or important, that his father never indicated that Paul contributed to his father's life or happiness in any way, and that his father never demonstrated that he saw Paul as a valuable or competent person. Paul continues to assert that he will not be okay until his father confirms him, shows interest in him, *proves* to him that he is indeed worthwhile, that he did not intend to make Paul feel that he is a miserable wretch of a person, nor does he need Paul to persist in conforming to this belief. Paul alternately grieves the loss of a family life he never had, and then fiercely maintains that he must keep on Leonard so that some family life can yet develop. If he stops or gives up, there will be nothing—they might as well all die.

Much of our time together during the early phases of therapy was spent going over various relationships at work, with Paul obsessing on how badly he manages things, and how imperative it is that he find ways of relating more positively to work colleagues. He is certain that he alienates them, that he forces people somehow to think that he is weak, inadequate, incompetent, and a slob.

Paul feels he is different from other people, somehow weird or not quite human. He frequently despairs that he will never be okay, that he will never be a whole, competent, and satisfied person. On these occasions of despair he makes it clear that it is my job to reassure him, to *prove* to him in some way or another that he is a worthwhile person and that there is a way out for him.

THE ORGANIZING TRANSFERENCE

Implicit in Paul's conviction about the nature of our interactions is the setup for the emergence of the organizing transference. The belief is firmly in place that no matter how much I try to relate to, value, or humanize him, Paul will never be able to accept that he is good, worthwhile, warm, caring, generous, worthy, or loving. So no matter how I may reach out to him, no matter what connections I may try to form with him, no matter how affirming I may wish to be with him, the writing is on the wall in terms of the organizing transference. The connection will somehow be broken by his succeeding in making me feel disgusted by him, tire of his continuous provocations, or come to see him as desperate and boring so that ultimately I will hate him.

During the early treatment phases I attempted in many ways to imagine how it was that Paul managed to prevent interpersonal contact or to break interpersonal connections once formed. I listened closely when he talked about his relationships with his family members, his business colleagues, his long-term friends, and his living partner— trying to determine how he manages not to sustain or actively to break connections.

I have on occasion been able to show Paul from countertransference material various ways in which, if he *wanted* to be more warm and engaging with me as he says he does, he could be relating to me more intimately or creatively, but that he isn't. That is, there may be a particular sequence of events, comments, or discussions in which I am trying to take a position, trying to give Paul ideas, or trying to find a place of importance for myself in the conversation with him. In one way or another he manages not to take me in, not to take in what I have to say, or not to show me that he values me or that he appreciates what I have to say. When I've been able to work from a countertransference position of feeling thwarted, put off, stymied, or ignored in the here-and-now, I seem to have been fairly successful at orienting him to what our task is about. I might point out how he could be responding to me more warmly or caringly, or how he could be working on making me feel better about my role or my contributions, but that he isn't. Paul appears momentarily taken aback but recovers quickly and acknowledges what I have just said about how I am doing in our interaction. He seems to grasp how that may be true and shows signs of recognition of how or why I might be feeling a certain way. In these moments he also seems appreciative for the contact, which he feels through my forthrightness, honesty, and insistence. But then he quickly moves on again, not quite knowing how to sustain a conversation in a relational mode unless I persist in leading him, pulling him back, or confronting his veering away from interpersonal contact again.

8/24/89 NOTES: ONE YEAR INTO THERAPY

Following a lively discussion about Paul's parents and some relationships he was having at work, we began to formulate what I believe are going to be important aspects of the organizing transference.

> *Paul:* As people encounter me, I subtly behave in ways so as to discourage or at least not to encourage the connection. I feel this scary, paranoid distortion and I am unable to bridge it by showing kindness, warmth, or generosity, or by being at ease with the other person. In this distortion I feel that they don't like me, or that they want to use me, to abuse me, or to cheat me. I then subtly withdraw. This clearly comes from Louise. Later, like with Sue at work, the other person and I are glued together in an unstated but conscious contempt and mutual hatred. Maybe *she* doesn't really feel contempt or hatred for me. But I feel it coming from her, and so I give her contempt and hatred and *make* her hate me.
>
> *Larry:* I hear you saying that when a person, perhaps even a neutral person who neither loves nor hates you, moves into your life

and is giving neutral or perhaps even lukewarm "getting ac-
quainted" responses, your paranoid delusions take over and you
feel that they hate you or want you dead—like Louise. You then
radiate coldness or distance, which alienates the other into a
standoff, with each waiting for the other to show warmth and
generosity to bridge the gap in the relationship.

Paul: And then I'm stuck. I can't go across any bridges. My distortion makes me afraid, and so we play a standoff game. I'm
scared of them and they of me. Unless that person clearly and
affirmatively reaches out we're not sure if we can trust each
other. I can't initiate warmth and generosity, no way. The best
people can see of me is that I'm withdrawn and scared—even
if they see I have an honest intent. But I *can* appreciate their
warmth and generosity. What I do have to stand on in relationships is that as a person I'm honest, reliable, and intelligent, and
that I *can* appreciate their warm overtones—even if I'm scared,
standoffish, or appear more openly cold and hostile.

Larry: When the other person firmly reaches out to you and an
atmosphere of safety is established then bridges can be made and
there can be a flow. But usually you actively and unconsciously
shut down the possibility of any connection.

Paul: Especially in my professional work.

Larry: It's not just that you're shy and afraid.

Paul: No. I'm forbidden to reach out. *It's as though there is a force-
field from outer-space that paralyzes my brain. Injecting terrified anxiety feelings into me. An outside force setting up an overriding terror
that totally prevents me from sharing intimately, warmly, generously,
affectionately, or presenting myself in a positive light.* I have to be
passive, awaiting their judgments and pronouncements on me—
which are bound to be bad. Even if their estimations of me aren't
negative at first, I *make* them bad. I actively make people see
me in a bad light. That's the important part—*I force people to
see me as bad.*

Larry: I feel you're trying to do this to me right now. [The actual
struggle which Paul has snared me in during this hour is trying
to keep him focused on dynamics that relate to us rather than
to talk about his parents or work colleagues. But that does not
come through clearly in these notes. I only wrote down the for-

mulations that emerged, but I am feeling caught in a struggle
to keep him focused and in dynamic contact with me.]

Paul: I'm trying to throw you off? *Not just as something passive?* To
make you have bad feelings toward me?

Larry: No. *You are actively thwarting our connection right now* by the
way you interrupt or prevent me from engaging in conversation,
by changing the subject or diverting the focus before I've had
an opportunity to digest your ideas or respond thoughtfully.

Paul: I've told you I put myself down. I don't show pride. I degrade
myself. I act negative, whiny, depressed. I act paranoid, like
they're taking advantage of me. I act hurt. I put on my martyr
thing. [He sidesteps my comment. But I pull him back.]

Larry: I think it's even more subtle than that. I have the image
of two people with neutral or lukewarm feelings toward one another, wanting to get to know each other, and slowly approaching each other as though they are getting ready to do a relationship dance. There are invisible tendrils of relatedness silently
reaching out . . .

Paul: (Interrupting) *And I have scissors that snip them off!*

Larry: Exactly!

Paul: (Veering off slightly) If someone seems to me to be acting coldly toward me I take it personally—I believe they don't
like me. I believe they hate me and that in subtle ways they
act differently—hurt, defensive. Then I get all hurt and angry when they may only be in a bad mood, or perhaps tired,
or perhaps impatient, or are feeling something that has nothing to do whatsoever with me. I take it personally. I'm not
going to give in to them. I give them the cold shoulder. For
example, at work maybe they're looking bored, withdrawn, or
sleepy. I feel they hate me. When I'm feeling paranoid and defensive, it affects my behavior. It starts an icy-cold Mexican
standoff and then they cannot approach me and they begin to
think bad things about me—that I'm weird or strange or that
I dislike them when, in fact, I'm severely afraid or suspicious
for no reason at all.

Larry: How do the snippers come out? [Again I pull him back to
where I want the conversation to go—that is, to how he actively
thwarts connection.]

Paul: If anyone seems displeased, annoyed, or whatever, then they get an exaggerated personal reaction from me, like they have hurt me, and that's how I shut them out.

Larry: But if the other person puts out positive tendrils?

Paul: I still get paranoid anxieties—I get scared, timid, and that drives me crazy. Like, "You *must* think I'm a horrible person. And if you don't, I will do things that will convince you that I'm not worthwhile."

Larry: I think you're doing it here and now with me. You're cutting me off.

[Note that here I'm focusing on the immediate struggle. I felt I had a complex formulation about two people approaching each other and what might happen in the interaction, but at every attempt to continue to reach out and give him my picture Paul interrupts with his elaborating but diverting comments. I am aware at this moment that *no matter how important what Paul is saying is, he is disrupting my thoughts, thwarting my reaching, and threatening my inner cohesion from where I am reaching toward him.*

Because I now have considerable experience in being led astray by Paul, in being diverted from a potential connecting course with him, I have the courage to follow the countertransference distress. More often than not in the past when Paul has done this to me I've used my self psychological training, decentered from myself and my intent, and tried to grasp his subjective position at the moment. But I've slowly realized that merely decentering, following Paul's lead, and achieving empathy with his immediate content simply doesn't cut the mustard. Something profoundly different is at stake. Empathy on a broader basis is required.[1] It is not simply the disjunction of two subjective worlds that needs to be understood and articulated. Rather, Paul is actively and with (non-conscious) intent disrupting my inner world of motivation so that any possibility of emotional connection is destroyed in favor of an intellectualizing and useless discussion. I've been trying for some time to pin-

---

1. In Appendix F, I address the paradox of empathy with the organizing transference, the technical problem being that empathic attunement is aimed at interpersonal connection—exactly what is terrifying in the organizing transference.

point how Paul succeeds in doing this. I feel successful during this session in having found a possible opportunity to show him how this operates—even as we talk about it in an intellectual manner. I am aware that Paul's brilliance and articulateness is frequently used in this way—to distract me, to derail me, to disarm me, and *to cause an inner collapse of myself.* That is, his seemingly good-natured efforts to relate to and to expand upon what I have to say are in fact functioning to collapse or fragment me and my intent to connect to him. This has happened frequently, and I feel I now have the opportunity and the courage to protest.]

Paul: I interrupt. I don't let people finish their sentences.

Larry: You actually cut off what might become a flow between you and me of ideas and feelings.

Paul: I'm so anxious, I just spurt things out. Particularly if I feel that they don't like me. [At this point by my inquiring and interrupting I am forcing Paul to talk *to me.* It feels significantly better and he seems more alive. Paul is now smiling and looking directly into my eyes, which he seldom does.]

Larry: I know you feel you do this, snip off tendrils of potential connection, when you are feeling negative toward someone. But I think the pattern is even more pronounced and devious in positive situations.

Paul: I get so pleased someone is responding positively that I spit out a lot of things. I start babbling like a baby. Overjoyed that someone likes me, I liven up and start a rapid stream of babble. [Which he is doing at the moment!]

Larry: And in so doing you cut off the positive tendrils, because of the Leonard and Louise living inside. You snip off the connections. (He looks puzzled.) I'm not interested in the behavior or the content of your conversation as such, because you always maintain a stimulating conversation. I'm more interested in the soul activity of *exactly how* you manage to snip the connections.

Paul: I start babbling like a baby, and then they say . . . , for example, Sue at work says, "Shut up. Leave me alone. You're interrupting my thoughts. Go away."

Larry: And so the Louise you identified with in infancy, who is still living inside of you, has snipped those connections, has forced the relatedness flow to stop. You comply with the inner Louise's instructions to break the threatening connection by needless babbling. And in so happily babbling you destroy the potential tendrils of real connection. You now do with Sue or with me what you once experienced being done to you by Louise. By being overly excited and overly solicitous you destroy any possible positive bridges that might be useful in building a relationship. With Sue you confuse her. With me you derail me into talking psychobabble with you. And you do so cleverly, intelligently, good naturedly, and in such a way that it goes almost unnoticed. But still Sue or I feel somehow cut off, confused, or lost track of.

9/21/89 NOTES: THE SADISTIC SOCIOPATH

Paul: I've been thinking about the sadistic sociopath I've often told you about that's inside of me. I've told you that when I hear or read about one of these serial killers who is a crazy, sociopathic, sadistic maniac that somehow I feel a kinship with him. What I've realized is that this image comes from Leonard. This week I've had many images arise in my memory of times when I experienced Leonard as being cold, calculating, sadistic, and destructive of me.

Larry: You're saying you've identified with that killer maniac that you as a child experienced your father as being?

Paul: Exactly. I don't think he meant to be deliberately cold, cruel, or destructive of me. He just didn't know any better. He experienced my being in the world as an ongoing threat to him in that I would demand some kind of relatedness from him. And since he didn't know how to respond to relatedness demands, my overtures were a threat to him and he was somehow roused to sadistically put me back in my place of not demanding something from him that he couldn't give or that threatened him.

Larry: And does this internal self image of the sociopath killer also go back to your mother and how she related to you?

Paul: Possibly, but I'm not sure just how.

Larry: As you were talking I was thinking that she also didn't mean to be cruel or to mistreat you. But remember that in the notes she made when observing you as a baby we could see that you were experiencing her at the time as cold, cruel, sadistic, and frightening and how angry you were about it when we read together the notes of how she related to you. Her withdrawn, cold aloofness was experienced by you as active cruelty and caused you to cry out in anger and then to collapse in fear.

Paul: She always gave the message that I was not to be alive, not to need her. That I was a bad, evil, mean child because I threatened her sense of sanity when I needed her to mother me. She should never have had children because she had no idea how to relate to them. My presence in her life could only have been experienced by her as a torture—an agonizing threat she had no means of responding to. No wonder she did whatever she could, cruel or not, to get me to back off, to leave her alone, to stop demanding response from her. I was left feeling like a monster trying to kill her whenever I needed something, some attention, some love, some care from her. Because that's how she experienced my need to relate to her as monstrous—she saw me as a monster!

Larry: So you've identified with the psychopathic killer in your father and the killer monster in your mother? The part of them that was experienced as coming at you startlingly, menacingly, and sadistically so that those reaching, relating tendrils of yours would retreat, stop demanding, and ultimately die out? What was once an instinctive retreat becomes part of your personality as you identify with their aggression?

Paul: Yes. Why couldn't I have identified with the good and the positive things in them instead of the aggressive?

Larry: Because the good things in an infant's or child's environment are simply taken for granted as what is needed, as the way things are supposed to be. But when there is a frightening or traumatic situation the child attempts to master it somehow. At the earliest phases of life that mastery entails somehow limiting or *becoming* that traumatizing agent—by identifying with it, for the purpose of understanding its nature. A primitive "monkey see, monkey do" imitative learning occurs in the earliest months and years of life in the areas in which the child is taken aback, hurt, or otherwise traumatized. You identified with the cold, cruel, sadistic, sociopathic killer that you experienced your parents being—each in their own way.

6/16/90 NOTES: A COUNTERTRANSFERENCE INTERPRETATION

I was disturbed after our session yesterday. I needed to write, feeling that the dynamics we are experiencing are something I need to try to capture. I wrote the following paragraphs:

"At this point we can continue to intellectualize pointlessly about various matters of concern to Paul, or I can attempt an empathic drop into my feelings—those stirred up by Paul and our relationship. It's much easier to go along with the topics he brings up but they go nowhere. I often feel on the verge of tears being with Paul. Exactly what the tears are about seems just beyond conscious grasp. There is a sadness that we cannot interpenetrate more deeply and freely and both enjoy and benefit from this process of being with each other, and exchanging with each other. Paul frequently complains that I am not giving him enough, that we need a breakthrough. When I press him to elaborate what exactly he needs from me he becomes frustrated and wants to withdraw, to give up. He explains that he needs a more aggressive, affirmative approach from me to draw him out. That somehow I have to know how to get him out of his mess.

"Last night I began our session by recalling how unhappy he was with me on Monday. He asked me to define that, to talk us back to Monday as he usually does. He likes me to initiate discussions to get us going. I felt I had a purpose in trying to revive Monday and a place where I wanted to try to go in terms of what I wanted to tell him. I wanted to free associate myself a bit about the countertransference in specific directions that might bring him out in some new ways. I started, 'Ever since we began, I've had a series of half-formed images, many of which I have from time to time tried to speak . . .' But Paul was off and running and I never got to finish. Paul talked the whole hour, and at the end commented with slight criticism that I had not said one single thing this session. I agreed.

"I was on the verge of tears during the entire session. I was wanting somehow to tell Paul how important a person he is to me, how I do deeply value him, how I do like him, how I respect him, how I do find him important to me and need him. But I was not able to speak up in the session. Or I was not being allowed to say how I felt. But the tension created in me during the session caused me to experience more about my predicament than I had been able to feel before.

"Content-wise I wanted to share the half-baked images that have been gradually forming from the beginning of our relationship of simply wanting somehow to be Paul's relating partner, to share days with him, to be totally involved and enmeshed with him—the sense being one of totally containing him, enveloping him, guiding him without leading him, of being an external structuring influence that would foster his growth without directing his unfolding process. The image that I've had is to be present, interested, attentive, and encompassing as a total supportive net. I have had fantasies of standing next to Paul at the proverbial party punchbowl where he hangs out feeling lost and lonely—and silently egging him on under a concerned and watchful eye, evaluating with him his every move, his every reaching out, his every feeling, his every pain, his every withdrawal—to be a silent supportive partner. All the things Paul believes he is I know he is: good-hearted, sympathetic, eager to contribute, desirous of beneficial interactions, charitable, kind, loving, worthy, and so forth. My role would be through my very presence and strength of being to expect, even to insist, that Paul live out in spades all that we both know he is. My watchful eye and presence would not permit him to back down, to withdraw, to wimp out in any way. And if he was struggling or floundering my presence would be his stay, his compass, his life support as he found new and creative ways to move forward on his own. The tone of all these images is one of wishing to surround, to support, and to envelop what is already there in a way that it strengthens itself, so that what is Paul can become realized and enriched through vibrant interactions with people.

"Affect-wise these various images—from being in his home with him, to going to work with him, to being in social settings with him, to sharing family life with him—are accompanied by almost choked-off tears. At times the tears seem to be of sympathy or empathy with him at how miserable his life and interactions always have been for him. The feelings are of pain of the kind he has on several occasions expressed in a cracked voice or tears during our sessions. At other times my choked-back tears seem tears of joy—like I'm on the verge of finally finding my lost baby or perhaps even my lost mother. But the holding back, the choking-back quality still prevails today almost like it did in last night's session."

This is as far as my writing got. I knew that I hadn't quite said all that I wanted to, that I hadn't quite let my thoughts take me where they wanted to go—but I had run out of time. In the beginning of the next session Paul opened with a fantasy that he had completely alienated me yesterday and that I was going to tell him he was hopeless, I couldn't work with him, and our relationship was over. He said sooner or later this always happens in relationships. The fact that I had ended the hour yesterday rather quickly without reassurances, that he had talked so much, and that I had not had a chance to talk led him to believe that I was going to throw him out today.

I explained that we were on similar wavelengths but that I had not arrived at a wish to throw him out, that instead something else had happened. I read the above paragraphs to him and a lively discussion ensued. I was hoping that the unfinished countertransference thoughts would emerge and crystallize in the discussion. Paul seemed enlivened by my interest, but not quite sure if he could trust it. He attempted to minimize it by various means that I systematically confronted. I told him I wasn't going to let him get away with doing to me what he does to everybody else. He was not going to push my interest and feelings away—like he had almost done yesterday. I am going to remain emotionally present, no matter how hard he tries to send me away. At the end of the hour, we had a discussion in which I pressed until Paul acknowledged that indeed my interest and concern did feel good. He was reluctant at first to admit it, but when he finally did he flashed a bright smile. Once again, *my insistence that we stay together served an interpretive purpose—as if to say, "You believe we cannot be interested in or enjoy each other but it is not true."* The countertransference content seemed to register my feeling lost, lonely, and shut out, helpless to find Paul (my mother). I clearly did not want to participate in this tendril-snipping relationship style Paul first learned with his mother.

Interestingly, what crystallized out of my countertransference musings was not any clarification of the content—regardless of its source.

Rather, the position I defined for myself left me feeling that I *must* reach out to engage him—something Paul cannot do when he is in a similar place of stifled yearning. This engagement seems to illustrate how what begins as organizing-level breach of contact or withdrawal in infancy undergoes a later transformation into a symbiotic style that is, through projective identification, represented as a symbiotic scenario in the transference–countertransference exchange. Such a speaking of the countertransference is actively interpretive in that I am doing what he could not do—saying what he could never say. De facto, by speaking the countertransference feelings I am refusing to accept the infant role representation being projected into me. In this way I stand against and refuse the scenario that Paul has internalized and replicated in our relationship. A Kleinian might say that I had found a way of interpreting the projective identification.[2]

AN OVERVIEW OF THE WORK BEING CONDUCTED

When I teach about the nature of the organizing-level transference and how to begin teasing it out, working it, and ultimately interpreting it, I always begin by emphasizing the long prodromal period that is often required to establish safety within the relationship. I have seen instances in which two, three, or more years have been required for the establishment of a sense of safety—given the extent and the nature of the damage suffered in early life and the person's ability and willingness to revive the early relational trauma in therapy. This early period often resembles a search in the spirit of the characters of Kafka's novels and short stories. The developmental metaphor would be an infant searching for a nipple to connect with, for a maternal presence within which to begin a safe, satisfying, and nurturing rhythm. The prodromal safety-searching in this type of therapy can seem endless. Many times therapists express surprise that the client keeps coming without any apparent purpose or "progress." Many times the prodromal period seems tiresome, boring, or tedious to the therapist because the content

---

2. This particular way of speaking the countertransference as an interpretation of symbiotic level transference is elaborated in Hedges 1992.

centers on nonhuman concerns, paranoid delusions, somatic preoccupations, disorientations in time and space, or other contents that I often term—for the sake of clarification—"little green men." My reason for wishing to stigmatize the incessant searching filled with psychotic or organizing content as "little green men" is to be able to point out the relative uselessness of therapeutic discussions about the content. The therapist hears an unending series of escapades at the office, in bed, with the children, or in the recovery group. There are countless stories about the past, fears about alien abductions, memories of molestation and ritual abuse, switches into other personalities, stories of physical and psychological symptoms, or sagas of all kinds of childhood trauma. The content many seem of crucial value to the client because it is all he or she knows to talk about that in some way *expresses* (note I do not say "represents") the nature and extent of the internal distress. But the therapist who has done much work with these endless stories full of organizing or psychotic content knows full well that no therapeutic progress ever comes directly from a discussion of "little green men" content. *The therapist's dilemma is that he or she is compelled to maintain rapport by talking about the little green men while at the same time being aware that so long as we're talking about these green men we will never be able to get to or work with the crucial aspects of why the person is in therapy, that is, his or her essential inability to form and to sustain human contacts that permit personal growth, enrichment, creativity, and enjoyment.*

In the present case the little green men revolve around intrigues at work, telephone calls with father, worries about mother and siblings, concerns about his career curve, and doubts about household details, weekend expeditions, vacations, conferences, business meetings, and so forth. But the central problem around which all the little green men revolve is that Paul simply does not know how to initiate or to sustain full, ongoing, interpersonal emotional connections with other human beings. Paul lives in a Kafkaesque world in which people, scenes, pressures, and forces move in a vaguely incomprehensible, incoherent, or chaotic way that he tries to bring order to with his movements and thoughts. The Kafkaesque search for connection with other people is reminiscent of the fundamental search of all mammals for the breast. Mammals, I am convinced, are born with the genetic instruction: "find a warm body or die."

Following a thirty-year study of autistic children in England, Tustin (1986) wrote a provocative paper entitled "The Rhythm of Safety." In discussing this paper at a pre-publication conference with a group of therapists in Paris in 1985, Mrs. Tustin reminisced that it was an experience of watching her grandniece nursing her new baby that inspired the paper. Tustin said she had completely forgotten that in the nursing process the breast and the nipple are as active and questing as the mouth. She observed her grandniece and infant move into a position where the sucking began and continued until one or the other was a bit uncomfortable. Then they shifted positions slightly so the sucking could begin again, and again. They were both trying to get into position so the rhythm of relating could begin—a rhythm in which two human beings mutually and interactively participate. Each time the rhythm began, the two bodies relaxed. Tustin called it the "rhythm of safety," and felt that this fundamental rhythm of human interaction served as a prototype for the connections that are essential for the later development of the human mind. All mammals attach to the warm body. But human beings have the capacity to fully and dynamically connect in special ways, mind to mind. One might even say that the very means through which the human mind is passed down through the generations are initiated through such mutually satisfying connections. The earliest bridge, says Tustin, is the sensuousness involved in mother's ministrations to the baby. It is through the baby's sensual potentials that the mother appeals to the baby and draws the baby to her slowly, carefully, empathically, so that the various rhythms that two connecting human bodies must share can begin. Two bodies and their capacity for sensuous experience allow for a bridge that comes to link two minds and then gives rise to mental and relational movement and enjoyment.

It has been my understanding from the outset of my work with Paul that some fundamental difficulty arose in his earliest relationship to his mothering partner or partners. The inference is that from time to time in Paul's infancy there seemed to be bits of rhythms and bits of understanding that led to certain kinds of connections and certain understandings between this child's mind and the mind of his mother and later between this child and the mind of his father. These early successful bridges seem not only to account for the large area of solid development that Paul has achieved, but also may account for why he is able to sustain certain forms of interconnectedness when another person strongly and affirmingly initiates and makes effort to sustain the connection. But the overriding deficit that Paul suffers from can be conceptualized as a difficulty in finding, sustaining, and enjoying contact with the maternal body—and through her body, her mind, and then with other minds.

It is the caregiver, the parent, the human mind as it has evolved through the millennia who knows that each baby must be carefully brought into connection with the mind of the group in order to develop its full relational capacities. Each mother who shares the group mind, the culture, and its emotional language extends through human empathy—in her own way, through her own personality—this group mind, this accomplishment of introducing the human race to her baby. And it is her empathic extension of her mind—first experienced by her baby through sensuous physical ministrations and later through psychological attentiveness and attunement—that allows each baby to bridge the gap from what we might distinguish as the ordinary life of a mammal, to the special, cherished, and sacred life that is possible for humans. That as fathers we are typically not more involved in the early emotional caregiving process clearly limits at present our individual and cultural mental experiences.

It has only recently been possible for us to extend our psychoanalytic thinking to the earliest months of psychic life, both inside of mother's body and to life shortly after birth, in order to understand how emotional experiences from this era become transferred into later relationships.[3] Some have called this earliest of mental structures the "psychotic" transference. Others speak of "the transference psychosis." I have chosen to call it the "organizing transference." The organizing transference is so named because the infant's first task is to organize channels to the environment. The first channels are physical, to mother's body, for bringing nutrients and taking away wastes. Later the channels are to mother's mind, bringing mental and emotional nurturance and allowing for an evacuation of tension or a relief from unpleasant emotional experience. In certain people these earliest trans-

---

3. For a history of the development of psychoanalytic thinking leading up to the definition of "the organizing transference," see the "Foreword" by James Grotstein in Hedges (1994c).

ference memories have played critical, formative roles in the development of their lives, their selves, and their relationships.

Babies come into the world prepared to create interpersonal bonds in a variety of ways. All individual caretakers with their own specific personalities and life circumstances inevitably fail in various ways to stimulate the baby's full bonding potential. So to a certain extent organizing experiences and organizing transferences are seen to be universal. But when there is a major disruption in the mother–child bonding process, for whatever reason, then significant scars are left in the form of somato-psychic memories—living memories of trauma. *Memories of infantile trauma record in the body and mind the ways in which the child dare not reach out to the environment for fear of being retraumatized.*

The study of fundamental learning principles in all advanced species indicates that when aversive stimulation is experienced in response to certain searching activities, the searching in that direction extinguishes rapidly. Reviving early traumatic somato-psychic memories so that these areas of contact aversion can be made subject to conscious, contemporary redefinitions with the prospect of evolving fresh possibilities in self-and-other relating is the goal of psychoanalytic study of these organizing transference memories.

TECHNICAL CONSIDERATIONS

In my technique I am aiming to bring into the here-and-now focus of Paul's and my relationship the specific patterns of aversion that were presumably developed in infancy in relation to his mother and father and that have remained active in his personality, making it difficult for Paul to live in the world of human beings in as satisfying or productive a way as he might enjoy.

In the material thus far presented, the main metaphor that we have been able to develop together is the metaphor of tendrils reaching out and his somehow snipping those tendrils so that he doesn't allow connections to take hold. The expressions of aversion Paul presented in the first two years of therapy have taken on the metaphoric qualities of his having been seen as needy or monstrous by his parents so that he has come to see himself as a monster. The lasting effect is either that other people are perceived as monsters or that his own reaching out is perceived as monstrous. The other expressive metaphor Paul has offered is that of an evil sociopathic killer lurking darkly inside him. It would seem that this expresses what Paul first experienced from his mother and perhaps later from his father as he attempted to reach out and found that his very sense of aliveness was killed off by the way in which they received his reaching. He has internalized that life-killing destructive tendency (of both self and other) and expresses it as fear of a serial killer lurking inside.

My aim with Paul is to continue focusing on our relatedness and the ways in which he experiences me as doing something to frighten or hurt him, and the ways in which he somehow manages to put a limit, curb, or governor on his own extensions toward me, so that we don't effectively and consistently connect. *Over the long haul the goal is to promote connections so that we can study the ways in which Paul manages either to foreclose the possibility of a sustained connection or to arrange a disconnection.*

This technique is not aimed at fostering or strengthening Paul's capacities for relationship as such. Therefore, the goal is *not* simply offering ego support while he learns to sustain connections. Rather, encouraging, seducing, or fostering connections allows the establishment of *a frame of reference* against which the many means of avoiding or rupturing connections can be analyzed. No matter how supportive or educational this technical approach may appear on the surface, the depth purpose is to establish a consistent frame for securing and analyzing the organizing-level disconnecting transferences and resistances.

THE "BABY AND MOTHER ARC" METAPHOR

I had been thinking about Paul one weekend and had a formulation that I thought was particularly apt. On Monday, early in the session, I began to try to pass my formulation on to him. But, not unlike a session that has been previously reported, I experienced my attempt to express myself as consistently thwarted by Paul. Silently I began focusing on the countertransference in terms of the frustration I was experiencing, the discouragement I was feeling, and my easy willingness to let him just go on and to give up expressing myself. At the same time, I was aware of my very strong desire to say what I had to say, and so to connect and somehow to get him to see *me*, to understand *me*, and to take in what *I* had to say. In my countertransference reverie I was trying to follow the full range of emotions that accompanied these thoughts as I would, from time to time in the hour, once again attempt to speak—only to be overridden by Paul's response. At length, I fell mostly into silence, and at the end of the session Paul commented that he was aware I hadn't said much and that he felt disappointed by my lack of response.

I was awakened the following morning by a very upsetting dream. I was enraged, my body was shaking, my fists were clenched, my jaw was tight, and I was sweating. Only a very few times in my life have I ever been so absolutely enraged as I was upon waking. There was nothing left of the dream imagery or of exactly what I was enraged at. But I had the distinct impression that the dream related to Paul and to emotions stirred up in session the evening before. I was troubled most of the day about it, trying to recall the dream content. Without my usual waiting to see what Paul had on his mind the next day, I said I had been awakened by a dream. Paul asked immediately if I was angry with him. When I inquired why he had asked that, Paul reported that he had not allowed me to talk the day before and that he thought I would be angry with him. I told him that my dream itself was lost but that the point of it seemed to be the stimulation in me of murderous rage occasioned by experiences of repeated frustration during our last session. But that I somehow felt my rage was *on his behalf*, that the missing piece in the things he had told me yesterday about his childhood was his rage. It seemed to me that I was dreaming it for him. I felt the rage in my countertransference frustration somehow belonged to him. Paul resonated with it quickly, first with his father—how enraged he is that his father won't listen, giving me several examples. Then Paul gave examples with his mother.

In the aftermath discussion of my dream and the countertransference reverie from the day before that I told him about, a metaphor developed between us. I began by imagining a young baby attempting to do something, striving to achieve something, perhaps learning to stand—feeling its feet on the ground, its hands in mother's hands, and then eagerly bouncing up and down, fully delighted in the feel of the muscles involved in standing and bouncing. Then the baby is feeling a great sense of triumph, laughter, joy, and power as a total connection is experienced between the ground, his overall skeletal structure and musculature, mother's hands, eyes, smile, and mind, and the fullness of mother's body and her groundedness. The baby feels joyously enlivened by a powerful energy arc linking two grounded minds and bodies. But then for some reason mother suddenly becomes disturbed, preoccupied, or frightened and the connection is broken between the baby's body, the baby's ground, and her mind, body, and grounding. Paul angrily interrupted, "She scared me!" He then reminded me of some of the cruel and startling things Louise had done to him that were recorded in the notes she had kept on him as a baby. So the metaphor evolved that just at the moment when the baby Paul was reaching, extending, and joyously feeling his power in being connected to his mother, Louise would, for her own reasons, become frightened by the connection and in some way or another startle, scream at, make grimaces, or do something to cause Paul to collapse suddenly and cower in terror. *The expectable murderous rage toward his persecutor had become instantly foreclosed by a startle response, fear, and collapse. The entire cycle of searching, reaching, feeling fleetingly connected to, and then collapsing or darting away was internalized so that both startle and rage are foreclosed from experience. The baby simply knows that grounded relating is treacherous.*

This metaphor has proven useful to us. The active ingredients include baby feeling its body, power, strength, and attunement with its mind—and baby reaching toward mother and bouncing—joyously feeling powerfully attuned to the ground and to mother's mind in dynamic harmony. At that moment what must be destroyed (in transference memory) is the connection to the mind of the mother/other. The internalization of this rupture demands not only destruction of the connection to the mother but, because of the startling and sadistic quality of it, the child's connection to himself, to his own grounding, and to his own body. What is retained in body memory is a crushing constriction that spells "never go there again." Never feel joy or triumph in your strength, in your relatedness capacity, or in your creative potential. Because if you do, I (mother) will startle, frighten, and abandon you in this moment of achievement and you will collapse devastated, no longer grasping for me, no longer needing me or demanding a relationship that scares me because I cannot understand or tolerate it. Paul added, "*I learned to approach her in a self-effacing, self-negating manner so that she would not be threatened by my needs or by my presence. I still do that with everyone—I make sure I am experienced by others as a friendly but nondemanding, nonthreatening blob.*" I felt as if we were connected and bouncing joyously together by the end of the session, both of us determined not to let fear, rage, and collapse intervene.

7/13/90 NOTES: THE "FAILURE TO THRIVE" METAPHOR

After studying the difficulties that the two of us were having trying to establish a connection and what the things were that got in the way for some time, I had a consultation with some parents and a baby that provided me with another metaphor for our work that I introduced.

Briefly, both parents brought their 6-month-old baby diagnosed with a "failure-to-thrive syndrome" into my office. Special kinds of feeding had to be provided for the child during the early months, because of problems with a stomach valve. At one point the child was actually taken away by a doctor, hospitalized, and fed to keep it from dying. At 6 months, the baby weighed little more than ten pounds. The baby was a "good" baby, but appeared quite confused, unfocused, and uncoordinated for a 6-month-old child. The baby was placed quietly on the floor of my office in a little car seat. When there were signs of fussing the mother nervously jiggled the car seat with her foot until the baby quieted. Rather than paying attention to each other or to the baby, who was making signs of needing recognition, the parents were focused on competitively telling me about the multiple medical problems, the hospitalizations, and about how criticized they had felt by various doctors and friends. At one point the baby was clearly wanting to eat. The mother did not respond. Father began angrily attacking the mother because he believed the baby should be fed on demand and was telling her so while searching me for approval. The mother, however, wasn't about to be pushed into feeding this baby, by him or by me, and began to talk about the group that she has joined that has a philosophy where "you teach the baby to eat when you want it to eat," so you "don't spoil it" or "don't let it get away with" things. While mother and father were arguing with each other trying to tell me about problems with the baby, problems with feeding, and their differences in philosophy, the baby was becoming increasingly distressed and no one was attending to it.

I am aware that I have a baby in front of me who has been diagnosed as on the verge of death and its parents are busy arguing about a philosophy of feeding, each angrily blaming the other and seeking support from me. At last the mother took the baby and managed to get the prescribed four ounces of milk into the baby with a medicine dropper. Then she held the baby awkwardly on her lap for awhile. Most striking was that there was no molding between the mother and the baby's body, no rhythm, no eye contact, and no mutual empathy.

In ordinary circumstances when a mother is holding her baby, she will hold it in close to her body, close to her bosom, and then begin tucking in this leg here or that arm there until the baby is all nestled comfortably and safely and focused on the mother's face, the mother's smile, the mother's voice, the mother's breast, the bottle, or whatever so that there is a sense of the baby's body and mind being collected, safe, and in connection with and related in a focused manner to the feeding, nurturing, maternal body and mind. In contrast, this baby's arms and legs were dangling in awkward, loose, and uncoordinated positions. It could not hold its head up. Its eyes were open but unfocused, never seeming to know quite where the mother or the father was, and unable to hold anything steadily in its vision. Nor was it being helped by either parent to focus its attention or its needs. At one point, the mother picked the baby up, faced it out and away from her, and attempted to burp it in a most awkward manner by jiggling the baby. Indeed, whenever the baby seemed to have a need the manner of approach to the baby was one of startling it, jiggling it, bumping it, or burping it. They succeeded mostly in managing the baby like a problem, but not in a way that the baby was going to be able to make use of comfortably.

Paul quickly grasped the power of this metaphor in terms of his parents not having the slightest idea of what to do with a baby, being, as they must have been, so caught up simply with the difficulty of trying to relate to themselves and to each other. But Paul added that it was even worse with him because of the way that his mother actively intruded by frightening him, purposefully driving him away at any point when he was about to become coordinated, or focused on her—which

she experienced as too threatening. Louise would feel forced to do something *to destroy* the coordination efforts he was making to connect with
her. Then he gave a series of memories of ways in which his father,
whenever Paul would turn to him with a need or a desire to be related
to, would in some way or another also make sure no connection occurred—usually through some sort of cynical, critical, devaluing, or
disinterested remark.

During the course of this discussion with Paul, the *process* of our
interaction became more important than the content.

After Paul made some opening remarks I told the baby story. As
usual he began immediately—although he had listened to the story
attentively and saw the relevance of it—to go off in free association to
other areas. I felt perturbed because once again Paul was thwarting my
attempt to be present with him and his issues and to call him to relate
to me. As I report this feeling I fear the reader will think that I personally need to control the hour or that I can't follow changes in subject
gracefully. But I assure you that I have followed Paul's endless jumps
and shifts until I have realized that *merely following Paul's lead is to collude
with the operant delusion, with the resistance to experiencing his transference
disconnections*. That is, staying with his content shifts feeds the resistance to connecting with me in a way that would allow for the emergence of transference (memory) experiencing. I began to express my
distress at our current process. Paul took me on in terms of his new
content because he thought what he was bringing up was very relevant
to his issue. He protested my wanting to stay with us and our process
here as tangential; he felt that what he had to say about his mother,
his father, and various other important things was very much to the
point. It took me some time to assure him that the things he was wanting to bring up were certainly important and relevant, but that they
were not to the point of the immediate present moment. I had to keep
focusing on what was happening to us, drawing him back and pointing
out that, at this moment in time, there was a leg dangling over the edge,
or an arm reaching out toward nowhere. This dangling part was certainly crucial to the body, but it had to be brought into direct connection in the here-and-now with me or we were not going to be able to
make collaborative use of it. Somewhat reluctantly through a series of
protests and responses Paul began to allow himself to become drawn in

toward me and toward our mutually developing discussion about how he manages to remain unfocused in life in various situations, but most importantly with me.

I said that I was struggling to make certain that he was safely held close to me without dangling arms and legs and with a focus on me so that we could be with each other. Thus the silent process of the hour was the most important feature, although the parallel content we were discussing allowed the process to move steadily closer toward a tighter connection. Toward the end of the hour Paul began to calm and to relax, and there was more smiling and contentment on his face than usual. So I had "won" my point and "forced" a connection. But Paul also wanted to be certain that the areas of content that I had so cavalierly dismissed were being set aside only for the moment because, in my view only, they were not immediately salient to us here and now. I directed our attention to *what the mother must bring to this process of holding. Paul helped me with this by mentioning caring, determination, concentration, focus, a willingness to enjoy, and a willingness to be in reverie with the child. We also formulated what the child must bring.* The child must be willing to be present, willing to be fed, willing to be nurtured, willing to have its arms and legs moved into a relaxed position, and willing to enjoy the maternal presence and focus. Even as we were talking about it Paul was slowly allowing this process to happen. I felt strangely parental and victorious.

At the end of the hour I insisted on his reviewing how he felt now, highlighting the pleasure he felt that we had a good discussion, that I had brought a metaphor to him that he could work with and enjoy, and that our discussion helped us come together more. He acknowledged that he liked it, that he felt I was on track, and that I was with him and he with me. But more than simply insisting that he acknowledge his pleasure, I also acknowledged my gratitude to him for bringing to our process the willingness and spirit of cooperation that he did. It was very important to me to know that he was willing to let us connect and to do the work that we were doing, and I derived a great deal of pleasure and satisfaction from our time together. As the mother/analyst in this process I need from him this spirit of cooperation and I feel benefited and gratified by it—even as I feel I have offered him something very special in return.

7/17/90 NOTES: THE NEXT SESSION

Paul came for his session with a violent headache behind his eyes, in both of his temples, and in the back of his neck. He seemed like he was in a terrible fog. He slumped down in his chair and in a groggy state with half-opened eyes said, "Where were we?" I waited a bit to see if he was willing to talk about the headache, the neck ache, or the fog, or why he wanted me to begin. I reviewed for him that our last session was one in which we engaged in a process of mutual cooperation far greater than usual during the hour and wondered if that were related to the present headache. I said, "Are the parents inside your head some- how forbidding us to continue our cooperative relating?" He complained that my comment was thin, feeble, and not too convincing.

Paul has for some time been contemplating a major step forward in his career that requires a vote of confidence from a number of his corporate peers and supervisors. He had talked today with several of these people and was dreading telephone conversations and letters to others. Partly because of his grogginess this hour I felt seduced into the conversation and began pushing a bit, expressing my opinion that he ought to be doing such and such with regard to phone calls, letters, and memos—tackling the whole relationship problem in a very aggressive manner. Then he listed in a somewhat complaining and whining way all the various reasons why he shouldn't do this, or can't do that, or how someone may react badly to his overloading the situation. Paul and I ended up locked into discussion with my pushing hard for him to fur- ther his best work and relational interests and with him dragging his heels. It felt as though I were giving loud and clear voice to a part of him that he was afraid to speak but was demanding that I speak. Paul then complained that his feelings just weren't in it. That he has no enthusiasm for this "relating project." I tell him that *his* feelings don't have to be in it at the present time because he has engaged me in such a way that *my* feelings are in it, that I am feeling *for him.* I give him a speech expressing confidence in his abilities, in his achievements, and in the direction that he's going and where we have to go together. At some point Paul protests that he sees all of this, but that he feels the inertia—and then suddenly reminds himself, "But I'm not a baby." I assure him that we "must override his internal parents that continue to pull him back to babylike incompetence." I pressed a little more, letting him know I wasn't going to let up on my insistence. He was slumped and downcast—"Why aren't I feeling any good feelings about myself?" I answered, "Because you've given the good feelings to me to feel for you, and I do feel them. You are forbidden to have good feelings. You do not have experiences of feeling good about yourself moving forward. You have shown me that at least for the time being, until we figure this out, it is *I* who must do the pushing and have the good, the positive, and enthusiastic feelings about and for you. This tension that only seems to be between *us* will hopefully bring *your* internal conflict out of hiding and destroy the power of the internal parents that want you to be an incompetent, dejected, and miserable baby." Some life stirred momentarily but silently in Paul.

CONTENT MODULES AND INTENSITY

As our relationship developed I began to notice that Paul often carried on what were more or less monologues, and that these were difficult for me, possibly because they left me out, or possibly because they bored me. After one particularly frustrating session, the term "content modules" came to my mind. In context, I was formulating how we had a dozen or more topics that we tended to talk about. My image was, I can "switch him on" and he goes into a content module with a little almost prepared speech. The "tape recording" then runs with the volume slightly amplified in a somewhat boring monotone or with gradually increasing intensity until Paul has once again said a sequence of things that he has already said in various ways before. We've been together long enough now so that I practically know his "content modules" by heart. It's not that they aren't modified, added to, or deepened, because they are. And the contents do, in and of themselves, seem important and undergo continuous revision. But on the evening when I thought "content modules," I was feeling particularly frustrated because during the previous session I hadn't been able to get a word in edgewise or to attempt to connect to him without his shifting rapidly into yet another content module. I thought Paul might as well be telling me about the little green men on Mars, we seemed so unrelated.

The next session I shared my thoughts and introduced the notion of "content modules," which he immediately grasped and elaborated as "prepared or canned speeches." Paul knew immediately what I was talking about and seemed pleased that I had mentioned it and captured it with a phrase. But when I attempted to relate *the function* of the content modules to the foreclosure of interactions between us he countered, almost as if feeling blamed, with comments to the effect that it was my job to come up with more useful and overarching synthesizing comments that could lead us to a breakthrough. If all *he* could do, he said defensively, was to repeat familiar things, it was because *I* wasn't doing a good enough job tying things together. His tone was, on the one hand, serious and accusative. But on the other hand, it also carried a slightly humorous and self-reflective note. I told Paul that what had drawn my attention the previous evening to content modules was actually the level and intensity of his voice—as if he were giving a speech rather than talking with me. He immediately brightened and recognized that when he gets on a roll he becomes physically animated and that his voice increases markedly in volume and intensity. The interpretation that I was trying to make was that in feeling somewhat put off or withdrawn, I was in some way shielding myself from the intensity of his voice and the persistent push of the content modules so that it was difficult for me to come forth and relate to him. Paul's intensity and content modules were foreclosing contact by forcing me to pull back. His immediate association was that by kindergarten people were already complaining about his loud voice and his persistent wide-eyed staring at them. Paul had alluded to these things before. But this is the first time that he could relate the voice and the staring to his *being an infant and Louise withdrawing with his learning to increase his intensity into a demanding or shrill voice or staring to try to get her attention so that he could have at least something from her. Louise had been experienced as being irritated by his demands and actively thwarting his needs for contact.*

I could see how increased intensity or clamor might be an infant's way of attempting to draw the attention of a withdrawing or inattentive mother. But I wondered if *the function of the loud voice, the staring, and the intense speech had come to serve instead to alienate the person Paul was seeking to address.* He insisted that the function of the intense communication was to reach out to a retreating other, namely his mother. But not wanting to let him get away with simply blaming his socially awkward intensity on a historical Louise, I talked about how he now carries Louise inside of him and into our relationship by means of this intensity so that he can't possibly have an extended conversation with me. *Paul is so anticipating my abandonment or rejection of him that he has to bombard me with content modules full of intensity. Paradoxically this clamoring bombardment ensures in advance my withdrawal, thereby acting out his earliest relation with Louise.* I said I had become conscious of how wearing his various forms of intensity are, whereupon he went into another content module of how Leonard and Louise wanted him to be defective and so he now conforms by being a defective mess for everyone. I told him that may be true, but that I was more concerned with the *way* in which they, living on in his behavior, continue to make a conversation between us nearly impossible. We made a good connection around how internalized parents affect him so he cannot connect freely with me.

Paul slept restlessly the night after that connecting conversation. The following morning in his hypnogogic state a series of frightening, grim, and bleak images emerged that I failed to make note of but that expressed his unconscious, terrified withdrawing reactions to our connection. Paul knew that I was somehow "to blame" for these terrifying dreams and did accept the interpretation that his internalized mother was once again trying to scare him away from feeling good about our connecting.

THE COUNTERTRANSFERENCE: OVERWHELMED AND EXHAUSTED

After a brief holiday break with several missed sessions Paul returned with a series of fresh episodes to fit in to various content modules. I tried several times to make comments or to intervene, but was unsuccessful. In the countertransference I felt myself withdrawing and exhausted, quite unable to muster up the energy to force myself into Paul's awareness or into an interaction with him.

I reported my countertransference sensations to him first off in the following session when once again he began with his hands folded saying, "Well, what now?" I told Paul that I had become aware of feeling overwhelmed by him, of feeling unable to integrate all of the various things he has to tell me, of often feeling unable to follow him when he goes from content module to content module, and of frequently feeling unable to integrate his diverse associations in a way meaningful to me. By way of analogy I indicated that often when I'm with a person talking about his or her life over a period of time a series of themes emerge that the two jointly construct and in which I can feel safe and integrated as a part of the mutually evolving creative conversational process. By contrast, with Paul it is more as if his content modules are all over the map and I easily become confused and overwhelmed as he rapidly switches. Not infrequently I become unable to make coherent comments that have the power to bring us together in a common focus, although I know he is expecting me to come up with a synthesizing view.

When I say rather daring things like this to Paul, he quickly picks up on them, sees where I'm coming from, and expresses pleasure and gratitude in various verbal and nonverbal ways that I somehow seem to be on to him. He said, "So then you're just ready to give up on me as a hopeless case?" Humorously I told him he was not going to be so lucky as that. He then insisted that it was my job to take more initiative and to be aggressive and assertive in affirming him. That is what he needs in order to feel more cohesive and to be more coherent. I told Paul that at various times when I have given him very positive affirmations, have shown him what a valuable person he in fact is to me, and have demonstrated how I do regard him with admiration as a good person—that he has been completely unable to make use of my comments. He knew from previous discussions that that was true.

I then attempted two somewhat contrasting interpretations of my experience of the previous hour. I said my first thought had been that in feeling overwhelmed, confused, and needing to retreat that I was feeling the subjective position of little Paul in relationship to his parents who overwhelmed him as an infant with *their* agendas because they were completely unable to have mutually engaged conversations with him. He resonated immediately and added some current examples. The second interpretive possibility was that, just as with his voice intensity, his staring, and his content modules, the bombarding way he addressed me yesterday serves to break off or to foreclose the possibility of a conversation of a mutually meaningful connection. What we are witnessing is the presence of Louise in the room standing between us, with him screaming wide-eyed and insistently at her, and her not hearing him. His insistent and intense content modules are his way of keeping the disconnecting Louise alive in his every relationship. Paul liked both interpretations.

I said the break in the energy arc between us had been occurring at the level of my internal integration. That is, Paul knows how to produce in me—through wide-eyed intensity and overload—a kind of withdrawal, disorientation, and fragmentation such that a communication link cannot be achieved or maintained by the two of us. By approaching me or Louise with intensity he can expect an automatic overload, withdrawal, or tendril-cutting. But the break is in fact produced or provoked *by him.* He no longer needs a live Louise to cut him off or to withdraw. *Paul now carries Louise implicit in his approach behavior to others that functions to replicate her fragmentation and withdrawal in others (and in this case me).*

At a dozen places in the foregoing conversation Paul attempted to rush off into one of his content modules. I steadily refused to go with him to new topics. I told him he was confusing me, that I wasn't going to let him fragment me today, and that we could talk about this or that later or tomorrow. Then he would quickly dart away again with another association to a separate but related content module. After calling him back a half-dozen times, I permitted myself to become a bit impatient and irritated with him, telling him very firmly that I was not going to let him get me confused today like he did yesterday. It was a good conversation. We both enjoyed it and both tracked the events the whole time. He is catching on, learning to connect, and he likes it. I like it too. Paul smiled, "Now you know how they made a wreck of me!" I answered, "I certainly do!"

PUSHING THE "TALK BUTTON"

An interesting variation of the content module activity emerged in the week that followed. On one evening I was more tired than usual when Paul arrived. I caught myself waiting to "push the talk button" to move Paul into a content module so I didn't have to struggle trying to relate to him. I told him so. He looked shocked and turned pale. "But that's not right, just getting me to talk so that you don't have to do anything!" "I know, but that's what I want to do! So what would you like to talk about?" "I'm not going to do it. I'm paying you and you have to do your work!" "Not if I can trick you into leaving me alone!" "How long have you been doing this to me?" "I don't know, I just noticed it tonight!" "I'm going to really have to keep my eye on you—you're worse than they are!" We both laughed.

FEARS AS CAUSAL OR FUNCTIONAL?

One day a discussion about Paul's fears took a turn where I was able to show him that I had a different view than he did of what he was doing. He viewed his fears and delusions as making it impossible to reach out to people *because* he feared they wanted him to be incompetent, see him as useless, feel him to be dangerous, or want him dead. I said that I do not think at this point in his life that the fears are causative, but rather that they *function* to make contact impossible. That is, *Paul approaches wanting to reach out but his basic belief is that contact will traumatize him. I maintain that the bad feelings, confusion, intensities, and fears arise to prevent whatever contact could transpire.* He (attempting to break contact by devaluing me) impatiently said he had told me that a thousand times. I insisted that he had not. And that my reframe had an important but subtle implication for how we think and work together. Paul couldn't see what difference it made whether the life-long fears caused the withdrawal or whether in order to break contact and justify withdrawal he conjured up old fears. I spent some time attempting to show Paul that if we believed that he couldn't reach out *because of* what he was afraid of, then the content of his fear is very important. But if we believe that *the simple act of reaching out is internally forbidden because contact with Louise had been traumatic in infancy, then the exact nature or content of the fear is of less importance.*

I told Paul we know the situation that is central to his delusion first evolved when he was an infant reaching out to Louise. Most of the time Louise had to fend off his reaching because it frightened, threatened, or disturbed her. She did this by traumatizing him somehow so that he learned never to reach out. Now when he comes to the threshold of a relationship possibility he automatically anticipates retraumatization from the act of reaching. Paul then added, "and it doesn't even have to be a real person. Like the times I can't even get out of bed in the morning to face people at work and become overwhelmed with morbid, confusing, psychotic, and paranoid ruminations. Or if I have to get something going at work that requires my initiative, I wander around lost for days like I'm in a drugged state."

> *Larry:* So the metaphor for my reframe is that you approach the threshold of a possible relationship encounter, of an uncertain interaction. You know the other is there and you want to reach across, to put out a bridge for communication or connection.
>
> *Paul:* But I'm terrified by the uncertainty. I'm afraid because Louise and Leonard . . .
>
> *Larry:* No! We can't get lost in the content, the "whys" of your fears. It is simply that in your uncertainty your fundamental delusion arises—your fear of retraumatization. *Then* your mind backpedals. The fears, the content modules, shifting moods, the high intensities—everything we have looked at that gives you trouble—suddenly click into place and come to your rescue to save you from the trauma of uncertainty stimulated by the desire or need to reach out.
>
> *Paul:* But if the other person first reaches toward me . . .
>
> *Larry:* That's often different, then you feel fine. Or then you wreck the relating with overeagerness.
>
> *Paul:* This is crazy. We've got to get to the bottom of *why* I flip-flop in my moods all the time. I can be having a good day and suddenly I'm faced with the prospect of talking to someone and I fall off a cliff into doom. I drop into the torture of a bottomless pit with images of monstrous, murderous, and hellish demons that frighten me always. But then someone can come up to me—and it doesn't have to be much. Maybe they just smile and say "hello" in a friendly way and I'm happy as a lark again. I have no control over these terrible mood swings, these flip-flops. I feel totally helpless to control my fears and moods.
>
> *Larry:* I know you *feel* a slave or victim to your fears and mood swings, that you *feel* like a leaf tossed in the wind—helpless and out of control. But a critical part of my reframe says that this simply isn't true.
>
> *Paul:* (Surprised) It isn't?
>
> *Larry:* No! Absolutely not. According to the way I'm coming to see you, I believe that these mood swings are something *you* do, states that you accomplish. *You* are the active agent in deter-

mining whether you plunge into hell or soar into heaven. You are not helpless—though I know it seems that way.

Paul: So I'm the agent, I'm in control of these moments, these moods?

Larry: Yes! When you approach this metaphoric threshold to reach out into uncertainty you're paralyzed with fear—for only *one* reason: You were deeply traumatized as an infant every time you reached toward Louise. *Now you are terrified of simply reaching out, of actively bridging toward contact with anyone.* The multitude of fears you know about and obsess over are your mind's way of pulling you back from the brink of terror. *The delusion is that it's safer to retreat into confusion and psychotic fear than it is to push across the threshold and live in the real world of relationships.*

Paul: That's why you have to help me feel like I'm a good, worthwhile, generous person with something to offer so that I'll have the self-esteem and confidence to reach out.

Larry: No! All of that can only follow, can only be *the cumulative result* of having the courage to reach out and cross the threshold into real relating rather than retreating into an internal world of fearful fantasies. You do not have to feel good and worthwhile to do that—you only have to be brave and reach! After you learn how to muster the courage and to relate skillfully on a regular basis you will begin to feel better about yourself.

Paul: So that I will have good, safe, and positive experiences, so I will learn that it's okay to relate, so I'll know that people are good and want to relate to me, and so I'll know I won't be hurting them if I do.

Larry: No! People are not necessarily safe and good, and your reaching out may indeed disturb or frighten them. That's not the point here. *The delusion you must have the courage to confront is your belief that it's better to retreat into inner fantasy—no matter how fearful or depressing—the way you learned to do as an infant—than it is to venture into the real world and to risk it.* Reality can be pretty bad and it can be pretty good. But you now have the ability to handle it either way. As an infant you could not handle a frightening or traumatizing real world so you collapsed, went inside, and then experienced the mood-filled internal fearful fantasies. It was better to be inside your head and body suffering from mood swings than to risk reaching out. Unless, of course, Louise *clearly* reached smilingly toward you—then you could brighten and function realistically for a while, until she became overwhelmed or preoccupied again.

Paul: But I'm not in control of my moods, they determine whether it's safe to reach or not.

Larry: Not so! You only *feel* like a leaf blowing in the wind. Every time you're faced with the need or desire to reach out, *you* activate fears to prevent it. But if someone reaching affirmatively toward you puts out a strong bridge for contact then you venture out of the inner fearful darkness into a happy, light, and interpersonal environment in which you feel great and do well—at least for awhile! She did give you the positive illusion that you could perk up and everything would be great—but that isn't entirely true either.

Paul: Then what I need is for people to reach toward me with good and positive intent.

Larry: No! You only think you need that. You are perfectly capable of handling stupid, sour, or even mean people in the real world. But because as an infant you could not handle the harshness or the frightening world that met your reaching, you delusionally believe you can only function in the real world if people are nice to you. It's simply not true. There are plenty of rotten people in the world with mean and destructive intent and you can perfectly well handle them.

Paul: Can I?

Larry: Absolutely! As it stands you don't know that because at the merest possibility of a relationship you might be able to reach out to, you change mood and retreat to an inner world of obsession, fear, depression, mania, or delusion.

NOTES 2/15/91: DELUSIONS, ILLUSIONS, AND REALITY

What follows is a summary of a three-week working-through period in which some interesting images and metaphors were developed. We had discussed at length how Paul avoids real connecting experiences by either devaluing or overidealizing himself unnecessarily.

350 / *Terrifying Transferences*

With the negative delusions on the one hand, and the positive illusions on the other, I had the format I needed for beginning to focus on the importance of "living in the real world." It took Paul awhile to grasp where I was going with "living in the real world," as he really didn't like it at first. I found myself talking about driving in the middle of the road, keeping one's eyes on the road, putting one step in front of the other, and being aware at all times of the work of relating. I asserted that he regularly escapes from the nitty-gritty of everyday living by dropping into despairing delusion, or conversely by fleeing into idealistic hopes and illusions for himself. By the second or third hour of this week Paul was quite irritated at me for harping on trying to be realistic. He felt that what I was trying to promote was absolute drudgery and hard work. He maintained that life had to be more fun than just all of this serious keeping your mind on business. I had to allow that the way I had presented my notion of living moment-to-moment in the real world might seem somewhat boring, or dreary, or drudgery. But I said it was not my intent to present it in that light but rather to say I do feel that keeping one's mind on the business of being with oneself and with other people does require a certain amount of discipline and work, particularly when you are not in the habit of doing it.

I was, of course, trying to create a paradigm for us to think about the realistic relationships he has with people at work and in his social life. What I had been able to formulate for myself, but not until this week been able to find a convincing way of communicating to him, is that every time there is a relationship pressure of any type, Paul's tendency is to escape the realistic relational demand. Whether it's doing supervision, talking with a colleague, making a phone call, planning a trip, or simply reading and writing, Paul does his best to avoid other people making relationship demands on him. He often accomplishes this by dropping into despair or racing off into idealizing fantasies.

We talked about a number of concrete examples in his day-to-day life. Paul kept skittering away and I kept pulling him back. I kept pressing against the abstraction of "relatedness demands," putting pressure on him to connect, to engage, to deal with the other person in a real interpersonal give-and-take way. I relentlessly maintained that he did everything in his power to avoid relationship situations.

One particular subordinate of his, Arthur, had been a concern to Paul for many months. This particular man has shown an inclination to be lazy, not to take his work seriously, to slough off, to say he has done things when he hasn't done them, and to actually out-and-out lie about a number of things. But Paul has been very reluctant to supervise him in an adequately limiting manner, and as a result has lost a great deal of time and work from the man. Although Arthur has a sarcastic, lackadaisical attitude, there is something about his inability to maintain concentration and determination in his work that Paul identifies with so that Paul has kept hoping that with empathic treatment the man will come around. Over a number of months, I have continued fairly actively to challenge Paul on why he is letting this man take advantage of him. We have reviewed how much it is costing his company to keep Arthur on. I have made many suggestions in terms of directions he might go to seek consultation from colleagues or outside management experts on how to set definite guidelines for the man, and how to begin managing and supervising Arthur in a more effective way so that either he could be gotten rid of, or so he could come to realize that he had to shape up and produce. But all of my efforts in questioning or making suggestions aimed at bringing some clarity, sanity, and responsibility to the supervisory situation have been fought in a variety of ways, and regularly backed away from by Paul.

During the last session of this first week I am reporting, however, I got a very interesting report about Paul's changing relationship with Arthur. It seemed that Paul's ability to relate more determinedly and creatively with Arthur had followed the more determined relating that he had experienced me doing with him. On the morning of this day, Paul had finally pinned Arthur down about a particular work project that had been delayed, put off, and sloppily performed for some time. Paul sat down with the man for one solid hour, and the two of them, side-by-side, worked painstakingly together in getting this particular project operating. Time and again the man would want to veer off the project and Paul would pull him back. Halfway through the hour the man was perspiring rather profusely, but Paul stayed right with the work situation. By the end of the hour he himself was sweating quite a bit. As Paul described the blow-by-blow details of this hour of two people working together, I picked up on each detail from the standpoint of two people staying realistically engaged with each other around a very definite, realistic, and worthwhile project. I empathized with what a strain it had been on both of them to stick with it. I highlighted the realistic, step-at-a-time process, doing just what one could manage so that the other could follow, and so forth. Both people were pleased with the considerable progress they had been able to accomplish together during this brief time, but Arthur quickly escaped to lunch with some other employees.

Throughout I was enthusiastically supporting Paul in terms of his willingness to engage Arthur, to stay with him through difficulty, to force the man to be creative, and to force himself to stay in a supervisory role. I further supported him in his successive confrontations with the man until it became increasingly clear to both of them what was going on. Paul had a real sense of victory and was pleased to be able to report all of this to me. He hadn't opted out of the fray like he usually does. I made some attempt to relate it to the general discussion that we had been having this week about relational demands and how he would typically do anything he could to avoid those demands. But in his interaction with Arthur he was facing the problem head on, and we both had a sense of victory. Our time was short and I failed to predict the emotionally disastrous sequelae based upon his successful week-long connection with me and his intense connections to himself and to Arthur.

The following Monday Paul came in looking a disaster. He had had an absolutely terrible weekend, "the worst of my entire life." He said, "You just don't understand how absolutely terrible these feelings are. We have to devise some new system so that you can understand what it's all about. All that talk last week can't even begin to touch how bad things can be for me. The whole weekend and all of its misery were somehow connected to you, to what we did last week." He couldn't pinpoint exactly how the bad weekend was related to last week but he knew it was and that in some way *I* was to blame.

Paul described having had what he called numerous "paroxysms of rage" throughout the entire weekend. They would periodically be at Leonard, at Louise, and at Arthur. His voice tone throughout telling me was very intense. He was deeply disturbed, his breathing would seize up, and he was seriously concerned about how bad things were. There was in his voice a strong but desperate pleading tone. Several times I thought Paul was going to break into tears as he told me about the miseries of his weekend. At other times his entire body began to move toward a boiling rage as his face got red and he got into a full, guttural tone, almost like an animal ready to attack. The attack was at the world, at life, at his situation and almost at me—but he couldn't quite focus any of it. The Arthur episode had set off a very powerful, deep, body, lifelong rage in him. Paul was unhappy with me because I don't understand how his parents want him to be, how they forced him to conform to their miserable expectations for him. I cautiously but definitively expressed my delight that he had allowed himself to have this rough experience, that the rage was long overdue, and that his discomfort is very important to our work. He protested that he couldn't do it. "The feelings have to stop. I can't stand these feelings. They're absolutely terrible. If this is our work I don't want it." I assured him that the feelings must not stop, this is the most real he has ever been, and he's waited a lifetime for this rage and despair to begin to emerge. I endorsed his temptation to lay his anger at my doorstep because it was indeed our work last week that had set this off, that released these powerful sensations, and that tormented his body in such terrifying and painful ways. I said I was sorry I had not predicted this outbreak because knowing it was likely to come might have made it easier on him and more accessible to self-observation.

After this first round of visceral expression, with my reinforcing it, saying that it had to go on and his insisting that it had to stop, Paul told me that, oddly enough, on both days he got five or six hours of very good, solid, and creative work done. Usually when he gets upset at anybody he can't work because he obsesses and goes into despair. I interpreted the creative productivity to be the result of his knowing *where* the problem was coming from, knowing that it wasn't him, knowing that he did not have to be incompetent "for them," and that then he could go ahead and do what he enjoyed doing—good, hard creative work. I told Paul that I was sorry this was so painful and that he was so miserable. But he's been holding onto this rage since infancy and he has to bring it out now. "No, I want to be positive, good, warm, loving, and caring. I don't want to be rageful and despairing."

I pointed out that in his descriptions of his paroxysms of rage over the weekend he never fully directed his rage at me. He said "No," and that he himself had wondered why, because he knew that I was somehow "to blame" for this upset. Then he told me, "I had a dream on Saturday night toward the morning." The dream:

I was in a new place. All of my old friends and colleagues from my previous company were there and there was a new and expanded space. My old colleagues and even my competitors were all there, and somehow or other they were all working under me cooperatively and harmoniously. All was going well, with the work going properly forward and it was good. There was love and warmth together, cooperation together.

Then Paul immediately insisted somewhat impatiently that we have to have a breakthrough, that he can't have feelings like this going on, that he would go crazy, that he cannot stand these feelings, that it's not possible for him to feel them and that they have to stop. I insisted that the flow of feeling was essential, that it was possible, that he *could* tolerate it, that even while he was in the midst of the worst he got more creative work done than ever. I interpreted the dream in terms of the new, expanded space and the pulling together of a number of difficult relationships under his own control with a sense of positive, creative warmth, cooperation, harmony, and love. I further interpreted that the conservative, unconscious part of his nature is reacting violently to his newfound sense of connecting to himself and to others.

My insistence on sustaining connection with Paul constitutes my interpretation of the disconnecting transference. In a similar vein, I coach him in parallel relationships. Actually forcing a shift, a change in his relatedness mode, brings the sky crashing down, causes a painful somatopsychic regression or fragmentation in which confusing, disorienting, terrifying sensations arise that mark a shift from his tried-and-true nonrelatedness patterns. None of the details or content formulations per se are critical—rather the process of formulating, suggesting, pressing, and coaching serves to frame the moment of nose-to-nose relating that Paul is terrified of but is slowly being brought toward tolerating.

THE DELUSION UNMASKED: "YOU'RE RIGHT! I AM A MONSTER!"

It's as though the planets are now lining up in such way that a major earthquake is beginning to rumble. Despite the fact that I'm basically a "nine-to-five" analyst who seldom "takes work home," I had a restless night after seeing Paul and wakened the next day churning with, "what's going on now." Let me name the planets that are lining up so ominously.

The first planet is the easiest. We are about to take a two-week holiday break. Whenever Paul and I have had rumblings before it has been in relation to a weekend or holiday break.

The second planet coming into place is the organizing transference. I have been dreading it since we began our work together. I find myself wanting desperately to deflect its intensity away from myself. As the ground under our feet starts to rumble I can feel deep, angry, bodily tensions building in Paul that want to aim themselves directly at me. There is a lifetime of pain, neglect, and despair that carries with it incredible rage—at Leonard, at Louise, and now in transfer at me. I don't want it. I want to try to talk him out of it, to smooth things over, to remind Paul that it isn't really me he's wildly and murderously enraged at. But the rageful transference is here. And it is inevitably me who occupies the place of the next failing love object—how will I manage? It's scary. I hate to be raged at. No matter how much I understand the rage, when it's directed at me I shrink and cower inside.

This morning in my hypnogogic state I was having vivid memories of previous experiences when I have been called upon to stay with a person through rageful episodes, some of which went well, and others that didn't. The pain of anticipated failure always lurks in the background. It feels rotten to work hard at something and then not to be able to make it—not to be able to contain the enormous energy of the rage directed at me. After the fact, when the therapeutic process has gotten somehow derailed, one thinks of a million reasons why what went wrong happened—one obsesses, licks one's wounds, makes resolutions for the future. But the bottom line is that one feels all of one's resources were not enough to save the day. Then the inevitable self-blame, self-pity, the search for others to blame and the frenzy to define how the circumstances simply could not be overcome. I don't want to get in over my head with Paul and then feel failure again as I have several times with others in the past in both my professional and personal life. But there is no way to pull out now, no way to retreat, no way to call off the appointment with the uncontained rage of the organizing transference. I hate it.

But there is another part of me, maybe the main part, that feels in a challenge situation. Like I'm in a marathon race or championship game or a debate—all of my resources are mobilized and my wits are finely honed for the battle. And that's what it is. It's not a battle with Paul—he and I are allies; he is depending on me, on my strength, courage, and skill. The battle is against his hidden or not so hidden psychosis. One goes on in therapy day in and day out pretending that the moment of truth will never come and then it does—and then is now. Are we really there? Maybe this will be another pseudo-crisis and things will settle down again the way they have so many times before. We aren't really ready yet, are we? Maybe I'll be able to shift him into more content modules or keep pushing the talk button until the intensity subsides and the earthquake settles and wait for a later planetary alignment.

This morning I was also remembering containment moments with my daughter in her early months when on several occasions she was experiencing intense distress. I would arrive home. She had been restless all day and driven my wife to distraction. It was my turn. I knew my calming role with my wife and we would get to that later. But now Breta's body was tense, her voice shrill, her back arching, her little arms pushing me away, her mouth refusing to suck the bottle offered. Slowly I would envelop her—just how I'm not sure I could say. But my mind, my mental determination to bring calm, would assert itself gradually in waves of forceful caring toward the tiny little struggling, out-of-control being, fighting her the whole way like slowly reeling in a fish, playing it, giving it slack, letting its energy dominate, and gradually wearing it down with persistence and determination to win. And of course I always would—I would find a way to join her level of tension, her rhythm of protest, her output frequency until I could slowly begin to modulate the distress, slowly reel her in, slowly pace her, slowly dominate the frenzy with calm, with containment, with peace and relaxation. Like spreading a large canopy—myself—and covering, protecting an unimaginably huge area. How moments like this try one's soul and how you pray for no outside interference! But I remember earaches that lasted the whole night through in the rocking chair. I would be dying for sleep and for calm myself. And just about the time we were ready to drift into peaceful togetherness some noise or some inner pain would set the turmoil off again. I would struggle to contain my instinct to sleep, my instinct to hate, my instinct to rage at frustrations I had no power to control. In this way I learned empathy for mothers who are horrified at fantasies of wanting to kill their babies, at parents with limited resources who literally beat and batter their babies.

How strong are we? How much can we take? When do we give up? How can we live with the terror of being unable to manage, of going out of control, of breaking down ourselves? In psychotherapy the unconscious transference goal of the client is to provoke a total replication of the original failure and breakdown in order to promote a total adult recall of the infantile trauma through re-experiencing the unbearable fragmentation in the present. Not until the breakdown is fully accomplished in the presence of and with the cooperation of the witnessing therapist can the two know together the power, the terror, the agony of the unspeakable infantile trauma—can the two establish consciousness (knowing together) of the devious and destructive forces that have been silently wreaking havoc behind the scenes for so long. Will I be able to mobilize Paul's inner resources in order to stem the tide or will the rage and murderous, retaliatory aggression win the day? I have had it go both ways. There are too many unknown and irrational factors and too many chance factors operating to be able to reliably predict the outcome.

Entering the fray with Paul is, at some deep level, very frightening. I not only face the possibility of defeat, but I fear the inner danger of giving my all to it and, in the process, collapsing in breakdown and failure myself. The danger puts me immediately into contact with my experiences as an infant—giving my all to find her, to attract her, to seduce her to come to me, to save me with life-sustaining connection, but then breaking down in utter failure because she wanted me to manage my needs on my own. I really don't want to do this. I don't want to have to experience Paul's organizing transference, which is bound to be violent and impactful. But isn't that what every performer says to him or herself just before the curtain goes up? What every champion says at the start line? "I really don't want to do this."

The third planet coming into alignment is Paul's real parents. They arrived from the East coast for a holiday stay with relatives and asked him to call last Saturday night. He hasn't been able to. He doesn't want to call, to talk to them, to see them yet he feels he must. How dynamically important this theme is at the moment I can't be sure. But time and again in the past when Paul has struggled to connect emotionally with one or the other parent I have firmly assured him that he is simply expecting more than they can give. Paul has protested—almost in tears—"Well, then, the only thing to do is just never to see them again, to give up, to never have a family, to let them die of old age never having learned how to connect to anyone." He always says this in a horror-stricken manner, reminding me that each of his siblings has come to the conclusion that the parents are intractable. Each sibling has given up on them, basically refusing to talk with them, doing only token service to annual family occasions in a superficial way.

The worst planet lining up is the one precipitating a staggering incapacity in Paul. This is his struggle with an employee to whom he has given heart and soul to helping for the last eight months. He supervises her in a situation that's threatening to end in disaster. Paul has done everything in his power to make it possible for this deeply disturbed and distraught woman to work productively and pleasurably for him. But he is clearly up against overwhelming odds. Edith appears to be irretrievably helpless, fragmented, and desperate. She goes from one pathetic illness or weakness excuse to another, hardly showing up at work, arriving hours late, leaving early, claiming her full salary, and not reporting or making up missed time. He is totally unable to be firm, to draw boundaries, to hold limits, or to state expectations clearly because he alternately feels sorry for her and then fears that it's his needing something from her, his pressuring her to perform, his provoking her with sarcastic criticism that is incapacitating her. In short, he has a perfect emotional replication of Louise and he is completely crippled in face of the weak, helpless, sick demeanor Edith presents to him.

Last Wednesday it all fell into place with my confronting/supporting him the entire session on how he must firmly manage Edith. He saw it and had been slowly moving in that direction for a number of weeks. I was firm and almost harsh in not letting him blame himself for her failures, for her irrational rages, amd for her basic incompetence. Throughout the hour Paul stammered as he struggled to stay connected with himself and with me around the problem of Edith, which we both knew was a living representation of the central problem of his life. We had made deep and intimate contact in the process and he had made use of it.

After our session Paul was restless and couldn't sleep all night, returning to disturbing sexualized fantasies and his long-standing nightmarish beliefs that he is somehow weird, strange, inhuman, and perverse—that something is truly and deeply wrong with him. He was impatient and angry with me the next day, clearly understanding that our interactions the day before had catapulted him into the chasm of despair that has been his lifelong nemesis. But Paul did have a good talk with Edith that day in which he spelled out firmly and in detail how he saw their problems. We had a lively, intense, and heated discussion most of the hour in which I firmly insisted that he was on the right track, that he must hold Edith to the line, and that he must be firm with the expectations and deadlines he has set for her today. Paul was distressed, in agony, and openly angry with me for pushing him, for insisting on clarity, for refusing his repeated statements that he is incompetent, deformed, defective, and psychotic. At times he was actually screaming and shouting directly and ragefully at me—really letting me have it for a number of things. I stayed with the rage that I wasn't helping him, that I too taxed him, that I shouldn't expect so much of him, and that I wanted him dead just like his parents. It was intense, direct, passionate, and contactful as I parried every thrust inviting more until his anger was spent—knowing the duel had been a contactful challenge for both of us—the best and most meaningful connection ever.

On Monday, Paul appeared blanched and more pent-up than I had ever seen him. He looked tight, nervous, and terrible. Thursday (after our last session) he had tossed and turned all night, sleeping badly. In the shower Friday morning he suddenly found himself obsessed with the statement, "You're right. I am monstrous!" The statement was addressed to everyone—to his parents, Edith, his colleagues, me, and the whole world of people who, the minute they see him, think the worst. In the ensuing discussion Paul hit his thighs hard several times, banged his chest with his fist hard, and finally slapped his face—all strong, spontaneous, somewhat alarming self-abusive behaviors I had never witnessed from him before. The abusive internal parents were alive and well—and now becoming defined and known.

Paul was angry at me and at how true it was—that he is a monster and there is nothing to be done about it, no hope of change. He hates himself. He might as well give up. At one point he sneaks in, "and you think so too." But I was ready and promptly refused to endorse the delusion. I repeated that he is not defective, only delusional about his monstrousness and lacking in a set of relating skills—something that we could work together on his developing. I repeated my belief that he is committed to messing up every possible relational situation by insisting that he is a monster, but that I absolutely refuse to endorse his cruel and self-destructive delusions about himself.

SESSION 8/7/91: THE BOOTSTRAP EFFECT

Fear takes strange and surprising turns in the organizing experience. Paul began today with a dream:

I was going to visit a therapist in this tall, vaguely confused sort of structure or building. He was late to start off with. Then when he appeared he was in a wheelchair with a disheveled suit, greasy skin, and mussed hair. It also seemed that he was confused or deranged. That's all.

I burst out laughing while Paul showed initial reluctance to point to me as the therapist in the dream. I was glad for the image because it promised to help us. It seemed no problem to feature me as the one he was hoping would help him. But after entering this confused structure and waiting too long, he found me crippled, deranged, repulsive, and pathetic. Paul didn't want to see the crippled, disheveled therapist as me nor did he like the idea of interpreting the dream as a role-reversal transference. For the rest of the session I struggled to interpret the role-reversal possibility. Paul kept misunderstanding me as somehow saying that he's the one who is really crippled, repulsive, crazy, and pathetic—something he simultaneously does and does not want to believe! I was (defensively) denying that I was saying this was his self-representation, and also pointing out that this is what he does—that is, struggles with me—just before breaks. This was the last session before a twelve-day vacation. My being offensively defensive was turned to more proof of how pathetic I saw him as being. He persisted in returning to the well-worked thematic demand that I had to believe in him and to affirm that he was worthwhile and good in order to contradict the message his parents gave him.

In the countertransference the power of the dream image echoed in my mind. What if he were correct—that in addition to being slow and late I am inept, crippled, and incompetent in my relationship with him? I worried I might not be able to turn the tide, that I might fumble around too long so that he finally becomes disgusted and gives up on me, abandoning me in my reaching out to him position. I would once again feel the crushing weight of failure. Other failures of a lifetime flashed before my mind. His by now persistent and perturbing broken-record insistence that I *do* something positive, that I show concrete evidence of getting a broader picture was interspersed with a barrage of sweeping criticisms of how many times he has tried to show me that he is in fact much better off than I believe him to be. Paul is furious that I might actually believe the "miserable incompetent wretch" facade he projects.

Being speechless, exasperated, and in an inner mire of frustration with Paul was by now familiar to me, so I attended to the fear of really being a crippled, repulsive, deranged, and pathetic therapist who was miserably failing. But, as usual in the endlessly repeated scenarios that characterize the therapeutic relationship, there was one fresh detail offered by the dream: namely, that Paul approaches the structure and the therapist with hope, with the expectation of "cure." I wondered aloud if that was how his parents approached him as their first-born, male child? I worked my interpretation unsuccessfully a number of times until two minutes before stopping time when he again pinned me to the wall with proof that I see no hope for him—that he *is* indeed crippled, pathetic, and disgusting. He repeated that he needs me to prove to him that he's worthwhile. I said he was deliberately mishearing me so that our holiday could begin on a sour note—just as I had predicted he would! Glancing at the clock, hoping for more time, he asked me to clarify because he didn't understand. We did take a little extra time because the stakes seemed so high.

Gathering my second wind I pushed forward, victoriously sensing that I had successfully hooked him.

> *Larry:* I cannot give you what you need to feel fulfilled, real, and good as a person. Only you can do that. And I believe that indeed you are doing just that. Slowly but surely you have come here hour after hour for almost three years working very hard

to show me the horrible trauma that you endured as a baby. Last week we were noticing an atmosphere between us in which I blame you for not making me a wonderful therapist and you blame me for not giving you what you need to be wonderfully alive. The mutually accusatory atmosphere is familiar to all of your relationships and goes back to infancy. The way we relate and the stories and dreams you bring are your way of bootstrapping yourself out of the terrible pit you have always felt yourself in. Inch by inch as you expand our relatedness and as we find new ways to discuss it—*you* are filling in the gap of self-worth that you believe I must fill in for you. [He is listening intently, apparently following] In the dream today you suggest that your parents approached their baby with hope—with the expectation that the lifelong emptiness each of them in their own way had experienced would be filled by you. They hoped that the baby's affirming responses to them would somehow fill in the internal gap, the painful hole they had always known. They hoped that having a beautiful baby would cure them. When the baby failed to parent them in the ways they needed and had hoped for, they saw the baby as weak, disgusting, damaged, crippled, and pathetic.

Paul: They've always seen me that way. They even both scapegoated their own therapists as failures.

Larry: You as the baby, of course, did your best to engage them, to please them, to get them to love and to approve of you. But your overtures were crushed.

Paul: They convinced me I was weak, disgusting, pathetic.

Larry: And so you transfer that to me—that I see you that way—when in fact I see you as an extraordinarily bright, competent, and creative person working hard to remember those early patterns by bringing them alive in our relationship. Then you take on their role—demanding that I, as little Paul, do something to prove that you (as Leonard and Louise) are not an empty, fragmented basket case. But being weak, pathetic, and crippled how can I?

Paul: I'm crushing you in the same way they crushed me?

Larry: Exactly. You're trying (by demanding that I do something to affirm you) to fill in the deep void. But I, Larry, am not a baby realistically fearing being crushed by abandonment and death if I don't satisfy you. I know that I cannot fill in your emptiness, that only you can do that. I further know that by using me as a reflecting instrument you are indeed finding and creating who you are. I will not conform by being a crippled, pathetic, disgusting therapist. I refuse to satisfy you by warping who I am to please you, as you had to do for them as a baby. Instead, I hope to show you your conforming patterns and thereby to watch you slowly realize that in essence you are not who they forced you to believe you are. That you are indeed a bright, loving, well-intentioned man who wants to love and be loved.

Paul: How will I know that?

Larry: You already do. Remember when we started compared with tonight—there's a world of difference in how you regard yourself and, therefore, in how you behave toward and relate to me. (He nods) You're filling in your own gap. Yes, you need me. But not to tell you that you're a good and worthwhile person as you believe you do. You need me to live out with you the crushing, crippling death-threatening circumstances of your infancy so that you can "remember" what happened and feel whole—you are bootstrapping yourself very well. Only *you* can prove your goodness and worth.

But, as is to be anticipated following a holiday break or in the wake of making new connections, over the next period Paul's determination, effectiveness, and clarity began to wane. Having gotten up a full head of steam myself for the shifts he was making, I soon found myself getting exasperated with Paul's failure to do a good follow-through on the many new courses he was beginning on. The countertransference this time begins to center on sensations in my hands and wrists with the distinct feeling that I want to shake him or strangle him to get him to straighten up and fly right. Undoubtedly this is his sense with his parents and clearly his parents' sense about him—murderous exasperation. Paul's moods fluctuate from moving effectively, to collapsing in despair, to making excuses for others, to being amused at my stated frustrations. But we're slowly moving forward into transformation and we both know it—three inches forward and one inch back!

AN EDUCATIONAL OR SUPPORTIVE APPROACH VERSUS AN ANALYTIC APPROACH

For conceptual clarity it is often helpful to distinguish between two diametrically opposed processes of growth and development. The first is an educational model, a positive and constructive one in which support and reinforcement allow new patterns of thought and behavior to be learned. In contrast, the analytic model is a breaking-down or destructive model in which previously established patterns of thought and behavior have an opportunity to be brought into full awareness so that their power and influence can be diminished or relinquished. In psychoanalysis the goal has always been to find ways of framing old patterns of emotional relatedness so that they enter into full consciousness in the here-and-now relationship dimension of the analytic process. Freud and the classical psychoanalysts specified the ways in which a frame for securing neurotic (5-year-old, triangular, family) relatedness issues can be created. Kohut has specified somewhat different ways for framing narcissistic (3-year-old, self-to-selfobject) relatedness patterns for analysis. Winnicott, Little, Mahler, Kernberg, and many others have participated in creating framing techniques for securing for analytic scrutiny the so-called borderline or symbiotic (self and other) relatedness scenarios. Searles, Giovacchini, Tustin, Grotstein, and Hedges have each specified ways in which organizing or psychotic (earliest months of life) relatedness patterns can be framed for analytic transformation. The organizing relatedness pattern (the so-called transference psychosis) exists as modes of avoiding, fleeing from, rupturing, or failing to sustain interpersonal connection.

The technique for framing organizing patterns of relatedness consists of:

1. establishing an analytic environment in which interpersonal contact can be tolerated with a sense of safety; then
2. promoting various forms of interpersonal relationship and connection; and finally
3. studying the transferential patterns of avoiding, breaking off, or fleeing from the discomfort and terror experienced as a result of anticipated, achieved, or sustained interpersonal connections.

Organizing-level patterns of relatedness that interfere with personality expansion and growth are assumed to arise from disruptive focal or strain trauma experienced in earliest infancy. Therefore, it can be expected that considerable time will be required to slowly bring these deepest, most basic relatedness patterns into the interpersonal focus and dialogue of an analytic relationship. I will conclude my report on Paul by briefly describing two relational images and experiences that illustrate his movement toward analytic transformation.

THE FREEWAY OF LIFE—THE THIRD YEAR OF THERAPY

Following a number of interactions that had an increasing sense of personal connection between Paul and myself, I again began pressing him toward more engagements with other people in various places in his life. While Paul knows that learning how to establish better interactions is essential for his well-being, he has remained mired down in the delusion that others have negative views of him, don't want to relate to him, and wish he would go away or die. After a series of significantly more successful efforts on the socializing front, Paul developed a freeway phobia one weekend when visiting his parents. He had never experienced driving difficulties before. He was in the center lanes of a large freeway with traffic moving rapidly in all directions and was struggling to make sense of all of the lanes and signs when he became acutely panicked and had to take the first opportunity to get off the road and calm down. Over the weeks as he elaborated the phobia Paul talked about how "You can't afford to think about what you're doing on a freeway if you want to negotiate complex driving situations—you have to intuitively just move and make decisions based on knee-jerk kinds of instantaneous judgments. If you once look back over your shoulder and think of how fast each vehicle is coming, where they're going, and how you'll negotiate between them while trying to keep your direction and lane movements clear, you'll immediately become confused." I interpreted Paul's freeway phobia as a representation of the freeway of life and of complex and real relationships. We considered jointly how much driving a freeway is like negotiating relationships—if you stop to think about things, or explore frightened or paranoid feelings that may come up in the course of a conversation, you immediately become lost and panicked and have to pull out of the relating scene.

Over several months we noted many examples in which Paul had to withdraw from relationships to avoid confusion and fear. But no sooner did we become able to contextualize each phobic episode in the day or week of social interactions or in our relationship than Paul would quickly retreat to—"But what if I'm really in the middle of a freeway and become truly paralyzed with fear and then I become unable to pull off and I crash into other cars? That could really happen, you know. I could kill myself and everybody else! It might get so bad I can't go anywhere or even come to see you." I regularly interpreted Paul's fear of becoming frozen with life-threatening fear as *the very mechanism he uses to justify not moving forward*, not going ahead and flying by the seat of his pants trying intuitively to do the best he can—both on the freeway and in relationships in life. I accepted no excuses. I said he could pull off the freeway any time he needed to. Or while he was learning to be brave, he could try an anti-anxiety medication to give him the courage to try out new interpersonal experiences. I have from time to time wished to get Paul involved with a third-party case monitor, so a consulting psychiatrist would indeed be welcomed by me into our interaction. I again brought up the idea. But Paul was reluctant to pursue a medication evaluation, preferring to wing it in new situations. He continued stretching himself in a variety of ways and tolerating a backlash of freeway anxiety. The phobic anxiety was clearly serving to signal Paul of the dangers of the spontaneous relating he was increasingly engaging in, and to remind him that interpersonal connections feel terrifyingly dangerous—as though they might kill him or others at any time.

THE BANQUET OF FLESH

The final relational image to be discussed began after a series of more intense personal engagements had occurred with me around Paul's increasingly effective social interactions. The background to the episode to be described has already been touched on lightly. Paul has had a way of getting into a cycle of devaluing himself in various ways, citing many personal interactions and his recurring belief that others see him as an ineffective, weak, confused, miserable wreck. The images, the people involved, and the negative qualities vary considerably, but the downward spiral of Paul's self-criticism invariably drones on in an similar vein ending with the surprise line directed at me—"and you think so too!"

During the course of our time together I have gone through various phases of responding to this challenge thrown to me. In the early phases I would protest that I had no such view, that in fact I liked him very much, saw him as competent, and respected him in every way, and so forth—depending on whatever barrage of self-criticism he had just offered. But Paul always had me in some way because he would quickly quote something potentially critical that I had said earlier in the session or on some previous occasion. He would give the line a deadly negative twist to prove that I indeed did think ill of him. That he was right, that it was true that I saw him as a sloppy miserable wretch or a ne'er do well. At first I would go into momentary confusion at his misinterpretation of what I had said. Then I learned to confront him and to dispute what he was imputing to me—and then to reaffirm him. But these downward spirals of self-criticism followed by a gauntlet thrown down to me continued. At times I tried to go with whatever negativity might have been implicit in my former comments. Then I would attempt to show Paul that my meaning was essentially positive—but he would remain unconvinced, nonplussed, or skeptical. After a while I got frustrated and tried to point out the double bind Paul put me in on these occasions. At other times I would get angry with him, insisting that he was deliberately distorting. Then I would try to show what his motivation might be for needing to see me as a harsh critic of his at that particular point in time. I tried various ways of exploring meanings, of looking for contextual cues, and of attempting to align Paul on the side of studying the interaction—all to little avail. Something was not yet understood.

Eventually I could feel myself squarely in Paul's trap every time he laid it. I then simply lapsed into looking at him inquisitively in response, trying to get him to elaborate what had just transpired between us and why. Paul wasn't uncooperative in these searches for meaning, but he always somehow got back to the refrain that I indeed hated him and I that I had said it clearly in so many words, no matter how much I tried to deny it. Of course we tried various transpositions of Louise and Leonard transference, which led up to the following events.

After a particularly social but frustrating weekend Paul had the following dream:

> I was going somewhere with Jerry (whose passivity all weekend had messed up a series of plans). We were in some European city, maybe Paris, and were supposed to be going to eat at this rather elegant cafe or restaurant. When we arrived we were shown the sideboard where two live horses were laid out, sedated and with their eyes covered so they couldn't see what was happening. We were handed these knives or meat cleavers and a plate in a nonchalant way. Like what you were supposed to do for your dining pleasure in this elegant bistro was to chop off chunks of meat—live flesh to eat. Like it was supposed to be some sort of delicacy and we were expected to simply go along with it. I recognized the scene as bizarre, as something I simply didn't want to do. I was immediately nervous and looking around, like maybe there was some vegetarian dish instead! I woke up very upset and began thinking about my relationship with Leonard.

In Paul's associations to the dream he emphasized the element of passivity, that he was simply *expected* to go along with this horse's ass kind of banquet. He and Leonard are always figuratively taking chunks out of each other's flesh and it's supposed to be okay, the proper and pleasurable way to relate. In the dream the two horses are laid out, sedated, and blindfolded so they won't actually see or feel what's being done to them (the passive position). Paul could see that the underpinning was, of course, the scenarios with Louise in which each person had to be the destruction of the other while both pretended that everything was as it should be. Paul said he has always felt forced to passively comply with this sort of bizarre and monstrous feasting on flesh that was in vogue in his family.

My interpretations focused in a congratulatory way on Paul's actively deciding to turn away from his lifelong pattern of feasting on flesh—this scenario of mutual cannibalism—to something different, namely to nourishing and healthy vegetables. We both laughed. We processed this dream in a variety of ways for several sessions.

A week later Paul started into another one of his downward spirals of self-criticism. By now well-accustomed to the horror of watching him rip himself limb from limb in these tirades, I watched with the fresh image of a flesh-eating banquet in the back of my mind. This time I saw the gauntlet coming a good three minutes before it landed squarely in front of me. I was lying in wait, in almost open-mouthed amazement, watching Paul's downward spiral of self-effacement with horror, knowing he would soon launch his surprise attack on me. I wish I could remember the exact content, but I was swimming in the increasing intensity of the moment. Paul suddenly looked up directly at me and said his usual, "and you think so too." But I was ready. I went with it. I continued his vicious, destructive banter along the lines of the same content he had just provided me with. I told him that it was true that I hated him, that he was indeed worthless, psychotic, delusional, despicable, a miserable wretch, and so forth. Paul was stunned. But grasping my ploy, he quickly added, *"You take your pleasure and amusement from watching me tear myself down and slowly self-destruct."*

I immediately fell into a pit. In this quick and brief exchange we had deepened the emotional material to a horrifying low. Paul added, *"And you do it so you can feel secure in your superiority."* I was truly stunned. I remember thinking, *"I have to go here, I have to feel this."* And I did. As the two of us sat in momentary silence I let my body and my mind drop into the experience of taking my pleasure and amusement from watching Paul self-efface and self-destruct in front of my very eyes. I enjoyed it. I actually allowed a full sense of cannibalistic glee and destructiveness to overcome me. Paul tried to talk—but I waved him off to shut him up. My mind swam in timeless delight and horror—images of Caesars languishing in decadent delight in the Roman Circus swirled. I saw slaves being slaughtered and eaten by lions. I thought of Nero, of Rome Burning, of Hitler, of lines of Jews, the ovens, of Sade, of naked savages chewing on human bones. Tears welled up in my eyes. My stomach churned in violent upheaval. I stammered, trying to speak what I was experiencing—voice quaking, facing the wide-eyed Paul. I slowly came to myself. *"I can't do it! I won't do it! I refuse this god-forsaken banquet of flesh—show me the vegetables!"* We laughed but were both taken aback—shaken by the truth and violence of the moment and by our mutual willingness to go there. Vegetables were a welcome comic relief. *"As a child you had no choice. You were led to this flesh-eating banquet and expected to partake. It was all that was offered. You had no way of knowing that there was a better way. You were drugged and blinded and told to eat. But I'm not a child. Nor am I passive. This flesh-eating banquet you led me to is a bizarre horror and I will have nothing to do with it. I will not eat!"* I had to repeat the lines forcefully several times to rescue myself from the emotional pull of the pit, the swirling horrors, the timeless spinning, and the disgusting nausea of destruction. *"I saw it. I felt it. It was terrifyingly real and horrible. I won't go there with you. I absolutely will not!"*

Dreams represent the conservative part of our primitive minds and they are the last to give way to deep character change. When Paul was wakened from the dream by his refusal to be passively led into cannibalizing on chunks of flesh, I understood his anxiety as his fear of turning away from the table that has always been laid for him. When Paul again tried to take me to that bizarre flesh-eating banquet table I finally grasped at an experiential body level what has been perhaps Paul's deepest truth. Terrified, horrified, I yelled, *"Horse's ass, I won't go there with you!"* Paul and I were together at last. We both were refusing to be passively traumatized.

For a lifetime Paul has feared relationships based on the template of a drugged and blinded cannibalistic scenario. But until now he has been compelled to return repeatedly to being the self-destructing sacrifice for his internal parents' amusement, pleasure, and self-aggrandizement. It was the only way of relating that he knew. Early in life Paul learned to turn the experience around, to reverse the roles and to sacrifice his experiences of others by destroying the very links and emotional possibilities that might set him free and allow him to grow.

Paul's deep pattern was yielding at last.

17

Summary and Conclusions: The Place of Terrifying Transferences in Human Realities

A GENERAL BACKDROP FOR CONSIDERING HUMAN TERROR

The dawn of the third millennium of Caesar Augustus' calendar sees a strange new light permeating Western Civilization. The new enlightenment is not entirely novel to Eastern Civilizations but because of our history it is now being noted and formulated differently than in, say, Taoism or Buddhism.

We are ever becoming more aware that things we have always assumed about our nature and our surroundings cannot possibly be so simple as we have imagined them. Our primate mentality, which has sought to understand the nature of such things as a banana, a tree, an enemy, or a child, found its formal expression in seventeenth-century Newtonianism and nineteenth-century objective science. But the advent of twentieth-century relativism, quantum mechanics, and chaos theory has forced us to question all previous assumptions about human realities as we have defined them. And to question all of our former methods of studying them.

We now know that human existence is inextricably tied to far-flung forces in the universe that we can neither clearly understand nor even easily observe or formulate. We also know that we can no longer objectively study our realities or our minds as an ape might study a banana. We find increasingly that we must settle for a series of interlocking but partial understandings of the forces and dimensions operating within us and around us, and that we must cultivate interesting points of view or perspectives from which we can make provisional observations and draw perennially tentative conclusions (Hedges 1983). Further, we find that we will likely have to relinquish altogether our persistent hope for a Grand Unified Theory, on the basis of it being, in principle, not possible to formulate the large scheme of things without encountering inherently gross inconsistencies and contradictions.

Not only have studies in physics and chemistry radically changed, but biological and evolutionary theory itself is now being reformulated along entirely new lines, so that we are coming to see life forms as evolving in specific environmental niches, each with its own self-regulating systems responding to other self-regulating systems (Maturana and Varela 1987, Varela et. al. 1995, von Forester 1962). Information theory, which has produced for us complicated computer systems and networks, has also changed how we view ourselves, our evolution, and our complex, interrelated, and ever-changing neurological systems. In short, the third millennium begins without our having a stable sense of what is real in human life.[1]

In psychotherapy and psychoanalysis we are coming less to assume that we know the *nature* of the human mind as we come increasingly to formulate it in terms of interpersonal listening dimensions that are known to have the power to transform individual human lives. That is, as we slowly succeed in freeing ourselves from the truth-seeking approaches of nineteenth-century objective science, we are increasingly immersing ourselves in various forms of systematic sub-

---

1. A detailed survey of the findings of quantum and chaos science and their implications for psychotherapy and psychoanalysis can be found in Hedges (1992).

jectivity and what Robert Stolorow and his colleagues (1992, 1994) have called intersubjectivity.

Whatever else may be said about human mind, we now believe it is formed in relation to other interacting minds, and that mind and its transformations are inextricably enmeshed in human relationships and the human relationship potential. At every stage of our existence we can be seen as organizing, disorganizing, and reorganizing our somato-psychic processes according to the demands of relationships as we perceive them at the time. In his 1997 book, *Cracking Up*, Christopher Bollas has formulated this ongoing and generative human activity of creating interpersonal tension and meanings and then of relaxing and allowing mutually created meanings to dissolve into laughter and tears as a vital human mental process.

TERROR

Terror—the fear of fear itself, the fear of ceaseless physical and emotional pain or vulnerability–is a universal part of human experience, though clearly our past individual experiences with fear and with uncontrolled terror undoubtedly color the way we each anticipate fear and defend against it. Most, but certainly not all, experiences of uncontrolled terror occur prior to the third or fourth year of life, by which time a child generally develops enough ego and self strength to master rudimentary forms of fear management. Fears of dismemberment, disease, death, incapacity, immobilization, fragmentation, and/or emptiness may at times be realistic to our personal life circumstances or may serve as images for representing or expressing otherwise unrepresentable or inexpressible mental and physical memories or states. Archetypal themes such as abduction, ritual abuse, incest, out-of-body experience, dissociation, depersonalization, past lives, and multiple selves can also serve as expressions of preverbal and otherwise unrememberable agonizing and dreaded somato-psychic experiences. *But since we now understand that human experience never occurs outside of some mental-relational context, we can also understand that memories of infantile traumas are inevitably attached to, paired with, and understood in some relational context, and that later similar relational contexts tend to revive anticipatory fears, pre-defenses, and experiential modes that were once attached to ear-*

lier terrifying experiences. Such fears, pre-defenses, and experiential modes can be expressed in a variety of somato-psychic ways that serve to crystallize, concretize, and represent in conscious awareness many otherwise unrememberable and unrepresentable experiences.

In psychotherapy and psychoanalysis we openly invite people to *remember through relating.* We expect an array of developmentally based fears to arise in the course of the intimate therapeutic relationship. In fact, it might even be said that the purpose of psychotherapy is to set up an intimate interpersonal situation designed to facilitate the arousal of previously experienced relational-fear responses so that their unthinking and automatic qualities can be brought to light, examined, and to a greater or lesser extent, relinquished.

From conception forward, fetuses and infants are subjected to a series of unsettling, frightening, and, if uncontained, terrifying experiences. Whether from intrauterine causes such as toxemia and genetic aberrations or from psycho-physical trauma, fetuses and babies withdraw, constrict, and/or slump and wither when confronted with overwhelming stimulation. Fraiberg (1982) has characterized the expectable responses to traumatic experiences of the mammalian newborn as the pre-defenses of fight, flight, and freeze. We now understand that whether we conceptualize in terms of the schizoid (withdrawing) defenses (Klein 1957), or mammalian pre-defenses (Fraiberg 1982), or somato-psychic constriction and withering (Hedges and Hilton, in press), that *the infant's response to overwhelming stimulation is traumatic and is invariably experienced as relational, as occurring in the context of a relationship with someone present or absent.*

The psychological theory of transference predicts that traumatic experiences will be recalled in some way when similar relational circumstances arise, prevail, or threaten. Consequently, in any ongoing relationship it is only a matter of time before a person begins to anticipate experiences occurring that have characterized previously experienced dreaded and avoided relationships. The psychotherapeutic relationship thus moves inexorably toward the re-experiencing of life's most primitive experiences of terror within the context of the relationship. Whether such terrors are allowed to develop over time is a function of the willingness and ability of the analytic speaker to relive the terrifying experiences in the context of a current intimate relationship, and one function of the skill of the analytic listener lies in being able and willing to welcome and interpret the resistance to re-experiencing the terror in the transferred here-and-now relationship.

COUNTERTRANSFERENCE TO
ORGANIZING-LEVEL TERROR

Countertransference responsiveness has traditionally been conceptualized as being an impediment to or a potential interference with the analytic process when dealing with relatedness issues internalized during the oedipal period of triangular (5-year-old) relating (Freud 1910, 1915). Countertransference responsiveness has been seen as facilitative in the recognition and analysis of narcissistic issues internalized during the (3-year-old) era of self-consolidation (Kohut 1971). Countertransference replications of (4- to 24-month-old) relatedness scenarios internalized through interactions with early caregivers have been seen as expectable if not essential in the analysis of borderline or symbiotic relatedness issues (Bollas 1987, Hedges 1983, 1992, Little 1981). Countertransference reactions encountered in the analysis of the earliest relatedness strivings, developmentally defined as the period in which the fetus or neonate is organizing nurturing and other meaningful channels to the human milieu, have been studied by Giovacchini (1979), Searles (1979), Grotstein (1981), Tustin (1981), and Hedges (1983, 1992, 1994 a,c).

Hedges (1994c) summarizes the most common countertransference reactions to organizing or psychotic level transferences as follows: (1) the belief that the person is sick, crazy, evil, or untreatable and must be managed with support, medication, exorcism, or lockup; (2) the fear that the intensity of the psychotic anxieties will become directed at the person of the analyst or the process of analysis; (3) the mobilization in the analyst of his or her own primitive organizing experiences and anxieties; and (4) an emotional withdrawal of the analyst *out of empathy with the deep terror* which threatens as a result of intense or sustained interpersonal connections. Countertransference terror can be expected to take any of these forms. I often find myself saying to a therapist in the throes of a heavy countertransference reaction, "There's a reason why more than eight million such people were burned at the stake as witches over a five-hundred-year period. Primitive anxiety sets off unspeakable terror responses in us and a desperation to do something about it!"

CONCLUSIONS

Clinical experience over the decades since 1911, when Freud first published his interpretation of Judge Schreber's memoirs of his psychosis has shown that much time is required for the person in analysis to feel safe enough to trust the analyst and the analytic situation to contain the disruptive elements of terror, the pre-defensive reactions to it, and the analyst's countertransference responses. Several of the case studies in this book have been chosen to illustrate the long and arduous task of establishing a safe context for terror to be interpersonally remembered in the transferential here-and-now. Other cases illustrate the tentative beginning of contact and the terror responses that occur on the way to establishing more reliable connections through interpersonal mutual cuing systems and symbiotic scenarios. And cases are provided to show various ways in which the primitive terrifying transferences can be lived through and worked through by analytic speaker and listener.

Throughout I have emphasized the disruptive effects on the therapist of the impact of primitive terrors and the importance of clearly establishing a frame in which terrors can be experienced, and of arranging for outside resources in terms of medication, hospitalization, peer consultation, and a third-party case monitor to keep track of the ongoing process and to provide a continuous reality perspective on the developing transference–countertransference engagement. This work cannot be safely done without auxiliary resources to assist both client and therapist.

In *Working the Organizing Experience* (1994c) my colleagues and I have presented a series of critical listening dimensions and techniques for work with organizing or psychotic transferences and have specified an expectable path to the establishment of interpersonally organized psychic experience. Eight in-depth case studies are provided by *In Search of the Lost Mother of Infancy* (1994a) to illustrate the types of organizing experience that often appear in clinical practice and to show how they can be responded to. *Terrifying Transferences* has sought to elucidate the unpredictable and disruptive elements of primitive terror as it inevitably appears in the working-through process with organizing transferences and countertransferences—whether they exist in small pockets of an otherwise well-developed personality or are pervasive in the personality makeup.

It is now up to the reader's imagination, courage, creativity, and determination to use these rough maps as listening perspectives to forge new and creative pathways into this truly new frontier of the human mind, the organizing experience.

APPENDICES

APPENDICES

Appendix A

The Dual Relationship
in Psychotherapy

The Problem of Duality

INTRODUCTORY COMMENTS: THE RISE AND FALL OF THE "DUALITY" CONCEPT

In 1973 The American Psychological Association Code of Ethics, in an effort to curb sexual exploitation in the psychotherapeutic relationship, opened Pandora's box when it coined the term "dual relationship." Since then, like Pandora's miseries, which spread evil throughout the world, every aspect of the psychotherapeutic relationship has been colored with continual concern, frustration, and doubt. The faulty shift of ethical focus from "damaging exploitation" to "dual relationships" has led to widespread misunderstanding and incessant naive moralizing that has undermined the spontaneous, creative, and

Reprinted with permission from *The California Therapist*, May/June, July/August, September/October 1993, originally titled "In Praise of the Dual Relationship."

unique aspects of the personal relationship that is essential to the psychotherapeutic process.

The atmosphere in the community of practicing psychotherapists that has been created by ethics committees and licensing boards now amounts almost to hysterical paranoia. It is as though some sort of witch-hunt is afoot, and no practicing therapist has a clean conscience when guilt is being dished out about the subtle potentials of dual relating! The bottom line is that dynamic and systems-oriented psychotherapies cannot be practiced without various forms of dual relating and every therapist knows this. But we have wrongly been told that dual relating is unethical.

The good news is that the pendulum has started swinging back and a hefty dialogue clearly lies ahead of us. The American Psychological Association (APA) Insurance Trust maintains that not all multiple roles are dual relationships. But the implication is still that "duality" may be unethical. The recent code of ethics for the California Association of Marriage, Family, and Child Counselors categorically states that "not all dual relationships are unethical." And the revised (December 1992) APA Code of Ethics at last returns us to sanity:

> In many communities and situations, it may not be feasible or reasonable for psychologists to avoid social or other nonprofessional contacts with persons such as patients, clients, students, supervisees, or research participants. Psychologists must always be sensitive to the potential harmful effects of other contacts on their work and on those persons with whom they deal. . . . Psychologists do not exploit persons over whom they have supervisory, evaluative, or other authority such as students, supervisees, employees, research participants and clients or patients. . . . Psychologists do not engage in sexual relationships with students or supervisees in training over whom the psychologist has evaluative or direct authority, because such relationships are so likely to impair judgment or be exploitative. . . . Psychologists do not engage in sexual intimacies with current patients or clients. . . . Psychologists do not accept as therapy patients or clients persons with whom they have engaged in sexual intimacies [and] do not engage in sexual intimacies with a former therapy patient or client for at least two years after cessation or termination of professional services. . . . The psychologist who engages in such activities after the two years following cessation or termination of treatment bears the burden of demonstrating that there has been no exploitation, in light of all relevant factors. [¶ 1.17]

Thus, after twenty years of grief, the term *dual relationship* as an ethical definition has been entirely eliminated from the revised APA code. The current ethical focus is on remaining mindful of the ever-present possibility of damaging exploitation. But the malignant concept of dual relationship that the APA introduced and has now eliminated has infected ethics committees, licensing boards, and malpractice litigation everywhere. We still have a major battle ahead to undo the severe damage done to the psychotherapeutic relationship by the pejorative use of the term *dual relationship*.

THE CASE FOR DUAL RELATIONSHIPS

As the pendulum swings back, such writers as Kitchener (1988) and Tomm (1991) argue that dual relationships need to be considered more carefully. Here are the main points that have emerged to date. (1) Dual relating is inevitable and offers many constructive possibilities. (2) Dual relationships are only one way an exploitative therapist or an exploitative client may take advantage of the other. (3) Metaphors are mixed when duality is treated as a toxic substance that "impairs judgment." (4) A priority of emphasis on the professional *role* serves to diminish personal connectedness, thereby fostering human alienation and endorsing a privileged role hierarchy. (5) Exploitation in relationships is always exploitation and unethical regardless of whether it occurs in a dual context. (6) Multiple connections that cross boundaries between therapy, teachings, supervision, collegiality, and friendship can be celebrated as part of the inevitable and potentially beneficial complexities of human life. (7) The power differential in any relationship can be used to empower the personal and/or professional development of both parties as well as to exploit them. (8) A frequent therapeutic goal involves helping students, supervisees, and clients understand and negotiate the multiple and shifting layers of human relatedness and human relational systems. (9) It is preferable to humanize and to democratize the therapeutic relationship rather than to encumber it with unnecessary trappings of professional expertise and higher authority. (10) The therapeutic role can be misused by cloaking it in paternalistic, patronizing attitudes of emotional distance and myths regarding the superior mental health of practitioners. (11) Incompetent and exploitative therapists are the problem, not dual relating. (12) What is needed by therapists is classification and discussion of the subtle kinds of exploitation that can and do occur in professional relationships, not a naive injunction against dual relating. (13) To categorically prohibit dual relationships reductionistically implies that there is no continuity or overlap in roles in relationships and that therapy can be separated from the person of the therapist. (14) Dual relationships are inevitable and clinicians can conduct them thoughtfully and ethically, making whatever happens "grist for the mill." (15) Dual relationships represent an opportunity for personal growth and enriched human connection that benefits both parties. (16) Human connections evolve spontaneously and change over the course of time naturally and unpredictably, and therapy need not block this natural process. (17) Duality provides an important pathway for corrective feedback, potentially offering improved understanding and increased consensuality. (18) Duality opens space for increased connectedness, more sharing, greater honesty, more personal integrity, greater responsibility, increased social integration, and more egalitarian interaction. (19) Dual relating reduces space for manipulation, deception, and special privilege, gives more opportunity to recognize each other as ordinary human beings, and reduces the likelihood of persistent transferential and countertransferential distortions. (20) Interpersonal boundaries are rarely rigid and fixed, but rather fluctuate and undergo continuous redefinition in all relationships, including the therapeutic relationship, which deliberately focuses on developing consciousness of boundary fluctuations and discussing such changes. (21) Dual relationships represent, after all, the exact kinds of complex interpersonal situations that our professional skills were developed to study and enhance, so as to increase the beneficial possibilities of human interactions and transformations.

Since these points have been discussed at length by the writers mentioned above, I will move on to other areas that I believe need to be elucidated. Being trained as a psychoanalyst, I will bring to bear on the subject various considerations of duality that have emerged over time in the psychoanalytic literature. These ideas seem relevant to consider in all dynamic and systems-oriented therapies. I leave it to others to bring forward ideas that have emerged from their own areas of specialization.

PSYCHOANALYTIC CONSIDERATIONS OF DUALITY

Duality: The Essence of Transference Interpretation

The very heart and soul of psychotherapy, transference, and transference interpretation, by definition, always constitute some form of dual relationship. Freud's initial definitions of psychoanalytic technique (1912, 1915) revolve around the "love" relationship that begins to form between physician and client in the course of psychoanalytic free association. Freud suggests the image of an opaque mirror to describe the neutral stance that the analyst seeks to achieve vis-à-vis the patient's neurotic conflict. Freud's images make clear the ultimate impossibility of ever attaining perfect mirroring or perfect neutrality. Despite the analyst's attempt to form a real relationship based on mirroring and neutrality, relationship expectations brought from the client's past would inevitably begin to make their presence felt. The decisive moment in psychoanalysis, and in all derivative psychotherapies, is that in which the duality is at last recognized and successfully interpreted by the psychotherapist. There exists at this moment the "real" relationship that has evolved over time between two people. But another reality is suddenly recognized and defined by the transference interpretation. In the former reality the analyst has a caretaking, curative role and the client has an obligation to relate to real needs of the analyst including fees, attendance, and respect for the setting that supports and protects the personal and professional life of the analyst as well as the client. But when transference reality can be discerned and discussed by two, the therapist functions in a completely different relationship to the client—one of professional interpreter of the emotional life of the client, which is brought to the real relationship set up by the analytic situation. At the moment of interpretation the analyst steps into the role of a third party viewing the realistic interaction of the two and comments on a heretofore hidden reality—the transference, or the resistance, or the countertransference.

The Working Alliance

Over time, the nature of this dual role of the analyst has received considerable attention in the psychoanalytic literature. Greenson

(1965), acknowledging the "real" developing relationship, speaks of "the working alliance" to acknowledge the *realistic collaboration and mutual respect of two*. Greenson's formulations stand as a correction of the faulty belief that the client's attitudes and fantasies are mostly transference distortions—when in fact a significant real relationship develops quite apart from the professional task of transference interpretation.

"Acting Out" Childhood Transformations

Bollas (1979) further clarifies the nature of the real relationship by pointing out that Freud (unwittingly and forgivably) designed the psychoanalytic listening situation in order to "act out" with his patients the earliest caretaking roles of parenting, so as to promote the transformational aspect of psychotherapy. The transformational role of the analyst is a realistic role distinctly different from that of transference interpreter. Psychoanalytic transformation occurs by means of this dual transforming/interpreting relationship. Following Winnicott's (1975) developmental approach and Modell's (1976) notion of the "holding environment," Bollas places the transformative element of psychotherapy less in a context of interpretive correction and more within a context of the therapeutic experience as it actually, realistically evolves. He refers to this transformative process as "psychoanalysis of the unthought known."

Transference Experience Arises from Realistic Relating

Schwaber's (1979, 1983) clarifying work arises from an orientation emphasizing the subjective aspects of self. Her ideas focus on the role that the *reality* of the analyst and the analytic relationship play in evoking transference. She, following Kohut (1971, 1977), emphasizes the reality of the ongoing nature of the relationship that evolves in the psychoanalytic listening situation. Transference from past experience is to be discerned on the basis of something the analyst actually did or did not do and the emotional reaction that the analyst's actual activities elicited. Schwaber highlights the real relationship based upon the analyst's effort to listen and to respond as empathically as humanly possible. Transference is then thought to be perceivable against the backdrop of failures in the analyst's empathic understanding. That is, the analyst actually engages or fails to engage in real interpersonal activity, the disruptive results of which the analyst could not have possibly foretold. According to this view, the working through of the "self-object" or narcissistic transference constitutes a new edition, a novel interpersonal reality that the analyst and client have now to address with new and different understanding and interpretation. Thus, not only is transference discernible by virtue of aspects of the real relationship coming up for discussion, but the working through is seen as an entirely new and evolving form of personal relationship.

The Transference Neurosis

The notion of cure in psychoanalytic theory revolves around Freud's definition of transference neurosis. The (neurotic) conflicts from the past come to be actually re-experienced in the present and are experienced by the client as the realistic situation. They are, by Freud's definition, complex unconscious features never fully interpretable as such. The ultimate unresolvability of the transference neurosis is widely misunderstood by those who wish a happy sunset at the end of analysis. But in Freudian analysis there are always interminable aspects to analytic work, and the transference neurosis in certain respects lives on indefinitely (for discussion see Hedges 1983, Chapters 3 and 4).

Mutative Interpretation

Strachey (1934) quotes Melanie Klein as saying that analysts are generally reluctant to give mutative interpretations (those that promote change) because full instinctual energy would thereby be directed *realistically* at the person of the analyst. This situation is feared and avoided by analysts who fail to interpret so the full power of transference comes into focus in the here and now. Thus, the two key curative agents in psychoanalysis—the establishment of the transference neurosis and the mutative interpretation—both function to bring past emotional experience to bear on and to intensify the *reality* of the present interpersonal relationship. These two realities will never become completely sorted out. One's past emotional life forever colors present relationships. Thus, psychoanalytic doctrine holds that the duality between the realistic present and the transferential past can never, in principle, be eliminated from human relationships. Psychoanalysis serves the purpose of shedding light on many aspects of these dual realities.

The Corrective Emotional Experience

Another line of psychoanalytic thought revolves around the notion of "corrective emotional experience" (Alexander 1961). Various realistic and active procedures may be introduced into the relationship for the purposes of promoting or maintaining the analysis (Eissler 1953, Ferenczi 1952, 1955, 1962). But the need for such reassurance, suggestion, or gratification later will have to be analyzed as transference. According to this view, the client's emotional past was flawed and the therapist is (realistically) going to be able to provide a better (corrective) emotional experience. The analyst by this view may actually step out of his or her usual role as analyst and "do things," intervene in active ways to help the client relate to the therapist and to stay in therapy.

Classical analysts who oppose active techniques maintain that the refusal by the analyst to engage in active, helpful interventions (which serve to strengthen the ego by support and suggestion) is what makes psychoanalysis different from all other "more supportive" psychotherapeutic and counseling techniques. Analysts who advocate the need for active intervention under certain circumstances implicitly recognize that the therapeutic action of psychoanalysis requires various forms of duality to become effective. This line of thinking asserts that psychotherapy and counseling, as distinguished from classical psychoanalysis, definitely and inevitably include the duality that characterizes the more active psychoanalytic techniques. It took Bollas (1979) to point out that even classical technique implicitly includes a setting in which transformational experiences from early childhood are acted out in a supportive way by the analyst. Dual relationships thus form the backbone of all dynamically oriented psychotherapies.

In Praise of the Dual Relationship

ESSENTIAL DUAL RELATEDNESS IN DEVELOPMENTAL PSYCHOTHERAPY

It is a moot question whether psychotherapeutic clients today are more primitive or disturbed than in the past or whether our therapeutic knowledge now enables us to see more clearly the more regressed aspects of human nature. In either case, the facts are that people who come to psychotherapy today present for analysis many very early developmental issues that have come to be called "borderline," "narcissistic," and "character" problems.

In general, there is a greater subjective sense of reality in the analytic relationship the further down the developmental ladder one finds the issue being attended to in psychotherapy. Winnicott (1949) points out that the earlier in development the impingement on the infant's sense of "going on being" is, the shorter the span of the ego—meaning the less that can be considered at any one moment in time. Thus, when early developmental issues arise in therapy, less reality testing is available, and only a greatly narrowed picture of the world and the analytic relationship is possible. In today's psychotherapy, many early developmental issues are activated. Consequently, a narrow, concrete, subjective experience may well take on a fully formed reality sense, when in fact only a small segment of the overall reality context is being considered.

At the psychotic or primary organizing level of human personality there is the risk of a complete breakdown of the sense of complex shared realities when the "transference psychosis" emerges in the therapeutic relationship for study (Little 1981, 1990). All people have deep layers of psychotic anxiety that may need to be activated at some point in therapy. This means that in any analysis a psychotic core may emerge for brief or extended periods of time during which the client's usual capacities to test reality and to abstract from broad experience may be impaired such that the analyst may become part of a delusional transference experience—possibly one that can threaten the therapist emotionally and realistically.

At the opposite end of the developmental spectrum, psychoanalysts learned early that symbolic interpretation serves in (oedipal, 4- to 7-year-old level) neurosis to permit a return of the repressed, which is recognized as one's own self that has been declared to be nonexistent for so long. In neurotic issues the capacity for reality testing and high-level abstraction and symbolization make the work easier to think about and safer for both parties.

At the selfobject (narcissistic, 3-year-old) level the analyst is perennially responsible for and often blamed for realistic empathic failures. Technically, the analyst takes responsibility for the activities in question, at which time the person in analysis can generally be helped to distinguish between interpersonal realities as they have actually occurred and the emergence of selfobject transference. Kohut (1977, 1984) is clear that actual, realistic, resonating understanding is the key therapeutic feature at this level. Interpretive verbalizations ("summarizing reflections") follow realistic interactional understanding. Kohut's selfobject transference concepts (1971, 1977) demonstrate clearly that blurring of self-and-other boundaries is prerequisite to being able to analyze the narcissistic transferences based upon self-other failures in early childhood that left the self with structural defects.

At the level of symbiotic (borderline, 4- to 24-month-old) issues, dual realities are more difficult to tease out. It requires considerable time and actual relating to establish interpersonal symbiotic scenarios as visible in transferences that become somehow replicated in the therapeutic relationship. In my work I have dealt extensively with the complicated interactional sequences and dilemmas that therapists encounter in responding to symbiotic (borderline) transferences (Hedges 1983b, 1992). Interpreting the countertransference becomes a critical aspect of responding to the many projective identifications encountered in this work.

Thus, at each of the four major levels of self-and-other relatedness the dual relationship mechanism is required for psychotherapy, although just how duality operates is different at each developmental level.

THE NECESSARY INTERPENETRATION
OF BOUNDARIES

The theoretician exciting the most interest today in clinical circles is Winnicott (1958, 1965, 1971), who, from his studies of the early mother–child relationship, demonstrates clearly the way the boundaries between the two mix and mingle and how this mixing and merging must be replicated when studying early developmental issues in the transference–countertransference relationship. Infant research (Stern 1985) further underlines this mixing of boundaries at early developmental levels. Little's (1990) deeply moving account of her own analytic work, which led to a complete psychotic breakdown in her analysis with Winnicott, demonstrates this aptly. No one makes clearer than Winnicott the importance of the actual reality of the therapist and the setting. His work demonstrates that the therapist *must be realistically available* to the client for long periods while restricted areas of the personality have an opportunity to expand. In his focus on early developmental issues he demonstrates that interpretation can only follow actual involvement and improvement. This kind of duality is essential to the transformation of all primitive mental states.

LOSS OF REALITY TESTING IN THE
"NEGATIVE THERAPEUTIC REACTION"

When aspects of the organizing (psychotic, schizoid) level become activated, the person in analysis often develops the *conviction* of special, privileged understanding regarding the reality of the therapeutic exchange. Reality no longer is a matter for mutual discussion, or for consideration by various standards of social consensus, or for contradictory or varying viewpoints. "This is real, don't give me any bullshit, you are shooting secret cosmic rays from behind your chair at me." "This is incest, you have damaged me irreparably by allowing me to feel close to you." "Because you have stepped out of your neutral role and given me advice, opinion, suggestion, or help, you are in a dual relationship with me. I cannot seek consultation with a third party as you have asked because I would be ashamed at how I seduced you into actually helping me grow. You are the guilty party because you have the power and should have known that revealing personal aspects of yourself and reaching out to me in realistic and 'helpful' ways would be experienced by me (in transference) as incestual and abusive. Your 'good nature' and 'willingness to help me grow' are devious things you do for self-aggrandizement, to make your own ego swell with pride. You have exploited me for the sake of your own ego, your narcissism. You have damaged me by overinvolving yourself in my therapeutic growth. I demand recompense for the violations you have indulged yourself in and the damage you have done. You seduced me (or let me seduce you). Now you will pay." No amount of objective feedback, attempts at rational discussion, or weighing of considerations is possible at such a shocking moment and there may not be another moment in which these psychotic transference convictions can be discussed before an ethical complaint or a lawsuit is filed.

At the moment of the negative therapeutic reaction symbolic speech and discourse are replaced by destructive concretization. Rage or lust is mobilized and with it a clarity of understanding about reality that is subjectively experienced as right, good, monolithic, absolute, and beyond dispute or discussion. A moral crusade characterized by vengeance and righteous indignation is on. The therapist is the enemy, the perpetrator of crimes, the exploiter. Evidence is gathered, much as one gathers evidence to support a paranoid pseudocommunity, in order to support and bolster his or her views against the alleged misbehavior of the therapist. If no moderation or mediation softens the position before accident intervenes, we see suicides, destructive mutilation, and homicides, as well as legal and ethical claims facing the therapist *as a result of good therapeutic mobilization of unconscious organizing affects.* The therapeutic activation has succeeded. But the cure has failed and the therapist is in realistic danger. Our focus for the future must be on how to understand and prevent such dangers.

Freud has formulated that the failure to de-idealize the analyst in time leads to a "negative therapeutic reaction" (Freud 1918, 1923, 1933). The dual relationship becomes not one in which transference and countertransference realities can be secured and discussed as a special reality that two can share as somewhat different from or resultant from other aspects of the real relationship, but as *the* reality that the person in analysis is privileged to know, a reality in which the wickedness and self-interest of the (parent) therapist is believed to have gotten out of hand.

As our experience with the emergence of psychotic transference (even in better-developed personalities) expands, the need becomes increasingly clear for the presence of a case monitor of some sort to follow the course of treatment so that when reality controls are lost by the client in psychotic transference, a third party who is knowledgeable about the course of the treatment and who has some relationship with the client is able to intervene to prevent such a dangerous and destructive negative therapeutic reaction.

Since all people have experienced an early developmental (organizing or psychotic) period with constricting limits and constraints, all people are subject to psychotic anxieties and transferences—meaning that the therapist is, in principle, never safe from the destructive emergence of an abusive psychotic transference that is experienced as very real by the client and that is aimed at the therapist's person. No amount of good judgment ahead of time is fail-safe protection against such potential disaster. Viewed from this angle it is always an error to trust the good will, good nature, and truth searching qualities of the client since they can suddenly be reversed in a psychotic episode.

The analyst is always in danger of becoming the target of psychotic anxieties that cannot be surmounted. If the patient was abused as an infant or young child, this abuse will likely emerge as some form of primary identification in the psychotic transference. The subjective experience is so real it cannot be interpreted successfully and the therapist becomes the victim. Therapists facing misconduct charges regularly report that they "never would have dreamed therapy could have produced such a miscarriage. She [the client] seemed like such a trusting person of good will, and of upstanding moral character. She was so involved in her therapy, so respectful of her analytic partner. How could such vengeance and hatred be directed at me, the very person who has probably done more for her in terms of opening herself up than anyone she has ever known?"

This is the problem. The therapeutic work did succeed in loosening the moralizing and idealizing defenses and in easing up the stifling rigidity of the symbiotic character structure. Indeed the traumatized, annihilated true self began to emerge with all of its raw, infantile power, lust, and rage, but while it was still identified with its aggressor in a very primitive way. The transference interpretation not only succeeded, but when the therapist (according to transference script) failed, the structure opened to the murderous psychotic rage of infancy. The idealizing tendency that has made for such an angelic self and unshakable idealization of the analyst collapses suddenly, and the way things have been going the analyst is in deep trouble if he or she has in any way trusted the good nature of the patient and extended various active interaction measures that can appear to a third party as "not avoiding an unethical dual relationship."

THE DANGERS TO THERAPISTS RAGE ON UNCHECKED

As our therapeutic tools for bringing out early traumas improve, practicing psychotherapists are headed for deeper and deeper trouble. The dual nature of psychotherapy cannot be denied or minimized and the active role of the therapist required in working with earlier developmental layers of the personality moves the dynamic psychotherapist inexorably toward an ill fate. Social consciousness-raising increasingly holds the teacher, minister, physician, and psychotherapist accountable for their activities. Deep working, well-intentioned psychotherapists face the danger that their best, most well-conceived efforts to help will be experienced as violent or incestuous intrusions that they "should have known" about in advance and "should have" taken measures to forestall.

Perhaps we should ask where the phrase "should have known" appears in any single piece of responsible therapy research or even in a single theoretical tract on the nature of psychotherapy? Such a claim is completely untenable and unsupportable. The literature on predicting violence and suicide has repeatedly demonstrated how poor our best-trained experts are at ever predicting even very strong variables. No one who seriously practices in-depth psychotherapy is likely to use such a phrase as "should have known." What may evolve in psychotic transference is never known in advance. Who are those who would tell us what we should or should not have known? After the fact, like Monday morning quarterbacks, they sit in armchairs saying what we should have known or done; meanwhile, strange and idiosyncratic transference configurations unfold hourly in our consulting rooms.

The misplaced focus by licensing boards and ethics committees on dual relationships when damaging exploitation is the issue has meant that therapists can no longer simply consider what such events as attending a client's wedding, attending a lecture or social event in a client's presence, offering a helpful book or cassette, giving or receiving token gifts or touch, or sending a birthday or sympathy card may mean to a client in the context of the therapy. Rather, the dual relationship witch-hunt has come to mean that we must concern ourselves with what precautions to take so that legal and ethical questions can never arise. The only tool we really have at our disposal in psychotherapy, the spontaneity of ourselves, has thus been tarnished and is in danger of serious damage.

Given the absurd state of affairs currently prevailing, the orientation now required by therapists who think developmentally and who work dynamically (1) begins with the realization that in-depth psychotherapy always depends on the successful evolution of a dual relationship, (2) realizes that heretofore questions of meaning and interpretation have been foremost in our practice, and (3) concludes that now (considering the dual relationship panic) we must reorient our thinking to protect ourselves from accusations that could dangerously be held against us for doing exactly what we aim to do—exploiting the potential of dual relatedness for the purpose of studying human nature and freeing our clients from the bondage of the past. What a fine kettle of fish this is!

Fortunately, the pendulum has begun to swing back to a position where we can begin relying once again on clinical considerations rather than naive moralizing and absurd misconduct rulings to guide our therapy. But for the present we are stuck having to water down what we do for fear of censorship by ethics committees and licensing boards. We are clearly in the midst of a major crisis in the practice of our discipline.

Our growing expertise in elucidating the deepest, most primitive and crazy aspects of our clients and of ourselves is expanding at the very moment when the therapeutic dimension we most depend on—dual relatedness—has come under social, legal, and ethical censorship. It is by no means clear how we will come to grips with these and many related issues.

Regulatory boards and ethics committees in their eagerness to provide rules for the practice of psychotherapy have rapidly moved toward positions that, if allowed, threaten to obliterate the essence of clinical work, which relies on the dual relationship. Viewed from this vantage point our fear of the boards and therefore our tacit support of their trends registers a resistance on the part of therapists to enter the new terrain of enriched psychotherapeutic relatedness.

UNAVOIDABLE DUALITY

The essential duality involved in psychotherapy can be considered from many angles. The views on duality presented here serve to contrast (1) the real, moment-to-moment, spontaneous, mutual need-fulfilling aspect of the actual, contractual relationship that evolves over time between two people, with (2) the symbolic, interpretive relationship in which two gradually come to stand apart, as it were, from their real, spontaneous relating and speak in such a way as to characterize from a third-party point of view the manner and quality of their relating. Two create pictures and stories that describe (as if from an outside or objective point of view) what is happening between them and why. This interpretive, third-party, symbolic relationship that two share enables each to speak his or her subjective reactions arising from within the real relationship in such a way as to consider the emotional load (left over from past emotional relationships) that each may be adding to their ongoing appreciation of the other and the relatedness.

The essence of the interpretive art at the symbiotic, borderline, or character level is a confrontation of the person's refusal to have such a dual relationship with the therapist and therefore with all emotionally significant others (Hedges 1983, 1992). The merger sense that lies at the root of virtually all clinical syndromes in treatment today resists treatment by relegating the reality of the therapist and his or her personality functioning to one of relative unimportance. This resistance functions to prevent the actualization of the symbolic duality that makes human development possible. The decisive interpretive move with symbiotic (borderline) issues comes when the therapist can say,

"But I am not you and I am not your wished for (or feared) other. I am a real person relating to you. I am unique, different from anyone you have ever known. I have shown you that I can relate more or less as you wish me to. But for myself, I do not think or react as you might expect or wish me to. It is not necessary for you to be disappointed, enraged, or hurt as you once were when you were on the verge of discovering your mother was a separate person. Differentness is something that can be celebrated. It is possible for you to learn to relate realistically to me and to others in ways that are different from your experience of the past. You are perfectly capable of seeing the two of us as we realistically relate to each other and to form ideas and feelings about us and our ways of relating."

NECESSARY SUBJECTIVITY

We no longer believe there is any such thing as an objective analyst (Natterson 1991). No one knows in advance how transference and countertransference will unfold and therefore unconscious transference and countertransference feelings cannot be limited and regulated in advance. This is especially true for the evolving countertransference that is projected onto the therapist at the level of the spontaneous interaction that recapitulates the early (borderline) mother–child symbiotic relationship. What evolves as a second relationship to the one based upon conscious contract is a joint fantasy relationship that two collaborate in creating (Spence 1982).

Natterson's (1991) text illustrates clearly how patient and analyst communicatively achieve an intense oneness and fusion, how subjective features from the analyst's past come into play in the countertransference, and how at the same time each is able to individuate and differentiate more completely from the experience than either was able to do before their work together. Natterson shatters the myth of the value-neutral therapist, exposing it as a fictive assumption. He makes clear that

all human two person transactions share fundamental meaning: *each party attempts to influence the other* with his or her view of the universe, to persuade the other of the rightness of his or her view. . . . this basic power orientation of dyadic relationships makes it natural for moral influences to be invariably significant components of the therapists' activity. [p. 28, italics added]

The interaction of the basic beliefs of patient and therapist are inseparable from the human fantasies and yearnings of each. Natterson (1991) views the psychoanalytic encounter as a dyadic impingement in which each person influences the other. "Their respective fantasies and desires, values and goals, are engaged in continuous struggle, through which both persons are continuously changing. This intersubjective experience should be regarded as the basic precondition for any theoretical understanding of psychotherapeutic processes" (p. 29). Natterson's brilliant work highlights the duality between the real relationship and the emerging transference–countertransference relationship.

It is time that we be clear that transference, countertransference, resistance, and interpretation as we have come to understand them, de facto rest upon the existence of a dual relationship. It behooves us to remember that all beneficial effects of psychotherapy arise in consequence of the dual relationship.

Duality as Essential
to Psychological Cure

AN ANTHROPOLOGICAL INSIGHT INTO
HOW PSYCHOTHERAPY "HOOKS INTO THE FLESH"
THROUGH DUAL RELATIONSHIPS

The French anthropologist Claude Lévi-Strauss (1949) in a chapter titled "The Effectiveness of Symbols," undertakes a penetrating definition of the psychoanalytic task, revealing from an anthropological and sociological viewpoint the necessarily dual nature of the psychotherapeutic endeavor.

Lévi-Strauss reviews the first available South American magico-religious text, an eighteen-page incantation obtained by the Cuna Indian, Guillermo Haya, from an elderly informant of his tribe (original source: Holmer and Wassen 1947). The purpose of the song is to facilitate unusually difficult childbirth. Its use is unusual since native women of Central and South America have easier deliveries than women of Western societies. The intervention of the shaman is thus rare and occurs only in the extreme case of failure to deliver and at the request of the midwife.

The song begins with the midwife's confusion over the pregnant woman's failure to deliver and describes her visit to the shaman and the latter's arrival in the hut of the laboring woman, with his fumigations of burnt cocoa-nibs, his invocations, and the making of *nuchu*, sacred figures or images carved from various prescribed kinds of wood that lend them their effectiveness. The carved *nuchu* represent tutelary spirits who become the shaman's assistants. He leads the *nuchu* to the abode of *Muu* (inside the woman's body). *Muu* is the goddess of fertility and is responsible for the formation of the fetus. Difficult childbirths occur when *Muu* has exceeded her functions and captured the *purba* or soul of the mother. The incantation thus expresses a quest for the lost soul of the mother, which will be restored after overcoming many obstacles.

The shaman's saga will take the woman through a victory over wild beasts and finally through a great contest waged by the shaman and his tutelary spirits against *Muu* and her daughters. Once *Muu* has been defeated, the whereabouts of the soul of the ailing woman can be discovered and freed so the delivery can take place. The song ends with precautions that must be taken so that *Muu* cannot pursue her victors (an event that would result in infertility). The fight is not waged against *Muu* herself, who is indispensable to procreation, but against her abuses of power. After the epic saga, *Muu* asks the shaman when he will come to visit again, indicating the perennial nature of psychic conflict that can be expected to interfere with childbirth.

Lévi-Strauss comments that in order to perform his function the shaman is, by cultural belief, assigned supernatural power to see the cause of the illness, to know the whereabouts of the vital forces, and to use *nuchu* spirits who are endowed with exceptional powers to move invisibly and clairvoyantly in the service of humans.

On the surface the song appears rather commonplace among shamanistic cures. The sick woman suffers because she has lost her spiritual double, which constitutes her vital strength. In traveling to the supernatural world and in being aided by assistants in snatching the woman's double from a malevolent spirit and restoring it to its owner, the shaman effects the cure. The exceptional aspect of this song, making it of interest to anthropologists and psychoanalysts alike, is that "'Muu's way' and the abode of *Muu* are not, to the native mind, simply a mythical itinerary and dwelling-place. They represent, literally, the vagina and uterus of the pregnant woman, which are to be explored by the shaman and *nuchu* and in whose depths they will wage their victorious combat" (p. 188). In his quest to capture her soul, the shaman also captures other spirits, which govern the vitality of her other body parts (heart, bones, teeth, hair, nails, and feet). Not unlike the invasive attention of the psychoanalyst, no body part is left unattended to.

Muu, as instigator of the disorder, has captured the special "souls" of the various organs, thus destroying the cooperation and integrity of the main soul, the woman's double who must be set free. "In a difficult delivery the 'soul' of the uterus has led astray all the 'souls' belonging to other parts of the body. Once these souls are liberated, the soul of the uterus can and must resume its cooperation" (p. 190). It is clear that the song seeks to delineate the emotional content of the physiological disturbance to the mind of the sick woman. To reach *Muu*, the shaman and his assistants must find "*Muu*'s way," the road of *Muu*. At the peak moment when the shaman has finished his carvings, spirits rise up at the shaman's exhortation:

> The (sick) woman lies in the hammock in front of you.
> Her white tissue lies in her lap, her white tissues move softly.
> The (sick) woman's body lies weak.
> When they light up (along) *Muu*'s way, it runs over with exudations and like blood.
> Her exudations drip down below the hammock all like blood, all red.
> The inner white tissue extends to the bosom of the earth.
> Into the middle of the woman's white tissue a human being descends.
> [Holmer and Wassen, cited in Lévi-Strauss, p. 190]

"*Muu*'s way," darkened and covered with blood, is unquestionably the vagina and the dark whirlpool the uterus where *Muu* dwells.

Lévi-Strauss comments that this text claims a special place among shaman cures. One standard type of cure involves an organ that is manipulated or sucked until a thorn, crystal, or feather appears, a representation of the removal of the malevolent force. Another type of cure revolves around a sham battle waged in a hut and then outside against harmful spirits. In these cures it remains for us to understand exactly how the psychological aspect "hooks into" the physiological. But the current song constitutes a purely psychological treatment. For the shaman does not touch the body and administers no remedy. "Nevertheless it involves, directly and explicitly, the pathological condition and its locus. In our view, the song constitutes a *psychological manipulation* of the sick organ, and it is precisely from this manipulation that a cure is expected" (p. 192).

Lévi-Strauss observes that the situation is contrived to induce pain in a sick woman through developing a psychological awareness of the smallest details of all of her internal tissues. Using mythological images the pain-induced situation becomes the symbolic setting for the experience of conflict. "A transition will thus be made from the most prosaic reality, to myth, from the physical universe to the psychological universe, from the external world to the internal body" (p. 193). The mythological saga being enacted in the body attains sensory and hallucinatory vividness through the many elements of ritual—smell, sound, tactile stimulation, rhythm, and repetition.

What follows in breathless (hypnotic) rhythm and rhyme are more and more rapid oscillations between mythical and physiological themes "as if to abolish in the mind of the sick woman the distinction which separates them, and to make it impossible to differentiate their respective attributes" (p. 193). Spirits and events follow one another as the woman's total focus becomes the birth apparatus and the cosmic battle being waged there by the invasion of the shaman and his spiritual helpers who bring illuminating light into the birth canal. The presence of wild animals increases the pains that are thus personified and described to the woman. Uncle Alligator moves about with bulging eyes, crouching and wriggling his tail. He moves his glistening flippers that drag on everything. The Octopus arrives with sticky tentacles alternately opening and closing, contracting and expanding passageways. The black tiger, the red animal, the two colored animals are all tied with an iron chain that rasps and clanks against everything. Their tongues are hanging out, saliva dripping, saliva foaming, with flourishing tails and claws tearing at everything.

According to Lévi-Strauss the cure consists in making explicit a situation originally existing on an emotional level and in rendering acceptable to the mind pains that the body otherwise refuses to tolerate. The shaman with the aid of this myth encourages the woman to accept the incoherent and arbitrary pains, reintegrating them into a whole where everything is coordinated and meaningful. He points out that our physicians tell a similar story to us but not in terms of monsters and spirits but rather in terms we believe like germs, microbes, and so forth. "The shaman provides the sick woman with a *language*, by means of which unexpressed, and otherwise inexpressible, psychic states can be immediately expressed" (p. 198). The transition to the verbal system makes it possible to undergo in an ordered and intelligible form an experience that would otherwise be chaotic and inexpressible. The myth and its hypnotic power enable the woman to release and reorganize the physiological processes that have become disordered in the woman's sickness.

THE DUAL RELATIONSHIP CURE

Lévi-Strauss (1949) explicitly contextualizes this shamanistic cure as psychoanalytic in nature. The purpose is to bring to a conscious level conflicts and resistances that have remained unconscious, with resulting symptom formation. The conflicts and resistances are resolved not because of knowledge, real or alleged,

> but because this knowledge makes possible a specific experience, in the course of which conflicts materialize in an order and on a level permitting their free development and leading to their resolution. This vital experience is called *abreaction* in psychoanalysis. We know that its precondition is the unprovoked intervention of the analyst, who appears in the conflicts of the client *through a double transference mechanism* as (1) a flesh-and-blood protagonist and (2) in relation to whom the client can restore and clarify an initial (historical) situation which has remained unexpressed or unformulated. . . .
> The shaman *plays the same dual role as the psychoanalyst.* A prerequisite role—that of listener for the psychoanalyst and of orator for the shaman—*establishes a direct relationship with the patient's conscious and an indirect relationship with his unconscious.* This is the function of the incantation proper. But the shaman does more than utter the incantation; *he is its hero, for it is he who, at the head of a supernatural battalion of spirits, penetrates the endangered organs and frees the captive soul.* [pp. 198–199]

The shaman, like the psychoanalyst, is thus enabled by the dual relationship to become (1) the transference object induced vividly in the patient's mind, and (2) the real protagonist of the conflict, which is experienced by the patient as on the border between the physical world and the psychical world. In this dual situation in which pain is deliberately induced by the practitioner, the psychoanalytic client eliminates individual myths by facing the reality of the person of the analyst. And the native woman overcomes an organic disorder by identifying with a mythically transmuted shaman.

Lévi-Strauss notes that the shamarita cure is a counterpart to psychoanalytic cure. Both induce an experience through appeal to myth. The psychoanalytic patient constructs a myth with elements drawn from his or her personal past. The shamanist patient receives from the outside a social myth. In either case the treating person fosters the emergence of a storyline that cures by giving language to experience. The effectiveness of symbols guarantees the parallel development in the process of myth and action.

Lévi-Strauss provides a fascinating argument that aligns the shamanism of ages past with the modern activities of psychoanalysis and psychotherapy. His arguments go considerably beyond Freud and into areas being explored in psychoanalysis and psychotherapy today, in which an inductive property of symbols permits formerly homologous structures built out of different materials at different levels of life—organizational processes, unconscious agency, and rational thought—to be understood as profoundly related to one another. Lévi-Strauss points out that the individual vocabulary of the cure is significant only to the extent that the unconscious structures it according to its laws and thus transforms it into language. Whether the myth is a personal re-creation or one borrowed from tradition matters little; the essential structure of language and the unconscious is the locus of the power of the symbol. Any myth represents a quest for the remembrance of things past and the ways those remembrances are structured in the unconscious. "*The modern version of shamanistic technique called psychoanalysis thus derives its specific characteristics from the fact that in industrial civilization there is no longer any room for mythical time, except within man himself*" (pp. 203–204).

The purpose of reviewing this anthropological analysis of psychoanalysis and psychotherapy as knowledge of the symbolic function inherited from shamanism is to highlight the inherently *dual* relationship involved in psychological cure. The shaman/analyst is first of all realistically involved with the person in conscious and unconscious ways so as to evoke a second-order relationship, the mythical transference in which the shaman/analyst becomes hero, protagonist in an inner drama, a conflict, a quest for possession of the soul. The drama proceeds by putting private experience into symbols that have the power to transform the inexplicable, the unintelligible, the inchoate, and the irremediable into a series of epic narrations that two can share together. It is only to the extent to which the shaman/analyst succeeds in establishing a real relationship that the epic journey in search of the soul through mythic transference, resistance, and countertransference becomes possible.

If an attorney should happen into the hut midway in this woman's process to cure with papers for her to sign, she no doubt would produce a stillbirth or die in childbirth from inability to stay with the symbolic. He would, of course, be on hand to bring action against the shaman for negligence. A judge and jury with no way of understanding the power of the symbolic or the subtle operations of transference could hardly be expected to show much mercy for the poor shaman left with only the incantations bequeathed him by wise forefathers, a handful of hand-carved stick figures, and cocoa incense. Perhaps his songs, smoke, and hocus-pocus will be viewed as harmless enough. But that he had formed a dual relationship with the woman, had become by virtue of his social role an authorizing personage in her life, and furthermore was actually fraternizing with her family and midwife, thus (no doubt) exploiting the hapless victim for personal aggrandizement of his narcissistic needs—may indeed be dimly viewed by administrative judges as he is charged with responsibility for stillbirth, a faulty delivery indeed.

Or should this woman by chance attend a recovery or incest survivors group midway in the move to the symbolic she may come to recognize the very real sense of penetration she feels from her shaman/analyst and begin reliving traumas of the past that have been revived by this penetrating therapeutic relationship of the present. The therapeutic relationship may become so terrifyingly real that she enters a negative therapeutic reaction with her heretofore idealized shaman. She soon is encouraged by well-meaning group members to file suit against him for failing to maintain his boundaries by his attending her wedding, sniffing cocoa incense with her, failing to stop her from reading his journal articles, and not preventing her from attending his classes at the local university. The shaman is judged negligent because he "should have known" that dual relationships are damaging. He should have known that she would in the long run prove insufficiently motivated, insufficiently endowed for the process, or easily derailed by accidental outside influences so that she would be unable to move to the level of the symbolic required for cure. The tragedy: the dual relationship that is the primary vehicle requisite for carrying the symbolic cure had been put securely in place, but patient constitution, concentration, or motivation to effect a transition to the transferential symbolic proved insufficient. Outside instigators empathically tapped into her negative psychotic transference feelings toward the shaman and urged her to file a complaint to avenge herself—as it turns out, for childhood abuse now attributed by transference to the shaman.

Those who know little or nothing of the subtleties of psychological cure can only point to what remains from aborted processes and rush in with judgments. How are we, who are charged with the sacred function of utilizing the power of the transferential symbolic for benefit of suffering humans, to protect ourselves from tribal administrators who have little or no knowledge of our function and no awareness that our art involves wielding the symbols of the gods in *real* relationships such that people forget the difference between ordinary reality and the mythic in order to bring to bear the power, function, and effectiveness of the symbol for the purpose of relieving psychological and physiological suffering. Caught midway when only the reality aspect is so far in play, or stopped short because the willingness or capability to enter the symbolic is lacking, we can indeed look like negligent fools! *But if we give up the dual relationship we relinquish the wisdom of the ages!* Then we become reduced to the same sense of impotence of those who seek to reaffirm their self-identifications and power by sitting in judgment over people and processes they cannot hope to understand.

PERSONAL OPINION

For over twenty years my primary business has been consulting with therapists and analysts about difficult clinical work. I have witnessed a rising swell of horror and fear among professionals as stories circulate about atrocities perpetrated by governing boards under the name of "administrative justice" and acts of ethics committees that appear to be operating as kangaroo courts. If even a small number of the reports that reach me are accurate (and I believe they are) we are all indeed in a precarious position.

The shocking findings of the social consciousness movement regarding real abuses by therapists have taken us all by surprise. Our professional organizations have reacted as quickly as possible in order to recognize the hazards of damaging and exploitative dual relationships and to take measures to rectify wrongs and to prevent future abuses. Only now are there beginning signs that boards and ethics committees are coming to appreciate the extreme subtleties and complexities of dual relationship issues.

I have hoped to bring to the attention of the community of practicing therapists the central position of duality in our work in order to challenge thinking further so that injustices can be prevented and so that future regulatory efforts can take into account the inevitable blurring of boundaries that transference and countertransference interpretation necessarily entail.

I offer the following suggestions for consideration in evolving safeguards against abuse while honoring the dual relationship inherent in the practice of psychotherapy.

1. When any direct or indirect contact outside the formal therapeutic setting exists between therapist and client, a consultant should be sought out regularly (at two- to six-month intervals) to evaluate and comment on the course of therapy. This is especially important in training programs where the trainee is likely to see or hear much that will necessarily color the therapeutic relationship. It would also seem critical in small communities where various forms of outside contact are inevitable.

2. Any roles that might be unavoidable outside the formal therapeutic relationship need to be kept somehow in the public eye. Some provision for periodic review with a third party should be obtained to evaluate how the therapy is proceeding.

3. In the name of protecting privacy and confidentiality, all *appearances* of dual relationship that might potentially be seen by third parties and conceivably by reported boards and committees for open investigation should be avoided. It is understood that "pure" work is to be preferred over "complicated" work but that work with various outside influences and complications (spouses, insurance companies, employers, government agencies, etc.) tends to be the rule rather than the exception. Complications cannot be assumed to be damaging exploitations. Multiple roles do not constitute unethical relationships that are exploitative and damaging. But avoidance of appearances and use of third-party consultation can help keep the distinction clearer and work to avoid confidentiality breaks through investigation.

4. Qualified experts should render opinions to regulating bodies. At present most individuals serving on regulatory boards and ethics committees, so far as I can tell, do not possess advanced specialty training that qualifies them to make judgments about the subtleties of the dual relationship necessarily involved in depth transference and countertransference work without outside expert consultation. If this is true, then these individuals are operating unprofessionally and unethically. For most purposes persons serving on regulatory boards and ethics committees need not possess the advanced expertise in the dual nature of transference–countertransference work needed to be able to identify therapist's abuses of the professional relationship. But (a) when subtleties are involved, (b) when therapists have sophisticated and enlightened rationale for various interventions based upon the dual nature of transference work, or (c) when a therapist's professional reputation and personal life are to be profoundly affected by claims that they do not honor as valid, we cannot afford as a profession to allow people without advanced training and professional expertise to stand in judgment of matters they cannot possibly be qualified to understand.

One way to correct the current threat that therapists live under as a result of cries and accusations of unethical dual relationship is to create panels of expert consultants who can demonstrate advanced understanding of the complexities of transference–countertransferene relationships. Experts in panels of three could be called upon to evaluate aspects of investigations in which subtle aspects of dual relationship are in play and to render expert opinion to regulatory boards and ethics committees.

5. An alternate approach to the expert consultant model is for the therapist needing protection to have some recourse to settling the dispute in civil court where discovery and due process is guaranteed—as it is generally not under administrative law. We know that all too often ethics committees and governing boards are prey to political pressures and various pre-established biases so that a therapist acting in good faith and upon sound judgment may not get fair treatment. Governing boards are certainly in a dual relationship position! Consumer interests and fear of publicity resulting in adverse political effects are too apt to color judgments against the therapist when subtleties of depth work are involved. While a judge and jury certainly do not constitute peers in terms of depth understanding, at least there is some hope of an un-

biased, unpolitical, fair judgment. With either the client or the governing board as plaintiff and the governing board acting as judge and jury the therapist de facto loses the civil rights guaranteed by the Constitution of the United States. As it stands in most states, therapists have no civil rights and no recourse to due process. We are potential prey to political pressures and victims of governing hierarchies without recourse to adequate defense.

6. Some therapists have pointed out that a jury certainly does not represent peer opinion, so that arbitration panels of persons sophisticated in aspects of depth therapy are to be preferred over civil courts.

DEFINING QUALIFIED EXPERTS

The position I have taken is that there are many kinds of transferences, countertransferences, and resistances that operate silently in psychological treatment. Cure itself is dependent upon the successful discernment and utilization of dual relationship variables. There is no provision in any currently existing licensing law that I am aware of that ensures training or licensing as a psychotherapist involves expertise in understanding and interpreting transference and countertransference phenomena. The California Research Psychoanalyst Law[1] does, however, specify compliance with a set of nationally and internationally recognized standards for such training. Expertise in transference, countertransference, and resistance analysis as reflected in this law is thought to be attained by exposure to (1) extensive (five years) didactic training *beyond* ordinary licensing requirements, (2) a minimum of 400 hours of personal didactic transference analysis, and (3) a minimum of three apprentice training cases with at least 50 hours of supervision each for a total of 200 post-licensing supervisory hours studying transference, resistance, and countertransference phenomena as they operate in three specific cases and two years of case conference supervision. When an individual becomes certified at this level and practices analytically for an additional five years, he or she attains the status of training analyst

---

1. Business and Professions Code *Research Psychoanalysts* Chapter 5.1 (added by Stats 1977, Ch. 1191) Section 2529 2529.5.

and is *only then a fully qualified expert* with enough experience to teach, supervise, and analyze others in the refined aspects of transference interpretation. This is the level of training and experience recognized the world over by psychoanalysts that constitutes expertise in transference and countertransference analysis.

Other schools of psychotherapy have yet to codify in law what comparable level of experience might qualify one with expertise to make judgments in this highly technical area of knowledge. Can we name any single board or ethics committee member with ten years of comparable advanced training and practice that might ethically qualify him or her to render the professional opinions now being made in this area? Administrative judges have no training at all and yet cavalierly remove licenses based on their evaluation of subtleties that in the profession require roughly fifteen years of advanced training to assess. A person would certainly not have to be a registered psychoanalyst to have sought out extensive and intensive training and practice in understanding the power and subtleties of transference and countertransference, but to date this law stands as the only public recognition I am aware of as to what such expertise might look like, or of how qualified individuals might be legally and ethically identified.

CONCLUSION

I do not wish my remarks to be misunderstood as accusatory in nature or tone. Blame is hardly appropriate at the level of peer review or professional regulation. We have been rapidly overtaken by a rush of new and important social consciousness issues. I have already suggested it may be our own reluctance to enter deeper therapeutic involvement, which so many of our clients desperately need, that accounts for our fear at present.

I hope my thoughts on the inevitability of the dual relationship in psychological cure will sound a precautionary note in quarters where it is sorely needed. I am calling for a more careful examination of the nature of duality, not only for therapist protection but, more importantly, in order to focus our attention on the dual nature of our work so we can develop even further its importance and potency for the benefit of those who seek out our professional skills.

Appendix B

False Accusations against Therapists: Where Are They Coming From, Why Are They Escalating, When Will They Stop?

THERAPIST AT RISK

Over the past five years I have reviewed more than forty psycho-therapy cases in which serious accusations have been made by clients against their therapists. Since in most instances the therapists sought consultation after the disaster had occurred, I could only empathize with them, offer some possible explanations for what had gone wrong, and wish them luck in their ongoing struggle to survive the damaging rav-ages of the accusatory process.

The majority of these therapists had already had their licenses re-voked or suspended by the time I saw them and many had been through lengthy and costly litigation. Others were dealing with losing their jobs and professional standing as well as their homes and personal invest-

Reprinted with permission from *The California Therapist*, March/April 1995.

ments. The malpractice insurance that therapists carry does not cover the enormous expense involved in fighting an accusation at the level of a licensing board, a state administrative court, an ethics committee, or a civil case in which an allegation of sexual misconduct is involved.

Most of the therapists whom I met with were seeking to gain some clarification as to what had happened to them. Many had read "In Praise of the Dual Relationship" (Hedges 1994b and Appendix A) where I had written about the emergence of the transference psychosis in which the client loses the ability to reliably tell the difference between the perpetrator in the infantile past and the present person of the treating therapist. After the publication of that article, twenty-two therapists from five states traveled long distances with no other purpose than to simply tell me about the disastrous experience that had befallen them and to see if I could shed light on what had gone wrong. Many accused therapists expressed the hope that I would pass their stories on to other therapists, advising them of the serious dangers currently facing us. I then published a series of these frightening vignettes in a book addressed to therapists on the subject of memories recovered in psychotherapy, *Remembering, Repeating, and Working Through Childhood Trauma* (Hedges 1994b).

"IT CAN'T HAPPEN TO ME"

My main business for many years has been working with therapists from many different orientations. Much of my time is spent hearing difficult cases in which transference and countertransference problems have developed. It is clear to me that most therapists are living in denial of the severe hazards that surround them in today's psychotherapy marketplace. Often when I have raised a word of caution regarding the potential dangers of a hidden psychotic reaction emerging and becoming directed at the therapist I hear, "I'm not at all worried about this person suing me, we've been at this a long time and we have a really good relationship." I find this attitude totally naive and dangerous. No one knows how to predict the nature and course of an emergent psychotic reaction and no one can say with certainty that he or she will not be its target.

Each therapist who told me about a disaster in his or her practice took great pains to tell me about the essentially good relationship they had succeeded in forming with the client. Repeatedly I heard how, in the face of very trying circumstances, the therapist had "gone the second mile" with the client or had done unusual things in order to be helpful to the client. I frequently heard how a therapist had made special concessions because the client had "needed" this or that variation or accommodation "to stay in therapy." In almost every case I heard that for perhaps the first time in this client's life he or she had succeeded in forming a viable relationship with another human being, the therapist. I was invariably told how, right at the moment of growing interpersonal contact or just when the relationship was really getting off the ground, "something happened" and "the client inexplicably turned against me." Or, "an accidental outside influence intervened and the therapeutic relationship was destroyed," resulting in a serious accusation being hurled at the therapist. Is there a pattern in these apparently false accusations of therapists? If so, what is it and how can we learn from it?

THE PROBLEM OF CONSIDERING ACCUSATIONS FALSE

To speak of "false accusations" is to take a seemingly arbitrary point of view regarding an event that is happening between two people. One person points the finger and says, "In your professional role of therapist I trusted you and you have misused that trust to exploit and damage me." The accused may be able to acknowledge that such and such events occurred, but not be able to agree on the meanings of those events or that exploitation or damage was involved. If we had a neutral or objective way of observing the events in question and the alleged damaging results, we might indeed see a damaged person. But would we be able to agree beyond the shadow of a doubt that the observable damage is a direct causal result of exploitative acts by the accused?

In the type of allegation I am defining as "false accusation," it is not possible to establish a direct causal link between actions of the

414 / Terrifying Transferences

therapist and the damage sustained by the client. Nor is it possible to establish beyond the shadow of a doubt that the activities of the therapist in his or her professional role were exploitative. I am aware that in certain ways this definition may beg the question of what is to be counted as false when separate points of view are being considered. But I also believe that accusations as serious as professional misconduct carry a heavy burden of proof so that the question of true or false requires the establishment of a satisfactory standard of evidence—a standard that frequently seems to be lacking in accusations against therapists. My position, drawn from impressionistic experience, is that there are many therapists who are currently being accused of damage they are not responsible for. So what is the nature of the damage being pointed to and where did it come from?

PHILOSOPHICAL BIAS OR A PERSONAL BLIND SPOT?

Many therapists for a variety of reasons have developed a personal or philosophical bias in their work against systematically considering the concepts of transference, resistance, and countertransference. In choosing to disregard these complex traditional concerns and to embrace more easily grasped popular therapeutic notions, a therapist may unwittingly be setting up his or her own demise. All schools of psychotherapy acknowledge in one form or another the transfer of emotional relatedness issues from past experiences into present relationships. Resistance to forming a living recognition of the influence and power of transference phenomena is also widely understood. And countertransference reactions to the client and to the material of the therapy are universally recognized. The personal choice involved in not noticing and studying what may be happening in these dimensions of therapeutic relatedness does not make them cease to exist. It simply means that one is using personal denial or rationalization for keeping one's head buried in the sand and remaining oblivious to what dangers may be approaching as the relationship deepens.

THE BROADER CONTEXT:
MEMORIES OF ABUSE AND PSYCHOTHERAPY

The problem of false accusations made against psychotherapists is perhaps best understood when considered within the broader context of false accusations that arise from memories "recovered" in the course of psychotherapy. Elsewhere I have written on the importance of taking recovered memories seriously and have reviewed a century of research and study on the problem (Hedges 1994b,d). Some key ideas will be included in the discussion that follows.

Recent shifts in public opinion have mandated changes in all sectors of our society aimed at correcting age-old patterns of abuse. People who have been subjected to damaging treatment have felt encouraged to speak up and seek redress for the wrongs done to them in the past. Memories of painful experiences that individuals have tried not to think about for many years are being revived and abusers are being confronted with the effects of their deeds. This vanguard of the civil rights movement has generated public indignation and a call for more effective laws and judicial procedures to limit widespread abuses of all types.

But along with the revival of painful memories of abuse that people have done their best to forget, another phenomena has moved into the public arena—"recovered memories" that emerge in therapy with compelling emotional power but exist to tell a story that could not have or did not occur in the exact or literal manner in which the abuse is so vividly remembered. On the basis of such memories, usually recovered in some psychotherapy or recovery-group setting, accusations on a large scale are aimed at people who claim not to be perpetrators of abuse. As of August 1994, the False Memory Syndrome Foundation in Philadelphia boasts more than 15,000 members claiming innocence for the crimes of which they are accused.

Highly respected public figures as well as ordinary, credible private citizens known in their communities to lead basically decent lives are having the finger of accusation pointed at them. Among this group of otherwise credible people who are being accused are numerous well-established individuals in the mental health field and in all of the other helping professions including nursing, medicine, law, the clergy, teachers, scout leaders, child-care workers, and choir leaders—in short, all people in our society vested in any way with trust in caring for others. New laws in more than half the states have changed the statute of limitations to read, "three years from when the abuse is remembered," though it is not yet clear whether such laws will stand up in court. By now accusations based on memories recovered in hypnosis, "truth serum" interviews, recovery groups, and psychotherapy are coming under sharp criticism—partly because so many of the accusations are so outlandish, partly because a sizable number of memories have proved faulty, and partly because of the witch-hunt atmosphere surrounding the recovered-memory controversy, which threatens widespread injustice if responsible social controls are not forthcoming.

But accusations against therapists are usually carried out in confidential settings—administrative hearings, ethics committees, and civil cases that are confidentially settled—so that the process and the outcome of these accusations is still largely a matter of secrecy, with the result that therapists do not yet know where the danger is coming from or what its nature is. A state and national grassroots movement has begun on a large scale that aims to bring into the light of day many miscarriages in justice for therapists.

There are clearly many issues to sort out in the recovered-memory accusation crisis before we can regain our individual and collective sanity on this subject. In *Remembering, Repeating, and Working Through Childhood Trauma* (Hedges 1994b) I review the research on the phenomenon of memories recovered in therapy, concluding that if these memories are not taken seriously in the context in which they emerge then we will indeed have a disaster on our hands.

PSYCHOTIC ANXIETIES AND RECOVERED MEMORIES

I relate a large class of recovered memories to primitive or "psychotic" anxieties that I assume to be operating to a greater or lesser extent in all people. My basic thesis is that, while we are now aware of much more real abuse than has ever been acknowledged before, this widely reported class of memories surfacing in psychotherapy today is not new. Psychotherapy began more than a century ago with the study of recovered memories of incest. Clearly the client has experienced some terrifying and traumatic intrusions—often in the earliest months of life, perhaps even without anyone really being aware that the infant was suffering subtle but devious forms of cumulative strain trauma. Memories from this time period simply cannot be retained in pictures, words, and stories—rather the body tissue itself or the characterological emotional response system retains an imprint of the trauma. Psychotherapy provides a place where words, pictures, and somatic experiences can be creatively generated and elaborated for the purpose of expressing in vivid metaphor aspects of early and otherwise unrememberable trauma.

Psychoanalytic research since 1914 (Freud) has shown how "screen" and "telescoped" memories condense a variety of emotional concerns in a dream-like fashion. "Narrative truth," which allows a myriad of emotional concerns to be creatively condensed into stories, images, somatic sensations, and cultural archetypes, has been well studied (Schafer 1976, Spence 1982) and understood to be the way people are able to represent in comprehensible form memories from early life that could otherwise not be processed in therapy. All of these different types of constructed memories have long been familiar to psychoanalysts and *serve as expressional metaphors for deep emotional concerns that are otherwise inexpressible.*

Memories recovered during the course of psychotherapy need to be taken seriously—considered and dealt with in thoughtful and responsible ways by therapists, not simply believed in and acted upon. I maintain that a therapist who takes a simplified recovery approach of "remember the abuse, be validated by being believed, and then confront the abusers" is not only involved in a devious and destructive dual relationship but is actively colluding in resistance to the emergence of developmentally early transference experiencing and remembering with the therapist.

TRANSFERENCE REMEMBERING

The most powerful and useful form of memory in bringing to light those primordial experiences is reexperiencing in the context of an intimate and emotionally significant relationship with the psychotherapist the traumatic patterns of the early experience. I call the earliest level of transference experiencing with the psychotherapist the "organizing transference" (Hedges 1983, 1992, 1994a,c,d) because the traumas occurred during the period of life when an infant is actively engaged in organizing or establishing physical and psychological channels and connections to his or her human environment. Other psychoanalytic researchers speak of the "psychotic transference" or the "transference psychosis" that frequently appears in the therapy of people who are basically nonpsychotic.

Given the intensity of the primitive organizing or psychotic transference that is being brought to the psychotherapy situation for analysis and the actual dangers to the therapist that this kind of work entails, it is not difficult to understand: (1) why many counselors and therapists without training or experience in transference and resistance analysis are eager to direct the intense sense of blame away from themselves and onto others in the client's past, (2) why so many therapeutic processes end abortively when transference rage and disillusionment emerge and psychotic anxieties are mobilized, and (3) how therapists can so easily become targets for transferentially based accusations of abuse. If personal responsibility for ongoing internal processes cannot be assumed by the client and worked through, then the blame becomes externalized onto figures of the past or onto the therapist of the present. Continuing externalization of responsibility for feeling victimized and/or not adequately cared for is the hallmark of therapeutic failure.

FOUR KINDS OF REMEMBERING AND "FORGETTING"

Psychoanalysts and psychologists have no viable theory of forgetting, only a set of theories about how different classes of emotional events are remembered or barred from active memory. "Forgetting impressions, scenes, or experiences nearly always reduces itself to shutting them off. When the patient talks about these 'forgotten' things he seldom fails to add: 'As a matter of fact I've always known it; only I've never thought of it'" (Freud 1914, p. 148). Of course, there are many things around us that we do not notice and therefore do not recall. Further, much of our life's experience is known but has never been thought about. Much of this "unthought known" (Bollas 1987) can be represented in stories, pictures, and archetypes of the therapeutic dialogue and understood by two. Even if sometimes "a cigar is just a cigar," psychoanalytic study has never portrayed human psyche as anything so passive as to be subject to simple forgetting. How then do analysts account for what appears to be "forgotten" experience? Based on a consideration of the development of the human relatedness potential, psychoanalysts have evolved four viable ways to consider personality structure and to understand the different kinds of memories associated with each.

FOUR DEVELOPMENTALLY BASED LISTENING PERSPECTIVES

In order to discuss the nature of the primitive mental processes at work in false accusations I need to establish a context by reviewing briefly the four developmental listening perspectives that have evolved in psychoanalysis for understanding four distinctly different types of transferences, resistances, and countertransferences (Hedges 1983). These listening perspectives are most often spoken of as four developmental levels, stages, or styles of personality organization, though we understand that every well-developed person may be listened to with all four perspectives at different moments in the therapeutic process. In considering false accusations against therapists our attention will be drawn to the fourth or earliest developmental form of transference remembering.

1. In *neurotic personality organization*, the subjective sense of a 5-year-old child's instinctual driven-ness is remembered in transference, along with intense fears of experiencing sexual and aggressive impulses toward anyone so intimate as the analyst, because such intensity was forbidden in the family, social, or triangular structure. At the level of neurotic personality organization *secondary repression* is brought about by self-instruction against socially undesirable, internal, instinctually driven thought and activity. *Note that the definition of repression does not include externally generated trauma but only applies to overwhelming stimulation arising from within the body.*

2. In *narcissistic personality organization* a 3-year-old's intense needs for admiration, confirmation, and inspiration in relation to his or her parents or selfobjects are central to transference memories. The natural narcissistic needs are enshrouded in shame regarding the desire to be at the center of the universe. At the narcissistic level *dissociation* operates, in which certain whole sectors of internal psychic experience are (defensively) walled off from conscious awareness in the main personality because they cannot be integrated into the overall span of the main personality. *Dissociated aspects of self experiences are not forgotten and are not considered unconscious. Rather their presence in immediate action and consciousness is dependent upon the interpersonal situation present at the moment.*

3. In *borderline personality organization* (the 4- to 24-four-month-old level) transference remembering is rooted in the replication of a set of symbiotic or characterological emotional scenarios within the therapeutic relationship. Resistance memories mitigate against living out the positively and negatively charged emotional interactions in the therapeutic relationship so that they can achieve representation and then be removed or relinquished. At the symbiotic or borderline level *ego–affect splitting* operates in which mutually contradictory affect states give rise to contrasting and often contradictory self-and-other transference and resistance memories that are present or not depending on the interpersonal context. The split-affect model of early memory used in understanding symbiotic or borderline personality organization postulates the presence in personality of mutually denied contradictory ego-affect states which represent specific transference paradigms based on internalized object relations (Kernberg 1975). *Whether a split ego state is or is not present in consciousness is dependent upon the way the person experiences the current interpersonal relationship situation. This means that what is remembered and the way it is recalled is highly dependent upon specific facilitating aspects of the relationship in which the memory is being recalled, expressed, or represented.* As such, transference and resistance memories represented in split ego–affect states are always incomplete and subject to distortions by virtue of the lack of integration into the overall personality structure.

4. In *personalities living out the earliest organizing processes* (from 4 months before to 4 months after birth), what is structured in transference memory is the rupturing or breaking of attempts to form sustained

organizing channels to the other. Resistance takes the form of terror and physical pain whenever sustained contact with a significant other threatens. At the organizing developmental level *primary (neurologically conditioned) repression* (Freud 1895) acts to foreclose the possibility of reengaging in activities formerly experienced as overstimulating, traumatic, or physically painful. *It is the organizing level of transferences, resistances, and countertransferences that usually give rise to false accusations.*

Primary repression characteristic of the organizing period of human development is a somatic event based on avoidance of experiences that are perceived as potentially painful (Freud 1895). McDougall (1989) points out, "Since babies cannot use words with which to think, they respond to emotional pain only psychosomatically. . . . The infant's earliest psychic structures are built around nonverbal 'signifiers' in the body's functions and the erogenous zones play a predominant role" (pp. 9–10). Her extensive psychoanalytic work with psychosomatic conditions shows how through careful analysis of manifestations in transference and resistance the early learned somatic signifiers can be brought from soma and represented in psyche through words, pictures, and stories. McDougall illustrates how body memories can be expressed in the interpersonal languages of transference, resistance, and countertransference.

Bioenergetic analysis (Lowen 1971, 1975, 1988) repeatedly demonstrates the process of bringing somatically stored memories into the here-and-now of transference and resistance in the therapeutic relationship. In bringing somatically stored memories out of the body and into psychic expression and/or representation, whether through psychoanalytic or bioenergetic technique, considerable physical pain is necessarily experienced. The intense physical pain encountered is usually thought of as resulting from therapeutically "breaking through" long-established aversive barriers to various kinds of physical experiencing that have previously proven frightening and were then forsaken. That is, *the threshold to more flexible somatic experience is guarded by painful sensations erected to prevent future venturing into places once experienced as painful by the infant or developing toddler.* The therapist who tells me, "these memories must be true" (i.e., vomiting, shaking, convulsing) seems not to realize that *it is the physical manifestations that are the memory from infancy—not the images or stories which the client generates in order* to metaphorically express or represent what that trauma was like to her or his infant self.

FOUR DEVELOPMENTALLY DETERMINED
FORMS OF MEMORY

Childhood memories recovered in the psychoanalytic situation fall into four general classes that correspond to the four types of personality organization just discussed:

1. *Recollections* of wishes and fears of oedipal (triangular, 4- to 7-year-old) relating, which take the form of words, pictures, and stories;
2. *Realizations* of self-to-selfobject (3-year-old) resonances, which take the form of narcissistic (mirroring, twinning, and idealization) engagements with the therapist;
3. *Representations* of self and other (4- to 24-month old) scenarios —in both passive and active interpersonal replications, which take the form of actual replications of mutual emotional engagements with the therapist;
4. *Expressions* of the search for and the rupture of potential channels or links to others (4 months before and after birth), which take the form of emotional connections and disconnections. It is this last class of memories that interests us in considering the problem of false accusations against therapists.

THE RUPTURE OF CONNECTIONS TO THE OTHER

The earliest transference and resistance memories are those from the "organizing" period of relatedness development (Hedges 1983, 1992, 1994a,b,c,d). In utero and in the earliest months of life, the fetus and neonate have the task of organizing channels to the maternal body and mind for nurturance, evacuation, soothing, comfort, and stimulation. Infant research (Tronick and Cohn 1988) suggests that only about 30 percent of the time are the efforts made by an infant and mother successful in establishing that "rhythm of safety" (Tustin 1986) required for two to feel satisfactorily connected. *The many ways in which an in-*

fant fails in securing the needed contact from its (m)other become internalized as transference to the failing mother. These disconnecting transference modes become enacted in the relationship with the therapist.

Because the biological being of the baby knows (just as every mammal knows), that if it cannot find the maternal body it will die, any serious impingement on the infant's sense of continuity of life, of "going on being" (Winnicott 1965) will be experienced as traumatic. An internalized terror response marks once-failed channels of connection with a sign that reads, "never reach this way again." Such traumatic organizing-level transference memories are not only pre-symbolic, but preverbal and somatic. *Resistance to ever again reexperiencing such a traumatic, life-threatening breakdown of linking possibilities is expressed in somatic terror and pain that mark "where mother once was and where I must not go again."*

Winnicott (1965) points out that early impingements on the infant's sense of continuity with life oblige it to react to environmental failure before the infant is fully prepared to begin reacting and thinking. The result of premature impingement is the formation of a primary persecutory mode of thought that forms the foundation of subsequent thought processes. That is, traumatic impingement on the infantile (omnipotent) sense of "going on being" insures that the first memory that is destined to color all later memories is that "the world persecutes me by intruding into my mental space and overstimulating (traumatizing) me. I will forever be on guard for things coming at me which threaten to destroy my sense of being in control of what happens to me." As a lasting imprint this earliest memory is essentially psychotic or unrealistic because the world at large offers many kinds of impingement. And searching the environment tirelessly for the particular kind of primary emotional intrusion that once forced the infant to respond in a certain way not only creates perennial paranoid hazards where there may be none, but causes the person to miss other realistic dangers that are not being scanned for because of this prior preoccupation of the sensorium. A person living out organizing states will do so without her or his usual sense of judgment, perception, or reality-testing capabilities so that inner fears and preoccupations cannot be reliably distinguished from external features or forces, with the result that the person may be temporarily or perennially living in frames of mind that are in essence psychotic in nature though this may not be obvious to others.

FEAR OF BREAKDOWN

Winnicott (1974) has shown that when people in analysis speak seriously of a fear of a breakdown or a fear of death, they are projecting into future time what has already been *experienced* in the infantile past. One can only truly fear what one knows about through experience. Terrifying and often disabling fears of breakdown and death are distinct ways of remembering traumatic experiences that actually happened in a person's infancy. *What is dreaded and feared as a potentially calamitous future event is the necessity of experiencing through the memory of the evolving psychoanalytic transference the horrible, regressive, and once death-threatening breakdown the person experienced in a dependent state in infancy.*

The fear of breakdown (from the infant's view) manifests itself in many forms as resistance to reexperiencing in transference the terror, helplessness, rage, dependency, and loss of control once known in infancy. Therapists and clients alike dread disorganizing breakdowns during the therapeutic process so that there are many ways in resistance and counterresistance that the two can collude to forestall the curative experience of remembering by reliving the breakdown experience with the therapist. One way for a therapist to collude with resistance to therapeutic progress is to focus on external perpetrators or long-ago traumas to prevent having to live through deeply distressing and frightening breakdown recreations together in the here-and-now therapeutic relationship.

The breakdown fear a person felt in infancy lives on as the somatic underpinning of all subsequent emotional relatedness but cannot be recalled because (1) No memory of the experience as such is recorded—only a nameless dread of re-experiencing the dangers of infantile dependence and breakdown, (2) the memory of the breakdown experience itself is guarded with intense pain, somatic terror, and physical symptoms of all types, and (3) the trauma occurred before it was possible to record pictures, words, or stories, so it cannot be recalled in ordinary ways but only as bodily terrors of approaching breakdown and death.

But massive breakdown of functioning is not the only kind of trauma known to occur in infancy.

CUMULATIVE STRAIN TRAUMA

Masud Khan's (1963) concept of "cumulative trauma" adds a new set of possibilities to those already discussed. Beginning with Freud's early studies of childhood trauma (1895), psychoanalysis has studied a series of possibilities regarding how the human organism handles overstimulation arising from the environment as well as from *within* the body. As early as 1920 Freud envisioned the organism turning its receptors toward the environment and gradually developing a "protective shield." "*Protection against* stimuli is an almost more important function for the living organism than *reception* of stimuli. The protective shield is supplied with its own store of energy and must above all endeavor to preserve the special modes of transformation of energy operating in it against the effects threatened by the enormous energies at work in the external world" (p. 17). This protective shield later develops into consciousness, but even so remains somewhat ineffective in protecting from stimuli arising from within the body so that (secondary) repression finally evolves in the oedipal-age child. But one way the infant organism attempts to protect itself from overwhelming internal stimuli is to project them into the outer environment and treat them "as though they were acting, not from the inside, but from the outside, so that it may be possible to bring the shield against stimuli into operation as a means of defense against them" (p. 17). Thus internally generated somatic or instinctual stimulation (both sexual and aggressive) is experienced as coming from the outside or from the other, rather than from one's own body.

The "false memory syndrome," whether directed at perpetrators from the past or at the therapist in the present, appears to originate in earliest infancy (pre- or postnatal) when environmental stimuli cannot be effectively screened out, or when strong internal stimuli are projected to the exterior in an effort to screen them out. *In either case, due to the operation of primitive mental processes, the environment is "blamed" by the infant for causing stimulation that cannot be comfortably processed—though blame may be objectively inappropriate to the circumstances.* For example, one accuser's early problems were traced back to a "placenta abruptio," a detachment of the placenta from the uterine wall giving rise to a period of prenatal life without nourishment or evacuation. Often accusations are traceable to shortages of oxygen in utero, to early problems in feeding, to infant allergies, to surgeries and medical procedures early in life, to incubators, to pain caused by accident or infection, to severely depressed mothers, to marital distress of the parents, or to an endless array of stressful early life events that were not deliberately cruel or abusive.

Khan (1963) holds that "'the strain trauma' and the screen memories or precocious early memories that the patients recount are derivatives of the partial breakdown of the protective shield function of the mother and an attempt to symbolize its effects (cf. Anna Freud, 1958)" (p. 52).

Khan (1963) also points out that the developing child can and does recover from breaches in the protective shield and can make creative use of them so as to arrive at a fairly healthy and effective normal functioning personality. But the person with vulnerabilities left over from infantile cumulative strain trauma "nevertheless can in later life break down as a result of acute stress and crisis" (p. 56). *When there is a later breakdown and earlier cumulative strain trauma can be inferred, Khan is clear that the earlier disturbances of maternal care may have been neither gross nor acute at the time they occurred.* He cites infant research in which careful and detailed notes, recorded by well-trained researchers, failed to observe traumas that only retrospectively could be seen as producing this type of cumulative strain trauma. Anna Freud (1958) has similarly described instances in which "subtle harm is being inflicted on this child, and . . . the consequences of it will become manifest at some future date" (p. 57).

Many symptoms and/or breakdowns in later life, occasioned by conditions of acute living stress, have their origins in infancy. The adult experience of believing that one has suffered a vague, undefinable, and/or forgotten earlier trauma is attributable to the cumulative effects of strain in infancy caused by environmental failure to provide an effective stimulus barrier during the period of infantile dependency. At the time, there may have been no way of knowing what kinds of stimuli were causing undue strain on the infant because they were not gross and they were operating more or less silently and invisibly. Or the circumstance may have been beyond the parent's capacity to shield, as in the case of medical problems, constitutional problems, or uncontrollable environmental problems such as war, food shortages, concentration camps, family discord, and similar situations. But the key consideration for our present topic is that *when a person in later years, under conditions of living stress, produces memories of the effects of the cumulative strain trauma, what is remembered is abstracted, condensed, displaced, symbolized, and represented visually in screen memories that operate like dreams so that an accurate picture of objective facts is, in principle, forever impossible to obtain from recovered memories.*

In expressions of searching for and breaking off (*primary repression of*) the possibility of contact with others, the early traumatic ways the nurturing other ruptured or failed to sustain contact live on as transference and resistance memories that interfere with subsequent attempts to make human contact that would lead toward full emotional bonding. *Organizing (or psychotic) transference memory involves the search for connection versus a compulsion toward discontinuity, disjunction, and rupture of connections. The resistance memory exists as the person's automatic or inadvertent reluctance to establish and/or to sustain consistent and reliable connection to the other (which might serve to make interpersonal bonding of these somatic experiences a realistic possibility).*

Case Illustration: Switching Personalities

It is this organizing experience, and the reluctance to permit or to sustain here-and-now connectedness experience, that I and my clinical colleagues have researched and written about extensively. A brief example of what an organizing-level transference disconnection might look like in a clinical situation suggests a direction for consideration.

A therapist working with a multiple personality presents her work to a consultant. After an overview of the case is given, the consultant asks for the therapist to present "process notes" (event by event) of the next session for review. The therapist begins reading the process notes, telling how her client, Victor, began the hour and how the client gradually zeroed in on a particular emotional issue. The therapist hears the concerns and very skillfully empathizes with the client's thoughts and feelings. Suddenly "little Victoria, age 4" appears in the room. The "switch" is significant in all regards and the therapist now listens to what the alter, Victoria, has to say. The consultant asks how the therapist understands what has just happened. The answer is that Victor felt very understood in the prior transaction and in the safety of the presence of the understanding therapist a more regressed alter (Victoria) can now appear. This kind of event is ubiquitous in the treatment of organizing experiences—an empathic connection is achieved by the therapist and there is a seemingly smooth and comfortable shift to another topic, to a flashback memory, or to an alter personality. The therapist had to work hard to achieve this connection and feels gratified that his or her interpretive work has been successful. The therapist feels a warm glow of narcissistic pleasure that is immediately reinforced by the client's ability to move on to the next concern.

Wrong!

When organizing or psychotic issues are brought for analysis, what is most feared on the basis of transference and resistance is an empathic interpersonal connection. This is because in the infantile situation the contact with the (m)other was terrifying in some regard. A more viable way of seeing the interaction just recounted is to realize that *the successful empathic connection was immediately, smoothly, and almost without notice ruptured with the shift!* The therapist may fail to see what happened for perhaps several reasons: (1) the therapist is a well-bonded person and assumes unwittingly that empathic connection is experienced as good by everyone; (2) the therapist doesn't understand how organizing transference and resistance operate and so is narcissistically pleased by the apparent connection he or she has achieved; (3) the client is a lifetime master at smoothly and efficiently dodging interpersonal connections—across the board or only at certain times when organizing issues are in focus; (4) a subtle mutual seduction is operating in the name of "recovery" in which resistance and counterresistance are winning the day with both parties afraid of personal and intimate connectedness, presumably because of its intense emotional demands; (5) the personality switch, sudden flashback, or change of subject focuses on the historical causes of the dissociation or some other red herring; or (6) the search for memories and validation forecloses the possibility of here-and-now transference experiencing of the emotional horror of infantile trauma and breakdown and how the connection with the therapist is stimulating its appearance. In all of these possibilities the tragedy is that the very real possibility of bringing to life and putting to rest traumatic memory is lost by the therapeutic technique being employed.

Case Illustration: Marge

In *Remembering, Repeating, and Working Through Childhood Trauma* (Hedges 1994b), I report a series of vignettes brought to me by therapists in trouble. The following is reported by a male therapist with fourteen years of experience (pp. 288–292).

I saw Marge for two and a half years. She came to me after her children were grown and left home. She was a chronically depressed housewife in danger of alcoholism. A psychiatrist prescribed medication for her but she kept going downhill. Nothing I could do or say seemed to help. She didn't want to go to work or school to bolster her skills. She belonged to church, which was group enough for her. She worried if her husband was having affairs on his sometimes week-long business trips. She mostly stayed home, watched television, ate, and slept.

On the day that later came into question Marge was more depressed and despairing than I had ever seen her. Many times she had spoken of having nothing to live for, and of being despairing because no one cared about her and life was meaningless. The few friends she had she couldn't talk with. Marge said she was ready to end it all. Inside myself during the entire session I had to continually assess the seriousness of the suicide threat. It seemed serious. I could see that today I was going to have to obtain a contract for her to call me before she did anything to hurt herself. But could I trust her even that far? Was I going to have to call the paramedics or police before I let her leave? I tried everything I could think of but could achieve no connection.

Marge had sat on the end of the couch further away from me than usual today. With ten minutes left I asked her if I could sit on the couch near her for a few minutes, thinking that perhaps that might help. She assented with some faint signs of life. A few minutes later, in desperation I asked if it would help her feel more safe if I put my hand lightly on her shoulder. She thought she might like that and shortly perked up enough for me to let her leave safely. Now, Dr. Hedges, I have four children. I know what a father's reassuring hand can mean and what it feels like—and I swear to God that's the way it was. I also believe that was the way she received it at the time because we seemed to connect and she took heart. We continued therapy some months and Marge began to get better, to relate to people more, and to take night classes. It seemed like some sort of turning point in our relationship, like we had passed through a crisis together.

To make a long story short, her husband lost his job, her insurance ran out, and I drastically cut my fee so we could continue meeting. After some months she was doing much better and the financial situation was getting even worse so she decided to take a break from seeing me, but the door was left open for her to continue her therapy at a subsequent date if she chose. Several years later I closed my practice entirely and left the clinic where I had been seeing Marge to take a full-time job with a managed care company. She wanted to be seen again and found how to contact me. I explained to Marge over the phone the reasons why I could not continue working with her—at that point I had no office, no malpractice insurance, no professional setup in which I could see her. She was enraged. I had always "promised to love her and to see her no matter what," she claimed. She wrote a threatening letter to the director of the clinic where I had previously seen her. He asked if we three could meet together. She was insinuating I had behaved inappropriately with her, had hugged and kissed her and made all manner of promises to her—none of which was true. All of it was apparently fabricated from that one incident and her sense of my ongoing commitment while working with her. This meeting with the clinic director settled her down a bit and she recanted the things she had said in the letter. He tried to arrange for her to see another therapist, which she refused to do.

Shortly thereafter Marge caught her husband in what she was sure was a lie about some woman he was involved with at work. Again she demanded to see me. I spoke with her on the phone, and again tried to assuage her rage that I could not see her. She was in a tirade of how I was abusing her. By this time she had been in an incest survivors' group for awhile and she had gained plenty of validations for her rage at her abusive parents and so was much freer to rage at me. I supported her anger and I gave her appropriate referrals.

The next thing I know an armed investigator from the state licensing board shows up at my work with an attache case and a lot of questions. Marge had written a letter alleging sexual misconduct. I was not allowed to see the letter of accusation. You know we have no civil rights in administrative proceedings. When accused we are presumed guilty until proven innocent. But I did discover that she accused me of making love to her on my couch for a whole hour, promising her unending love and devotion, and then that I had made her promise not to tell. The "promise not to tell" part clearly linked her current delusional accusation to her childhood molestation.

Whatever Marge told the licensing board, my attorney tells me I am in deep trouble because I'll never be able to prove it didn't happen. I have some notes, but ten years ago we didn't keep many notes so I don't know what good they will do. And anyway I don't keep notes on things that don't happen! I'm told I may lose my license to practice psychotherapy. And if she wins at this level there's malpractice settlement money waiting for her to go after. I'm really worried. I have a good job and a family to support. If charges of sexual misconduct are made I could lose my job and everything I own trying to defend myself.

We were doing good work and we both knew it. We got to many of the really terrible things that happened to her in childhood. I had her on her feet and moving in the world again and I think I could have gotten her out of her deep and lifelong depression and low self-esteem if the insurance money hadn't run out. And now this.

I came to see you because when I read your paper, "In Praise of the Dual Relationship," and I got to the part about the psychotic transference I suddenly saw what had happened. You said something to the effect that the tragedy is that the therapy has succeeded in mobilizing deep psychotic anxieties in the transference. But that then reality testing becomes lost and the therapist is confused in transference with the perpetrator of the past. That really happened. We were never taught about such things in school. Do you have any ideas about how I can get myself out of this jam?

Commentary

The most disruptive and dangerous thing a therapist can do when working with an organizing transference is to successfully connect to the person without adequate working through of the resistance to the emotional connection. Yes, this man saved the day and didn't have to hospitalize his patient. He succeeded in calling her "back from the brink." But he is deluded in thinking that such a connection is experienced as good by people who are living an organizing experience. I think she never forgave him for approaching and connecting when she wanted distance. And then he became fused with her psychotic fantasies as yet another perpetrator. Her distress that she cannot have him further fuses him to the image of the neglectful, tantalizing, or teasing perpetrator. Also, physical touching for the purpose of providing comfort or reassurance is never a good practice, because if it is not misunderstood as a seductive invitation it will surely be seen as a replication of an abusive penetration. I do see one certain, carefully defined potential use for interpretive touching in work with organizing or psychotic transference (Hedges 1994c). But interpretive touch is a carefully calculated concretized communication given at a critical and anticipated point in time when the person is having a hard time sustaining a connection and clearly understands the communication. The problem that the licensing board will have no way of understanding is that the therapy was going well until outside forces interrupted, plunging Marge into despair that her therapist successfully connected with. The psychotic transference then operated to fuse his contact with contact in childhood that was traumatic.

THERAPISTS AT RISK

I hope I have succeeded in drawing attention to how precarious our current situation is. We have learned how to follow people deep into their infantile psychotic anxieties in order to provide an opportunity for reliving and therapeutic mastery of the problem of emotional contact in the context of an adult psychotherapy relationship. But the possibility of a negative therapeutic reaction looms large. In *Working the Organizing Experience* (Hedges 1994c), I specify a series of features that characterize the development of the transference psychosis, elaborate on common subjective concerns of the person living an organizing experience, and provide a series of technical issues to be considered by therapists choosing to do long-term, intensive psychotherapy. The companion casebook, *In Search of the Lost Mother of Infancy* (Hedges 1994a), provides a theoretical and technical overview of working the organizing experience as well as lengthy and difficult in-depth case study reports of long-term work with organizing transferences reported by eight psychotherapists. The working through of the organizing transference or transference psychosis is demonstrated when it exists as the pervasive mode of the personality as well as when it exists only in subtle pockets of otherwise well developed personalities.

Clients who were traumatized early in life are at risk for the development of a negative therapeutic reaction in the form of a transference psychosis that can be suddenly, surprisingly, and destructively aimed at the person of the therapist. False accusations against therapists will not stop until therapists become knowledgeable about how to work with the primitive processes of the human mind.

Appendix C

Prevention of False Accusations against Therapists

All professionals working in trust relationships are subject to being falsely accused by people with whom they work or have worked. But psychotherapists are especially vulnerable to being falsely accused since the nature and purpose of psychotherapy is to reactivate for examination in the present therapeutic relationship the deep and damaging scars left over from past emotional relationships. A close examination of false accusations as they arise in the psychotherapeutic relationship can provide a revealing "slow motion" view of the accusatory process in general as it affects other helping professionals.

A false accusation can be functionally defined as an allegation in which "it is not possible to establish a direct causal link between actions of the therapist and the damage sustained by the client. Nor is it possible to establish, beyond the shadow of a doubt that the ac-

Reprinted with permission from *The California Therapist*, July/August 1997.

tivities of the therapist . . . were exploitative" (this volume, pp. 413–414). Since allegations of professional misconduct are so serious and so potentially devastating to the professional, insisting on a rigorous burden of proof is essential.

It seems that false accusations against therapists are seldom made by people intending to lie or by people simply seeking settlement dollars. False accusations against therapists, especially those presented to ethics committees and licensing boards, are usually made by people who truly believe that they have been damaged in some significant way by the accused. In many cases people who make false accusations are seeking some form of public recognition and/or punishment for damage they feel they have been the victim of. They often seek confrontation, humiliation, and revenge against the trusted professional they have identified as the perpetrator of some deep form of abuse against them.

But if people issuing false accusations are in some sense operating in good faith, if a direct and unambiguous causal link cannot be established to the person of the accused, and if clear evidence of exploitation is lacking, how can we understand the nature of these malicious and vindictive accusations? And how can psychotherapists and other professionals take steps to protect themselves from being falsely targeted?[1]

The most direct answer to the riddle of false accusations is that a deep transference reaction has been activated in the trust relationship. The most fundamental concept of psychotherapy is "transference," whether one thinks of it in terms of "parent tapes," "business left over from the past," or the experiences of one's "inner child." A century of psychotherapeutic study has revealed a human tendency to transfer over-learned emotional habits and fears from significant past relationships into the emotional context of present trust relationships.

First studied by psychotherapists were the so-called oedipal transferences left over from dysfunctional family relationships experienced in the 4- to 7-year-old developmental period. Then therapists studied

---

1. The question of prevention is addressed in detail from a number of vantage points in Hedges and colleagues (1997). The central ideas from this book are presented by the authors in a series of audio and videotape cassettes available through The Listening Perspectives Study Center, 1439 East Chapman Avenue, Orange, CA 92866. Fax/Phone (714) 633-3933.

the narcissistic transferences left over from the 3-year-old period in which needed affirming, confirming, and inspiring others failed in some way. During the 1970s and 1980s, therapists studied the borderline transferences left over from faulty or abusive relationships experienced during the character-forming period from 4 to 24 months of age.

Only in the last decade has it been possible to spell out in transference terms how significant emotional traumas dating from the months immediately preceding and following birth tend to live on in people's bodies, their personalities, and their relationships. These primitive emotional experiences that become lived out in later life in trust relationships are referred to as "organizing transferences," "transference psychosis," or "psychotic transferences," whether they are pervasive in the personality or only exist in small pockets.[2]

It is now clear that infantile trauma leaves significant emotional scars that cannot be remembered in ordinary ways because the growing child's capacities for memory are in nascent stages of development. *Remembering of infantile trauma is accomplished by repeating in significant trust relationships destructive emotional experiences from the primeval past.*[3]

The key feature of the organizing transference is a deep-seated terror of genuine interpersonal contact. This terror of personal connection with a trusted other relates to the person's earliest love relationships, which were in one way or another experienced as overstimulating, frightening, traumatic, damaging, or hurtful. *As the person reached out in infancy to organize a channel of connection for nurturance, stimulation, and love, something happened to traumatize the reaching so that the basic (almost neuronal) memory comes to read, "never reach out for that kind of connection again."*

The helping professional, especially the psychotherapist, who reaches out and succeeds in establishing a personal connection with the client thus traumatized in infancy puts him or herself into serious jeopardy. The reason? The deeply ingrained prohibitions against ever again connecting in a dependent and vulnerable way have now been broken, violated by the personal contact promoted by the trusted professional.

---

2. For a comprehensive historical, theoretical, and clinical overview of transference psychosis and the organizing transferences see Hedges (1994a,c).

3. See Hedges (1994b), where I review a century of psychoanalytic research into the phenomena of "recovered memories" as they relate to infantile trauma.

The client has been successfully drawn into relinquishing his or her fundamental defenses and has been retraumatized in the process as the frightening memories reappear in various forms of physical and mental anguish.

At the time of the establishment of the primordial prohibition against future interpersonal emotional connections, a sense of reality appreciation had not yet developed. *When the prohibition is later broken, the primitive body memory of the infantile trauma is reactivated and there is an instantaneous confusion and fusion of the perpetrator of the past with the helping person of the present who has reached out and in some way emotionally touched the person.* The sense of terror, panic, abuse, damage, and exploitation that was originally associated with the infantile perpetrator is now associated with the "violator" of the present—the well-intended helping professional.

In understanding infantile transferences it is important to remember that single focal events as well as prolonged emotional strains equally function as psychological traumas in infancy, though caregivers may not interpret the situation as traumatic to the infant at the time. Also, many events in infancy—such as incubators, adoptions, allergies, surgery, fevers, and family upsets—are likely to be experienced by the baby as traumatic. In the baby's mind the world is not going as it should and blame is hurled at the world through the baby's angry accusatory cry. The infant is angry and helpless in face of life's abusive circumstances, but the adult whose body is shaking with a flood of traumatic memories is no longer helpless and wishes to strike out to end the pain and to punish the wrongdoer. *As the memories pour out in terror, the fear and blame become displaced as they do in dreams and are then attached to the only other person present—the person who is "responsible" for the reactivation of the pain and terror, the therapist or helping professional!*

What are some measures that can be taken by the therapist to guard against his or her clients' experiencing the therapeutic process as traumatic?

1. Be cautious about who you take on. Are they truly suitable for once-a-week outpatient work? What forms of extra care are they likely to need? Are you prepared to respond to that need? Remember, pulling out or deintensifying later will likely replicate the traumatic infantile experience that produced the initial prohibition against later inti-

macy, thereby increasing the danger of an accusation. Also remember that "going the second mile" or the third or fourth mile to try to be with or to rescue someone in a deep regression is very hazardous because the situation is likely to be reminiscent of some aspect of a desperate infancy. The plea is always for "more." But providing "more" runs the risk of forcing a connection to "save" the person when what they are running from is the possibility of an emotional connection that will catapult them into traumatic, regressive, body-shaking memories of early trauma and abuse. When they get there it will be you who is accused of the intrusive abuse! This is the precise nature of the organizing transference and potential disasters for therapists can be predicted.

2. Remain mindful of the dangers of organizing transferences or transference psychosis through extensive documentation, use of consultants, and use of a third-party case monitor who also sees the client occasionally, conferences the work with you, and takes careful notes.[4]

3. Document all peculiar actions and verbalizations that might contain primitive transference material. Document any physical contact and any countertransference disclosures carefully in terms of the therapeutic context, aim, reaction, and transference implications.

4. Avoid going "beyond the call of duty." It invariably plays into the transference psychosis and creates unnecessary risks for the therapist without providing appreciable gains for the client. Don't be a detective helping your client dig up graveyards or search old dusty cellars for proof of "remembered" abuse. Stay in your consulting room, keep your hands to yourself (unless you are certified to do body work), and remain in a professional role at all times—regardless of how desperately you are petitioned to do otherwise! Avoid recommending magical crystals, shamanistic journeys, peasant wizards, or other unorthodox techniques if you know what's best for you. Be cautious what reading materials you suggest and what professionals you refer to. Carefully document any irregularities of technique, explaining in your notes the reasons for your decisions and the client's reactions.[5]

---

4. Use of a case monitor is discussed in Hedges (1994c).

5. These suggestions reflect the kinds of things that attorneys and attorneys general focus on to fault therapists. A series of case study disasters is reported in Hedges and colleagues (1997).

5. Do not collude with the resistance to transference remembering by encouraging "recovered memories" and passively going along with acting out on the basis of them. Recovered memories are at best dubious these days and hypnosis or chemical interviews are risky as well. Make sure that all unusual processes are carefully thought through, your thinking documented, experts obtained, third-party and/or videotaped monitoring arranged, and that all questions are processed thoroughly with the client.

6. Remember that *borderline clients are afraid of abandonment*, but that *people working in psychotic areas of personality—no matter how much advanced development they may have achieved—are terrified of connection. Never allow emotional connection to occur without carefully working through the transference fears associated with that connection. Document the forms that resistance to contact takes and work on the transference-based terrors of connection.*

7. Be aware that countertransference reactions to organizing or psychotic transference include not only an irrational fear of the power of the client's psychotic reactions, but frightened confusion on the part of the therapist when the client fails to reach out for the contact you offer.

CONCLUSION

Virginia Wink Hilton (1993), in "When We Are Accused," points out that a three-part response to accusation arises almost instinctively from most of us: (1) Denial—"I didn't do it," (2) defense—"I did the best I could," and (3) blame—"She knows better than this, this accusation is pathological." The real problem, says Hilton, is that an accusation often is aimed, somewhat successfully, at a core emotional wound of the accused, at a blind spot or Achilles' heel. Until the accused is able to work through the core wound as it is active in the present relationship, it is unlikely that he will be able to give a satisfying response to the accuser who "knows" she is somehow right.

Hilton charts a course for us:

1. Avoid denial, defensiveness, and blame.
2. Use consultation to work through the core wound the accusation touches in oneself.

3. Show the person that you know how deeply he or she has been wounded by you or by the position you have taken.
4. Provide some reassurance that this particular kind of injury can somehow be averted or softened in the future—that is, that "this won't happen again to me or to someone else."

Hilton (1993) also believes that the most sensitive moment in the accusatory process is when the client first broaches the accusation with you. First, she says, it takes a lot of courage to confront someone you believe is or has been abusing you. And secondly, given that transference distortions are likely to be in operation and the high probability that the accusation will be aimed at a core wound of the accused, it is important to make every effort to "get it"—to grasp what the person is saying, to show an understanding of how they feel you have hurt them, and to acknowledge how determined they are to see to it that you do not hurt them or anybody else in this way again.

"Getting it" the first time correctly and extending deep empathy can save professionals a lot of expense and grief! It's no skin off your back to acknowledge that you now see that what you did (or didn't do) caused hurt to them—and to make matters worse, *you* of all people who "should have known." Acknowledge that despite your best intentions, your judgment failed to show a full understanding of where they were coming from. "No wonder this hurt so much."

Appendix D

Informed Consent for Limited Physical Contact

I, _____, hereby grant permission to my therapist, _____ to engage in limited forms of physical contact with me as a part of our ongoing psychotherapy process.

I understand that the purpose of therapeutic touching is to actualize for study, in concrete physical forms, certain basic aspects of human contact which I may have been deprived of or which may have been distorted in my personal development.

I understand that the purpose of therapeutic touching is not for gratification of physical longings, nor for providing physical comfort or support. Rather, the specific forms and times of the limited physical therapeutic contact are aimed towards understanding issues around the

---

Reprinted with permission from *Working the Organizing Experience* (Hedges 1994c).

approach to, the achievement of, the sustaining of, and/or the breaking off of human emotional contact.

I understand that limited forms of physical contact such as handshakes, "A.A. type" hugs, occasional hand holding, and other token physical gestures are not uncommon as a part of the interpersonal process of psychotherapy. However, other forms of touching are more rare and need to be clearly understood by both parties and discussed in terms of their possible meanings.

I understand that many professional psychotherapists believe that physical contact of any sort is inappropriate because it fails to encourage verbalization and symbolization of exactly what meanings might be implicit in the physical touch.

I understand that sexual touching of any type is unethical, illegal, and never a part of professional psychotherapy.

I understand that many aspects of the psychotherapeutic process, including the possible value of limited physical contact, cannot be established as clearly beneficial on a scientific basis. But I also understand that physical contact has many values in human relationships and that to categorically exclude it from the psychotherapeutic relationship may be detrimental to my therapeutic process when the critical focus for study needs to be around concrete and personal experiences of meaningful and sustained interpersonal contact.

I HEREBY AGREE THAT SHOULD I HAVE ANY MISGIVINGS, DOUBTS, OR NEGATIVE REACTIONS to therapeutic physical contact or to the anticipation of such, that I will immediately discuss my concerns with my therapist.

If for any reason I experience concerns which I am reluctant to discuss directly with my therapist, or if I feel unsatisfied with our discussion, I HEREBY AGREE TO SEEK IMMEDIATE THIRD PARTY PROFESSIONAL CONSULTATION FROM A LICENSED PSYCHOTHERAPIST OF MY CHOICE OR ONE WHO IS RECOMMENDED BY MY THERAPIST. This part of the agreement is to ensure that no misunderstandings or uncomfortable feelings arise as a result of physical contact or anticipation of therapeutic physical touching.

I understand that I may at any time choose to discontinue this permission by a mutual exchange of written acknowledgments indicating that permission for therapeutic physical contact is revoked.

I HAVE CAREFULLY READ ALL OF THE ABOVE PROVI-
SIONS AND HAVE DISCUSSED THEM WITH MY THERAPIST.
ANY QUESTIONS OR MISGIVINGS I HAVE ARE WRITTEN IN
THE SPACE PROVIDED BELOW.

Client or Patient	Date
Therapist or Analyst	Date

ADDITIONAL SPECIFIC REQUESTED PROCEDURES:

Request	Initial	Date
Request	Initial	Date
Request	Initial	Date

SPECIFIC QUESTIONS, MISGIVINGS, AND CONCERNS:

Appendix E

Informed Consent for Long-Term Psychotherapy

Regarding a Case Monitor, Medical Care, and Termination Plans

Psychotherapy that lasts for more than twenty sessions or six months necessarily involves an ongoing relationship between you and your therapist. One of the purposes of long-term, intensive psychotherapy is to allow your past emotional patterns to emerge and to be understood as they affect current relationships, particularly the therapeutic relationship. If there is the possibility that early or deep trauma of any kind affected your development, then as a part of your therapy you may need to review or to re-experience the emotions that were attached to that trauma.

Experience with revived memories of early abuse, deprivation, and trauma tells us that these memories are usually confusing, frightening, and/or upsetting. Experience in psychotherapy further tells us that such early memories are not usually recorded only in ordinary recollections, pictures of the events, or stories, but in the ways we experience relationships and in various muscles and tissues of our bodies. Thus, when these memories emerge in the here-and-now to be looked at they will be manifest in the ways you experience your therapist and/or the ways you experience your body and mind in reaction to therapy or to the therapeutic relationship.

There are three main dangers of intensive, long-term, relational psychotherapy:

1. You may begin to experience your therapist as somehow frightening, dangerous, neglectful, or not "on your side" in some way in the therapy process.

2. You may experience body reactions that represent early memories—such as agitation, distress, apathy, addictions, depression, eating and sleep difficulties, confusion, suspiciousness, or other physical symptoms intruding into your life in various ways.

3. You may feel a strong urge to flee, emotionally or physically, from your therapy so as to avoid further emergence of bad memories or negative experiences.

Psychotherapists have developed standard ways of addressing these potential dangers:

1. There may come a time when your confidence in your therapist or in the therapeutic process begins to get shaky. It is important that you first bring this up with your therapist and then, if your concerns continue, to arrange with him or her to seek out a third-party professional case monitor or consultant with whom to discuss your misgivings. Your therapist will help you locate a mutually agreed upon health professional who is familiar with this kind of work and who can listen carefully to what problems are coming up with your therapist or with the therapy process and make appropriate suggestions and recommendations. If your therapist at any time believes your emotional reactions are threatening to you or to your therapy in any way he or she will insist that you immediately consult a mutually agreed upon case monitor.

2. An increase in any physical symptoms or adverse emotional reactions during the course of long-term psychotherapy usually signals the emergence of early traumatic memories. For your well-being and safety it may be essential for you to have immediate medical and/or psychiatric evaluation and to remain under the care of a physician for

a period of time. If your therapist at any time feels that the physical or mental reactions emerging in the course of treatment may potentially endanger you in any way he or she will insist that you go immediately for medical and/or psychiatric consultation.

3. Should you wish to terminate treatment before you and your therapist mutually agree upon a beneficial time, it may be that you are unconsciously wanting to avoid the emergence of long-hidden traumatic memories. For example, you may experience your therapist as somehow failing you, as repeating previous insults or abuse to you, or as not being interested in you, not being emotionally available, not understanding you, or not liking you. You may then abruptly want to stop seeing your therapist in order to avoid the emotional pain and/or perceived dangers of dealing with these issues. Your first remedy would likely be to consult a mutually agreed upon case monitor in order to discuss the issues coming up with your therapist or your therapy process. A part of this consultation will be that your therapist and case monitor will communicate with each other about the relevant issues. Additionally, it is of crucial importance that you be willing to continue at least five to ten therapy sessions so that you, your therapist, and your case monitor can adequately discuss your reasons for wanting to stop therapy and try to reach a joint understanding on what these reasons may mean to you and to your ongoing therapy process. If your therapist feels your decision to terminate therapy is abrupt or may be related to the revival of early traumatic memories, he or she may insist that you consult a case monitor and then continue for a series of five to ten additional sessions before terminating.

INFORMED CONSENT AGREEMENT

I have read the above considerations for entering into long-term, in-depth relational psychotherapy. I understand that certain dangers may be expected to appear over time in relational therapy. I have discussed the dangers and the usual safeguards listed above with my therapist so that I understand them. If any of the above-mentioned conditions occur: (1) the loss of confidence in the therapy or the therapist, (2) the emergence or increase of physical or mental symptoms, or (3) the wish to terminate before a mutually agreed upon time, then I agree to abide by the three safeguards listed above, that is: (1) to consult with a third-party professional case monitor, (2) to consult with a medical/psychiatric practitioner, and/or (3) to attend five to ten regular termination sessions.

I further understand that this informed consent and other written requests that my therapist may make from time to time pertaining to my well-being and safety must be agreed upon in order to enter further into or to continue long-term psychotherapy. Failure to comply with any requirements which are designed to safeguard me and my therapy process will be grounds for my therapist to give me a five to ten sessions notice of termination.

_____

Client Signature   Date

_____

Therapist Signature   Date

Please Retain a Signed Copy of This Agreement

Appendix F

Achieving Optimal Responsiveness with Early Developmental Trauma[1]

Abstract. This paper points to a technical problem that frequently arises in the working-through process when various forms of infantile trauma are involved in the formation of the transference. Infantile trauma is remembered somato-psychically through a tendency to avoid, rupture, or flee from any and all interpersonal contact that might conceivably be re-traumatizing. The dominant technical approaches of the past two decades have included some form of empathic resonating, holding, or containing—based on the general understanding that fear of emotional abandonment is central to most early psychological states. But if the primordial transference structure is based upon a terror of interpersonal contact, an empathically containing technical approach is bound to give rise to various potentially serious abreactions, one of

1. Presented at the 21st Annual International Conference on the Psychology of the Self, San Diego, CA, October, 1998.

which is that the therapist may become the target of serious accusations. Countertransference responsiveness may be called into play in the service of resistance to the analysis of organizing transferences.

OPENING CONSIDERATIONS

We take the infant's primary task, both in utero and after birth, to be that of organizing and establishing reliable channels of connection—first to the maternal body and later to the maternal mind. Workable dynamic connections between the developing infant and the caregiving human environment are a given when considering the slowly evolving processes referred to as attachment, bonding, and intrapsychic symbiosis. But we know that many things can and do go wrong in the process of establishing mutually engaged connections with the mother/other that serve the infant's growth through satisfying attunement.

We can formulate three broad classes of failure in the early infant–caregiver connecting process:

1. Failures arising when the infant extends in some way and does not experience the possibility of being met by the caregiving environment;
2. Failures arising when the infant extends in some way and experiences pain and instinctive contraction or constriction as a result of the encounter with the painful environment; and
3. Failures accumulating over a period of time due to a persistent strain experienced by the infant in reaching out to or adapting to the connecting possibilities and/or requirements of the caregiving environment.

Infantile trauma can be effectively defined as any of these types of failure being experienced frequently, intensely, or cumulatively. We must assume that some mnemic record of significant failures exists that influences the infant's subsequent extensions or reaching-out attempts. Freud (1895) first formulated this problem in quasi-neurological terms when he spoke of a counter-cathexis being established against experiences of pain so that the developing organism does not extend in that particular way again.

A DEVELOPMENTAL CONTINUUM
OF TRANSFERENCE STRUCTURES

The history of the study of transferences begins with Freud and the classical psychoanalysts focusing on the complex emotional traumas, recorded during the oedipal period, which lead to repression and neurosis. Kohut (1971) and the self psychologists have extended developmentally downward our understanding of transference structures to include childhood traumas resulting from faulty mirroring, twinning, and idealizing experiences leading to narcissistic defects or deficits in the self structure. Mahler (1968), Kernberg (1975), Winnicott (1971), Little (1981), Giovacchini (1979), Bollas (1987), Stolorow and Atwood (1992), and Stolorow and colleagues (1994), as well as many others, have contributed fundamentally to our understanding of the yet earlier symbiotic or borderline level transferences resulting from a failure to fully individuate from self-and-other scenarios or patternings firmly established during the period of characterological development often called symbiosis. Grotstein (1981), Tustin (1981), Brandschaft (1988, 1994), Hedges (1983, 1994a,b), and others have elucidated and clarified the operation of transference structures resulting from the three above-mentioned types of failures occurring in the earliest processes of organizing psychological bonds. The effects of infantile trauma appear in psychotherapy as "primitive mental states," "breakdown experiences," "transference psychoses," or "organizing transferences." I will use Hedges' term *organizing transference* because the problem I wish to focus on relates to the transference memory of organizing channels of connection to the environment and experiencing those channels as being traumatically intruded upon or disrupted in infancy—either in focal or cumulative (Khan 1963) ways.

CONSIDERING DEVELOPMENTAL LINES
OF EMPATHY AND INTERPRETATION

As early as 1959, Kohut formulated the concept that introspection and empathy (vicarious introspection) operate as definers of the field of psychoanalysis. In his last address to the self psychology community at Berkeley in October of 1981, Kohut spoke of different kinds of empathy for different developmental levels of selfobject relatedness. He recounted a story of how some years before, in desperation, he had initiated fleeting physical contact with a very vulnerable woman as a fitting and workable empathic gesture for the moment. In keeping with his emphasis on a developmental line of selfobject relatedness and a corresponding awareness of the different types of empathy required to respond to various levels of selfobject needs, Kohut issued a challenge to his successors to formulate a developmental line of empathy and empathic interpretation since different forms of environmental responsiveness are required to achieve different developmental levels of self to selfobject resonance. Since that time our field has witnessed many contributions to the understanding of developmental forms of empathy and interpretation.

A TECHNICAL PROBLEM WITH THE ORGANIZING-LEVEL TRANSFERENCE

It is my purpose here to describe a technical problem in the application of empathic understanding in the working-through process of infantile traumas as they reappear in primitive, psychotic, or organizing-level transferences—whether the transference stems from a full-scale arrest in personality development or from only a "pocket" or limited area of early developmental fixation. The technical problem can be stated simply enough. But grasping its magnitude and range of applications is a formidable task.

The transference memory laid down in infancy by any of the three kinds of trauma mentioned above—feeling unresponded to, feeling injured, or feeling chronically strained to adapt—is by nature a somatopsychic structure that is designied to avoid, rupture, or flee from similar forms of empathic contact offered in the future (Grotstein 1994, Hedges 1994a,b). That is, the motivation set up by the original trauma in infancy is to avoid all or certain kinds of (empathic) connections that may prove to be similar to the kinds of connections originally experienced as traumatically empty, painful, or frustrating.

All therapists are familiar with the disconcerting clinical situation in which virtually every empathic gesture is systematically deflected, rejected, or abreacted to in some way—usually with discouragement, despair, disdain, or a hostile accusation. Many therapists find this phenomena puzzling, since our central technical emphasis for several decades has been on "containing" fragmented pieces of the personality or the self through establishing various forms of "empathic resonance," "emotional holding," or "intersubjective attunement." Why then does the effort of the therapist to achieve and to sustain empathic contact with these earliest transference structures persistently fall short?

Restating the problem, we might say that the central issue of most early developmental states relates to the attachment and bonding processes and that problems in accomplishing these processes manifest as a fear of some form of emotional abandonment. Technical procedures that address the fear of lack of attunement or the fear of abandonment are generally known to produce a calming or containing effect that allows the working-through process to continue. But if the psychic structure mobilized by the therapeutic relationship is genetically linked to infantile (pre-bonded) contact trauma, it is reasonable to expect that later attempts at contact through empathy, containment, and holding in the usual sense will be systematically avoided. That is, *if the primary motivation of the organizing level transference structure is to prevent, rupture, or flee from all possibilities of emotional contact similar to those that have proven traumatic in the past, then the therapist reaching out in an interested, caring, empathic, or containing manner will stimulate the fear of retraumatization through attempts at interpersonal contact and connection.* The technical problem is this: How does a therapist empathize with, interpret, and initiate a working-through process with a person who shrinks with terror at the slightest hint of an empathic, contactful approach from the other—despite "false self" (Winnicott 1952) and "mimical self" (Hedges 1994c) maneuvers to the contrary?

We can verbally conceptualize the problem of early transference structures based on infantile trauma in this somewhat sensible manner. But the organizing-level transference does not exist at a rational verbal level, nor can it be appealed to on a logical, sensible basis. Words such as mad, insane, crazy, psychotic, and untreatable have long been used to describe the complete sense of defeat that people experience when encountering in others psychic manifestations that go to any limit to avoid meaningful, mutually engaged connections and personal interactions. Not even a comprehensive lexicon of psychotic and borderline symptomology could do justice to the skill with which many people have learned to slither out of interpersonal connectedness completely unnoticed by others.[2]

NEGATIVE THERAPEUTIC REACTIONS

From the Anna O. specimen case of psychoanalysis (Breuer and Freud 1893–1895) through present case books, there is a running thread of mystery about analysands who have simply not been able to benefit from empathic contact offered by their analysts. Often formulated as "negative therapeutic reactions" (Freud 1918, 1923, 1933) with various explanations being offered for the failure of the therapy, it would now appear that many of these cases record instances in which the underlying transference structure was skillfully organized to prevent increasing interpersonal contact and connection at all cost.

THE TRANSFERENCE PSYCHOSIS

Brandchaft (1988, 1994) reports three cases involving what might be called transference psychoses. Though he formulates the work in terms of early affect communication and the problem of the analyst

---

2. Howard Bacal (personal communication, 1998) points out that my formulations as stated here join up with Fairbairn's concept of the "anti-libidinal" ego, which the patient harnesses to quell those aspects of himself that would launch an appeal to the parental figure to supply the emotional nourishment that he knows will not be forthcoming. These formulations also join with Guntrip's "schizoid citadel" within which the weakened self must hide from the "desirable deserter" or the "infinite exploiter," and with Balint's "basic fault," a structure that reflects an experience of archaic relatedness that has gone wrong. Self psychology theory also recognizes the need of some patients to "resist" the analytic treatment efforts by continuing to ward off the awareness of selfobject needs—in structures such as the vertical and horizontal split—in order to avoid expected retraumatization. Bacal comments that the material presented here underscores two aspects of these constellations that have not been adequately appreciated: first, the operation of a "transference structure" that actively prevents contact with the analyst and secondly, that empathic attunement in such instances may not be effective. He notes that "The challenge, in such cases, is for that particular therapist to find the response that is optimal (i.e., specific) to the therapeutic needs of the patient [and] that he or she is capable of providing that patient."

learning to tune into unusual, chronic, or intractable affect experiences, it seems likely that these cases and others like them might be additionally understood from the standpoint of an organizing transference structure operating to foreclose any and all feasible forms of contact and connection. Grotstein (1994) likewise cites many instances in the literature on psychotic and borderline states that might well be formulated as a transference-based determination not to allow meaningful interpersonal connections.

THE FEAR OF BREAKDOWN

Winnicott's final paper, "Fear of Breakdown" (1974), points to the place in an analysis where an analysand verbalizes a fear of breaking down, of being empty, or of experiencing deadness. Winnicott's interpretation is simply, "the breakdown has already happened." By this he means that a breakdown occurred in infancy that is being recalled by projecting the fear of traumatic despair and fragmentation into the imminent future. By implication, the mobilization of the organizing-level transference is pointing the person toward a somato-psychic remembering of the infantile agony and breakdown through a traumatic reliving of the experience in the analytic relationship. Based on experiences of traumatic infantile breakdown, the analysand intensely fears re-experiencing such a trauma in the working-through process and seeks all possible ways to avoid it.

THE ORGANIZING TRANSFERENCE
AND "FALSE" ACCUSATIONS

As the primordial breakdown experience is revived in transference remembering, an inevitable clinical result is that the analyst is accused of a variety of crimes that have caused or at least that have not prevented this deep sense of fragmentation, disorientation, and agony from recurring. The accusation that the analyst is the perpetrator of the traumatic experience can be considered a further manifestation of transference remembering. But like all transferences, these accusations do not exist in a vacuum—the analyst has indeed to acknowledge crimes of omission or commission that the analysand points to as valid aspects of the interaction that do indeed raise questions about whether or not the analyst can be trusted in the ways that the analysand has hoped for and desired. Further, the therapist is the perpetrator of relived infantile trauma experience, in that she or he has indeed encouraged the development of the intimacy of the therapeutic relationship that the person is experiencing as traumatic. But the intense sense of abandonment, betrayal, or victimization at the hands of the analyst can also serve as a transference resistance maneuver to avoid or to rupture feared interpersonal contact that is developing or that threatens to develop.

> The clamor [for "more," for how "you're not treating me right," for how "you're not giving me what I need," and for how "I can find somebody better who will"...] is an angry memory of what I needed and didn't get. *But the conditioned clamor-memory now functions in the service of preventing intimate or reciprocal interconnections that in the past were known to be traumatic.* [this volume, pp. 39–40]

The sense of victimization can also lead to a negative therapeutic reaction and to an acting out of the accusatory process in other arenas such as licensing boards, ethics committees, and courts of law (Hedges 1996, Hedges et al. 1997).

THE TECHNICAL IMPASSE

This threatening moment of somato-psychic breakdown, which is a form of transference remembering, gives rise to a point of technical tension that often leads to impasse or disaster. The analyst expects that if his or her empathic failures can be acknowledged and that if a connection to the fragmented and fragmenting self can be made appropriately and in time, then an empathic link will allow interpersonal resonance to resume or to become more deeply established. The analyst expects that the offer of empathic connection through the acknowledgment of empathic breach will bring relief to the horrible sense of loneliness, fragmentation, alienation, agony, and abandonment that is being experienced by the analysand. But this is not so when an organizing transference is operating. Even when attempts at containing empathic connection do succeed in momentarily quelling the storm, they do not hold long before another outbreak of accusatory despair or rage emerges, often accompanied by frank psychotic symptoms, a negative therapeutic reaction, and/or an acting out of the transference-based demand for reparation or revenge—often in the form of "false accusations."

EMPATHY AND COUNTERTRANSFERENCE RESPONSIVENESS

Since the early 1950s the analyst's emotional responses to the analysand and to the analytic process have undergone considerable study. It has seemed useful to many to conceptualize the relatedness dimension of psychoanalysis along developmental lines, since the concept of transference implies a series of internally structured relationships, and since humans experience relationships differently at different stages of emotional development. If forms of transference relatedness and corresponding modes of empathic attunement are conceptualized along a developmental continuum from more basic to more complex, then the analyst's expectable emotional responsiveness to the transference can likewise be organized along that continuum. It makes a certain intuitive sense to think in terms of different modes of emotional relatedness being expectable or appropriate when interacting with an infant, a toddler, a 3-year-old, or a 5-year-old.

Countertransference responsiveness has traditionally been conceptualized as being an impediment to or a potential interference with the analytic process when dealing with relatedness issues internalized during the oedipal period of triangular (5-year-old) relating (Freud 1910, 1915). Countertransference responsiveness has been seen as facilitative in the recognition and analysis of narcissistic issues internalized during the (3-year-old) era of self-consolidation (Kohut 1971). Countertransference replications of (4- to 24-month-old) relatedness scenarios internalized through interactions with early caregivers have been seen as expectable if not essential in the analysis of borderline or symbiotic relatedness issues (Bollas 1987, Hedges 1983, 1992, Little 1981). Countertransference reactions encountered in the analysis of the earliest relatedness strivings, developmentally defined as the period in which the fetus or neonate is organizing nurturing and other meaningful channels to the human milieu, have been studied by Giovacchini

(1979, 1997), Searles (1979), Grotstein (1981), Tustin (1981), and Hedges (1983, 1992, 1994a,c).

Hedges (1994a,c) summarizes the most common countertransference reactions to organizing- or psychotic-level transferences as follows:

1. The belief that the person is sick, crazy, evil, or untreatable and must be managed with support, medication, exorcism, or lockup;
2. The fear that the intensity of the psychotic anxieties will become directed at the person of the analyst or the process of analysis;
3. The mobilization in the analyst of his or her own primitive organizing experiences and anxieties; and
4. An emotional withdrawal of the analyst out of empathy with the deep terror that threatens as a result of intense or sustained interpersonal connections.

The third countertransference reaction above, mobilization of psychotic or organizing anxieties in the analyst, especially interests us in a study of empathy or optimal responsiveness (Bacal 1998). We might say that all human infants extend into the caregiving milieu expecting satisfying and satisfactory responsiveness, and that when the environment fails in one of the ways mentioned earlier—by providing frustrating unresponsiveness, traumatic injury, or chronic strain—the infant experiences various forms of disorganization, confusion, fragmentation, pain, contraction, constriction, and/or terror. We would, therefore, assume that somato-psychic mnemic traces of the consequences of faulty relational responsiveness in infancy are a more or less universal part of human experience and human relational memory. Thus, when an analyst extends empathy repeatedly or in extraordinary ways and finds her- or himself repeatedly or intensely frustrated, emotionally unresponded to, rejected, abandoned, ignored, devalued, or attacked, it is only a matter of time before primitive anxieties and the defenses against them are likely to become mobilized to one degree or another in the analyst.[3] This means that careful attention to counter-

---

3. Following Selma Fraiberg (1982) I have discussed the basic mammalian responses of fight, flight, and freeze as defensive or predefensive maneuvers that serve to ward off psychotic anxieties (Hedges 1994a,c).

transference responsiveness is critical to analyzing and working through organizing-level transferences.

Further, given the propensity toward various forms of fragmentation and mobilization of primitive anxieties and defenses in people reacting to organizing- or psychotic-level transference manifestations, it is reasonable to assume that this human tendency will be used in psychoanalysis in the service of resistance to transference remembering. That is, individuals whose organizing transference need is to avoid, rupture, or flee from various kinds of interpersonal connections are likely to learn to use the fragmenting and disconnecting potentials of others to accomplish their purposes. In practice this might mean that a particular feature of the analyst's personality or way of working or responding would be engaged or related to in such a way as to cause momentary disruption in the sense of mutual interconnectedness. That is, the analyst's modes and capacities for empathy itself—as ways of establishing emotional attunement—may well become (purposefully, nonconsciously) targeted in order to disarm, disorganize, or in some way fragment the analyst so as to foreclose the possibility of analyzing the organizing transference.[4]

THE PARADOX OF EMPATHY WITH THE ORGANIZING EXPERIENCE

If the very tool that the analyst most prizes, empathic attunement, is doomed to failure in the organizing-level transference because the analysand experiences a deep terror of empathic connection due to primordial traumatization by early experiences of intersubjective connection, how do we proceed from here?

A Transference Illustration: Raging at the Therapist

The first case example is from a woman therapist who has been seeing a female client for three years twice a week. An intense therapeutic relationship has developed. The client is a very bright and so-

---

4. The lengthy cases of Sandy (Hedges 1994a) and Paul (Chapter 16 of this book) illustrate in detail this use of countertransference responsiveness in the service of resistance to working through the organizing transference.

phisticated woman, a professional. She lives in the world very comfort-ably in regard to everyday matters but she suffers privately from hav-ing a "multiple personality." The most troubling switch is when she, without apparent reason, goes into a rageful self. Her therapist sought consultation in a crisis after she got a telephone call following their last session saying, "I'm not coming in any more because there's something wrong with our relationship." The therapist inquires about the nature of the problem. She says, "I can tell you feel there's something wrong with my relationship with Naomi." Naomi is a lesbian woman the cli-ent has developed an intimate relationship with. She continued, "You don't think it's right, or you think there's something wrong with Naomi. There's no point in our going any further as long as you think that way." She's angry, shouting at her therapist, and then she lists a number of other things. "You don't listen this way . . . and you're not that way . . . ," a tirade of angry complaints and accusations leveled at the person and the practice of the therapist that the therapist has never heard before.

The therapist is in a state of shock, feeling she may never see the woman again. She is not even clear about what might have been said to upset her. She cannot link her abrupt disruption to anything. The therapist asked, "What makes you think I don't like Naomi? I've always been supportive of your relationship with Naomi." But the client is certain the therapist disapproves of Naomi and the relationship. As far as the consultant could ascertain the therapist has no such negative feelings about the relationship and has no personal biases against les-bianism. In fact, the therapist seems glad her client has found a friend. The therapist is in crisis because she has been able to schedule a tele-phone appointment with her client but is anxious about how it may go. She tells the consultant that her client is basically not lesbian. She's had three or four relationships with women but they've been relation-ships in which she is looking for soothing contact with a woman, pos-sibly in order to feel mothered. She can't develop relationships with men because she doesn't know how to relate to men. She's confused and frightened by men. She's talked at various times about how even though she's having a sexual relationship with a woman, she doesn't feel that she's lesbian. She doesn't feel like other lesbians. The client feels certain she's really not a lesbian. At one point the therapist had said, "I really don't think you're a lesbian either." It occurs to the con-sultant that this could be where the organizing transference became attached, that is, in the therapist's attitude that she's not lesbian. The consultant asks, "How have you developed your view? From all you've told me of her relatedness capacities, she's emotionally 3 months old. We have no idea what lesbianism means to her, and we have no idea what her future may be. She's developed no real sexual identification yet and therefore no stable gender identity." The therapist immediately resonates with that. It seems the client is experiencing some breach in empathy. She has determined that her therapist has an attitude that she's not really a lesbian. Now she claims the therapist disapproves of Naomi and of her relationship with Naomi. Her therapist has learned how to work the organizing experience very skillfully. For months the two have worked over many connecting and disconnecting experiences in other relationships, though she has not been able to work the organizing transference directly with her therapist—at least not until now. In a series of parallel transferences the two have been studying the ways she connects and disconnects daily with people. She says, "I feel fully connected with people. I see people. I talk to people. I move in a social world. Superficially I do very well, but at some other level I know I'm not connected." She has the conviction that her mother "gave me away" in the seventh or eighth month in utero, and that what she's been striving for ever since is to be bodily reconnected to mother, to be sustained in a physical relationship. The suggestion is that there was once a connection, but that mother broke the connection. The analytic speaker has no idea how to make or to sustain mental connections. She has presented one critical traumatic memory: when she was perhaps 2 or 3, she and her mother lived in quite poor circumstances—in maybe one room with a bathroom down the hall.

Her mother would often take her to the bathroom with her. One day her mother takes her into the bathroom. Her mother was carrying a baby at the time, which at that point was miscarrying, and the child witnesses her mother pull out the bloody fetus and flush it down the toilet. It was a vivid memory. The consultant asks the therapist, "Do you suppose her mother also tried to abort her? Because that seems to be what's coming up in the transference. The consultant remembers one man who had an endlessly recurring dream about desperately hanging onto the edge of a cliff, clinging to one root and about to fall to his death at any moment. His mother later confirmed that she had used a coat hanger several times in an attempt to abort him during the pregnancy.

His struggle to stay alive was vividly represented in the recurring dream. The consultant asks, "Do you suppose her memory is a screen memory? Or is it something she actually witnessed? My hunch is that the memory stands out so vividly because she believes 'that's what mother did to me. Mother flushed me down the toilet. Mother broke the contact and flushed me down the toilet in the same way.' Perhaps that's what she experiences you are doing to her right now. She has somehow succeeded in experiencing in transference that you're aborting her. She is using something in your demeanor toward her friend Naomi in order to project the organizing-transference wish to abort her into the therapeutic relationship."

The deceptive thing, and the reason this example is clear, and the next one even more interesting, is because when a therapist first starts tracking these organizing experiences in transference they frequently look like symbiotic (abandonment) material. The speaker says, "I'm leaving you because you failed me. You abandoned me and I'm never coming back." Yet, upon closer examination, we begin to realize that as the organizing transference begins to fit into place, the person waits for a moment in which she can re-create the organizing rupture in the relating. Here she recreates it by screaming accusations at her therapist about her attitudes and how bad she is as a therapist. Her intensity and abruptness as well as her departure from ordinary reality appreciation has left the therapist shaken. She says, "I've never been this shaken with this woman before. I'm worried I'll never see her again. I'm worried she'll never come back." It's not too difficult to infer, under the circumstances, that an unconscious fantasy may exist on the therapist's part of getting rid of her. She then says, "Oh, you know, there's another thing. I have been delaying all week returning her phone calls. She called me. I think, 'I've got ten minutes and I can call her. No, no, no. If I call her tomorrow I'll have fifteen, so I'll call her tomorrow.'" So she's aware she's pushing her away in that way. The therapist also said she had the fantasy of "Well, you know, she's threatening to be very difficult lately, and the truth of the matter is, if she didn't come back I suppose it wouldn't be the worst thing in the world for me." The client may have picked up some ambivalence in the countertransference that she reads as abortion fantasies, miscarriage fantasies. This is her way of accomplishing the disconnection. First inside herself, and then with her therapist.

There are two ways we may study the presence of the organizing transference "rupture in relating": in its passively repeated form and in its actively mimicked form. In the present example we might first infer that when the baby needed something, mother attempted in some reasonable way to give the baby what she needed but it wasn't right. Mother's attempts failed somehow. So the baby began screaming. We then picture this mother who, with limited resources, didn't know how to respond to the baby screaming. Maybe the child had an earache or whatever. Not being able to bear the tension, the mother leaves the scene so the child learns "when I scream mother leaves." So the analytic speaker now screams at her therapist with the expectation that she too will leave her. Her way of accomplishing the rupture is to scream. When the consultant suggested this to the therapist she quickly reviewed every relationship the client has had with a man. At the point in the relationship at which the client begins to feel connected to the man, suddenly she switches into this "other personality," which is a "screaming bitch" and starts screaming and yelling obscenities and accusations at them and so they can't stay around. She accomplishes the break by screaming accusations.

But the activity of actually accomplishing the break belonged to mother and so is somehow identified with, mimicked. According to this line of inference, did mother scream at the baby for misunderstanding her needs in the relationship, for not being responsive to mother's attempts to care for her? We don't know exactly how the primary identification with the mother who broke the contact operates from this limited material but it provides clues to future analytic understanding. The therapist is still left worrying, "But what am I going to do with this disconnection?" Since the therapist has been traumatized, as the mother may have been with the child's needs, she too seems almost ready to flush her down the toilet.

An alternative formulation might use Fraiberg's (1982) notion of "pre-defense." In observing interactions of neglected and abused children with their parents, Fraiberg noticed three almost biological reactions that serve to (defensively) control the stimulation: aversion, freezing, fighting (or flight, fight, or freeze). This woman's screaming at men and at her therapist might be considered a fighting response in the face of the anticipated abusive overstimulation and contact rupture that the organizing transference threatens to generate. (The following two vignettes will illustrate the flight and freeze tendencies.)

These interpretive hunches connect immediately with the therapist. Then she is ready to talk with her client about it all today. The consultant warns, "Don't rush into this material because one thing we know is that when people are in organizing states they can't handle much at any given moment that's abstract, that's verbal. Just be with her for now. You've learned from her rantings. You've seen the small window to her soul from your own shocked experience, which no doubt in some way represents her trauma as an infant. But if you start to talk about it too soon, you'll be introducing ego functioning into space where ego doesn't belong—which may have been her mother's worst empathic error. If so, then you become her psychotic mother by trying to be too helpful!" On the way out, she says, "You know, I just never know what to expect from these organizing people. I've been really gearing up for the worst." The consultant responds, "Well, maybe you'll have a difficult experience with her when you talk with her on the phone today. These people have a way of making it very hard on us." The therapist says, "But you know, it also occurs to me that maybe when I call her, at the other end, there will just be this still, quiet little voice that says, 'Hi, I've missed you.'" The following week she reports exactly that. She was able to stay with her client and help her feel how awful it was to think that her therapist in some way might disapprove of Naomi or think that a lesbian relationship wasn't right for her. The rupture had been repaired, the connection remade so she could continue to stay in therapy. But the crucial transference experience that appeared is by no means understood or worked through. This episode represents her first tentative foray into working the organizing transference directly with her therapist. Now the heat is temporarily over and the therapist has a clearer view of the nature of her client's disconnecting transference replication.

The organizing transference seems to be worked through in a series of waves or episodes. The therapist will be more prepared to act quickly next time. The interpretation will perhaps be possible in the non- or preverbal *way* the therapist stays with her in her rageful self and invites her (perhaps with extended hand) to stay connected and to live out together her terror of being with the therapist rather than to disconnect or rupture the connection with rage.

A Transference Illustration: Flight from the Therapist

The second example of organizing transference involves a woman therapist who has been seeing a client for three or four years. This client has been driving an hour and a half each week to see her therapist. The therapist says, "so there's a long umbilicus." The woman has presented the client as tenuous in her ability to maintain relationships. In the last six months she has talked frequently about terminating therapy because of money and distance. She canceled her sessions in bad weather and during the winter holiday rush.

On several occasions the therapist has empathically tried, "Well, okay, I can understand how busy you are and how far it is. You've accomplished a number of things in therapy, so if you want to consider termination we can talk about that." She even suggested helping her find a therapist who was closer. But that all became taboo. The client was allowed to talk about termination, but the therapist was forbidden to talk about it.

On the occasion in question the woman called during the Christmas holidays and without any warning canceled all future appointments. Her therapist made several phone calls in unsuccessfully attempting to reach her. She sent a Christmas card. She did everything she could to reach out to her. The therapist thought, "Well, maybe it's best that she stop and this is her way of stopping. Maybe I shouldn't be pursuing her." This laissez-faire attitude may be appropriate for listening to more differentiated forms of personality organization but is clearly not empathic when working an organizing transference in which the person cannot initiate or sustain connection. This therapist is an empathic and intuitive woman and so remained persistent in her attempts to restore the connection. They finally did connect by phone and the therapist found out what happened. The client said, "In the last session I was telling you about my friend Valerie and you turned away. Then I knew you didn't care for me and so there wasn't any point in my coming back."

As the incident was discussed in consultation, the consultant encouraged the therapist to attempt a review of events in order to try to get some idea of the content of what was being talked about with Valerie. Concrete images about contact ruptures serve us well in understanding organizing experiences. It is often important to ascertain exactly what was being talked about, and why turning away to pick up a cup of tea was seen as a rejection. Here, the woman has been slowly backing away, but not letting the therapist back away. The therapist can't talk about termination but the client is waiting for when the therapist turns at a critical moment so that the rupture of the organizing transference can be attached to the therapist's turning away activity. The consultant says, "She's found a way to live out the organizing transference of mother disconnecting. This is the window to the organizing experience we're waiting for. We wait for the moment in which the reenactment of the turning away, the breaking of contact, the rupture of experience happens in the transference." This episode might be mistaken for a symbiotic relating scenario or narcissistic breach in empathy—"Just when I needed affirmation from you, just when I need something from you, you turned away." It could be seen as splitting; it could be seen as abandonment; it could be seen as selfobject failure. But the consultant had heard developments in the case several times before, enough to realize that there was a deep organizing-level component. In response to the consultant considering the rupture as disconnecting transference, the therapist said, "You know, she's been married for twenty years. So I had always thought of her as basically symbiotic or borderline in her object relations. But now I recall a number of instances with her husband in which she must have been in an organizing pocket and experienced her husband as the psychotic mother." But now the rupture of relating had actually been re-created with the therapist. She says, "It's funny, during this time period she had moved. She called my recorder to leave her new phone number on it. And, you know, I didn't take the phone number off the machine before I erased the message." So the analytic listener is ready in some sense to let her die, too.

The therapist was fired up with these ideas because they seemed to make sense and to organize in her mind many past incidents. She was ready to go back and talk to her client about all of this. The consultant cautions her not to rush and tells her why. The therapist tunes in quickly and says, "I feel like where we're at right now is that we're both lying down in a playpen and I have to wait for her to come to me." The consultant reminded her the baby has to be allowed to find the breast. The transference to the psychotic mother will be reenacted again and again so there will be ample time to interpret. But she can use her new understanding to be with her client in new ways. The therapist was reminded of what she already knew from her studies of the organizing experience, that abstract verbal interpretations as such will not touch this very early transference. Interpretation at the organizing level must be a concrete activity, often manifest in physical gesture or interpretive touch at the specific moment when the analytic speaker is actually in the act of pulling away from contact, of (transferentially) creating a rupture. Viable interpretation of the organizing transference may involve an actual, physical, concrete reaching out of one person toward another in such a way as to communicate, "I know you believe you must break off our personal engagement in this way now. But it's not true. You have, as an adult, the ability to stay here now with me and to experience your long-standing terror of connectedness. How can you manage not to leave me now? Can we manage to remain in contact for just a few more minutes?"[5] Clients often deliberately and perhaps wisely conduct the early phases of therapy at quite some distance from the therapist by spacing appointments far apart and/or arranging long and difficult drives. They know that closeness can only be experienced by them as traumatic.

The therapist had arranged this consultation because she was concerned about her own anger. In the midst of all the client's coming and not coming, calling and canceling, connecting and disconnecting, the therapist had become enraged and said she was "just ready to kill her" when she sees her on Thursday. She even made a slip and said, "I have an appointment with her on Saturday." The consultation group laughed to think she doesn't want to see her so soon as Thursday. She's an excellent therapist, and of course she really does want to connect, but it is easy to understand the countertransference ambivalence. Ruptures in relating, which organizing transferences necessarily entail, stir up organizing experiences in the therapist.

A Transference Illustration: Frozen in Impotent Rage

In the third example of how organizing transference works, an emerging theme in the therapy of an otherwise very well-developed

---

5. For a discussion of "interpretive touch," which therapists often employ at critical moments of transference disconnecting, see Hedges (1994a,c).

woman has been related to the organizing period. This example is from a much later working-through period of the analysis and occurs in a personality much more capable of verbal abstractions than the previous two. The woman's mother, during the baby's first few months of life, was afraid to pick up her baby for fear of "breaking" her. It's been discovered through several years of intensive psychotherapy that there were many strengths this mother was able to stimulate in this child, but at the deepest psychic level there are connecting difficulties. The emergent theme over several weeks was the analytic speaker's rage, which occurs on a fairly regular basis in social situations when she knows that the person she's interacting with can indeed do more for her, and be more there for her, but somehow flakes out. In short, her rage is mobilized at people when they have potentially more to offer than in fact they are actively living in the current relationship. In a key session the woman develops the theme further. With her husband, she says, early in the marriage he was far more warm, far more giving, far more available than he is now, and how angry she is that he isn't more available when she knows he can be. She becomes exasperated to the point of feeling utterly helpless and frozen. With a close friend she indicates that what attracted her to the friend was that this other woman had so much to give. She's well-traveled and well-read. She's alive, active, versatile, a good conversationalist, and much more. But in a recent example, when her friend had a bout of flu and refused to get out of bed to go to the client's son's very first baseball game, "Then I don't see her any longer as what she could be or might be for me. And I become angry and disillusioned with her. Now I know what's been bothering me so much lately about her in our relationship. Too often she cancels, flakes out, or blobs out when I know she doesn't have to, when I know she has far more to give but is choosing not to. I become completely immobilized in impotent rage."

In the discussion of various examples that have occurred with her husband and her friend, she said, "Now I'm finding that when I'm enraged at the other person for not living up to their potential not only do I not get what they have to offer me, but I also see that when I'm enraged I am totally unable to take in, to get, to make use of what they can in fact offer me." She referenced some examples from previous transference experiences in therapy where she, in complaining bitterly about the therapist's seemingly endless unavailability over the holidays and weekends, was so preoccupied in her hours leading up to the holidays that she was unable to make use of whatever good experiences might be possible in the sessions. Her comment is, "Something always happens." The emphasis here is on the subjective statement of the disconnecting experience being impersonal. It's not, "I'm disappointed with the other," or, "The other lets me down," or, "The other fails to live up to their potential." It's "We're interacting and then *something happens* and the potential that is there isn't being lived out, and I fall into a lost state of sadness and grief that's usually manifested in instantaneous but frozen rage."

At this point in the session the client realized she has lost or repressed a further insight regarding her husband and friend that she was very excited about only a moment before when she connected to it. But just as quickly as the insight came it fled, and she was very disturbed for some time about having lost it. Late in the session she provided another example of some neighbors whom, when she first began to get to know them, she experienced as somewhat available. Now she experiences them more as users than givers. And while she acknowledges that this latter impression is no doubt also true in some ways, she cites several instances at the beginning of their relationship where the neighbors were very supportive, very helpful, very outgoing. But the man in the couple began on occasion to have other things that kept him away from doing things with them. And the woman began not being able to have lunch with the client often or visit over coffee. Before too long there were enough gaps in the relationship that it became unbearable to her. She says, "It's easy to say they aren't meeting my needs. I'll have to go elsewhere." But she realizes that this is not entirely the case. They do have some things to offer, but because they're not offering all that they can, she feels that "mysterious unbearable pain" again.

After a few thoughtful moments she said, "It sounds like a reason to break contact." The therapist quickly replied, "No, it's the way you break contact." She then said excitedly, "That's exactly what I lost. I was trying to formulate the problem with my husband and my friend in terms of how I break contact but I couldn't quite get there. If I'm always living in what a person could give me but isn't, then several things happen: One, I have reason not to relate to them. Two, I'm not relating to them at all but I'm relating rather to my fantasy. And three, they do have something to give or I wouldn't be relating to them, but in my distress and frozen anger I'm completely missing what they do have to give to me. I break the contact by being sad and enraged, complaining about what I'm not getting." At this point she slowed down and indicated that she was emoting very deeply, that she feels she's reached a very profound point. "I know somehow that this can change my life if I can finally get hold of it. If I can find some way of fully knowing about this, I will be able to change many things." Her therapist said, "It seems as though you've located the mechanism regarding how the contact is broken and how it relates to the early experiences of your mother who, much of the time, was there—so that you knew full well what things she could provide. But when she was preoccupied, or not able to give, or frightened about how she might harm the baby, she bowed out, leaving you stuck, knowing that she could give more but was not giving it. No wonder she reports that you were such a good baby and slept a lot!" The content of the transference is, 'You could be giving me more but you're not.' Then the woman said, "Now I know why my daughter seems to be left out of this dynamic. You know how I've always said with her it's somewhat different? Well, the difference is that I'm not expecting to be given to by her. I understand that her role isn't to give to me and so I'm much freer to relate to her without this pain coming up. The few instances in which I do lose it with her, I may feel that she's not giving me her full cooperation as freely and fully as I know that she can. But, in fact, I am able to take a great deal from her by simply being with her—by just being present while she's losing her baby teeth, or brushing her hair. I go to softball league with her and I receive through just watching." Her therapist said, "You do take what she has to offer." She responded, "Yes, but it's often very indirectly, just by enjoying being with her. Whatever she does is so wonderful and beautiful that it's a very rich experience just being by her side."

She then commented about the previous week's Thursday session. "I was concerned that you didn't know about my feelings of caring for you and how grateful I feel to you for just being here with me. I get a lot from you by just being with you even if you don't have a lot to give on a certain day." (The therapist had an obviously serious eye infection on that day and his spirits were a little off. It was something she detected and expressed concern about within the hour.)

"Now," she continued, "I find I'm a little scared about knowing all of this. Things keep clicking in my mind—more and more examples.

It's like my whole life is built on this single mechanism. No wonder I wasn't happy when John, my supervisor, failed to tune into me completely when I knew he could. If I finally identify this, I may be able to change. I'm excited, but I think I'm mostly very scared. I think the scare is that I won't remember this, I won't be able to take hold of it. I won't be able to make it my own." The therapist said, "No. The scare is that you *will* remember it. You are in the process of deep change and as you are changing you are coming face-to-face with a terror you have avoided all your life. The terror of having to encounter a real live person who has some good things to offer but who may not, for a variety of reasons, be willing or able to give fully in all areas. Sooner or later in every relationship you encounter this situation and it brings back the sad and rageful reactions you had to your mother during your earliest months of life. So you have been unable to continue relating, or you have given up the relating when the conditions are not met the right way. What you're scared of is actually allowing yourself to negotiate the uncertainties of relationships and to survive the positive possibilities as well as the painful disappointments that are bound to be a frightening and powerful consequence of fully knowing and living out what you are now discovering."

Each of these three examples serves to illustrate how the rupture of the organizing experience is repeated in transference. In each instance multiple interpretive possibilities exist. The decisive moment of organizing transference interpretation is not visible in any of these examples—in the first two because the relationship had not yet arrived there, and in the third because the in vivo interpretations had already begun and the woman was in a later stage of "owning" the interpretative work, though she expresses fear of losing it. The presence of Fraiberg's (1982) three "pre-defenses" of aversion, freezing, and fighting is suggested in these case vignettes, and may be seen as the clients' ways of achieving a rupture in contact which, due to transference projections, is threatening to become overstimulating.[6]

---

6. These three cases and further examples of the actual interpretive and working-through process (in the case of Sandy) are provided in Hedges (1994a, and reprinted in Hedges 1994b).

EMPATHY AND WORKING THROUGH
THE ORGANIZING TRANSFERENCE

When infantile trauma is a significant underlying component in the transference structure, we can anticipate an abreaction to usual technical attempts, which are designed to restore a working relationship through ordinary forms of empathic attunement. Instead, we can regularly anticipate that when empathic connections are achieved or even broached with the person in therapy or analysis that various forms of terror and withdrawal will follow. *Empathy in the broadest sense, or optimal responsiveness, then must include an awareness of and a working through of the danger of painful and overwhelming retraumatization that interpersonal contact and intersubjective connection often entail in the organizing-level transference experience.*[7]

A successful working-through process with an organizing-level transference necessarily includes an alliance in which two share the knowledge of the retraumatization danger and set out together to study the entire cycle set in motion by the transference revival of infantile trauma. The cycle includes how the person approaches, seeks, and sues for contact with the other, and how diverse relational modes and activities developed over a lifetime tend to foreclose the possibility of actually achieving and sustaining intimate, mutually engaged personal contact and/or connection. This avoidance of or flight from interpersonal connection might be manifest in various forms of dissociation, personality "switching," recovery of vivid memories, sudden upsurges of symptoms, accusations of faulty attunement, or any of a variety of somatic or psychic distractions (in the transference or countertransference response) designed to draw two people's attention from the fact that contact and connection in the present are being actively avoided, thwarted, ruptured, or fled from.

The joint study by analyst and analysand of the operation of transferential reliving of infantile trauma would ideally include attention to all relational attitudes and activities that function to alienate or deflect the attention of the analytic listener through various means so

---

7. My colleagues and I have provided numerous examples of how this difficult and distressing process can be accomplished (Hedges 1994a,b, and this volume).

that the listener appears somehow to be "responsible" for the breach. The working-through process necessitates two paying close attention to all activities of mutual contact search and avoidance—accompanied by a joint effort to maintain contact and connection in face of rising fear and in spite of the strong tendency—often felt by both participants—to allow contact to be destroyed, deflected, dissipated, or lost.

SUMMARY

Achieving optional responsiveness with experiences of infantile trauma necessarily includes studying the approach for interpersonal contact as well as the relational means utilized by both participants of the analytic dyad to effect breaches in contact. Achieving and maintaining optimal responsiveness to the organizing experience necessarily entails the concerted cooperation of both participants learning to establish and sustain interpersonal connection in the face of the primordial terrors and agony being remobilized, so that the effects of infantile trauma can be somato-psychically recalled and worked through in an analytic reliving process. Infantile trauma as a component of transference poses a paradoxical challenge for our ongoing study of the nature of empathy.

Appendix G

Organizing Experience Worksheet

Person's Disguised ID _____
Date _____

1. Bring fully to mind someone you know or work with but have a hard time staying emotionally connected to. Describe this person's relationship with you.

2. How do you experience this person's connections and disconnections? ____unavailable for connection, ____quick to break connection, ____unable to sustain connection, ____gets me to break connection. **Describe briefly. How are connections typically made and broken?**

3. Why do you think this person has a hard time connecting and holding onto connections?

4. Common Subjective Concerns of this person are:

____ I feel very crazy, like falling apart or dying.

____ I worry I won't be able to find you if I need you.

____ If I can't hold on the way I need to, I'll die.

____ I am overwhelmed by what seems easy to you.

____ I need not to be pressured or rushed.

____ There must be time and space for my expressions.

____ I must have continuity and safety with you.

____ I need to hear, see, smell, and feel your presence.

____ Please be available or don't tantalize me.

____ I need to have a total body experience.

____ I need you to be alive to me and my concerns.

____ Please respect my sense of time and space.

____ Don't expect me to have more ego than I do.

____ Show me in concrete ways how to hold onto you.

____ Please don't crush, kill, or abuse the child inside.

____ Don't agree to hold me if you intend to drop me.

____ Don't assume I'm connected   ____ (Other) _____
when I'm not.   _____
____ Please search for my sense of _____
life inside.   _____
____ Show me how to connect   _____
with myself and you.   _____

5. What kinds of expressions and symbols does the person use in regular self-expression that strike you as unusual, unique, or obsessive? What ongoing or over-concern does the person have with things such as religion, food, love, relationships, work, children, illness, morals, judgments of others? **How are these symbols and concerns used to connect, avoid, or rupture connections?**

6. What kind of nonhuman imagery does the person use fairly regularly? How does the person experience mechanical, impersonal, uncontrollable, mystical, economic, political, legal, and/or supernatural forces or movements in the world that determine things? How are people and relationships experienced as powers, forces, devices, diseases, or trends to be dealt with, controlled, or avoided? How are things in the person's life experienced as governed by impersonal or inanimate forces, strange happenings, or persecutory signs? **How does the person use nonhuman imagery to connect and disconnect from people?**

7. What kinds of physical sensations, preoccupations, or symptoms are mentioned often? How are body parts, physical symptoms, and health fears in one way or another a frequent concern? This can include focus on organ functioning, weight gain and loss, food and substance use and abuse, or obsessive concern with exercise and health, digestion and evacuation, and mental and physical deterioration or disease and aging. **How are compulsive concerns with physical matters used by this person to achieve, thwart, and destroy connections?**

8. How is the person's orientation in time and space less than reliable and consistent? What kinds of regular or periodic confusions, lapses, distortions, disorientations, or inconsistencies occur? When and under what circumstances does the person seem less than reliably and safely grounded? **How do orientation issues involved in this person's life relate to her or his connections and disconnections?**

9. What other ways have you observed that this person uses to avoid, rupture, dilute, or cut short emotional connections?

10. **Describe special moments when you and this person are clearly affectively connected.** What do those moments look like in terms of body involvement? What contents or kinds of events allow these special connections to occur? How are these moments lost or destroyed? How does the person change or dilute the subject, focus, or emotional impact of such connections?

11. **How does it seem this person uses "projective identification" or your "countertransference" response to achieve a minimizing, an avoidance or a breaking off of contact?** That is, in what ways is she or he using longstanding skills to push you away or alienate you emotionally? In what ways has this person skillfully ferreted out things in you that are easily mobilized and that can serve to disrupt the mutual emotional connection?

12. **Forgetting "usual therapeutic technique," what do you think you could do or say to get this person to hold on to these special moments of emotional connection with you for a little while longer?** What would it take to get her or him to stay with you a little longer?

13. What do you think would happen if you could encourage the person to stay connected longer? Be specific. In both bodies? In the emotions of two? In the sense of connection?

14. How is deep transference terror likely to manifest itself? What about countertransference terror? How will the two of you handle it?

15. As you have been considering inviting this person into more intimate relating with you what emotional reactions have you been having?

16. What body reactions have been occurring as you imagine getting closer to this person? What sorts of fears are arising for you and how are they manifest in various places in your body?

17. Why does this project seem like it just won't work? In what ways does it seem plausible?

18. What comes up for you now as you think of sharing these reactions with colleagues?

References

Alexander, F. (1961). *The Scope of Psychoanalysis*. New York: Basic Books.

American Psychiatric Association (1987). *Desk Reference to the Diagnostic Criteria from DSM-III-R*. Cambridge, England: Press Syndicate of the University of Cambridge.

Bacal, H. (1998). *Optimal Responsiveness: How Therapists Heal Their Patients*. Northvale, NJ: Jason Aronson.

Bick, E. (1968). The experience of the skin in early object-relations. *International Journal of Psycho-Analysis* 49:484–486.

Bion, W. R. (1977). *Second Thoughts*. New York: Jason Aronson.

Bollas, C. (1979). The transformational object. *International Journal of Psycho-Analysis* 59:97–107.

——— (1987). *The Shadow of the Object: Psychoanalysis of the Unthought Known*. London: Free Association Press.

Brandchaft, B. (1988). An intractable depression. In *Learning from Kohut*, ed. A. Goldberg, pp. 133–154. Hillsdale, NJ: Analytic Press.

——— (1994). To free the spirit from its own cell. In *The Intersubjective Perspective*, ed. R. Stolorow, G. Atwood, and B. Brandchaft, pp. 57–76. Northvale, NJ: Jason Aronson.

Breuer, J., and Freud, S. (1893–1895). Studies on hysteria. *Standard Edition* 2.

Deutsch, H. (1942). Some forms of emotional disturbance and their relationship to schizophrenia. In *Neuroses and Character Types: Clinical Psychoanalytic Studies*. New York: International Universities Press, 1965.

Eigen, M. (1992). *Coming Through the Whirlwind*. New York: Chiron.

Eissler, K. R. (1953). The effect of the structure of the ego on psychoanalytic technique. *Journal of the American Psychoanalytic Association* 1:104–143.

Erikson, E. (1959). Identity and the life cycle. In *Psychological Issues*, Monograph No. 1. New York: International Universities Press.

Fraiberg, S. (1982). Pathological defenses in infancy. *Psychoanalytic Quarterly* 51:612–635.

Freud, A. (1958). Child observation and prediction of development. Cited in *The Privacy of The Self*, ed. M. M. R. Khan, pp. 57ff. New York: International Universities Press, 1974.

Freud, S. (1895). Project for a scientific psychology. *Standard Editon* 1:283–388.

———— (1905). Three essays on sexuality. *Standard Edition* 6:125–244.

———— (1910). The future prospects of psychoanalytic therapy. *Standard Edition* 1:141–151.

———— (1911). Psycho-analytic notes on an autobiographical account of a case of paranoia (dementia paranoides). *Standard Edition* 12:12–24.

———— (1912). Papers on technique: the dynamics of transference. *Standard Edition* 12:92–108.

———— (1914). Recollecting, repeating, and working through (further recommendations on the techniques of psycho-analysis II). *Standard Edition* 12:145–156.

———— (1915). Observations on transference love. *Standard Edition* 12:159–171.

———— (1918). An infantile neurosis. *Standard Edition* 7:1–124.

———— (1920). Beyond the pleasure principle. *Standard Edition* 18:3–64.

———— (1923). The ego and the id. *Standard Edition* 19:3–68.

———— (1933). New introductory lectures on psycho-analysis. *Standard Edition* 22:1–184.

Giovacchini, P. L. (1979). Countertransference with primitive mental states. In *Countertransference*, ed. L. Epstein and A. H. Feiner, pp. 235–265. New York: Jason Aronson.

———— (1997). *Schizophrenia and Primitve Mental States*. Northvale, NJ: Jason Aronson.

Green, A. (1986). *On Private Madness*. London: Hogarth.

Greenson, R. (1965). The working alliance and the transference neurosis. In *Explorations in Psychoanalysis*, pp. 199–225. New York: International Universities Press.

Grotstein, J. (1981). *Splitting and Projective Identification*. New York: Jason Aronson.

—— (1994). Foreword. In *Working the Organizing Experience* by L. Hedges, pp. xvii–xxxiii. Northvale, NJ: Jason Aronson.

Hebrews 11:1. *The Holy Bible* (1967). New York: Oxford University Press.

Hedges, L. E. (1983). *Listening Perspectives in Psychotherapy*. Northvale, NJ: Jason Aronson.

—— (1992). *Interpreting the Countertransference*. Northvale, NJ: Jason Aronson.

—— (1994a). *In Search of the Lost Mother of Infancy*. Northvale, NJ: Jason Aronson.

—— (1994b). *Remembering, Repeating, and Working Through Childhood Trauma*. Northvale, NJ: Jason Aronson.

—— (1994c). *Working the Organizing Experience: Transforming Psychotic, Schizoid, and Autistic States*. Northvale, NJ: Jason Aronson.

—— (1994d). Taking recovered memories seriously. *Issues in Child Abuse Accusation* 6(1):1–30. Northfield, MN: Institute for Psychological Therapies.

—— (1995). False accusations against therapists. *The California Therapist* March/April, pp. 35–45. Reprinted in Hedges et al. (1997).

—— (1996). *Strategic Emotional Involvement*. Northvale, NJ: Jason Aronson.

Hedges, L. and Hilton, V. W. (in press). *The Seven Deadly Fears*.

Hedges, L., Hilton, R., Hilton, V., and Caudill, B. (1997). *Therapists at Risk*. Northvale, NJ: Jason Aronson.

Hilton, V. W. (1993). When we are accused. *Journal for Bioenergetic Analysis* 5(2):45–51.

Hunter, V. (1994). *Psychoanslysis Talk*. New York: Guilford.

—— (1996). Symbolic enactments in countertransference. In *Strategic Emotional Involvement*, ed. L. Hedges, pp. 25–37. Northvale, NJ: Jason Aronson.

Jacobson, E. (1954). The self and object world: vicissitudes of their infantile cathexis and their influence of ideational and affective development. *Psychoanalytic Study of the Child* 9:75–127. New York: International Universities Press.

—— (1964). *The Self and Object World*. New York. International Universities Press.

Kernberg, O. (1975). *Borderline Conditions and Pathological Narcissism*. New York: Jason Aronson.

Khan, M. M. R. (1963). The concept of cumulative trauma. *Psychoanalytic Study of the Child* 18:286–306. New York: International Universities Press.

Kitchener, K. (1988). Dual relationships: What makes them so problematic? *Journal of Counselling and Development* 67:217–221.

Klein, M. (1957). *Envy and Gratitude*. New York: Basic Books.

Kohut, H. (1959). Introspection, empathy and psychoanalysis: an examination of the relationship between mode of observation and theory. *Journal of the American Psychoanalytic Association* 7:459–483.

——— (1971). *The Analysis of the Self*. New York: International Universities Press.

——— (1981). *Summarizing reflections*. Paper presented at the UCLA Conference, "Progress in Self Psychology." Los Angeles, October 5.

——— (1984). *How Does Analysis Cure?* Chicago: University of Chicago Press.

Lévi-Strauss, C. (1949). The function and field of speech and language in psychoanalysis. In *Ecrits: A Selection*. New York: Norton.

Little, M. (1981). *Transference Neurosis: Transference Psychosis*. New York: Jason Aronson.

——— (1990). *Psychotic Anxieties and Containment: A Personal Record of an Analysis with Winnicott*. Northvale, NJ: Jason Aronson.

Lowen, A. (1971). *The Language of the Body*. New York: Collier.

——— (1975). *Bioenergetics*. London: Penguin.

——— (1988). *Love, Sex and Your Heart*. New York: Macmillan.

Mahler, M. (1968). *On Human Symbiosis and the Vicissitudes of Individuation*. Vol. I: *Infantile Psychosis*. New York: International Universities Press.

Mahler, M., Pine, F., and Bergman, A. (1975). *The Psychological Birth of the Human Infant: Symbiosis and Individuation*. New York: Basic Books.

Maturana, H., and Varela, F. (1987) *The Tree of Knowledge*. Boston: New Science Library.

McDougall, J. (1989). *Theaters of the Body*. London: Free Association Press.

Modell, A. H. (1976). "The holding environment" and the therapeutic action of psychoanalysis. *Journal of the American Psychoanalytic Association* 24:285–308.

Natterson, J. (1991). *Beyond Countertransference: The Therapist's Subjectivity in the Therapeutic Process*. Northvale, NJ: Jason Aronson.

Schafer, R. (1976). *A New Language for Psychoanalysis*. New Haven: Yale University Press.

Schwaber, E. (1979). *Narcissism, self psychology and the listening perspective*. Pre-presentation reading for lecture given at the University of California, Los Angeles Conference on the Psychology of the Self—Narcissism, October.

——— (1983). Psychoanalytic listening and psychic reality. *International Journal of Psycho-Analysis* 10:379–391.

Searles, H. F. (1965). *Collected Papers on Schizophrenia and Related Subjects*. New York: International Universities Press.

———— (1979). *Countertransference and Related Subjects*. New York: International Universities Press.

Spence, D. (1982). *Narrative Truth and Historical Truth*. New York: Norton.

Stern, D. N. (1985). *The Interpersonal World of the Infant*. New York: Basic Books.

Stolorow, R., and Atwood, G. (1992). *Contexts of Being: The Intersubjective Foundations of Psychological Life*. Hillsdale, NJ: Analytic Press.

Stolorow, R., Atwood, G., and Brandchaft, B. (1994). *The Intersubjective Perspective*. Northvale, NJ: Jason Aronson.

Strachey, J. (1934). The nature of the therapeutic action of psychoanalysis. *International Journal of Psycho-Analysis* 15:117–126.

Tomm, K. (1991). The ethics of dual relationship. *The Calgary Participator: A Family Therapy Newsletter* 1:3. (Reprinted in *The California Therapist*, Jan/Feb 1993).

Tronick, E., and Cohn, J. (1988). Infant-mother face-to-face communicative interaction: age and gender differences in coordination and the occurrence of miscoordination. *Child Development* 60:85–92.

Tustin, F. (1972). *Autism and Childhood Psychosis*. London: Hogarth.

———— (1981). *Autistic States in Children*. Boston: Routledge & Kegan Paul.

———— (1986). *Autistic Barriers in Neurotic Patients*. New Haven: Yale University Press.

———— (1990). *The Protective Shell in Childhood and Adults*. London: Karnac.

———— (1991). Revised understanding of psychogenic autism. *International Journal of Psycho-Analysis* 72(4):585–592.

Van Sweden, R. (1995). *Regression to Dependence*. Northvale, NJ: Jason Aronson.

Varela, F., Thompson, E., and Rosch, E. (1995) *The Embodied Mind*. Cambridge, MA: MIT Press.

von Forester, H. (1962). *Principles of Self-Organization*. New York: Pergamon.

Winnicott, D. W. (1949). Hate in the countertransference. *International Journal of Pycho-Analysis* 30:69–75.

———— (1952). Psychoses and child care. In *Through Paediatrics to Psycho-Analysis: Collected Papers of D. W. Winnicott*, pp. 219–228. New York: Basic Books.

———— (1953). Transitional objects and transitional phenomena: a study of the first not-me possession. *International Journal of Psycho-Analysis* 34:89–97.

———— (1958). *Through Paediatrics to Psycho-Analysis*. New York: Basic Books, 1975.

———— (1960). The theory of the infant–parent relationship. *International Journal of Psycho-Analysis* 41:585–595.

———— (1965). Birth memories, birth trauma, and anxiety. In *Through Paediatrics to Psycho-Analysis: Collected Papers of D.W. Winnicott*. New York: Basic Books.

———— (1971). *Playing and Reality*. London: Tavistock.

———— (1974). Fear of breakdown. *International Review of Psycho-Analysis* 1:103–107.

———— (1975). Reparation in respect of mothers' organized defense against depression. In *Through Paediatrics to Psycho-Analysis: Collected Papers of D. W. Winnicott*. New York: Basics Books.

Index